2005
The Supreme Court Review

200
The

"Judges as persons, or courts as institutions, are entitled to
no greater immunity from criticism than other persons
or institutions . . . [J]udges must be kept mindful of their limitations and
of their ultimate public responsibility by a vigorous
stream of criticism expressed with candor however blunt."
—*Felix Frankfurter*

". . . while it is proper that people should find fault when
their judges fail, it is only reasonable that they should recognize the
difficulties. . . . Let them be severely brought to book,
when they go wrong, but by those who will take the trouble
to understand them."
—*Learned Hand*

THE LAW SCHOOL

THE UNIVERSITY OF CHICAGO

Supreme Court Review

EDITED BY

DENNIS J. HUTCHINSON

DAVID A. STRAUSS

AND GEOFFREY R. STONE

THE UNIVERSITY OF CHICAGO PRESS

CHICAGO AND LONDON

INTERNATIONAL STANDARD BOOK NUMBER: 0-226-36251-5

LIBRARY OF CONGRESS CATALOG CARD NUMBER: 60-14353

THE UNIVERSITY OF CHICAGO PRESS, CHICAGO 60637

THE UNIVERSITY OF CHICAGO PRESS, LTD., LONDON

© 2006 BY THE UNIVERSITY OF CHICAGO, ALL RIGHTS RESERVED, PUBLISHED 2006

PRINTED IN THE UNITED STATES OF AMERICA

The paper used in this publication meets the minimum requirements of American National Standard for Information Sciences–Permanence of Paper for Printed Library Materials, ANSI Z39.48-1984. ∞

TO DAVID CURRIE

*On the occasion of his retirement
from the faculty but not from his work:*

*Peerless teacher and scholar
of the Constitution,
tireless colleague,
friend.*

CONTENTS

ERNEST A. YOUNG

JUST BLOWING SMOKE? POLITICS, DOCTRINE, AND THE FEDERALIST REVIVAL AFTER GONZALES v RAICH

Most assessments of Chief Justice Rehnquist's jurisprudential legacy have placed federalism firmly at its center.[1] And yet, a full decade after the Court's revival of limits on the commerce power in *United States v Lopez*,[2] grave doubts remain about the Chief's "Federalist Revival." Some of these doubts concern the advisability—both as a matter of judicial restraint and of substantive policy—of limiting national power. The doubts upon which I wish to focus here, how-ever, go to the seriousness of the Court's enterprise. That serious-ness might be doubted on two distinct grounds. First, many ob-servers have argued that the Rehnquist Court's commitment to federalism is unprincipled, that is, that federalism merely provides an instrument for the achievement of politically conservative policy

Ernest A. Young is the Judge Benjamin Harrison Powell Professor of Law at the University of Texas at Austin.

AUTHOR'S NOTE: I am grateful to Frank Cross, Dennis Hutchinson, Doug Laycock, and H. W. Perry for helpful comments, to Kim Olson and Elizabeth McKee for valuable research assistance, and to Allegra Young for indulgence and inspiration. I was the principal author of the Brief of Constitutional Law Scholars as Amici Curiae in Support of Re-spondents in No 03-1454, *Gonzales v Raich* (filed Oct 13, 2004), and my co-amici deserve credit for many of the doctrinal views herein; anything less than sensible in the present essay, however, should be attributed to me alone.

[1] See, e.g., Linda Greenhouse, *William H. Rehnquist, Architect of Conservative Court, Dies at 80*, NY Times (Sept 5, 2005), at 16; John O. McGinnis, *Reviving Tocqueville's America: The Rehnquist Court's Jurisprudence of Social Discovery*, 90 Calif L Rev 485 (2002).

[2] 514 US 549 (1995) (striking down the federal Gun Free School Zones Act).

results. This criticism generally comes with a prediction that the Court will abandon federalism at the moment it ceases to promote such results. Second, others have argued that the Court's federalism jurisprudence is unsustainable, that is, either that the doctrinal formulations employed are incapable of rolling national power back any significant distance, or that the Court simply lacks the resolve to take its federalism very far.

Last Term's decision in *Gonzales v Raich*[3] put the Court's seriousness to the test along both these dimensions. California legalized the use of marijuana for medicinal purposes—a position generally identified with politically liberal social policy. The national government, by contrast, has taken a more politically conservative line by barring marijuana use across the board. The question in *Raich* was whether the federal Controlled Substances Act could, within the limits of Congress's commerce power, prohibit the medicinal uses of marijuana that California wished to permit. Many observers predicted that the Court's "Federalist Five" would forget all about federalism in their rush to throw the book at pot smokers; some even wondered if the more liberal "Fab Four" might eschew their usually generous view of national power in order to help out the suffering patients.[4]

Raich also tested the sustainability of the doctrinal line taken in *Lopez* and *United States v Morrison*.[5] Whatever the symbolic value of striking down federal laws in the latter two cases, the actual statutes involved had little practical importance. *Raich*, by contrast, challenged the federal Controlled Substances Act—a veritable paradigm of a big important federal statute. Doctrinally, the arguments in *Raich* applied maximum pressure to the weakest points in the Court's articulated tests under the Commerce Clause. In particular, it was hardly obvious how to characterize the regulated activity for purposes of telling whether it was "commercial" or "economic" in nature, and the government was able to advance strong claims that barring even noncommercial uses of marijuana was "necessary and

---

[3] 125 S Ct 2195 (2005).

[4] See, e.g., Dahlia Lithwick, *Dude, Where's My Integrity? Medical Marijuana Tests the Supreme Court's True Love of Federalism*, Slate (Nov 29, 2004), available at http://www .slate.com/id/2110204/; Ann Althouse, *The Marijuana Case: A Great Test of Law and Politics*, Althouse (Nov 28, 2004), available at http://althouse.blogspot.com/2004/11/ marijuana-case-great-test-of-law-and.html.

[5] 529 US 598 (2000) (striking down a portion of the federal Violence Against Women Act as outside the commerce power).

proper" to a broader scheme for regulating the interstate market in illicit drugs. To affirm the Ninth Circuit, which had held Angel Raich's use of medicinal marijuana off-limits to federal regulation,[6] the Court would have had to broaden and deepen its Commerce Clause doctrine considerably.

This the Rehnquist Court declined to do, and in so holding it invited—and received—vigorous questions about its seriousness in federalism cases. Those questions come, moreover, at a time of major transition for the Court. As the Roberts Court gets under-way in the 2005 Term—and as the Court's most consistently pro-federalism member, Sandra Day O'Connor, rides off into the sunset—those of us who write about federalism can plausibly won-der whether we will soon be in the unenviable position of freedom of contract experts after 1937.

This essay addresses the question of seriousness in three stages. Part I argues that *Raich* was mostly encouraging from the standpoint of principled decision making; virtually all the Justices, after all, held to their established positions on federalism doctrine irrespec-tive of the political valence of the issue in the case. Part II is more pessimistic from a doctrinal perspective. I contend that doctrinal approaches were available to the Court that would have restricted national power in *Raich* without crippling national authority or mir-ing the Court in unavoidably subjective analysis; the Court simply chose not to take them. The only silver lining is that the case was a legitimately difficult one, such that the United States' victory should not necessarily be seen as a portent that the Federalist Re-vival has ground to a halt. I take up that predictive point in Part III, seeking to read the meager tea leaves available as to the future course of the Court's federalism jurisprudence.

I. A (Mostly) Good Day for Principle

The conventional wisdom before the Court handed down its decision in *Raich* was that the government would win[7]—which it did. Many observers expected *Raich* to confirm their long-held suspicions that the Court's federalism jurisprudence was merely a cover for the political preferences of the Justices. And, to some

---

[6] *Raich v Ashcroft*, 352 F2d 1222 (9th Cir 2003).

[7] See, e.g., Linda Greenhouse, *States' Rights Defense Falters in Medical Marijuana Case*, NY Times (Nov 30, 2004), at A20 (reporting on the oral argument).

extent, the Court's decision to change course in *Raich* might be viewed as confirming that hypothesis: Confronted with a politically liberal state advancing a politically liberal social policy, the mostly conservative Court upheld Congress's right to impose a more politically conservative solution. Peter Smith, for example, has written that "it is difficult to resist the conclusion that the outcome of the Rehnquist Court's final federalism decision was influenced by policy-focused instrumentalism."[8]

I have never had much sympathy for these sorts of explanations for judicial decisions. Although such claims are often dressed in the analytical trappings of political science,[9] it is frightfully difficult to prove that any given judicial decision was motivated by something other than the account offered in the opinion. Nor, in my view, is the political account a good guide to what happened in *Raich* itself. I begin with the Court's medical marijuana decision, then offer some more general observations about the political account of the Court's federalism cases.

A. A GLASS EIGHT-NINTHS FULL

The political or instrumentalist account of the Court's federalism cases is that the Justices favor federalism when it advances their political preferences, and they discard it when it does not.[10] Hence the Court's conservative majority limited national power in order to preserve the right to own or possess firearms—supposedly a "conservative" right—in *Lopez* and *Printz* (and the liberals dissented).[11] Likewise, a conservative majority suspicious of the rights of plaintiffs in litigation protected state governmental defendants from liability in state sovereign immunity cases like *Alden* and *Garrett* (and the liberals dissented).[12] In a range of pre-

---

[8] Peter J. Smith, *Federalism, Instrumentalism, and the Legacy of the Rehnquist Court*, 74 Geo Wash L Rev (forthcoming 2006).

[9] See, e.g., Jeffrey A. Segal and Harold J. Spaeth, *The Supreme Court and the Attitudinal Model Revisited* (Cambridge, 2002).

[10] See, e.g., Frank Cross, *Realism About Federalism*, 74 NYU L Rev 1304, 1307–12 (1999).

[11] See *United States v Lopez*, 514 US 549 (1995) (striking down the national Gun Free School Zones Act as outside the commerce power); *Printz v United States*, 521 US 898 (1997) (striking down portions of the Brady Act that "commandeered" state officials to enforce national gun control laws).

[12] See *Alden v Maine*, 527 US 706 (1999) (holding that Congress may not override state sovereign immunity when it acts pursuant to its commerce power, even for suits in state court); *Board of Trustees of the University of Alabama v Garrett*, 531 US 356 (2001) (holding

emption cases, by contrast, the liberals adopted a federalist pose in order to promote state governmental regulation while the more laissez-faire conservatives broadly construed less rigorous federal regulatory measures to supersede tougher state standards.[13] The *Raich* result surely fits this pattern: A Court that had used the Commerce Clause to limit federal initiatives of a liberal stripe suddenly experienced a change of heart when asked to shelter some California pot smokers from federal prosecution.

But the Supreme Court is a "they," not an "it,"[14] and the votes of the individual Justices paint a considerably different picture. The most obvious version of the political hypothesis would have expected Chief Justice Rehnquist, Justice O'Connor, and Justice Thomas to vote in favor of cracking down on marijuana use; likewise, that hypothesis would forecast the four liberals (Justices Stevens, Souter, Ginsburg, and Breyer) casting their votes against the government. Instead, all seven of these Justices voted to affirm their previously expressed legal commitments on federalism and the Commerce Clause. That hardly seems to vindicate the political hypothesis. Unless we expect perfection, *Raich* seems like a prima facie vindication of principle over politics. By this count the glass is neither half full nor half empty—rather, it is *seven-ninths* full.

One can, of course, quibble. The Chief Justice, already battling the cancer that would take his life a year later, might have sacrificed his lifelong love of law enforcement not for federalist principle, but rather for a different, and more personal, political preference for broad access to pain-mitigating drugs.[15] Justice O'Connor—likewise no stranger to cancer—has also noted the importance of

---

that Congress did not validly abrogate state sovereign immunity for suits under Title I of the Americans with Disabilities Act).

[13] See, e.g., *Lorillard Tobacco Co. v Reilly*, 533 US 525 (2001) (holding that federal warning labels on cigarettes preempted more extensive state restrictions on tobacco advertising); *Geier v American Honda Motor Co.*, 529 US 861 (2000) (holding that federal regulations phasing in airbag requirements for cars preempted state common law products liability suits); see generally Richard H. Fallon, Jr., *The "Conservative" Paths of the Rehnquist Court's Federalism Decisions*, 69 U Chi L Rev 429, 471–72 (2002) (observing that the Court's conservatives generally favor federal preemption of state law, and the Court's liberals generally oppose it); Ernest A. Young, *The Rehnquist Court's Two Federalisms*, 83 Tex L Rev 1, 30–32, 41–45 (2004) (noting the same phenomenon, and suggesting that this disparity reflects different views as to the point of federalism).

[14] Apologies to Kenneth M. Shepsle, *Congress Is a "They," Not an "It": Legislative Intent as Oxymoron*, 12 Intl Rev L & Econ 239 (1992).

[15] Personally, I do not find it at all plausible that the Chief's personal circumstances would have shaped his vote. I raise the possibility simply to highlight the indeterminacy of the political hypothesis.

access to pain relief.[16] And Justice Thomas's conservatism has shown a libertarian streak,[17] such that he might have voted as he did in order to further a political preference for rolling back regulation of private activity. These sorts of arguments, however, do more to undermine the political hypothesis than to save it. Many of us, as the Chief possibly did, harbor a variety of cross-cutting political preferences that may bear on a particular case, and the effect is to make the political hypothesis nonfalsifiable: Whichever way the Chief jumped, one could have constructed a political account of what pushed him. Likewise, my uncertainty about Justice Thomas highlights just how capacious our definitions of political ideologies like "conservatism" and "liberalism" really are. Given the availability of competing strands within each of these traditions, it is easy to formulate a political account either way in many (if not most) cases.[18] That makes it difficult to identify those cases in which any given Justice may have been tugged in opposite directions by politics and legal principle.

Most legal principles, moreover, have a stopping point, although different lawyers may disagree about that point's location. Justice Scalia voted with the pro-states majorities in *Lopez* and *Morrison*, but he concurred in rejecting the Commerce Clause challenge in *Raich*. Does that mean he was inconsistent, and that he placed the politics of drug control over federalist principle? Federalism is inherently about the balance between national and state authority,[19] and different people—as a matter of principle—will plausibly strike that balance in different places. Justice Scalia's commitment to a radical reordering of the current allocation of authority has always been a bit suspect: He is an "executive branch conservative" whose nonacademic legal career consisted largely of federal government service and whose academic career focused on federal

---

[16] See *Washington v Glucksberg*, 521 US 702, 736 (1997) (O'Connor, J, concurring).

[17] See, e.g., *Lawrence v Texas*, 539 US 558, 605 (2003) (Thomas, J, dissenting) ("If I were a member of the Texas Legislature, I would vote to repeal [the Texas anti-sodomy law]. Punishing someone for expressing his sexual preference through noncommercial consensual conduct with another adult does not appear to be a worthy way to expend valuable law enforcement resources.").

[18] Moreover, if we treat Justice Thomas as a politically motivated libertarian vote, then we may have to move Justice Kennedy into the "principled" column for voting *against* his own libertarian tendencies in *Raich*.

[19] See Ernest A. Young, *Making Federalism Doctrine: Fidelity, Institutional Competence, and Compensating Adjustments*, 46 Wm & Mary L Rev 1733, 1750–53 (2005).

administrative law.[20] It seems plausible that he thought it important to affirm the limiting force of constitutional text in *Lopez* and
Morrison without feeling any strong desire to roll back more significant federal statutes, like the Controlled Substances Act.[21] That
would hardly prove Scalia's vote was motivated by politics—rather,
it simply suggests that he has been pursuing a more limited principle of federalism than, say, Justice O'Connor.

Justice Kennedy's vote, on the other hand, does seem plausibly
explicable by the political hypothesis. He is well known for his
hostility to drug use,[22] and he may also be more sensitive than
most to another form of political pressure in the form of a desire
to appear statesmanlike by "moderating" the Court's federalism
jurisprudence.[23] (Query whether the latter is really a "political"
impulse at all, rather than a methodological commitment to incrementalism.[24]) The important point, however, is that the force
of the political hypothesis seems a bit attenuated when it can really
only account for one or possibly two votes in a major case like

---

[20] See Thomas W. Merrill, *The Making of the Second Rehnquist Court: A Preliminary
Analysis*, 47 SLU L J 569, 609–12 (2003). But see Bradford R. Clark, *The Constitutional
Structure and the Jurisprudence of Justice Scalia*, 47 SLU L J 753 (2003) (insisting that Justice
Scalia really does care about federalism). As I discuss further in Part III, Chief Justice
John Roberts and Justice Samuel Alito share a similar background.

[21] See Part III.C for a discussion of the various commitments that might prompt a
conservative jurist to care about federalism as a constitutional principle.

[22] See, e.g., Lyle Denniston, *Commentary: Justice Kennedy and the "War on Drugs,"* SCO-
TUSblog (June 6, 2005), available at http://www.scotusblog.com/movabletype/archives/
2005/06/commentary_just.html.

[23] Cf. David G. Savage, *The Rescue of Roe v Wade*, LA Times (Dec 13, 1992), at A1
(discussing Justice Kennedy's decision to pursue a moderate course in *Planned Parenthood
v Casey*). A defender of Justice Kennedy might plausibly ask why I am unwilling to attribute
to him precisely the same limited commitment to limiting national power that I attributed
to Justice Scalia. It is, of course, hard to know—this sort of psychoanalysis does not come
easy to lawyers, and my ultimate argument is that it is not worth doing. Justice Kennedy's
opinions both inside and outside the federalism area, however, indicate greater comfort
with the exercise of judicial power than Justice Scalia's do. Compare, e.g., *Roper v Simmons*,
543 US 551, 574–75 (2005) (majority opinion by Kennedy, J, overruling prior precedent
and striking down juvenile death penalty based "evolving norms of decency"), and *Lawrence
v Texas*, 539 US 558, 578–79 (2003) (majority opinion by Kennedy, J, striking down anti-
sodomy law under broad and unenumerated right to personal autonomy), with *Roper*, 543
US at 607–08 (Scalia, J, dissenting), and *Lawrence*, 539 US at 586 (Scalia, J, dissenting);
see also *United States v Lopez*, 514 US 549, 579 (1995) (Kennedy, J, concurring) ("But as
the branch whose distinctive duty it is to declare 'what the law is, . . . we are often called
upon to resolve questions of constitutional law not susceptible to the mechanical application of bright and clear lines."). It is thus easier to imagine that Scalia—as opposed to
Kennedy—would be uncomfortable with judicial implementation of a "necessity" requirement under the Necessary and Proper Clause, for example. See Part II.B (discussing the
necessity issue in *Raich*).

[24] See Cass R. Sunstein, *Foreword: Leaving Things Undecided*, 110 Harv L Rev 6 (1996).

this. Under the circumstances, the hypothesis would be more a biographical point about Justice Kennedy than a useful hypothesis about the Supreme Court as an institution.

Attitudinalists might respond, of course, by noting that Justice Kennedy has long been a swing vote on the court, and his influence is likely to increase with Justice O'Connor's departure.[25] Predicting the behavior of the "median Justice" thus will often mean predicting the outcome of critical cases. But the political hypothesis purports not only to provide a predictive tool but also to state a more fundamental truth about law and courts—that is, that legal principle does not constrain judges, and the doctrinal explanations offered in judicial opinions are simply post hoc rationalizations meant to mask the pursuit of naked political preferences.[26] The positions taken by an overwhelming majority of the Justices in *Raich* do not support that hypothesis.

Despite how the case came out, then, the glass is seven- or (more likely) eight-ninths full. Almost all of the Justices adhered to established positions on federalism and the Commerce Clause, notwithstanding an apparent shift in the political valence of this case from previous ones raising similar issues. One decent case, of course, is hardly enough to disprove the political hypothesis. As I discuss in the next section, however, that hypothesis has broader problems.

B. THE POLITICS OF THE FEDERALIST REVIVAL

The political hypothesis—sometimes called the "attitudinal model" by political scientists—suggests that politics, not legal principle, drives judicial decision making.[27] Judge Richard Posner

---

[25] See Paul H. Edelman and Jim Chen, *The Most Dangerous Justice Rides Again: Revisiting the Power Pageant of the Justices*, 86 Minn L Rev 131 (2001) (identifying Justice Kennedy as the "most dangerous" Justice of the 1994–2000 terms); Charles Lane, *Kennedy Seen as the Next Justice in Court's Middle*, Washington Post (Jan 31, 2006), at A4 ("Alito's arrival . . . may turn the O'Connor Court into the Kennedy Court.").

[26] See Segal and Spaeth, *The Supreme Court* at 86 (cited in note 9).

[27] See, e.g., id; Smith, 74 Geo Wash L Rev (cited in note 8). The attitudinal model is increasingly under siege in political science circles from practitioners of positive political theory (PPT), which rejects the attitudinalist's image of individual Justices largely unconstrained from following their political preferences in favor of a model of strategic Justices who are constrained by the choices made by their fellows and the other institutional characteristics of their environment. See, e.g., Daniel B. Rodriguez and Matthew D. McCubbins, *The Judiciary and the Role of Law: A Positive Political Theory Perspective*, in B. Weingast and D. Wittman, eds, *Handbook on Political Economy* (Oxford, 2006) (available at http://ssrn.com/abstract=875025); Forrest Maltzman, James F. Spriggs II, and Paul J.

recently endorsed this view, at least as it applies to constitutional cases in the Supreme Court, in his *Harvard Law Review* "Foreword."[28] Judge Posner aside, however, pursuit of political preference is certainly not how the judges say they decide the cases, and it is inconsistent with much anecdotal evidence from people who have worked with them. For example, when I went to clerk for a federal appeals court judge after wrestling with Critical Legal Studies for three years in law school, one of the very first questions that the judge asked me about a case was, "What's the right answer?" (I wanted to hug him.) Not surprisingly, most proponents of the political hypothesis seem to concede that judges do not consciously vote their political preferences; the proponents insist, rather, that the influence of politics is subconscious—but nonetheless dispositive.[29]

Because the political hypothesis takes this form, its plausibility depends heavily on its ability to predict results. Indeed, one of the attitudinalists' primary criticisms of the "legal model"—which posits that judges are constrained to follow the preexisting legal materials—is that the latter model is not "falsifiable" empirically.[30] Attitudinalists have thus assembled a vast database of Supreme Court decisions, coded according to their political valence, which are then correlated to the supposed political predispositions of the Justices.[31] While this approach is a valuable effort to introduce some analytical rigor into the usual speculation about why judges do what they do, it suffers from similar problems of indeterminacy to those that plague doctrinal analysis. This is not the place for a thoroughgoing critique of the attitudinal model. What I hope to do instead is to point up some conceptual difficulties with the

---

Wahlbeck, *Strategy and Judicial Choice: New Institutionalist Approaches to Supreme Court Decision-Making*, in C. Clayton and H. Gillman, eds, *Supreme Court Decision-Making: New Institutionalist Approaches* 43 (Chicago, 1999). The PPT perspective, however, shares the attitudinalist assumption that judges seek to maximize their preferences rather than seek some sort of legal "right answer."

[28] Richard A. Posner, *The Supreme Court, 2004 Term—Foreword: A Political Court*, 119 Harv L Rev 31 (2005).

[29] See id at 52; Segal and Spaeth, *The Supreme Court* at 433 (cited in note 9) (remaining agnostic as to the judges' conscious motives).

[30] See Segal and Spaeth, *The Supreme Court* at 46–47 (cited in note 9).

[31] The various databases are available at http://www.as.uky.edu/polisci/ulmerproject/sctdata.htm. For explanatory documentation, see Harold J. Spaeth, *The Original United States Supreme Court Judicial Database, 1953–2003 Terms: Documentation* (2005) (available at http://www.as.uky.edu/polisci/ulmerproject/allcourt_codebook.pdf).

political hypothesis and to illustrate the havoc wrought by those difficulties upon an effort to assess *Raich*.[32]

An effort to demonstrate that the political or policy preferences of the Justices control their votes in particular cases faces two basic problems of characterization: One must coherently characterize the preexisting preferences of the Justices, and one must also characterize votes in particular cases in terms that map onto the Justices' defined preferences. Some version of these two problems would arise regardless of the method by which the assessment proceeds; for an empirical project like the attitudinal model, the problems become problems of coding. Attitudinalists have thus undertaken to rate individual Justices as "conservative" or "liberal" and to code case votes in the same binary terms. If either set of coding criteria is unreliable or indeterminate, then the results of the model fall into serious question.

Take the Justices first. The leading attitudinalists derive the Justices' individual predispositions from surveys of newspaper coverage at the time of each Justice's nomination.[33] It is common knowledge, however, that initial assessments—by well-informed professionals, much less newspaper editorial boards—often turn out to be wrong. So it is unsurprising that the attitudinalist method produces some real howlers: Professors Jeffrey Segal and Harold Spaeth list the younger Justice Harlan as a strong liberal, Justice Powell as equally conservative as Justice Thomas, Justice Blackmun as *more* conservative than Justice Thomas, and Justices Stevens, Souter, and Breyer as moderate conservatives.[34] Not surprisingly, the attitudinalists do not actually seem to stick with these initial ratings. Segal and Spaeth's discussion of the Rehnquist Court, for example, consistently treats Justice Souter as a liberal, notwithstanding his conservative score based on their initial cri-

---

[32] The space devoted to the attitudinal model here is arguably disproportionate to its actual stature in political science. See, e.g., H. W. Perry, *Taking Political Science Seriously*, 47 SLU L J 889, 891 (2003) (observing that "many (I dare say most) public law political scientists, let alone political scientists generally, have never taken the attitudinal model that seriously"). The model's acceptance by influential legal scholars like Judge Posner, however, suggests that the model is worth taking on. Moreover, the Spaeth database of Supreme Court opinions has been employed more broadly by political scientists studying the Court from a variety of perspectives. To the extent that some of my objections go to the coding of that database, they implicate that broader body of work.

[33] See Segal and Spaeth, *The Supreme Court* at 321 (cited in note 9); Jeffrey Segal and Albert D. Cover, *Ideological Values and the Votes of U.S. Supreme Court Justices*, 83 Am Pol Sci Rev 557 (1989).

[34] See Segal and Spaeth, *The Supreme Court* at 322 (cited in note 9).

teria.[35] That sort of modification, however, opens the attitudinalists to the charge of circularity. If one reclassifies Justices' personal ideology based on their subsequent votes,[36] then one cannot then use the correlation between the Justices' ideology and votes to prove anything about causation.

A more fundamental problem with coding both the preferences of Justices and the valence of votes is that we lack any coherent definition of "liberal" or "conservative." Political theorists notoriously disagree about the meanings of these terms.[37] *Lawrence v Texas*,[38] striking down a Texas anti-sodomy law, was widely condemned by social and religious conservatives, yet it was applauded by libertarian conservatives.[39] If the coder's definition of "conservative" is capacious enough to include both social conservatives and libertarians, it becomes possible to code virtually any outcome in a case about privacy rights and the like as either conservative or liberal. The Court's decisions on cross-burnings[40] show a similar divide on the liberal side. Free speech liberals have long opposed any restrictions on expressive activity, yet other liberals more focused on the question of equality for racial minorities have strongly argued for such restrictions.[41] Again, the availability of a

---

[35] Professors Segal and Spaeth note, for example, that Justice Souter voted to strike down 42.3 percent of "liberal" laws and 74.2 percent of "conservative" laws without expressing any surprise that Souter voted against his predicted ideology, see id at 415–16 and Table 10.1. Presumably this is based on a perfectly plausible—but unexplained— judgment that he is actually part of the Court's more liberal bloc.

[36] I have seen no indication that the attitudinalists perform a reevaluation of newspaper assessments years into a Justice's tenure. See Jeffrey A. Segal and Harold J. Spaeth, *The Authors Respond*, 4 Law & Courts 10, 10 (Spring 1994) (conceding that their model "does not even attempt" to account for changes in attitudes).

[37] For an introduction, see the two companion volumes edited by Peter Berkowitz, *Varieties of Conservatism in America* (2004) (surveying "classical conservatism," "libertarianism," and "neoconservatism"), and *Varieties of Progressivism in America* (2004) (surveying different positions on the American left). I have catalogued the very divergent strands of conservatism elsewhere. Ernest A. Young, *Judicial Activism and Conservative Politics*, 73 U Colo L Rev 1139, 1181–1203 (2002).

[38] 539 US 558 (2003).

[39] See, e.g., Randy E. Barnett, *Restoring the Lost Constitution* 334 (Princeton, 2003) (applauding Justice Kennedy's opinion in *Lawrence* as protecting "liberty" rather than "privacy"). One might be tempted to write off libertarian outcomes as not conservative at all, yet the libertarian position is strongly identified with conservatism when it comes to economic regulation. Does anyone doubt that the attitudinalists should and would code *Lochner v New York*, 198 US 45 (1905), as a conservative decision?

[40] See *RAV v City of St. Paul*, 505 US 377 (1992); *Virginia v Black*, 538 US 343 (2003).

[41] Compare, e.g., Charles R. Lawrence III, *If He Hollers Let Him Go: Regulating Racist Speech on Campus*, 1990 Duke L J 431 (arguing for restrictions on hate speech), with

liberal argument for either result in many such speech cases means that coding the results for attitudinal model purposes involves a difficult question of judgment.

Equally important, the different factors used to code a case as "conservative" or "liberal" may cut in different directions within the confines of a single case. The Spaeth database, for example, codes a case as "liberal" if it invalidates a criminal conviction, and "conservative" if it limits national power on federalism grounds.[42] So what to do with a case like *Lopez*, which did both things at the same time? *Raich*, of course, would present precisely the same problem in reverse: The prevailing majority refused to enjoin enforcement of a criminal statute (conservative) but rejected a state-autonomy-based challenge to federal legislation (liberal).[43]

What is a coder to do in such situations? When the prearranged criteria conflict, one of two things seems likely to happen: The coders may resolve the conflict based on some gestalt judgment that would be difficult to articulate and defend.[44] Alternatively, the coders might analyze the doctrinal issues in the case to determine which dimension of the decision (e.g., *Lopez*'s restriction of national power or its windfall to the individual defendant) is more salient. But this approach accords a critical role to doctrine that the attitudinalists generally seem at pains to deny. In any event, the indeterminacy of coding cases and Justices casts considerable doubt on the attitudinal model's great strength—its strong predictive success. Without determinate coding criteria, we cannot be sure that the people com-

Nadine R. Strossen, *Regulating Racist Speech on Campus: A Modest Proposal?* 1990 Duke L J 484 (opposing such restrictions).

[42] See Spaeth, *Documentation* at 57–60 (cited in note 31).

[43] In fact, the current version of the Spaeth database classifies *Raich* as a "conservative" outcome—just as it classified *Lopez* and *Morrison*. See Harold J. Spaeth, *The Original U.S. Supreme Court Judicial Database*, available at http://www.as.uky.edu/polisci/ulmerproject/sctdata.htm.

[44] See Howard Gillman, *Separating the Wheat from the Chaff in the Supreme Court and the Attitudinal Model Revisited*, 13 Law & Courts 12, 17 n 12 (Summer 2003) (reporting a concession by Professor Spaeth that coding decisions are conducted "ad hoc"). It seems at least possible that, much as initial classifications of a Justice's ideological position seem to be revised in light of his votes in subsequent cases, difficult calls about whether to code a given case as liberal or conservative may be resolved by looking at *who* voted for and against the result. This would, of course, pose a similar circularity problem. See Segal and Spaeth, *The Supreme Court* at 47 (cited in note 9) ("[A]n attitudinal model that measures the justices' attitudes by their voting behavior and then explains their votes by their attitudes would . . . be unfalsifiable.").

piling the relevant databases are not doing so in a way that simply confirms what they expected to find.[45]

In the Commerce Clause cases, the Spaeth database seems to prioritize factors based on the specific result over structural views about federalism. The database classifies *Lopez*, *Morrison*, and *Raich* as all "conservative" decisions, presumably because the federal statutes struck down in the first two cases embodied "liberal" policies of gun control and gender equality, while the federal law upheld in *Raich* stifled a liberal California experiment in drug policy.[46] But thinking about the results in these terms simply is not very persuasive with regard to a number of key cases in the Federalist Revival. Does anyone really think that the Court struck down the federal Gun Free School Zones Act in *Lopez* because the Court was so pro-gun that it did not care about the safety of schoolchildren? Or that it struck down the civil remedy under the Violence Against Women Act in *Morrison* because the Court was pro-violence against women? Or that the result in *Seminole Tribe v Florida*[47] had anything to do with the Justices' preconceived political preferences regarding the Indian Gaming Regulatory Act? The more plausible account is that the Justices in the majority in these cases were acting on a more general preference for state autonomy and sovereignty over national power, and in fact the Segal-Spaeth database allows for coding decisions about federalism issues as "conservative" simply on the ground that they are pro-states. But on that sort of criterion, one can hardly classify *Lopez* and *Raich* as the same, given their diametrically opposed conclusions on Commerce Clause doctrine.

We might, of course, simply take the Spaeth database's classification of *Raich* as a conservative decision to be a mistake, given the decision's nationalist orientation. Peter Smith's account of the state sovereign immunity cases, for example, properly concedes that it is hard to assign any political valence to these cases in terms of their particular results.[48] While cases like *Kimel*[49] and

---

[45] See Gillman, 13 Law & Courts at 14–15 (cited in note 44) (suggesting that "maybe the books have been cooked a little bit to make the correlations a little better").

[46] See Spaeth, *Database* (cited in note 43).

[47] 517 US 44 (1996) (holding that the judicial enforcement provision of the Indian Gaming Regulatory Act was invalid under the Eleventh Amendment).

[48] See Smith, 74 Geo Wash L Rev (cited in note 8).

[49] *Kimel v Fla Bd of Regents*, 528 US 62 (2000) (striking down a provision of the Age Discrimination in Employment Act that sought to abrogate state sovereign immunity in damages suits brought under the Act).

Garrett[50] made it more difficult for federal rights plaintiffs to recover for discrimination, for example, cases like *Florida Prepaid*[51]
impinged on the interests of the business community in the intellectual property field, and cases like *Seminole Tribe* were so ambiguous as to whose ox had really been gored as to defy political
classification.[52] Leaving the sovereign immunity cases out, however,
would seriously weaken any argument that the Federalist Revival
bears a political stamp overall; as I have long argued, the sovereign
immunity cases are at the heart of the Rehnquist Court's vision of
federalism.[53] The obvious alternative would be to say that the immunity cases reflect a strong preference that state governments not
be subject to suit—a preference that is part and parcel of a "conservative" commitment to limiting national power.

This move, however, reveals a more fundamental difficulty with
many versions of the political hypothesis. The problem is that it is
hard to distinguish between a "preference" for federalism of the
sort just described and a good faith legal view about the meaning
of the Constitution. In the immunity cases, for instance, how much
conceptual daylight is there between a "preference" that states not
be subject to suit and a legal conviction that the Constitution contains a strong principle of state immunity?[54] One cannot prove the

---

[50] *Bd of Trs of the Univ. of Ala v Garrett*, 531 US 356 (2001) (striking down a provision of Title I of the Americans with Disabilities Act that sought to abrogate state sovereign immunity in damages suits brought under the Act).

[51] *Fla Prepaid Postsecondary Expense Bd v College Savings Bank*, 527 US 627 (1999) (striking down a provision of the Patent Remedy Clarification Act that sought to abrogate state sovereign immunity in damages suits for patent infringement); see also *Chavez v Arte Publico Press*, 157 F3d 282 (5th Cir 1998) (invalidating Congress's attempt to abrogate state sovereign immunity in copyright cases).

[52] It was highly unclear in *Seminole Tribe* whether the State of Florida was really better off once it had been held immune from suit under the IGRA. The Act was designed to permit states some say in regulating gaming on Indian reservations, and the anti-state suit provisions were designed to allow the tribes to compel states to negotiate agreements under which gaming proceeds. After holding that these anti-state suit provisions were invalid, the Eleventh Circuit held them severable from the remainder of the Act. See *Seminole Tribe v Florida*, 11 F3d 1016, 1029 (11th Cir 1994), aff'd, 517 US 44 (1996). The result was that a nonconsenting state would be cut out of the process entirely, and reg-ulations for gaming would be promulgated by the Secretary of the Interior. Id.

[53] See Young, 83 Tex L Rev at 2 (cited in note 13); Ernest A. Young, *State Sovereign Immunity and the Future of Federalism*, 1999 Supreme Court Review 1, 1–2.

[54] One frequent answer is to say that the immunity cases reflect a politically conservative hostility to civil plaintiffs. See, e.g., Erwin Chemerinsky, *Understanding the Rehnquist Court: An Admiring Reply to Professor Merrill*, 47 SLU L J 659, 665–69 (2003). That answer is problematic on several levels. In cases like *Florida Prepaid*, the unfortunate plaintiffs are, in fact, the very same sort of corporate business entities that conservatives usually stiff plaintiffs in order to defend. Moreover, one would expect a Court that was simply out to

primacy of political preferences over legal principle if one's definition of political preferences is so broad as to include legal principles.

The attitudinal critique in political science tends to an across-the-board assault on law as a meaningful determinant of judicial outcomes. In the legal literature, however, accusations that the Court behaves politically are often localized to particular doctrinal areas. As Peter Smith's recent essay demonstrates,[55] the Rehnquist Court's federalism jurisprudence is a particularly common target. But this sort of selectivity opens the instrumentalist account itself to the charge of instrumentalism. Why is the Court's federalism jurisprudence constantly critiqued as instrumentalist, while the Court's equal protection jurisprudence, for example, is not?[56] Professor Smith, to his credit, recognizes the problem and attempts an answer: Federalism cases, he says, are more troubling because federalism has been associated in the past with unsavory causes like slavery and segregation.[57] We should be more worried about instrumentalist judging, in other words, when the policy ends to be served are bad ones.

---

make states hard to sue to limit damages suits by plaintiffs against state *officers*. Cf. John Jeffries, *In Praise of the Eleventh Amendment—and of Section 1983*, 84 Va L Rev 47 (1998) (arguing that the availability of damages suits against officers largely eliminates the practical impact of state sovereign immunity on plaintiffs' ability to recover). Yet the Court has done little to guard the flank of *state* immunity by shoring up the common law immunities of individual officers; indeed, in perhaps the most important line of cases, it has refused to extend official immunity to private entities exercising functions delegated to them by governmental bodies. See *Wyatt v Cole*, 504 US 158 (1992); *Richardson v McKnight*, 521 US 399 (1997).

[55] Smith, 74 Geo Wash L Rev (cited in note 8); see also Erwin Chemerinsky, *Empowering States When It Matters: A Different Approach to Preemption*, 69 Brooklyn L Rev 1313, 1328 (2004).

[56] The most obvious example of instrumental instrumentalism is the widespread tendency to charge that the majority Justices in *Bush v Gore*, 531 US 98 (2000), voted to elect their favored presidential candidate, without leveling a similar accusation at the four dissenters, who are equally vulnerable to charges of partisanship. See, e.g., Jack A. Balkin and Sanford Levinson, *Understanding the Constitutional Revolution*, 87 Va L Rev 1045, 1049–50 (2001) (describing the majority as "[f]ive members of the United States Supreme Court, confident of their power, and brazen in their authority" and claiming the majority "engaged in flagrant judicial misconduct that undermined the foundations of constitutional government"—without any censure of the dissenters); Frank Michelman, *Bush v Gore: Suspicion, or the New Prince*, 68 U Chi L Rev 679, 689 (2001) (conceding that "the Bush v. Gore dissenters . . . . no doubt, had reasons parallel to those of the majority for preferring an opposite electoral outcome and hence for preferring an opposite legal outcome in Bush v Gore," but nonetheless concluding that "[t]he dissenters get an exemption because they all maintain that the Court should have denied or dismissed the writs of certiorari in the election cases").

[57] Smith, 74 Geo Wash L Rev (cited in note 8).

That ground of distinction will not do, for at least two reasons. First, it grossly distorts the complicated relationship between federalism and race over the course of our history. Henry Adams, for example, wrote over a century ago that "[b]etween the slave power and states' rights there was no necessary connection. The slave power, when in control, was a centralizing influence, and all the most considerable encroachments on states' rights were its acts."[58] In any event, most accept the modern nationalization of racial matters, so that current debates about state autonomy concern nonracial questions, such as gay marriage or air pollution control.[59] It is odd to criticize doctrine driven by policy preferences on these sorts of issues on the ground that federalism doctrine *used to be* driven (if it even was) by another set of preferences entirely.

The second problem is that more favored doctrinal adventures have also been associated with unsavory causes. How much of First Amendment doctrine has been developed in service of pornographers and the Ku Klux Klan?[60] How much Eighth Amendment doctrine has benefited brutal murderers?[61] Why do we so readily accept that a judge who allows the Nazis to march in a Jewish community is holding his nose and acting on principle, while presuming that a judge who invokes principles of federalism to shelter a state policy is in fact embracing that policy on the merits? I submit that it is far more plausible to view the academy as politicized on these questions than the judges themselves. Academics criticize as instrumentalist the decisions they do not like, and much of the academy has little use for federalism.[62] Under those circumstances, many if not most critiques of the Court's decisions as "political" are no more trustworthy than the opinions that they purport to debunk.

---

[58] Henry Adams, *John Randolph* 178 (Peter Green, 1969) (1898). See also Lynn A. Baker and Ernest A. Young, *Federalism and the Double Standard of Judicial Review*, 51 Duke L J 75, 143–49 (2001); Earl M. Maltz, *Slavery, Federalism, and the Structure of the Constitution*, 36 Am J Legal Hist 466 (1992).

[59] See Baker and Young, 51 Duke L J at 147–57 (cited in note 58).

[60] See, e.g., *Brandenburg v Ohio*, 395 US 444 (1969); *Reno v ACLU*, 521 US 844 (1997).

[61] See, e.g., *Roper v Simmons*, 543 US 551 (2005).

[62] See, e.g., Larry Kramer, *Putting the Politics Back into the Political Safeguards of Federalism*, 100 Colum L Rev 215, 290–93 (2000) (intemperately criticizing the Court's federalism cases). Although my observation pertains primarily to legal academics, the leading proponents of the attitudinal model in political science make little attempt to hide their own political contempt for the Rehnquist Court. See Segal and Spaeth, *The Supreme Court* at 430–31 (cited in note 9).

C. INDETERMINACY AND STRUCTURAL PRINCIPLE

In order to determine the realm of judicial outcomes that are governed by law, as opposed to politics, the political hypothesis must draw two difficult boundary lines. One is the line between determinacy and indeterminacy: The claim that law fails to constrain presupposes a definition of legal "constraint" or, conversely, when a judge should be said to be exercising "discretion." The second line divides political from nonpolitical arguments, so that we can tell which arguments are driving the decisions in particular cases. The mainstream legal literature has long recognized that neither of these boundaries is easy to demarcate; surprisingly, proponents of the political hypothesis seem to take them almost for granted.[63]

Take indeterminacy first. The attitudinalists seem to think that law loses any constraining or directive force whenever precedents can be cited on either side of a question. But the fact that one can write an argument that would avoid Rule 11 sanctions for either party in most Supreme Court cases hardly proves that one side's argument is not *stronger*, as a matter of law, than the other side's. It is no doubt difficult to factor the weight of precedent, or the multifarious factors that may make one textual reading or precedential authority more persuasive than another, into a political scientist's model. And yet eliminating these comparative judgments from consideration will lead the attitudinalist to find indeterminacy even in cases where most professional lawyers would say that one answer is clearly better than the other.

The fact that reasonable professionals will disagree about the right answer in many cases—and particularly in the atypical subset of constitutional cases that reach the Supreme Court—hardly proves that the Justices are unconstrained by legal principle. Judge Posner, for example, asserts that when the Court was asked last Term "to decide whether execution of murderers under the age of eighteen is constitutional," the Justices were "at large. Nothing compels a yes or no."[64] I would contend, however, that both the

---

[63] A related criticism notes that the attitudinalists' conception of "legal" decision making is a straw man, grounded in notions of "mechanical jurisprudence" that have been out of vogue for nearly a century. See Gillman, 13 Law & Courts at 12 (cited in note 44); Gerald Rosenberg, *Symposium on the Supreme Court and the Attitudinal Model*, 4 Law & Courts 3, 6–7 (Spring 1994).

[64] Posner, 119 Harv L Rev at 41 (cited in note 28).

majority and the dissents in *Roper v Simmons*[65] were meaningfully constrained by legal principle. Justice Scalia's dissent took the view that the Court should strike only those practices disapproved by a clear consensus of American jurisdiction, under which approach no one could plausibly say that thirty out of fifty states amounted to a "consensus."[66] Justice O'Connor's dissent and Justice Kennedy's majority opinion allowed a considerably greater role for "objective" moral reasoning, but disagreed as to how that moral calculus ought to play out.[67] Neither disagreement—over method, or over application—provides much comfort to attitudinalists. The fact that the Justices disagreed over which method of legal reasoning to adopt does not prove that either method fails to constrain on its own terms; the attitudinalist would need to show (somehow) that individual Justices shift back and forth between different methods in different cases depending on the political valence of the results. Nor does disagreement among Justices applying basically the same method demonstrate a lack of constraint. One could just as well say that one of the Justices (Justice Kennedy, in my own view) was mistaken. In any event, given the general similarity of political outlook between Justices Kennedy and O'Connor, it would be exceptionally difficult to show that the difference between them in *Roper* was a function of raw political preferences.

The most likely answer to these arguments would raise the other boundary question: Which arguments are "legal," and which are "political"? One might argue, for instance, that Justice Scalia's methodological aversion to moral argument is itself a political preference. Judge Posner makes a similar move in his "Foreword" when he counts as "personal or political" the methodological preference for rules over standards.[68] But now *everything* is a "political" preference. There is no way to distinguish, for instance, a methodological preference for rules from a preference for following precedent. At this point, of course, the attitudinal model is truly

---

[65] 543 US 551 (2005) (holding that the juvenile death penalty violates the Eighth Amendment).

[66] *Roper*, 543 US at 615–18 (Scalia, J, dissenting).

[67] Id at 561–64 (majority opinion); id at 590 (O'Connor, J, dissenting).

[68] See Posner, 119 Harv L Rev at 51 (cited in note 28) (suggesting that Justice Scalia's vote to strike down the Texas flag desecration statute is attributable to a "political" preference that "constitutional standards such as freedom of speech be recast as rules that have very few exceptions").

nonfalsifiable. Justices acting consistently with the legal model will simply be satisfying their own political preference for lawlike behavior.[69]

It might seem more plausible to suggest that the overtly moral arguments that moved Justices O'Connor and Kennedy in *Roper* are simply political preferences. The situation is considerably more complicated, however. Ronald Dworkin has famously argued that the general moral commitments of a free society are part of the legal background that must be consulted when more particular sources of law—text, precedent, and so on—run out.[70] Whatever one thinks of that approach in general, there is some warrant for it in the Eighth Amendment context, where both the morally freighted text of the Constitution ("cruel and unusual") and long-standing precedent ("evolving standards of decency") seem authoritatively to incorporate moral reasoning into the relevant legal rule. One may protest that these sorts of tests are no way to run a legal railroad, but that—again—is a normative disagreement about the content of the law.

General views about federalism may perform a similar function in a case like *Raich*. I have argued elsewhere that a general concern for balance between national and state power is readily identifiable in the Constitution.[71] This is a legal principle—a claim about the meaning of the Constitution—rather than a political preference exogenous to the case. Because the principle is general, however, it can offer legal direction even in cases where the immediate sources—constitutional text, direct precedent—run out.[72] As I discuss in Part II, the text of the Commerce Clause and the existing precedent would have permitted—but did not dictate—a more restrictive approach to Congress's commerce power. To the extent that the balance of power in twenty-first-century America has shifted in favor of the national power, the constitutional principle

---

[69] Judge Posner offers another avenue of nonfalsifiability when he hypothesizes that "voting against one's seeming druthers may be a calculation that the appearance of being 'principled' is rhetorically and politically effective. It fools people." Id at 51–52. Now any judicial behavior contrary to the attitudinal model can be written off as subterfuge, undertaken to set up some future opportunity to behave politically. This may, of course, describe how judges in fact behave (at least sometimes). But the possibility makes it impossible to disprove the assertion that politics is at the root of every decision.

[70] See Ronald Dworkin, *Hard Cases*, 88 Harv L Rev 1057 (1975).

[71] See Young, *Making Federalism Doctrine* at 1764–75 (cited in note 19).

[72] See id at 1775–99; Ernest A. Young, *Alden v Maine and the Jurisprudence of Structure*, 41 Wm & Mary L Rev 1601, 1638–51 (2000).

of balance would have supported this more restrictive tack. On the other hand, if one interprets the Constitution as a fundamentally nationalizing document,[73] then that interpretation would support the approach taken by the *Raich* majority. The important point for present purposes is simply that these are contending views about the law, not simply political preferences.

A final point about the preferences commonly imputed to the Justices by proponents of the political hypothesis: Why would one assume that the Justices place no value on the development of—and adherence to—a coherent set of legal rules? Political scientists in the interpretivist tradition have suggested that "justices acquire distinctive preferences, goals, or conceptions of duty by virtue of their understanding of the role of the Supreme Court in the political system," and that "the justices' concern about the maintenance of the institution's power and legitimacy mitigates their temptation to indulge their personal points of view."[74] Surely every constitutional lawyer has wrestled with the need to maintain some coherent distinction between law and politics, and one would think that this distinction might well be even more central to the professional identity of those lawyers serving as Supreme Court Justices. This "preference for law" may well be overridden in some cases, but why would one assume that it would *always* lose out to some marginal result-oriented preference having to do with, say, the implementation of the Indian Gaming Regulatory Act?[75]

For the attitudinalists, analyzing a Supreme Court decision like *Raich* in terms of its articulated legal reasoning requires "the fatuousness characteristic of Pollyanna."[76] Belief in the constraining force of law is an "unsophisticated view"; in truth, "the legal model and its components serve only to rationalize the Court's decisions and to cloak the reality of the Court's decision-making process."[77]

---

[73] See, e.g., Calvin H. Johnson, *Righteous Anger at the Wicked States* (Cambridge, 2005).

[74] Howard Gillman, *The Court as an Idea, Not a Building (or a Game): Interpretive Institutionalism and the Analysis of Supreme Court Decision-Making*, in *Supreme Court Decision-Making* at 65, 77 (cited in note 27).

[75] See *Seminole Tribe v Florida*, 517 US 44 (1996) (holding that the Indian Gaming Regulatory Act could not overcome the states' sovereign immunity).

[76] Segal and Spaeth, *The Supreme Court* at 1 (cited in note 9); but see Cross, 74 NYU L Rev at 1313 (cited in note 10) (advancing a more modest version of the political hypothesis and conceding that "[t]he law can and does constrain opinions to a degree").

[77] Id at 6, 53. Although I have cited Judge Posner as the most prominent recent proponent of the political hypothesis among *legal* academics, he does not go nearly so far: His claim that law fails to constrain is limited to constitutional decisions by the Supreme

But like most categorical claims in a complex world, this claim is wrong: Politics surely enters into Supreme Court decisions, but it is hardly the whole story. Neither the federalism cases in general, nor the *Raich* decision in particular, bears out the claim that the Court's decisions are driven by result-oriented political preferences.

II. A Bad Day for State Autonomy

The more interesting questions in *Raich* were doctrinal. The first two arose out of the fact that the federal Controlled Substances Act was a major federal statute governing a large class of activity. This gave rise to a problem of characterization: Is the "regulated activity"—which must be commercial under *Lopez*—the marijuana market generally? Or is it the medicinal use by people who grow it themselves in California? The second question arises if the latter characterization is accepted: To what extent can *non*-commercial activity be regulated as a "necessary and proper" means of facilitating a scheme of commercial regulation? Justice Stevens's majority opinion resolved the case by opting for a broad view of the relevant regulated activity. Justice Scalia's concurrence, by contrast, decided the case on "necessary and proper" grounds. These two doctrinal approaches seem likely to remain the primary battlegrounds in future Commerce Clause decisions.[78]

The third and more general question arises from the presence of a state regulatory regime dealing with the same subject matter as the federal one. Should this matter? Most efforts to articulate the values served by federalism, after all, stress the importance of allowing state governments to make their own distinctive policy choices. From that perspective, *Raich* was a far more important case than *Lopez* and *Morrison*, in which the states had not undertaken to dissent from federal policy. Given the structure of the Supremacy Clause, however, it is difficult to give weight to state policy judgments when they come into conflict with federal mandates. The facts of *Raich* offered some possible avenues for re-

---

Court. See Posner, 119 Harv L Rev at 40–41 (cited in note 28). But within that sphere, it is not easy to see where he differs from the attitudinalists in political science.

[78] See, e.g., Randy E. Barnett, *Foreword: Limiting Raich*, 9 Lewis & Clark L Rev 743, 744–50 (2005) (offering an array of doctrinal strategies for limiting *Raich* along these two doctrinal lines).

specting state policy divergence, but the Court largely ignored them.

A. THE CHARACTERIZATION PROBLEM AND AS-APPLIED CHALLENGES

Lopez and *Morrison* suggested that the key question in Commerce Clause cases is whether the activity that Congress has sought to regulate is "commercial" or "economic" in nature. Generally speaking, Congress may regulate items or persons in interstate commerce, the channels and instrumentalities of interstate commerce, or activities with "substantial effects" on interstate commerce.[79] The third category has traditionally been the most capacious, especially in light of the Court's holding in *Wickard v Filburn* that "substantial effects" must be assessed in the aggregate.[80] For example, the fact that the sale of a single stick of bubblegum has no appreciable effect on the national economy matters little, since the aggregate impact of all bubblegum sales is much more substantial.[81] The Court limited this aggregation principle in *Lopez* and *Morrison*, however, by insisting that it applied only when the regulated activity is itself commercial or economic in nature.[82] Most cases are thus likely to turn on the character of the regulated activity.

The Court had little trouble with this question in *Lopez* and *Morrison*: It found, without a great deal of disagreement on the point from the dissenters, that neither possessing a gun nor assaulting a woman is a commercial act.[83] The issue was considerably more difficult in *Raich*, however. The plaintiffs argued that their marijuana use was plainly noncommercial: They cultivated their marijuana themselves, so that it was neither bought nor sold—nor carried across state lines. They were thus not participants in any economic market for marijuana.[84] The U.S. government, on the other hand, insisted that the relevant activity was marijuana use in general, which generally does involve a purchase and sale and

---

[79] See, e.g., *Lopez*, 514 US at 558–59.

[80] 317 US 111, 127–28 (1942).

[81] See Datamonitor, *Gum Confectionery in the United States* at 9 (Feb 2004) (reporting that the value of the U.S. gum confectionery market was $2.296 billion).

[82] See *United States v Morrison*, 529 US 598, 613 (2000); *Lopez*, 514 US at 560.

[83] See *Morrison*, 529 US at 613; *Lopez*, 514 US at 561.

[84] See Brief for Respondents in No 03-1454, *Gonzales v Raich*, at 23–27.

is thus clearly commercial in nature.[85] These divergent charac-
terizations were reflected in the respective statutory schemes. The
federal scheme regulated marijuana use generally, while the state
regulatory regime sought to carve out a narrow class of purely
medicinal, homegrown consumption.[86]

The characterization problem in *Raich* was reminiscent of the
classic "level of generality" problem arising in the definition of
fundamental rights under the Due Process Clause.[87] Neither the
Due Process Clause nor the Commerce Clause says anything about
the appropriate level of generality at which to analyze any given
activity, and the manipulability of this choice generates both unpredictability and the potential for result-oriented decisions. The
Raich majority sought to avoid these pitfalls by deferring to Congress's choice of the appropriate level of generality. Because the
Controlled Substances Act regulated marijuana use generally, the
Court rejected California's attempt to carve out a particular subset
of that activity for distinctive treatment.[88]

This approach avoided the need for the Court to choose for
itself the level of generality at which to characterize the regulated
activity. There are several problems, however. One is that the
Court may, in fact, have misconstrued Congress's choice. The
question is whether medicinal use of marijuana is sufficiently distinct from ordinary recreational use as to constitute a separate
activity for regulatory purposes. The structure of the federal Controlled Substances Act suggests that medicinal uses are distinctive,
and it regulates them separately under Schedules II through V of
the Act.[89] Federal authorities have determined, of course, that
marijuana is a drug without any legitimate medical use, but that
determination is irrelevant to whether medical uses—where they

---

[85] See Brief for Petitioner in No 03-1454, *Gonzales v Raich*, at 40 ("For purposes of
defining Congress's power under the Commerce Clause in enacting the CSA, . . . there
is no basis for distinguishing marijuana production, distribution, or use for purported
medicinal purposes, as opposed to recreational (or any other) purpose.").

[86] Compare Compassionate Use Act of 1996, Cal Health & Safety Code § 11362.5, with
the Controlled Substances Act, 21 USC § 844(a). The CSA does expressly disclaim intent
"to . . . exclu[de] any State law on the same subject matter . . . unless there is a positive
conflict" such that the federal and state laws "cannot consistently stand together." 21 USC
§ 903.

[87] See generally Laurence H. Tribe and Michael C. Dorf, *Levels of Generality in the
Definition of Rights*, 57 U Chi L Rev 1057 (1990).

[88] See *Raich*, 125 S Ct at 2211–13.

[89] See 21 USC §§ 821–29; Scholars' Brief at 17–18 (cited in "Author's note").

are thought to exist—are sufficiently distinct from recreational uses to require separate regulatory treatment. On that question, Congress and California were in agreement, and the Court arguably should have deferred to that judgment by analyzing medical use as a distinct class of regulated activity for Commerce Clause purposes.

More fundamentally, a policy of deferring to Congress's choice of the appropriate level of generality makes Congress the judge of its own power. As the *Raich* dissenters recognized,[90] Congress can choose how generally to regulate, and under the majority's approach Congress can leverage a dubious regulation of noncommercial activity simply by casting the regulatory net more broadly. A narrow regulation of the content of high school science textbooks, for example, might not hold up as "commercial" under *Lopez*, but Congress could overcome this barrier by enacting a more comprehensive scheme regulating the purchase and sale of textbooks generally. Adrian Vermeule has argued that this sort of perverse incentive is endemic to the Court's Commerce Clause doctrine.[91] It is inevitable, however, only if the Court refuses to analyze whether particular subsets of activity are "commercial" notwithstanding the more general scope of Congress's regulatory scheme.

One escape from this dilemma would be through the Court's doctrine of facial and as-applied challenges. If the Court permitted as-applied challenges, then the constitutionality of federal regulation could be framed by the activity at issue in the particular case. Angel Raich used marijuana that she had grown herself for purely medicinal purposes; she did not buy, sell, or take the stuff across state lines. A traditional as-applied challenge would ask whether her activity was commercial. Hence, her brief began its discussion of the relevant class of conduct in the case by insisting that "Respondents are not challenging the constitutionality of the CSA on its face but only as it applies to the class of activities in

---

[90] See *Raich*, 125 S Ct at 2222 (O'Connor, J, dissenting) ("[A]llowing Congress to set the terms of the constitutional debate in this way, *i.e.*, by packaging regulation of local activity in broader schemes, is tantamount to removing meaningful limits on the Commerce Clause.").

[91] Adrian Vermeule, *Does Commerce Clause Review Have Perverse Effects?* 46 Vill L Rev 1325, 1333–36 (2001) (noting that because the Court permits regulation of noncommercial activity where such regulation is part of a "comprehensive scheme," the *Lopez* doctrine may encourage Congress to draft broader regulatory schemes to the detriment of the States).

which they are engaged."[92] Under this approach, the Court would not "choose" a level of generality, but rather accept the case as defined by the litigants. This is how most constitutional litigation proceeds.[93]

Assessing federal statutes as applied to particular plaintiffs would, of course, push in the direction of narrower frames, with the result that federal regulation would be more likely to be found unconstitutional in particular cases. That does not mean the courts would strike down federal law in many cases—the Court's definition of commercial activity remains extremely capacious,[94] and the government would retain the option of arguing that sweeping in subclasses of noncommercial activity is "necessary and proper" to fulfill the legitimate commercial goals of the statutory scheme.[95] Moreover, the as-applied nature of the challenge inherently lowers the stakes by permitting the federal regulation in question to continue to be applied to those instances of the regulated activity that are commercial in nature. The *Raich* majority squarely rejected this sort of analysis, however, and refused to permit constitutional challenges to carve out noncommercial instances of an activity from a broader regulation covering commercial and noncommercial instances alike.[96]

The Court's rejection of as-applied challenges in *Raich* is odd, given its stated strong preference for as-applied challenges in other areas.[97] It is even odder in light of the Court's recent decision in *Tennessee v Lane*,[98] in which the Justices in the *Raich* majority es-

---

[92] Respondents' Brief at 19 (cited in note 84).

[93] The question how to define the activity at issue in a particular case is distinct from the generality issue involved in identifying protected individual rights. See generally *Michael H. v Gerald D.*, 491 US 110, 127 n 6 (1989) (opinion of Scalia, J). In *Bowers v Hardwick*, 478 US 186 (1986), for example, one might have defined the regulated activity as "homosexual sodomy" because that is what the particular plaintiff had done, while still arguing that the interpretive question is whether the Constitution protects a more general right of sexual privacy.

[94] See Young, *Two Federalisms* at 135–37 (cited in note 13).

[95] I assess these sorts of arguments—which I believe provided the more persuasive ground for sustaining the statute in *Raich*—in the next section.

[96] See *Raich*, 125 S Ct at 2211–13.

[97] See, e.g., *United States v Salerno*, 481 US 739, 745 (1987) ("A facial challenge to a legislative Act is, of course, the most difficult challenge to mount successfully, since the challenger must establish that no set of circumstances exists under which the Act would be valid."); *Younger v Harris*, 401 US 37, 52–53 (1971). For a particularly lucid discussion of the Court's use of facial and as-applied analysis in federalism cases, see Gillian E. Metzger, *Facial Challenges and Federalism*, 105 Colum L Rev 873 (2005).

[98] 124 S Ct 1978 (2004).

sentially considered the ADA as applied to courthouse access cases, while refusing to evaluate whether the statute would be a valid exercise of the Section 5 power considered across the whole range of its applications.[99] *Lane*, however, was itself a departure from previous federalism cases that had tended to evaluate the full sweep of a statute rather than its application to individual instances. In *City of Boerne v Flores*,[100] for example, the Court's "congruence and proportionality" analysis focused on the entire sweep of the statute in question, not on its application to a particular plaintiff or even to a subclass of cases.

The use of facial analysis in Section 5 cases, however, has properly been influenced—at least implicitly—by the peculiar office of Section 5 as a vehicle for the legislative enforcement of constitutional rights. The worry in *Boerne* and its progeny is that Congress will use Section 5 to change the content of rights rather than simply to enforce them. This concern must be balanced, however, with deference to the institutional advantages that Congress enjoys with respect to enforcing rights in particular situations.[101] Because of its different fact-finding mechanisms, for example, Congress may be better at identifying practices that derive from unconstitutional discriminatory intent, even though they are facially neutral in form.[102] The doctrine has thus allowed Congress to act "prophylactically" by barring practices—such as a literacy test for voting—that it views as unconstitutional notwithstanding that a court would be unwilling to find the same practice unconstitutional.[103] The trick, of course, is to distinguish between cases

---

[99] *Lane* did not pursue a "pure" as-applied analysis because it did not ask whether the states' failure to provide access to the particular disabled plaintiffs in the case was unconstitutional; rather, it took a broad statute (requiring disabled access to public accommodations generally) and identified a much narrower subset of cases (those involving access to courthouses). It then assessed the constitutionality of the ADA as applied to this subset of cases. That, however, is a far cry from the ordinary facial challenge, which would have assessed the statute's entire range of applications.

[100] 521 US 507, 532–33 (1997); see also Metzger, 105 Colum L Rev at 894–97 (cited in note 97) (discussing the use of facial analysis in Section 5 cases).

[101] Lawrence Gene Sager, *Fair Measure: The Legal Status of Underenforced Constitutional Norms*, 91 Harv L Rev 1212 (1978); Melissa Hart, *Conflating Scope of Right with Standard of Review: The Supreme Court's "Strict Scrutiny" of Congressional Efforts to Enforce the Fourteenth Amendment*, 46 Vill L Rev 1091 (2001).

[102] See *Katzenbach v Morgan*, 384 US 641, 654–56 (1966) (noting Congress's "specially informed legislative competence" in identifying invidious discrimination).

[103] Compare *Lassiter v Northampton Cty Bd of Elections*, 360 US 45 (1959) (rejecting a constitutional challenge to literacy tests for voting), with *Morgan*, 384 US at 649 (framing the relevant question as, "Without regard to whether the judiciary would find that the

in which Congress is prophylactically enforcing the same constitutional principle as the Court has recognized, and cases in which
Congress is trying to overrule the Court's interpretations and
change the Constitution without going through the amendment
process (as the Court thought it was in *Boerne*).[104] This is where
facial analysis comes in: The Court looks to the entire sweep of
the statute—not just its application in a particular case—to determine whether Congress has generally tried to conform the
shape of its legislation to the constitutional principle recognized
by the Court. If that is the case, then the fact that the statute may
reach conduct that would not be unconstitutional in a particular
case is not fatal.

The fact that Congress is enforcing rights grounded in the Constitution also explains, in my view, the departure from ordinary
facial analysis in *Lane*. The Americans with Disability Act is generally considered an equality statute, enforcing the Equal Protection Clause. The problem then is that disability is not a suspect
class, so that broad statutory prohibitions of discrimination based
on disability are likely to prohibit far more conduct than would
the Constitution itself.[105] But in *Lane*, an additional constitutional
right was at stake: the right, grounded in the Due Process Clause,
of access to courts.[106] The subset of ADA cases that the Court
analyzed in *Lane* was thus carved out by the Constitution itself,
rather than arbitrarily chosen by the majority Justices. Surely it
makes sense to analyze the propriety of congressional enforcement
of a right with particular regard to cases implicating that right.[107]

Equal Protection Clause itself nullifies New York's English literacy requirement as so
applied, could Congress prohibit the enforcement of the state law by legislating under §
5 of the Fourteenth Amendment?").

[104] I take no position here on whether Congress *ought* to be able to enforce a different
interpretation of the Constitution than that which the Court would accept. Current case
law says Congress may not, and my subject here is how the Court enforces that principle
by use of facial analysis of Congress's statutes.

[105] See *City of Cleburne v Cleburne Living Ctr*, 473 US 432, 442–47 (1985) (refusing to
recognize the disabled as a suspect class); *Bd of Trs of the Univ. of Alabama v Garrett*, 531
US 356, 374 (2001) (emphasizing the absence of heightened scrutiny in holding that Title
I of the Americans with Disabilities Act was not a valid use of the Section 5 power).

[106] See, e.g., *Faretta v California*, 422 US 806, 819 n 15 (1975) (recognizing a criminal
defendant's "right to be present at all stages of the trial where his absence might frustrate
the fairness of the proceedings"); see also *Press-Enterprise Co. v Superior Court*, 478 US 1,
8 (1986) (recognizing the public's "First Amendment right of access to criminal
proceedings").

[107] Cf. Metzger, 105 Colum L Rev at 931–32 (cited in note 97) (concluding that *Lane*
properly applied ordinary rules of severability in holding that Title II of the ADA could

The point of this side trip through the Section 5 cases is to show that the considerations governing the use of facial or as-applied analysis in these cases are unique to Section 5. The commerce power, by contrast, is not delimited by principles found elsewhere in the Constitution; the question is simply what counts as "commerce among the several states." As-applied analysis would help to manage the otherwise intractable problem of defining the appropriate level of generality in Commerce Clause cases; the fact that such analysis is used differently in Section 5 cases is interesting but hardly dispositive.[108] Problems would remain, of course. As Gillian Metzger has suggested, an as-applied challenge may define the relevant class of activity "so narrowly as to not fairly constitute a discrete class."[109] But that risk evaporates in cases like *Raich* where both state and federal authorities have chosen to treat medical uses of a substance differently from other uses. In any event, the alternative—allowing Congress's choice to legislate generally to sweep in all sorts of noncommercial subclasses of activity—simply does too little to maintain balance between federal and state authority.

B. FALSE NECESSITY

The second important set of doctrinal issues has to do with Congress's authority to regulate noncommercial activities under the Necessary and Proper Clause. Justice Scalia's concurring opinion in *Raich* avoided the need to resolve the level of generality problem discussed in the last section by assuming, at least for the sake of argument, that the more narrow frame was appropriate. He thus conceded that, as in *Lopez* and *Morrison*, the regulated activity was noncommercial in nature.[110] But this did not auto-

at least be upheld as applied to court access cases). The Court very recently adhered to this approach in *United States v Georgia*, 2006 US LEXIS 759 (Jan 10, 2006), which upheld, as applied to persons alleging actual constitutional violations, the abrogation of state sovereign immunity in Title II of the Americans with Disabilities Act. See Sam Bagenstos, *Court Decides US/Goodman v. Georgia*, Disability Law (Jan 10, 2006) (available at http://disabilitylaw.blogspot.com/2006/01/court-decides-usgoodman-v-georgia.html) (observing that "[t]he Court's decision . . . made clear that the as-applied analysis in *Tennessee v. Lane* was not a sport").

[108] See Metzger, 105 Colum L Rev at 930 (cited in note 97) (concluding that "as-applied challenges generally remain available in the commerce power context"); Barnett, 9 Lewis & Clark L Rev at 745 (cited in note 78) (concluding that as-applied challenges remain available even after *Raich*).

[109] Metzger, 105 Colum L Rev at 929–30 (cited in note 97).

[110] *Raich*, 125 S Ct at 2219 (Scalia, J, concurring in the judgment).

matically make the regulation unconstitutional. Rather, he argued that Congress may regulate noncommercial activity where such regulation is "necessary and proper" to the regulation of a commercial market. This argument relied heavily on dictum in *Lopez* suggesting that noncommercial regulation may be appropriate if it is "an essential part of a larger regulation of economic activity."[111]

Justice Scalia began by noting the broad purpose of the CSA to "extinguish the interstate market in Schedule I controlled substances, including marijuana."[112] He went on to observe that "[d]rugs like marijuana are fungible commodities," and therefore "marijuana that is grown at home and possessed for personal use is never more than an instant from the interstate market."[113] The government had offered several more specific arguments along these lines in its brief. It claimed, for instance, that medical cannabis may substitute for other painkillers, thereby affecting the market for those drugs.[114] It also warned that any person arrested for marijuana possession would claim to have a medicinal purpose—a contention that would have to be negated beyond a reasonable doubt at trial.[115]

Some of these assertions were patently implausible as justifications for enforcing the CSA against medical patients. For example, the government's concern that medical patients allowed to grow their own marijuana would no longer have to buy painkillers in the ordinary commercial market—thereby affecting prices in that market, à la *Wickard*[116]—is of course relevant only if the government is trying to support the *price* of pain-relieving drugs. But some of the other arguments could not be so readily dismissed, such as the concern about problems of proof in distinguishing between medicinal and nonmedicinal users. Much thus turns upon

---

[111] *Lopez*, 514 US at 561. The majority likewise relied on this language, see 125 S Ct at 2209–10, but for the different argument that one cannot carve a subset of noncommercial activities out of a more generally defined regulatory statute.

[112] *Raich*, 125 S Ct at 2219. In noting that "[t]he Commerce Clause unquestionably permits this," id, Justice Scalia rejected any suggestion that a purpose to eliminate commerce would fall outside the Clause. I do not mean to challenge that view for purposes of the present argument.

[113] Id.

[114] Petitioner's Brief at 26–27 (cited in note 85).

[115] Id at 29–30.

[116] See *Wickard v Filburn*, 317 US 111, 128 (1942).

the standard of review for claims that noncommercial regulation is "necessary" to facilitate commercial ends.

The leading case on the meaning of "necessary and proper" is, of course, *McCulloch v Maryland*, which framed the scope of judicial review in exceedingly deferential terms:

> Let the end be legitimate, let it be within the scope of the constitution, and all means which are appropriate, which are plainly adapted to that end, which are not prohibited, but consist with the letter and spirit of the constitution, are constitutional.[117]

This standard, unfortunately, amounts to a blank check: At least as interpreted in later cases,[118] the *McCulloch* test requires courts to defer to any "rational basis" for legislation—it means, in virtually all cases, that Congress will be limited only by its own sense of self-restraint. The effect of the *McCulloch* test in federalism cases is thus to make the doctrine of enumerated powers dovetail with limits imposed on all government action by substantive due process. That hardly makes sense, given that a primary reason for discountenancing substantive due process challenges is their tenuous grounding in the constitutional text and structure—a problem from which enumerated powers challenges do not suffer.[119]

Rational arguments of "necessity" could easily have been made

---

[117] *McCulloch v Maryland*, 4 Wheat 316, 421 (1819).

[118] See, e.g., *Oregon v Mitchell*, 400 US 112, 286 (1970) (Stewart, J, concurring in part and dissenting in part) (citing *McCulloch* for the proposition that when Congress acts under its Section 5 power, "as against the reserved power of the States, it is enough that the end to which Congress has acted be one legitimately within its power and that there be a rational basis for the measures chosen to achieve that end"); *Scofield v NLRB*, 393 F2d 49, 53 (7th Cir 1968) (citing *McCulloch* for the basic rational basis test); *NLRB v Edward G. Budd Mfg Co.*, 169 F2d 571, 577 (6th Cir 1948) (same); *United States v Chen De Yian*, 905 F Supp 160, 163 (SDNY 1995) (same).

[119] Nor can equating the two sorts of challenges be grounded in long-standing practice. The Court has manifestly not applied a rational basis test to cases testing the limits of Congress's commerce power for much of our history. See, e.g., *A.L.A. Shechter Poultry Corp. v United States*, 295 US 495 (1935) (unanimously applying a more rigorous test). The more recent cases apply a rational basis test to Congress's judgment that a particular activity, taken in the aggregate, will have a substantial effect on interstate commerce, see *Hodel v Virginia Surface Mining & Reclamation Assn., Inc.*, 452 US 264, 276–80 (1981), but deference applies only to that single link in the doctrinal chain; it does not apply, for instance, to the analytically prior question whether the regulated activity is commercial in nature, see *Lopez*, 514 US at 567–68 (refusing to defer on this question). Moreover, during the century in which the *McCulloch* test was formulated, its "reasonableness" review of the relation between governmental means and ends had yet to take on the "rubber stamp" quality that it would assume after 1937.

in *Lopez* and *Morrison*, as the *Raich* dissents pointed out.[120] The government should have argued, for instance, that the Gun Free School Zones Act was a necessary part of an effort to stop sales of guns to minors. Since schools are where minors congregate, and since it is always difficult to catch buyers and sellers in mid-transaction, surely it would be rational to prohibit the very possession of a gun at school in order to stamp out playground arms deals. If *Lopez* and *Morrison* are to stand, in future, for anything more than a guide to writing government briefs, then the Court is going to have to limit its deference to such arguments.

Justice Scalia's concurrence in *Raich* was ambiguous on the extent to which the Court should be prepared to look behind the government's assertions and determine for itself whether any given noncommercial regulation is "necessary" to a broader scheme of commercial regulation. I have argued elsewhere that a *McCulloch* standard for implied powers, developed at a time when the express powers of Congress were interpreted quite narrowly, may make little sense under modern conditions.[121] Any attempt to tighten the standard of review, however, is likely to raise all the old concerns about second-guessing the policy judgments behind legislation that led to the repudiation of the *Lochner*-era jurisprudence.[122] And the inevitable inconsistencies that would arise in the application of an open-ended standard in this area will only worsen the criticisms, discussed in Part I of this essay, that the Court's federalism jurisprudence is political or instrumental.[123]

There are, however, at least two ways out of this dilemma. One is by way of clear statement: If Congress is to invoke the Necessary and Proper Clause in this potentially unlimited fashion, then at least Congress should make the judgment of necessity. This would substitute a process-based limit, derived from both the represen-

---

[120] See *Raich*, 125 S Ct at 2223 (O'Connor, J, dissenting).

[121] See Young, *Making Federalism Doctrine* at 1754 (cited in note 19). *McCulloch* also presupposed that some review would be available to foreclose Congress's use of the commerce power as a *pretext* for noncommercial ends. See 4 Wheat at 422 ("[S]hould Congress, under the pretext of executing its powers, pass laws for the accomplishment of objects not intrusted to the government; it would become the painful duty of this tribunal, should a case requiring such a decision come before it, to say that such an act was not the law of the land."). But that motive-based limit has been dead ever since the Court overruled *Hammer v Dagenhart*. See *United States v Darby*, 312 US 100, 116–17 (1941).

[122] See, e.g., *Lopez*, 514 US at 604–09, 614–15 (Souter, J, dissenting) (raising this worry).

[123] See Lawrence Lessig, *Translating Federalism: United States v Lopez*, 1995 Supreme Court Review 125, 170–75; Young, 46 Wm & Mary L Rev at 1836–40 (cited in note 19).

tation of the states in Congress and the procedural difficulties of federal lawmaking, for a substantive one.[124] In *Raich*, the only governmental necessity judgment consisted of an argument in a brief submitted by the Justice Department.[125] Insisting on a clear statement of Congress's intent, then, would have preserved the states' autonomy on the matter unless and until Congress could overcome the ordinary inertial barriers attendant on legislation and revisit the issue.

The other option would involve giving weight to the judgment of the state legislature—like Congress, a democratically accountable institution—that measures incorporated in the state scheme could minimize any detrimental impact on federal regulation of nonmedicinal uses. The rational basis test derived from *McCulloch* has its impetus in the institutional advantages that legislative bodies enjoy over courts—primarily in terms of democratic legitimacy, but also sometimes based on fact-finding capacity and policy-making expertise.[126] A case like *Raich*, however, involves not one legislature but two. If the Court is looking for a legislature to defer to, it could choose to defer to California's judgment that a limited class of medicinal users may be carved out from the general prohibition on marijuana without unduly undermining the overall regulatory scheme. The Supremacy Clause does not make Congress's judgments any wiser or more legitimate than a state legislature's, and those are the criteria of deference when a court is asked to assess the limits of lawmaking authority. In assessing whether Congressional legislation is enacted "pursuant to this Constitution" so as to trigger the Supremacy Clause, there is no a priori reason that a modest Court should not defer to the state legislature's judgments rather than to Congress's.

This last argument raises a broader question: To what extent should it matter, when assessing the limits of Congress's power, that a state legislature has chosen to approach a particular policy issue in a way that deviates from the federal program? Although I have suggested that *Raich* raised complex variations on the tests adopted in *Lopez* and *Morrison*, it was this added element of state policy divergence that made the case truly distinct from what had

---

[124] See Young, 83 Tex L Rev at 17 (cited in note 13) (discussing the effects of clear statement rules).

[125] See Petitioner's Brief at 22–35 (cited in note 85).

[126] See Hart, 46 Vill L Rev at 1104–05 (cited in note 101).

come before.[127] The Court's approach to this element, however, offered little ground for optimism that its federalism jurisprudence will evolve in a direction that would truly respect the valuable aspects of state autonomy.

C. DOES STATE REGULATION MATTER?

Defenders of federalism from a policy standpoint tend to stress the value of having state governments adopt and implement policies that diverge from one another and from the national government. Such divergence is a precondition of state experimentation and accommodation of diverse preferences.[128] It underlies values of political participation at the state level: What good is political participation, after all, if participants are not free to pursue their own policy agendas?[129] And policy autonomy powers what is, in my view, the most plausible account of how state governments foster liberty. On that account, state governments prevent the entrenchment of elites at the national level by providing a place where parties that are out of power at the center can nonetheless pursue their own policy agendas. Successes at the state level then allow these "out" parties to present themselves as plausible and competent alternatives in national elections.[130] None of this works, however, unless state governments have the freedom to go their own way on at least some issues of significance.[131]

Given the centrality of state policy autonomy to theoretical accounts of federalism, it is somewhat surprising that *Raich* was the first of the Rehnquist Court's Commerce Clause trilogy to involve a serious difference of opinion over policy between the national government and a state government. The federal regulation in *Lopez* was completely redundant with state laws barring

---

[127] The same element figured prominently in *Gonzales v Oregon*, 126 S Ct 904 (2006) (deciding whether the Attorney General had statutory authority to preempt Oregon's physician-assisted suicide law).

[128] See Young, 83 Tex L Rev at 53–58 (cited in note 13).

[129] See id at 58–63.

[130] See Ernest A. Young, *Welcome to the Dark Side: Liberals Embrace Federalism in the Wake of the War on Terror*, 69 Brooklyn L Rev 1277, 1286–87 (2004). For a similar view, see Heather K. Gerken, *Dissenting by Deciding*, 57 Stan L Rev 1745, 1759–69 (2005).

[131] See Young, 83 Tex L Rev at 63–65 (cited in note 13); see also Todd E. Pettys, *Competing for the People's Affection: Federalism's Forgotten Marketplace*, 56 Vand L Rev 329 (2003).

guns in schools.[132] And no one seriously thinks that the states were "pro-violence" or "anti-woman" in *Morrison*; indeed, thirty-six states filed an amicus brief supporting the VAWA's constitutionality.[133] If the point of federalism is to facilitate diverse regulatory regimes or state-by-state experimentation, then neither *Lopez* nor *Morrison* did much in furtherance of those goals. *Raich*, however, involved a state regulatory experiment reflecting a substantial divergence between the views of the state population and that of the nation as a whole.

The Court's majority, however, did not care. For them, the only question in the case was whether the law fell within Congress's enumerated power under Article I. The existence or nonexistence of a state regulatory scheme was completely irrelevant to this question: "Just as state acquiescence to federal regulation cannot expand the bounds of the Commerce Clause, . . . so too state action cannot circumscribe Congress' plenary commerce power."[134] This position is plausible in light of the structure of Article I and the Supremacy Clause. Federal law is supreme so long as it is grounded in the enumerated powers, and the supremacy effect of such law extends from the most weighty to the most trivial enactments. The text makes no allowance, for example, for weighing the importance of a state policy against a federal law provision that purports to trump it.[135] It was thus surely intelligible, under the current doctrine, to view the contours of California's regulatory program as irrelevant to the issue in *Raich*.

---

[132] *Lopez*, 514 US at 581 ("Indeed, over 40 States already have criminal laws outlawing the possession of firearms on or near school grounds.").

[133] Brief of the States of Arizona et al in Support of Petitioner in Nos 99-5, 99-29, *United States v Morrison* and *Brzonkala v Morrison* (filed Nov 12, 1999) (available at 1999 US S Ct Briefs, LEXIS 219); see also *Morrison*, 529 US at 653 ("The National Association of Attorneys General supported the Act unanimously. . . and Attorneys General from 38 States urged Congress to enact the Civil Rights Remedy, representing that 'the current system for dealing with violence against women is inadequate . . .'").

[134] 125 S Ct at 2213. The Court cited a variety of prior statements to the same effect. *United States v Darby*, for example, insisted that the commerce power "can neither be enlarged nor diminished by the exercise or non-exercise of state power." 312 US 100, 114 (1941). And *Wickard* said that "no form of state activity can constitutionally thwart the regulatory power granted by the commerce clause to Congress." 317 US at 124.

[135] See *Raich*, 125 S Ct at 2212 ("It is beyond peradventure that federal power over commerce is 'superior to that of the States to provide for the welfare or necessities of their inhabitants,' however legitimate or dire those necessities may be.") (quoting *Maryland v Wirtz*, 392 US 183, 196 (1968)); Ann Althouse, *Why Not Heighten the Scrutiny of Congressional Power When the States Undertake Policy Experiments?* 9 Lewis & Clark L Rev 779, 781 (2005) ("A federal law, however crude, trumps conflicting state law, no matter how carefully conceived and magnificently beneficial the state's policy experiment may be.").

I want to argue, however, that this view was mistaken. For one thing, it is surely ironic to hear those who have argued for the dramatic expansion of national power in the twentieth century as a necessary response to the practical necessities of modern governance suddenly become formalists when it comes to the Supremacy Clause.[136] If American federalism is to take account of modern institutional realities, then the development of state governments into large, sophisticated, and competent regulatory entities in their own right ought surely to be one of those realities. The critics of the Court's more formal doctrines are right when they say that federalism is a practical conception. To ignore the existence and activity of one of the world's largest regulatory jurisdictions—the great State of California[137]—is to blink functional reality in the worst possible way. One would have thought we were past the day when Justices could assert that state governmental authority "does not exist."[138]

Ann Althouse has worried that taking state regulation into account "would invite fifty states and innumerable cities to carve out exceptions of all sorts from important federal statutes that are unquestionably supported by the Commerce Clause."[139] But one need not propose some amorphous and open-ended balancing of state and federal interests to take state regulation into account. Doctrinally, recognition of the existence and capacity of state governments can and should occur through the "necessary and proper" analysis that considers when Congress may regulate matter outside the Commerce Clause in order to further a scheme of commercial regulation. It is one thing to say that any outright

---

[136] See, e.g., *Printz v United States*, 521 US 898, 941 (1997) (Stevens, J, dissenting) (arguing that federal commandeering of state officials is a necessary and practical response to modern crises). Critics of the Federalist Revival love to lambaste the Court for its excessive formalism. See, e.g., Matthew D. Adler and Seth F. Kreimer, *The New Etiquette of Federalism: New York, Printz, and Yeskey*, 1998 Supreme Court Review 71 ("The jurisprudence of federalism has been bedecked with formalistic distinctions . . . ."). For a convincing rebuttal, see Allison Eid, *Federalism and Formalism*, 11 Wm & Mary B of Rts J 1191 (2003).

[137] If California were an independent nation, its economy (with a gross state product of $1.5 trillion in 2004) would rank somewhere between fourth and tenth largest in the world. See "Economy of California" in Wikipedia, available at http://en.wikipedia.org/wiki/Economy_of_California.

[138] *United States v Belmont*, 301 US 324, 331 (1937) (asserting that state authority is irrelevant "[i]n respect of all international negotiations and compacts, and in respect of our foreign relations generally").

[139] Althouse, 9 Lewis & Clark L Rev at 789 (cited in note 135).

regulation of commercial activity is permissible, regardless of the presence or absence of state regulation. But it is quite another to say that state regulatory schemes are irrelevant to what federal measures are necessary under the "Sweeping Clause." "Necessity," after all, is a practical rather than a formal conception. Federal action may well be necessary when failure to act would leave a regulatory void; it may well be less necessary when state regulation is taken into account.

Consider, for example, the government's argument in *Raich* that the existence of any legal category of marijuana consumption would create daunting problems of proof in prosecutions of non-medicinal users.[140] Anyone arrested for recreational consumption would, of course, plead that they reserved their marijuana for "medicinal purposes," and federal prosecutors would have to negate this contention beyond a reasonable doubt. That seems like a pretty compelling argument, but it changes considerably when the state regulatory regime is added to the picture. Under that scheme, California provided authorized medicinal users with an optional ID card clearly stating that they were entitled to use marijuana under the state law scheme.[141] Persons arrested for recreational use would either have such a card or they would not. While more marginal proof issues might remain, the California scheme cuts substantially into the federal government's case for extending their scheme of regulation to noncommercial activity.[142] On these sorts of practical questions, the contours of state regulation ought to make a difference.

The majority opinion's insistence on the irrelevance of state regulation is particular depressing in light of its author. I have argued elsewhere that the Court's four putative "nationalists"—Justices Stevens, Souter, Ginsburg, and Breyer—actually harbor a meaningful conception of federalism that stresses the value of state regulatory autonomy.[143] Justice Stevens, in particular, has been willing to defend the authority of state governments to enact and implement their own policies in cases involving the preemption

---

[140] Petitioner's Brief at 30 (cited in note 85).

[141] Cal Health & Safety Code §§ 11362.7–11362.83 (2003).

[142] See Respondents' Brief at 38–39 (cited in note 84); Scholars' Brief at 28–29 (cited in "Author's note").

[143] See Young, 83 Tex L Rev at 41–45 (cited in note 13).

of state regulation by federal law.[144] As *Raich* demonstrates, these same values are at stake in cases about the constitutional scope of Congress's regulatory authority; Congress cannot preempt state law, after all, unless it has the authority to act in the first place. The Court's four liberals remain allergic to any suggestion that federalism is enforceable as a matter of constitutional principle, and yet it is hard to see how state regulatory autonomy can remain secure without some hard limit on Congress's power.

III. WORSE DAYS AHEAD?

Many observers will view *Raich* as the end of the Rehnquist Court's "Federalist Revival," especially when one sees it in conjunction with the Court's recent retreat in several important Eleventh Amendment cases.[145] Others will note the importance of the Controlled Substances Act and its clear range of constitutional applications, as well as the relative care with which the *Raich* majority analyzed its commercial impact, as evidence that the Court's jurisprudence is now "normalizing" or moderating; in a mature and meaningful Commerce Clause jurisprudence, after all, we would expect to see cases coming down on both sides of the line. This last section will try to read some tea leaves.

A. JUSTICE O'CONNOR'S QUESTION

At the oral argument in *Lopez*, Justice O'Connor asked Solicitor General Drew Days to tell her, if the Gun Free Zones Act was within the Commerce Power, what conceivable federal law would *not* be constitutional.[146] The transcript indicates that General Days

---

[144] See, e.g., *Geier v American Honda Motor Co.*, 529 US 861, 887 (2000) (Stevens, J, dissenting); *Lorillard Tobacco Co. v Reilly*, 533 US 525, 590 (2001) (Stevens, J, dissenting).

[145] See *Nevada Dept of Human Resources v Hibbs*, 538 US 721 (2003) (upholding abrogation of state sovereign immunity in the Family Medical Leave Act); *Tennessee v Lane*, 541 US 509 (2004) (upholding abrogation of state sovereign immunity in Title II of the Americans with Disabilities Act for plaintiffs denied access to the courts); *United States v Georgia*, 2006 US LEXIS 759 (Jan 10, 2006) (upholding abrogation of state sovereign immunity in Title II of the ADA for plaintiffs alleging constitutional violations); *Central Virginia Community College v Katz*, 2006 US LEXIS 917 (Jan 23, 2006) (upholding abrogation of state sovereign immunity under the Bankruptcy Code).

[146] Oral Argument in *United States v Lopez*, No 93-1260, 1994 US Trans LEXIS 107, at *4 ("If this is covered, what's left of enumerated powers? What is there that Congress could not do, under this rubric, if you are correct?").

had no answer to that question.[147] Not surprisingly, the majority opinions in both *Lopez* and *Morrison* stressed that, if the respective statutes in those cases were upheld, the Court would be left with no limiting principle for federal power at all.[148]

One can make the case that *Raich* presented the same situation. The dissenters argued with considerable force that the doctrinal moves made to uphold the Controlled Substances Act could also have been applied to uphold the Gun Free School Zones Act and the private right of action provision of the Violence Against Women Act.[149] Randy Barnett, who argued the case for Angel Raich, predicted afterwards that "[t]here will never be another successful Commerce Clause challenge to a federal statute in the Courts of Appeals if the Supreme Court accepts EITHER of the government's two theories."[150] My own view, however, is that the Court's back was not to the wall in the sense that it was in *Lopez* and *Morrison*. One can identify plausible federal statutes—for instance, a federal statute banning gay marriage—that would be exceptionally hard to justify on any of the theories offered in *Raich*.

My choice of gay marriage as an example is not simply an effort to tweak liberal assumptions (as fun as that is). Two aspects of gay marriage are important in this context: First, it is not a subset of

---

[147] See id at *4–5:

> General Days: Well, Your Honor, I'm not prepared to speculate generally, but this Court has found that Congress, for example, in New York v. United States could not regulate—could not require New York State to carry out certain responsibilities, because it was commandeering the instrumentalities of the State.

Justice O'Connor was unsatisfied by this reference to the anti-commandeering doctrine:

> Question: Well, the objection there was that it was objecting the State governmental machinery to operate in a certain way. The question here, it seems to me, is quite different. The question here is the universe of transactions that the Congress may reach.

Id at *5. No example of a transaction that Congress may not reach was offered by the government.

[148] See *Lopez*, 514 US at 564 ("[I]f we were to accept the Government's arguments, we are hard pressed to posit any activity by an individual that Congress is without power to regulate."); *Morrison*, 529 US at 615–17.

[149] See *Raich*, 125 S Ct at 2226 (O'Connor dissenting); see also Scholars' Brief at 23–25 (cited in "Author's note").

[150] Randy Barnett, *Adler on Importance to Federalism of Raich v Ashcroft*, The Volokh Conspiracy (Dec 1, 2004), available at http://volokh.com/posts/1101916887.shtml. Professor Barnett's more recent assessment seems somewhat less dire. See Barnett, 9 Lewis & Clark L Rev at 750 (cited in note 78) (predicting that, in the future, "the 'doctrine' established by the Court in *Raich* will seem remarkably narrow, fragile, and easy to distinguish or subtly modify").

a larger class of activity that seems plausibly commercial, as medical marijuana use is a subset of a larger market in illicit drugs. Second, a federal statute banning gay marriage would stand largely alone, unattached to any comprehensive federal marriage scheme. Perhaps Congress could assert sufficient links to the interstate economy to support such a scheme under the Commerce Power. (Anyone who has ever paid for a wedding has experienced the multiplier effect of a marriage vow on the market for goods and services.) But the political checks on comprehensive national regulation of marriage and family structure seem very strong.

The message of *Raich* may be that when Congress enters a regulatory field in a comprehensive way—for example, federal drug regulation—its incursion will be upheld, but that isolated regulations of noncommercial acts will not be. That would leave us with little hard limit on Congress's power, but the same rule would effectively multiply political checks on national action. The most formidable "political safeguard of federalism," after all, is opposition on the merits to any particular federal proposal; by foreclosing Congress from legislating narrowly, the likelihood and ferocity of political opposition to any given proposal should increase.[151] These dynamics will only increase in importance as the culture wars heat up. By impeding Congress's ability to single out particular practices for federal disapproval in areas otherwise left to state regulation, even the narrow limit described here would promote state-by-state experimentation and accommodation of divergent preferences. It is surely important that Congress lacks power to impose a national solution to current debates about marriage and similar issues.

Notwithstanding this silver lining, *Raich* most likely marks the outer bound of the Court's ambition in Commerce Clause cases. Apocalyptic predictions notwithstanding,[152] many of us have long argued that the Court's Commerce Clause jurisprudence was primarily symbolic in its importance and unlikely to go far.[153] A roll-

---

[151] See, e.g., Althouse, 9 Lewis & Clark L Rev at 789 (cited in note 135) (suggesting that it would have been politically difficult for Congress to legislate more broadly in *Lopez*).

[152] See, e.g., Charles E. Ares, *Lopez and the Future Constitutional Crisis*, 38 Ariz L Rev 825, 825–26 (1996) (asserting that *Lopez* had "opened the floodgates" for judicial limits on national power).

[153] See, e.g., Daniel J. Meltzer, *The Seminole Decision and State Sovereign Immunity*, 1996 Supreme Court Review 1, 63; Ernest A. Young, *Dual Federalism, Concurrent Jurisdiction, and the Foreign Affairs Exception*, 69 Geo Wash L Rev 139, 157–61 (2001).

back of the national regulatory state was never in the cards; there are simply too many precedential, institutional, and political constraints pressing the Court to uphold relatively broad federal power.[154] *Raich* may indicate that even minor incursions on the federal edifice are unlikely, and that except in cases where to uphold the federal act would remove any limit whatsoever, the Court will condone national action. As long as the next Solicitor General has any plausible answer to Justice O'Connor's question, he seems likely to prevail.

B. BATES AND THE COURT'S PREEMPTION JURISPRUDENCE

It may help to view *Raich* in conjunction with another important federalism case from last Term that has received significantly less attention: *Bates v Dow Agrosciences*,[155] in which the Court held that federal regulatory approvals under the Federal Insecticide, Fungicide, and Rodenticide Act (FIFRA)[156] did not preempt state common law claims against a pesticide company for failure to warn of the harms caused by its chemicals in certain types of soil. *Bates* is a significant case in at least two respects. First, its rejection of a preemption challenge to state law comes after a string of decisions holding state common law actions preempted by federal regulatory provisions.[157] Second, and without delving into the arguments on the merits, it struck many observers as a genuinely close case and thus an impressive win for opponents of federal preemption.

Despite the fact that *Raich* and *Bates* both involved agricultural production, somehow the FIFRA case did not have the same cachet among court watchers. I have argued elsewhere, however, that preemption cases are the most important of all for federalism

---

[154] See Cross, 74 NYU L Rev at 1313–26 (cited in note 10); Young, 83 Tex L Rev at 92–103 (cited in note 13).

[155] 125 S Ct 1788 (2005). See generally *The Supreme Court, 2004 Term—Leading Cases*, 119 Harv L Rev 376 (2005).

[156] 7 USC §§ 136–136y.

[157] See, e.g., *Buckman Co. v Plaintiff's Legal Committee*, 531 US 341 (2001) (holding that federal law preempted state law tort claims involving medical devices); *Geier v American Honda Motor Co.*, 529 US 861 (2000) (holding that federal safety regulations preempted state tort claims involving the failure to install airbags in cars); *Norfolk S. Ry. Co. v Shanklin*, 529 US 344 (2000) (holding that the Federal Railroad Safety Act preempted state tort remedies).

doctrine.[158] These cases have the most direct impact on the states' ability to make their own regulatory choices, and they often involve matters that, in their practical importance, far outstrip the policies at stake in Commerce Clause litigation.[159] *Bates*'s resolution of a close statutory question against preemption, and by a lopsided vote, is thus quite encouraging for those concerned about state autonomy.

It is hard to tell whether *Bates* and other encouraging cases decided in the last couple of years represent a retreat from the Rehnquist Court's "jurispathological" (apologies to Robert Cover[160]) approach to preemption of state law. In his partial dissent in *Bates*, Justice Thomas noted with approval that "[t]oday's decision . . . comports with this Court's increasing reluctance to expand federal statutes beyond their terms through doctrines of implied pre-emption."[161] On the other hand, I remain skeptical that the Court thinks of its statutory preemption cases—which are generally dominated by the details of the particular federal regulatory scheme at issue—as presenting a unified set of issues to be approached in a coherent fashion.[162]

The important point, however, is that if the Court would approach preemption cases in this way, then *Raich*-for-*Bates* might be the sort of trade-off that any advocate of state autonomy ought happily to accept. The Commerce Clause line was always unlikely to be drawn very tightly, and therefore Congress will continue to enjoy, for the foreseeable future, an exceptionally broad range of potential action. The most important questions will go to what happens within this broad area.[163] Those will not be constitutional questions, but statutory ones, but the background norms with

---

[158] See Young, 83 Tex L Rev at 130–34 (cited in note 13). See also Calvin Massey, *Federalism and the Rehnquist Court*, 53 Hastings L J 431, 508 (2002) (making a similar point).

[159] See Young, 1999 Supreme Court Review at 39–42 (cited in note 53); Ernest A. Young, *Two Cheers for Process Federalism*, 46 Vill L Rev 1349, 1384–86 (2001).

[160] See Robert M. Cover, *Foreword: Nomos and Narrative*, 97 Harv L Rev 4, 40–41 (1983) (identifying the "jurispathic" function of courts in killing off rival sources of law).

[161] *Bates*, 125 S Ct at 1807 (Thomas, J, dissenting).

[162] See Young, 83 Tex L Rev at 133 (cited in note 13).

[163] See *Egelhoff v Egelhoff*, 532 US 141, 160 (2001) (Breyer, J, dissenting) (stressing "the practical importance of preserving local independence, at retail, i.e., by applying pre-emption analysis with care, statute by statute, line by line, in order to determine how best to reconcile a federal statute's language and purpose with federalism's need to preserve state autonomy").

which the Court approaches these interpretive questions are likely to have extremely important implications for state regulatory autonomy.

C. OF TOADS, MACHINE GUNS, AND SUICIDE: PROSPECTS FOR THE
   ROBERTS COURT

The current Supreme Court Term will afford our first look at a post-Rehnquist federalism jurisprudence. As this article goes to press in February 2006, the Roberts Court has already decided a variety of important federalism cases. In *Gonzales v Oregon*,[164] the Court held that former Attorney General John Ashcroft's interpretive rule stifling Oregon's experiment with legalized physician-assisted suicide was an invalid extension of the Controlled Substances Act. On the more nationalist side of the ledger, *Central Virginia Community College v Katz*[165] and *United States v Georgia*[166] upheld Congress's power to abrogate state sovereign immunity under the Bankruptcy Code and the Americans with Disabilities Act, respectively. An array of important federalism cases remain to be decided as Justice Samuel Alito takes his seat. First up are two consolidated cases under the Clean Water Act that ask whether Congress's commerce power extends to certain sorts of wetlands.[167] Two cases under the Vienna Convention on Consular Relations will test the power of supranational courts to preempt state procedural law.[168] Still other cases raise important questions

---

[164] 126 S Ct 904 (2006).

[165] 2006 US LEXIS 917 (Jan 23, 2006). For an early analysis, see Kevin Russell, *News and Analysis on Today's Decision in Katz*, SCOTUSblog (Jan 23, 2006) (available at http://www.scotusblog.com/movabletype/archives/2006/01/news_and_analys.html).

[166] 2006 US LEXIS 759 (Jan 10, 2006). The Court's unanimous holding was limited to suits by disabled state prisoners complaining of ADA violations that also amounted to "actual violations" of the Fourteenth Amendment. See id at **9–13. For early accounts, see Bagenstos, *Court Decides* (cited in note 107); Lyle Denniston, *Court Rules on State Immunity, 2 Other Issues*, SCOTUSblog (Jan 10, 2006) (available at http://www.scotusblog.com/movabletype/archives/2006/01/court_adds_some.html).

[167] *Rapanos v United States*, No 04-1034, and *Carabell v U.S. Army Corps of Engineers*, No 04-1384. See generally Tony Mauro, *Justice Alito's Green Day*, Legal Times (Feb 8, 2006) (available at http://www.law.com/jsp/article.jsp?id=1139306710859).

[168] *Llamas v Oregon*, No 04-10566, and *Bustillo v Johnson*, No 05-51. On the interaction between international, federal, and state courts in the Vienna Convention context, see Ernest A. Young, *Institutional Settlement in a Globalizing Judicial System*, 54 Duke L J 1143, 1164–70, 1178–88 (2005).

of abstention[169] and the limits of state legislative control over redistricting.[170]

Many observers have predicted that appointments by President
George W. Bush are likely to accelerate the Court's efforts to limit
national authority.[171] My own view is that this is highly unlikely;
if anything, the losses of Chief Justice Rehnquist and Justice
O'Connor will yield a more nationalist court on federalism issues.
Despite her moderate instincts and reputation as a swing Justice
on many issues, Justice O'Connor was perhaps the Court's most
committed Justice on questions of state autonomy. And the Chief
Justice, while perhaps more accepting of national power in some
circumstances,[172] deserves to be described as the programmatic
architect of the Federalist Revival. From the states' perspective,
these Justices are virtually irreplaceable.

Nor are there strong grounds to believe that Chief Justice Roberts and Justice Alito will share their predecessors' commitment
to limiting national power, even if these jurists turn out to be as
"conservative" as many of their supporters no doubt hope. To see
why, it may help to posit three different grounds upon which a
Justice might support federalism as a constitutional constraint.
One would be a deeply felt attachment to a particular state political
community that generates a sense of state institutions as competent
and important, most likely coupled with a more fundamental identification with a home removed from the nation's capital. Justice
O'Connor, for instance, famously served in all three branches of
state government and retained a strong attachment to her ranch
in Arizona. She seems to have felt the importance of federalism

---

[169] *Marshall v Marshall*, 04-1544.

[170] See *LULAC v Perry*, 05-204; *Travis County v Perry*, 05-254; *Jackson v Perry*, 05-276;
G.I. Forum of Texas v Perry, 05-439. I have suggested elsewhere that the Texas redistricting
saga at issue in these cases may demonstrate how, contrary to conventional wisdom, political parties may subvert state autonomy at the behest of national political actors. See
Young, 83 Tex L Rev at 75 & n 351 (cited in note 13).

[171] See, e.g., Adam Cohen, *What's New in the Legal World? A Growing Campaign to Undo
the New Deal*, NY Times (Dec 14, 2004), at A32 ("If the Supreme Court drifts rightward
in the next four years, as seems likely, it could not only roll back Congress's Commerce
Clause powers, but also revive other dangerous doctrines."). Indeed, Jack Balkin and Sandy
Levinson have claimed that the nefarious purpose of *Bush v Gore*, 531 US 98 (2000), was
to ensure a string of Republican judicial appointments that would perpetuate the Court's
federalism "revolution." Balkin and Levinson, 87 Va L Rev at 1052–53 (cited in note 56).

[172] See, e.g., *South Dakota v Dole*, 483 US 203 (1987) (Rehnquist, CJ, writing for majority
upholding broad federal conditional spending power, over O'Connor's dissent).

in her bones, undergirding any intellectual attachment to constitutional principle.[173]

A second impulse derives from a commitment to constitutional fidelity. Whether or not one has any intrinsic brief for federalism, one might be uncomfortable with the notion that the Supreme Court can simply stop enforcing certain constitutional principles, as the Court arguably did with federalism between 1937 and 1995.[174] One need not believe in any radical restoration of a "Constitution in Exile" to think that courts should make compensating adjustments, in marginal cases, to move back in the direction of a constitutional balance that has been lost.[175] Chief Justice Rehnquist seems most likely to have fallen into this camp. Although the Chief spent sixteen years in private practice in Arizona, he also spent possibly formative stints in the national military and the federal executive branch. It seems likely that much of the Chief's dedication to federalism came not from personal experience or attachment but rather from a sense that judges should not be allowed to render large structural principles of the Constitution a dead letter.

The third impulse is a belief in incrementalism or minimalism as the preferred form of legal change. I have argued elsewhere that incrementalism is one of federalism's primary virtues: Whereas national action generally commits the entire nation to a particular policy course, limits on such action leave the states free to experiment, as well as to simply reflect the divergent preferences of their citizens.[176] Proponents of change must work one state at a time, and individual states can rely on the experience of their fellows in evaluating proposed reforms. Justice O'Connor and Justice Kennedy—another key voice for state autonomy in many cases, *Raich* notwithstanding—have both been described as "ju-

---

[173] To take another (purely hypothetical) example, one might feel similarly if one were a professor at a large state university in Texas and descended from Texas ranchers on one side and Texas football coaches on the other.

[174] See, e.g., Gary Lawson, *The Rise and Rise of the Administrative State*, 107 Harv L Rev 1231, 1233–37 (1994); Young, 46 Wm & Mary L Rev at 1764–75 (cited in note 19).

[175] On the "Constitution in Exile," see Douglas H. Ginsburg, *Delegation Running Riot*, Regulation, No 1, 1995, at 83. For an approach based on compensating adjustments, see Young, 46 Wm & Mary L Rev at 1748–62 (cited in note 19).

[176] See generally Ernest A. Young, *The Conservative Case for Federalism*, 74 Geo Wash L Rev (forthcoming 2006).

dicial minimalists," committed to deciding "one case at a time."[177] It is not surprising that they also tend to emphasize the advantages of state-by-state policy diversity in their opinions upholding state autonomy.[178]

I do not mean to exclude entirely the influence of other preferences—even political preferences, like a hostility to government regulation or to private plaintiffs, of the sort discussed in Part I. Nor do I mean to suggest that the impulses surveyed here are not themselves "political," at least in a sense. But that sense is far more nuanced than the political hypothesis can accommodate. Constitutional fidelity is surely grounded, to some extent, in conservative suspicion of radical change[179]—but it is also a legal interpretation of the obligation of the judge in constitutional cases. Affinities for state institutions and commitments to incrementalism are likewise views that may exist apart from strictly legal interpretations of the Constitutional text, history, and precedents, but to say that is hardly to accept the attitudinalist view. Almost every constitutional case involves, for example, practical judgments made with highly imperfect information. Cases about the scope of federal common lawmaking authority, for instance, involve judgments about the importance of policy uniformity on a given question;[180] the "necessary and proper" argument in *Raich* likewise involved a practical judgment about necessity. General views about the competence of state institutions and the desirability of policy diversity will inform these judgments. But this form of "political" influence informs the application of a legal standard—it does not serve as an alternative mode of decision that the legal arguments simply mask.

It must also be conceded that the impulses I have identified are far from absolute indicators. Justice Souter is often a minimalist,[181] and surely no Justice bears a stronger attachment to an outside-the-Beltway hearth and home, but no one has been a more determined opponent of constitutional restraints on national au-

---

[177] Cass R. Sunstein, *One Case at a Time: Judicial Minimalism on the Supreme Court* (1999); see also Kathleen M. Sullivan, *The Supreme Court, 1991 Term—Foreword: The Justices of Rules and Standards*, 106 Harv L Rev 22 (1992).

[178] See *Gregory v Ashcroft*, 501 US 452, 458 (1991) (O'Connor); *United States v Lopez*, 514 US 549, 581–83 (1995) (Kennedy, J, concurring).

[179] See Young, 46 Wm & Mary L Rev at 1772 (cited in note 19).

[180] See *United States v Kimbell Foods*, 440 US 715, 727–33 (1979).

[181] See Ernest A. Young, *Rediscovering Conservatism: Burkean Political Theory and Constitutional Interpretation*, 72 NC L Rev 619, 718–19 (1994).

thority. Chief Justice Rehnquist seemingly had little reason to care about federalism other than constitutional fidelity, and yet ended up leading the Federalist Revival. That said, one can plausibly infer that the strongest proponents of limits on national power will be Justices like O'Connor that combine two or more of these impulses, and that a bare impulse toward constitutional fidelity will often—but not always—be insufficient to make one an enthusiastic federalist. I have already discussed how Justice Scalia's vote in *Raich* may reflect a set of structural interests focused primarily on separation of powers, not federalism.[182] This should be relatively unsurprising: Nothing in Justice Scalia's background or professed methodology reflects any affinity for state governmental institutions or for incrementalism.[183]

Chief Justice Roberts's confirmation process was marked by concerns that he would roll back federal power to prehistoric levels. These concerns were engendered primarily by a dissenting opinion concerning a case that involved a Commerce Clause challenge to the Endangered Species Act.[184] There, Judge Roberts doubted Congress's ability to protect "a hapless toad that, for reasons of its own, lives its entire life in California."[185] But there is every reason to think, "hapless toads" notwithstanding, that Roberts is an executive-branch conservative in the mold of Justice

---

[182] See text accompanying note 20. Even in *Printz v United States*, 521 US 898 (1997)—surely Justice Scalia's most important federalism opinion—he grounds the doctrine that Congress may not "commandeer" state executive officials to enforce federal law not only in federalism but also in fears that Congress's appropriation of state executive personnel would undermine the federal unitary executive. See id at 922–23. Brad Clark has argued vigorously that Justice Scalia's commitments to federalism and separation of powers are complementary, see Clark, 47 SLU L J at 770 (cited in note 20), and I have little doubt that this is often true. My point is simply that his primary interest is in separation of powers, and that if push comes to shove he will prefer his established separation of powers commitments to any concern about federalism. In two important preemption cases, for example, Justice Scalia has emphasized his strong view of judicial deference to executive agency interpretations of law over important federalism concerns. See *Gonzales v Oregon*, 126 S Ct 904, 926 (2006) (Scalia, J, dissenting); *AT&T Corp. v Iowa Utils Bd*, 525 US 366, 378 n 6 (1999).

[183] See also Young, 72 NC L Rev at 681–86 (cited in note 181) (critiquing Justice Scalia's commitment to bright-line rules from a Burkean incrementalist perspective).

[184] See, e.g., *Scrutinizing John Roberts*, NY Times (July 20, 2005), at A22 (reporting that Judge Roberts "dissented in an Endangered Species Act case in a way that suggested he might hold an array of environmental laws, and other important federal protections, to be unconstitutional"). The case in question was *Rancho Viejo LLC v Norton*, 334 F3d 1158 (DC Cir 2003), in which Judge Roberts dissented from a denial of rehearing en banc. He stopped short of arguing that the ESA was, in fact, unconstitutional, and even offered an alternative rationale for upholding the statute. Id at 1160.

[185] Id.

Scalia.[186] Roberts's professional life, after all, has been spent either in the federal government or as a Washington lawyer preoccupied with questions of federal law; he has no record of participation in or commitment to the institutions of state government comparable to Justice O'Connor's. It seems quite plausible, for example, that Chief Justice Roberts would have voted with Scalia in *Raich*. This expectation seemed to be borne out by the oral argument in the first major federalism case of the Roberts Court, at which the new Chief reportedly "stepped forward . . . as an aggressive defender of federal authority to block doctor-assisted suicide."[187] And, in fact, when *Gonzales v Oregon* came down in January, the new Chief Justice joined Justice Scalia's dissent arguing that the Controlled Substances Act should be read to confer broad authority on the Attorney General to preempt state regulation of doctors.[188]

Judge Alito's considerably longer record of decided cases yields a few more hints of concern for state autonomy.[189] His dissent in *United States v Rybar*[190] argued that 18 USC § 922(o), which regulates the possession and transfer of machine guns, was an invalid exercise of the Commerce power. The *Rybar* dissent is a comparatively aggressive application of *Lopez*, and it suggests that Alito might have been with the dissenters in *Raich*.[191] Nonetheless, like Roberts's, Judge Alito's resumé has a strongly national tilt: Indeed, Alito has spent his entire professional life as an employee of the

---

[186] See Merrill, 47 SLU L J at 609–12 (cited in note 20).

[187] *Roberts' Debut: Right-to-Die Case*, St. Petersburg Times (Oct 6, 2005), at 1A.

[188] See 126 S Ct at 779–94 (Scalia, J, dissenting).

[189] For the breathless tone of concerns about Judge Alito's pro-states leanings, see *Another Lost Opportunity*, NY Times (Nov 1, 2005), at A26 (worrying about "Judge Alito's frequent rulings to undermine the federal government's authority to address momentous national problems").

[190] 103 F3d 273 (3d Cir 1996).

[191] The considerable attention devoted to Judge Alito's majority opinion in *Chittister v Dept of Community & Econ. Development*, 226 F3d 223 (3d Cir 2000), by contrast, seems misplaced. In that case, the Third Circuit held that the sick-leave provision of the Family Medical Leave Act was not a valid exercise of the Section 5 power, so that Congress could not abrogate state sovereign immunity for individual damages claims under the statute. Judge Alito has been criticized for not anticipating the Supreme Court's decision in *Nevada Dept of Human Resources v Hibbs*, 538 US 721 (2003), which upheld such abrogation for the family-care provisions of the FMLA. It will suffice to say that very few Eleventh Amendment aficionados expected *any* part of the FMLA to pass muster in *Hibbs*, and the provision that *Chittister* struck down is sufficiently more difficult to defend under Section 5 that two circuits have struck it down even after *Hibbs*. See *Touvell v Ohio Dept of Mental Retardation & Developmental Disabilities*, 422 F3d 392 (6th Cir 2005); *Brockman v Wyoming Dept of Family Servs*, 342 F3d 1159 (10th Cir 2003).

national government, much of that time as a Justice Department lawyer charged with implementing and defending national policy.[192] Despite concerns in the press that he may "envision a dramatic curtailing of national power,"[193] it is hard to see Alito developing into an ardent partisan of states' rights.

All this gives some reason to worry that the Federalist Revival, such as it was, may be drawing to a close. There is, however, a more optimistic scenario from the perspective of state autonomy. Five years ago, in the pages of this journal, I pleaded for the Federalist Five to adopt a more moderate approach to state sovereign immunity that might encourage the more Nationalist Four to support a judicially enforceable notion of enumerated powers.[194] The Court's recent decisions in *Hibbs* and *Lane* do, indeed, show at least some members of the Five moderating their positions on sovereign immunity and the Section 5 power.[195] But *Raich* reflects the Four's continued intransigence on enumerated-powers questions. The question is whether two new Justices can do any better at forging a consensus position that can attract support from across the Court's ideological spectrum.

To the extent that Roberts and Alito *do* care about federalism, they may turn out to be more effective advocates for it than the other pro-states Justices on the current Court. Justice O'Connor's affinity for open-ended balancing could hardly reassure Justices worried, as Souter and Breyer have been, about the ability of courts to identify principled limitations on federal power once they reopen the Pandora's Box of judicial review in this area.[196] Likewise,

---

[192] See the official White House biography at http://www.whitehouse.gov/infocus/judicialnominees/alito.html.

[193] Editorial, *Judge Alito on the States*, Wash Post (Nov 21, 2005), at A14.

[194] See Young, 1999 Supreme Court Review at 68–73 (cited in note 53).

[195] The two state sovereign immunity cases decided in January 2006 continued this trend. See *United States v Georgia*, 2006 US LEXIS 759 (Jan 10, 2006) (upholding abrogation of state immunity under Title II of the Americans with Disabilities Act, where the alleged statutory violation is also a constitutional violation); *Central Virginia Community College v Katz*, 2006 US LEXIS 917 (Jan 23, 2006) (upholding Congress's authority to abrogate state sovereign immunity under the Bankruptcy Code). *Katz* is particularly significant, as it cut back on the Court's earlier suggestion that none of Congress's Article I powers would suffice to abrogate state sovereign immunity. See *Florida Prepaid Postsecondary Educ. Expense Bd v College Savings Bank*, 527 US 627, 636 (1999). Justice O'Connor provided the fifth vote in *Katz*; Chief Justice Roberts joined Justice Thomas's dissent, which maintained the *Seminole/Alden* line on state immunities. Much will thus turn on the position that Justice Alito adopts in the next state sovereign immunity case.

[196] See *Lopez*, 514 US at 604 (Souter, J, dissenting); id at 627–28 (Breyer, J, dissenting).

Thomas's radicalism, Scalia's combativeness, Rehnquist's impatience with extended reason-giving, and Kennedy's sheer unpredictability created serious handicaps in this regard. As a seasoned doctrinal advocate known for his collegiality, Chief Justice Roberts may well be positioned to play a Brennan-like role—perhaps even reaching out to members of the Nationalist Four to forge the principled middle ground on federalism that has eluded the Court for so long.

The other half of a viable way forward, in my view, is for a solid majority of the Court to recognize that the values of constitutional federalism are implicated not only in cases that test the limits of Congress's power, but also in statutory construction cases that assess how far a given enactment has actually gone. I have already discussed the importance of preemption cases like *Bates* for preserving state autonomy.[197] On this score, the decision in *Gonzales v Oregon* upholding Oregon's physician-assisted suicide regime is encouraging. Especially after *Raich*, the primary restraints on the Commerce Clause will be political. Under those circumstances, it is important that the Court demand a relatively clear statement from Congress when it wishes to intrude into areas of traditional state authority (like medical practice). It is equally critical that federal preemptive authority actually be exercised by Congress, which is at least subject to political and inertial checks, rather than by executive actors that can act more easily and without input from the states' elected representatives.[198] Although it seemed relatively clear at the macro-level that Congress did not intend to grant a general regulatory power over medical practice to the Attorney General under the CSA, the structure of the Act was complex and included relatively open-ended delegations of power. The willingness of six Justices in the Oregon case to resolve these questions against the Attorney General bodes well for the survival of some elements of process federalism, notwithstanding the *Raich* majority's aversion to hard substantive limits on national authority.

CONCLUSION

There is some consolation in Justice O'Connor's descrip-

---

[197] See Section III.B.

[198] See Bradford R. Clark, *Separation of Powers as a Safeguard of Federalism*, 79 Tex L Rev 1321, 1433 (2001); Young, 83 Tex L Rev at 88–91 (cited in note 13).

tion of federalism as "our oldest question of constitutional law."[199] While the balance of power between the nation and the states has steadily shifted in favor of the former over the 230 years of our history, one need look no further than current debates over air pollution, gay marriage, and the death penalty to see that federalism remains a vital force in our polity. This is true notwithstanding considerable ebbs and flows in the willingness of the federal courts to enforce constitutional limits on national power. Even in the case of medical marijuana, state legislation remains a considerable practical impediment to the imposition of a uniform national drug policy.[200] On the constitutional side, much life remains in the anti-commandeering doctrine, state sovereign immunity, pro-federalism clear statement rules—and, I have argued, even aspects of Commerce Clause doctrine. It is, of course, far too early to tell whether the accomplishments of the Rehnquist Court will endure. But it is unlikely that *Raich* spells the end of the conversation.

---

[199] *New York v United States*, 505 US 144, 149 (1992).

[200] See, e.g., M. L. Johnson, *House Overrides Carcieri's Medical Marijuana Veto*, Boston Globe (Jan 3, 2006) (available at http://www.boston.com/news/local/rhode_island/articles/2006/01/03/house_members_override_carcieris_medical_marijuana_veto/) (noting that even after the Court's decision in *Raich*, "[f]ederal authorities conceded they were unlikely to prosecute many medicinal users, and Rhode Island lawmakers pressed on, passing their medical marijuana bill on June 7").

ELIZABETH F. EMENS

AGGRAVATING YOUTH: ROPER v SIMMONS AND AGE DISCRIMINATION

At the penalty phase of Christopher Simmons's murder trial, the prosecutor argued to the jury that Simmons's youth should be considered aggravating, rather than mitigating:

> Let's look at the mitigating circumstances. . . . Age, he says. Think about age. Seventeen years old. Isn't that scary? Doesn't that scare you? Mitigating? Quite the contrary I submit. Quite the contrary.[1]

The prosecutor's argument is striking. Indeed, when *Roper v Simmons*[2] reached the Supreme Court this Term, his argument was criticized in briefs, at oral argument, in the majority opinion, and in a dissent.[3] These words from the prosecutor played, I will argue,

Elizabeth F. Emens is Associate Professor of Law, Columbia Law School.

AUTHOR'S NOTE: My thanks to the following people for helpful conversations and comments on draft material: Ursula Bentele, Emily Buss, Sarah Cleveland, Geraldine Downey, Richard Emens, Jeffrey Fagan, Robert Ferguson, Victor Goldberg, Anil Kalhan, Alice Kessler-Harris, Sarah Lawsky, James Liebman, Martha Minow, Martha Nussbaum, Elizabeth Scott, Reva Siegel, Rachel Smith, Geoffrey Stone, David Strauss, Susan Sturm, Cass Sunstein, Jenia Iontcheva Taylor, John Witt, Kenji Yoshino, and participants in the 10-10 Workshop and the Law and Culture Colloquium at Columbia Law School. I also thank Sloan Speck for excellent research assistance, and the library staff at Columbia Law School, Beth Williams in particular, and at the University of Chicago Law School for their work obtaining key sources, including elusive trial transcript material from diverse locales.

[1] Transcript of Record on Appeal (filed Dec 19, 1994) at 1156–57, *State v Simmons*, 944 SW2d 165 (Mo 1997) (en banc) (No 77269) (hereafter "TT").

[2] *Roper v Simmons*, 125 S Ct 1183 (2005).

[3] For example, Brief for Respondent at *30, 2004 WL 1947812; Brief for NAACP Legal

a crucial role in the Court's decision that the Eighth Amendment prohibits states from executing people for crimes they committed when they were younger than eighteen.[4]

In the majority opinion, Justice Kennedy invokes this aspect of the prosecutor's argument to reply to Missouri's (and Justice O'Connor's) claim that juries should decide the relevance of youth on a case-by-case basis because youth is an inexact proxy for diminished culpability. Kennedy, in response, expresses his concern that juries will not be able to weigh an individual's age properly, and that the risk is thus too great that they will get it wrong, citing among other things the prosecutor's argument that youth should be an aggravating rather than a mitigating factor. He seems worried not only that juries lack the skill required to identify the cases in which youth should be treated as mitigating, but also that they will sometimes weigh youth in exactly the wrong way.

This concern seems surprising in an opinion that declares that the differences between juveniles and adults are so "marked and well understood" that we can draw a categorical rule based on age in the weighty context of the death penalty.[5] But, as Kennedy explains, there are numerous reasons to fear that juries may make mistakes when deciding whether the youth of a particular juvenile offender diminishes his culpability. Moreover, while sentencing someone to death incorrectly is always serious, mistakenly ending a young life may be even more so. Society justifies treating youth differently from adults in many contexts in part on the ground that youth will grow up and enter the majority class; an unwarranted execution of a young offender may undermine that system.

But it's not just the weight of the decision—whether to execute a young offender—or the potential number of errors—an unanswered empirical question—that, in Kennedy's view, requires a rule rather than a standard. Rather, the prosecutor's argument that youth is aggravating, rather than mitigating, highlights a peculiarly unacceptable type of error: the possibility of executing a young offender because a jury erred based on categorical disfavor; that is, because a jury treated a member of this vulnerable group worse

---

Defense Fund, et al, as Amici Curiae, at 18 n 26, 2004 WL 1636450; Transcript of Oral Argument at *10–*11, 2004 WL 2387647; *Simmons*, 125 S Ct at 1189, 1197; id at 1215 (O'Connor, J, dissenting).

[4] *Simmons*, 125 S Ct at 1200.

[5] Id at 1197.

precisely because he is a member of that group. To persecute when we should protect is to commit an error of great magnitude, especially in the domain of capital punishment. And so Kennedy embraces certain age-based stereotypes that mitigate culpability—that youth are more reckless, more susceptible to influence, and less formed in their characters—and uses those stereotypes to justify a prophylactic rule against executing any juveniles.

Read in its best light, Kennedy's opinion thus seems to turn on the insight that while age-based classifications are rational—they are a good proxy for various aspects of behavior—particular judgments based on age are not necessarily rational. To the contrary, our judgments based on age may be distorted, or even inverted, because of wrongheaded thoughts and, especially, feelings. In the context of death penalty sentencing, among others, we think we favor youth, and we think we should favor youth, but in reality we may disfavor youth. Kennedy's reasoning thus suggests that, in at least this context, the law must embrace a categorical rule to *align* how we treat young people under law with how we think we do and should treat them.

Kennedy's analysis of the "national consensus" question might be read to employ a similar logic. He concludes that a majority of states opposes the juvenile death penalty because he counts the states that completely outlaw the death penalty as opposing the juvenile death penalty. Justice Scalia argues in dissent that a state's general position on the death penalty does not bear on the question of whether a special rule should protect juveniles from the death penalty where it exists. Kennedy's contrary conclusion might be understood to rest in part on the very concern that animates his proportionality analysis: For a state to oppose the death penalty for adults but not for juveniles is both plausible and troubling for the same reasons that the prosecutor's argument that youth is aggravating is plausible and troubling. That is, juveniles are a less culpable included group of offenders, so if a state opposes the death penalty generally, it must (that is, it should) oppose it for juveniles. It would be normatively unacceptable, although possible, that negative attitudes toward and fear of juveniles would lead people to think juveniles deserve the death penalty when adults do not. In short, we require rules to align our legal treatment of juveniles with our favorable attitudes toward them.

This tension between the rationality of age-based classifications, on the one hand, and unacknowledged negative attitudes toward age-based groups, on the other, links *Simmons* to a frequently overlooked aspect of age-discrimination law. In the same month it decided *Simmons*, the Court concluded in *Smith v City of Jackson*[6] that disparate-impact claims are available under the Age Discrimination in Employment Act (ADEA).[7] But *Smith* also seems to suggest that because age is rationally related to many job requirements (i.e., age is often a good proxy for ability), and because age discrimination is not motivated by dislike or intolerance (as opposed to irrational stereotyping), the statute's reasonable factors other than age (RFOA) defense swallows up most disparate-impact claims.[8] *Smith* may be too sanguine, however, about the reasonableness of employment decisions that have an age-related disparate impact: Recent work in social psychology suggests that we dislike older people much more than we think we do.[9]

Thus, the principle underlying Kennedy's proportionality analysis—which also finds its way into his national consensus reasoning—could apply to ADEA jurisprudence: Age is a rational proxy for certain characteristics, but because we often overlook our negative attitudes based on age, we should be wary of the age-based classifications and effects we create. More may be behind our apparently rational calculations in the context of age than we are willing or able to admit. We may think we have neutral or positive attitudes, but negative attitudes and stereotypes may underlie our decisions without our knowledge. Standing by itself, this claim does not demonstrate that *Simmons* was rightly decided. But it does suggest that the decision is undergirded by a coherent and plausible rationale, one that has implications for other debates about the application of antidiscrimination principles.

The following discussion proceeds in five parts. Part I introduces the crime, the precedent, and the opinions in *Simmons*. Part II examines the majority's proportionality analysis, in which the Court concludes that youth's relevance in a given case should not be left to the jury. Part III applies these themes to the dispute between Kennedy and Scalia over how, in evaluating whether a national consensus opposes the juvenile death penalty, to count the states

---

[6] *Smith v City of Jackson*, 125 S Ct 1536 (2005).

[7] 29 USC §§ 621–34 (2000).

[8] *Smith*, 125 S Ct at 1540.

[9] See notes 216–19 and accompanying text.

that have outlawed the death penalty altogether. Part IV speculates on how the idea of irrational judgments about rational classifications might inform the analysis of cases arising under another prophylactic legal rule based on age, the ADEA. Part V concludes.

I. The Case and Its Context

A. THE CONTEXT

1. *The crime*. In 1993, when Christopher Simmons was seventeen years old and a junior in high school, he murdered a neighbor, Shirley Crook. He was the apparent ringleader of a plan with two other teens to break into a house, burglarize it, and, according to some of the witnesses at trial, murder the occupants. He supposedly told his friends that they could get away with it because they were juveniles.[10]

At 2 a.m. on Thursday, September 9, 1993, Simmons and his two friends met at the trailer of an older neighbor;[11] one boy

---

[10] 125 S Ct at 1187 ("Simmons assured his friends they could 'get away with it' because they were minors."); *State ex rel Simmons v Roper*, 112 SW3d 397, 419 (Mo 2003) (Price Jr., J, dissenting) ("Prior to the robbery, petitioner stated to his accomplice that they could commit a robbery and murder and get away with it because they were juveniles."). The accounts of what Simmons supposedly said in this regard vary. See, e.g., TT at 840 ("They said that they could do it; and [Simmons] said they could do it and not get charged for it because they are juveniles, and nobody would think that juveniles would do it." (quoting Brian Moomey, see note 11)); id at 99 (stating that Moomey will testify that he overheard Simmons saying to other teens that "nobody will think you guys are capable of this because you are juveniles" (quoting John Applebaum of the Jefferson County Prosecuting Attorney's Office)).

[11] 125 S Ct at 1187. The older neighbor, twenty-nine-year-old Brian Moomey, whom the neighborhood boys called "Thunder Dad," was an ex-con at whose trailer Simmons and his friends gathered and drank and did drugs. Moomey was a key prosecution witness at Simmons's trial; he came forward to supply evidence against Simmons after he heard that the police wanted to talk with him (Moomey) in connection with the murder. Simmons's brief makes the reader wonder how much influence Moomey had over the teens, and also what role was played by the third boy who abandoned the plan at the trailer—fifteen-year-old John Tessmer, a boy who, unlike Simmons, did have a record of past offenses, who was Moomey's "best friend" and "Number One Thunder Cat" (Moomey's words), and who was the other key prosecution witness, in addition to the police who testified about Simmons's confession. Brief for Respondent at *2–*3 (cited in note 3). Simmons's trial counsel testified at the postconviction hearing that the "talk in the neighborhood" was that "Moomey was letting young men drink in his house and that they were doing drugs there and that he would have them commit crimes for him." Transcript of Record on Appeal (filed July 18, 1996) at 383, *State v Simmons*, 944 SW2d 165 (Mo 1997) (en banc) (No 77269). Simmons's trial counsel also asserted that Simmons had told him that Moomey "was aware of what was going on and had helped plan it." Id at 433. The jury clearly did not doubt that Simmons committed the murder, and the trial transcript gives one little reason to question that conclusion, but parts of the story and the testimony give one pause about Simmons's motivation to rob and then to kill and his role in planning the events.

apparently abandoned the plan, but the other two proceeded to the Crook house and opened the back door by reaching through an open window. When Shirley Crook, home alone, called out "who's there?" Simmons recognized Crook: He had been in a minor auto accident with her just after he got his license. He thought she recognized him too, and, depending on which source you consult, this moment of recognition either confirmed his resolve to kill her, or inspired him to kill her in the first place.[12] Simmons and his friend duct-taped her mouth and eyes and transported her by van to a nearby river, where they bound her hands and feet with electrical wire, covered her face with a towel, and threw her in the river to drown.[13]

On the afternoon of September 9, Shirley Crook's husband returned from traveling and reported her missing. Her body was found in the river by a fisherman that day. The police picked up Simmons at school the next day; he'd apparently bragged to friends that he'd killed Crook "because the bitch seen my face."[14] In less than two hours, Simmons, in tears, confessed and agreed to perform a reenactment of the crime.[15]

2. *The courts.* Prior to *Simmons*, the minimum age for execution under the Eighth Amendment was sixteen. In 1988, in *Thompson v Oklahoma*,[16] a plurality of the Court had concluded that executing individuals who had committed their crimes before the age of sixteen constituted cruel and unusual punishment under the

---

[12] 125 S Ct at 1187–88; Brief for Respondent at *2 (cited in note 3). The prosecutor does not attempt to resolve the question of which account explains Simmons's actions; in his closing statement to the jury at the penalty phase, the prosecutor argued for the death penalty with these words: "Do it because when he broke in Shirley Crook's home, and she woke up, whatever his plans might have been before, something was solidified then, she was going to die. She was going to die because he didn't want to take the responsibility." TT at 1158.

[13] 125 S Ct at 1188.

[14] Id. The source for this quotation from Simmons is Brian Moomey (see note 11); TT at 842. Moomey failed to use this "bitch seen my face" expression in his initial four- to five-hour interview with the police—saying only that Simmons reported he had killed her because "she seen my face"—and explaining this omission by saying that the police officers had told him not to swear in front of them. TT at 864–69. As defense counsel drew out at trial, Moomey swore multiple times in his initial interview. TT at 866–67.

[15] Brief for Respondent *2 (cited in note 3) (noting that, in order to secure Simmons's confession, the police "accused [Simmons] of lying, falsely told him [an accomplice] had confessed, and explained that he might face the death penalty and that it would be in his interest to cooperate").

[16] 487 US 815 (1988) (plurality opinion).

Eighth Amendment.[17] The plurality based its conclusion on, first, the "evolving standards of decency" reasoning, which looks principally to trends in state legislatures, as well as jury verdicts and absolute numbers of executions, and, second, its own view that executing those under the age of sixteen did not further the proper purposes of the death penalty, because young people are not as culpable and are unlikely to be deterred by a potential death sentence.[18] Justice O'Connor concurred in the judgment, concluding that although she thought there was a national consensus on the matter, the evidence was insufficient to rule as such. Therefore, she reasoned, a state legislature that wanted to permit executions of those under sixteen had to make a clear statement to that effect, and Oklahoma's legislature had not done so.[19]

The next year, the Court handed down two related decisions on the same day. In *Stanford v Kentucky*,[20] the Court declined to extend the reasoning in *Thompson* to sixteen- and seventeen-year-olds, holding that no national consensus supported that extension.[21] And in *Penry v Lynaugh*,[22] on similar grounds, the Court held that the Eighth Amendment did not prohibit the execution of offenders who are mentally retarded.[23] Also relevant to our inquiry, the Court nonetheless found Penry's death sentence unconstitutional, because Texas law did not allow the jury to consider his mental retardation as a mitigating factor. The Court famously referred to mental retardation as a "two-edged sword" for Penry: "it may diminish his blameworthiness for his crime even as it indicates that there is a probability that he will be dangerous in the future."[24]

In 2002, the Court partially overruled *Penry* in *Atkins v Virginia*,[25] concluding that the Eighth Amendment prohibits executing mentally retarded defendants. By this time, "standards of decency" had apparently "evolv[ed]" sufficiently—as indicated by the

---

[17] Id at 818, 838.

[18] Id at 821–22, 824–25, 825 n 23.

[19] Id at 848–49, 857–58.

[20] 492 US 361 (1989).

[21] Id at 380.

[22] 492 US 302 (1989).

[23] Id at 340.

[24] Id at 324, 328.

[25] 536 US 304 (2002).

national consensus—to persuade the Court.[26] The Court also determined that in its own judgment, mental retardation sufficiently affected culpability and deterrability to render the imposition of the death penalty cruel and unusual.[27]

Inspired by *Atkins*, the Missouri Supreme Court in 2003 overturned Christopher Simmons's death sentence on the ground that *Atkins* had effectively overruled *Stanford*—because of similar national trends and diminished culpability and deterrability—and that it must therefore be unconstitutional to execute those who committed their crimes when they were under the age of eighteen.[28] The Supreme Court granted certiorari.

B. THE SIMMONS OPINIONS

1. *"As every parent knows": Societal maturation and the special risks of youth.* Kennedy's opinion for the Court comes in two (and a half) parts. First, the trend among states indicates that standards of decency have evolved toward the conclusion that it is cruel and unusual punishment to execute those who committed their crimes before they turned eighteen.[29] Second, youths are different enough from adults to require a rule prohibiting their execution because they cannot be reliably classed among society's worst offenders.[30] As an avowed afternote, the Court adds that international law and norms support its conclusion.[31]

The first part relies mainly on the trend among states, which looks somewhat like the "telling" trend against executing people with mental retardation observed in *Atkins*.[32] As of 2005, thirty states banned the juvenile death penalty, including eighteen that specifically banned the juvenile death penalty and twelve that banned the death penalty altogether; in 2002, at the time of *Atkins*, the breakdown with regard to mental retardation had been precisely the same, including eighteen states expressly banning the

---

[26] Id at 321.

[27] Id at 320.

[28] *State ex rel Simmons v Roper*, 112 SW3d 397, 399 (Mo 2003) (en banc).

[29] 125 S Ct at 1192–94.

[30] Id at 1194–98.

[31] Id at 1198–1200.

[32] Id at 1193.

death penalty for people with mental retardation and twelve with an overall ban.[33]

The size of the recent shift toward banning was much greater in *Atkins*, however, largely because in 1989 more states already prohibited executing juvenile offenders than prohibited executing people with mental retardation: After 1989, the number of states banning executions of mentally retarded offenders increased from two to eighteen, whereas the number banning the juvenile death penalty increased from thirteen to eighteen.[34] Because the trend is not as strong as in *Atkins*, the Court makes much of the consistent direction of the trend.[35] That is, no state had lowered the age for death eligibility between 1989 and 2005.[36] Quoting the Missouri Supreme Court, the Court notes that it would be "ironic" if the juvenile death penalty was deemed constitutional because its impropriety had been recognized more widely sooner.[37] The Court does not address the fact that some states had enacted laws, where none had previously existed, that permitted execution of those younger than eighteen when they committed their crimes.[38]

The second part of the opinion focuses on three ways that juveniles differ from adults such that "juvenile offenders cannot with reliability be classified as among the worst offenders,"[39] those for whom society's worst punishment is reserved. First, "as every parent knows," juveniles are comparatively immature, reckless, and irresponsible.[40] Second, juveniles are "more vulnerable and susceptible to negative influences and outside pressures, including peer pressure," in part because juveniles, as legal minors, have less control over their environments.[41] Third, the character of juveniles

---

[33] Id at 1192.

[34] Id at 1193; see also note 175.

[35] Id (citing *Atkins*, 536 US at 315 n 18).

[36] Id.

[37] Id at 1193–94 ("In the words of the Missouri Supreme Court: 'It would be the ultimate in irony if the very fact that the inappropriateness of the death penalty for juveniles was broadly recognized sooner than it was recognized for the mentally retarded were to become a reason to continue the execution of juveniles now that the execution of the mentally retarded has been barred.'" (quoting *State ex rel Simmons v Roper*, 112 SW3d 397, 408 n 10 (Mo 2003) (en banc))).

[38] See 125 S Ct at 1220 (Scalia, J, dissenting).

[39] Id at 1195.

[40] Id (citing these qualities as the reasons why juveniles may not "vot[e], serv[e] on juries, or marry[] without parental consent").

[41] Id.

is "not as well formed as that of an adult" and their "personality traits" are "more transitory, less fixed."[42] In addition to quoting its own past language about the nature of youth, the Court cites psychological literature on adolescent development and provides appendices detailing state laws prohibiting juveniles (defined in most cases as those under eighteen) from voting, serving on juries, and marrying without parental consent.[43] The Court concludes that these three differences "render suspect any conclusion that a juvenile falls among the worst offenders," because a juvenile's on-going struggle to define his (or her) identity "means it is less supportable to conclude that even a heinous crime committed by a juvenile is evidence of irretrievably depraved character."[44]

These differences indicate that "the penological justifications for the death penalty"—retribution and deterrence—apply to juveniles "with lesser force than to adults."[45] The Court says that retribution isn't proportional if "the law's most severe penalty is imposed on [those] whose culpability or blameworthiness is diminished, to a substantial degree, by reason of youth and immaturity."[46] And, the Court says, there is a lack of evidence to show that juveniles are deterred by the death penalty.[47] Indeed, the same characteristics that make juveniles less culpable make them less deterrable.[48] For example, juveniles are unlikely to engage in cost-benefit analysis (the Court ignores Simmons's comment about getting away with it because they are juveniles).[49] The Court nonetheless gestures in the direction of imagining what a young person's cost-benefit analysis might look like, noting that life imprisonment may be a particularly harsh punishment for a young offender, because more of life lies ahead.[50]

---

[42] Id.

[43] Id; see notes 121–22 and accompanying text.

[44] Id.

[45] Id at 1196.

[46] Id.

[47] Id.

[48] Id.

[49] Id ("In particular, as the plurality observed in *Thompson*, '[t]he likelihood that the teenage offender has made the kind of cost-benefit analysis that attaches any weight to the possibility of execution is so remote as to be virtually nonexistent.'" (quoting *Thompson v Oklahoma*, 487 US 815, 837 (1988) (plurality opinion))).

[50] Id (arguing that "the punishment of life imprisonment without the possibility of parole is itself a severe sanction, in particular for a young person").

The Court then entertains, without accepting, the argument that "a rare case might arise in which a juvenile offender has sufficient psychological maturity, and at the same time demonstrates sufficient depravity, to merit a sentence of death."[51] Missouri argues that this possibility calls for an individualized determination by juries—properly guided to consider aggravating and mitigating circumstances—rather than a "categorical rule."[52]

In a crucial passage, the Court responds that the risk is too great that a "youthful person" would be put to death "despite insufficient culpability."[53] This risk apparently exists because, first, the "brutality or cold-blooded nature of any particular crime" could overpower mitigating arguments, even where they should apply, and, second, "a defendant's youth may even be counted against him."[54] On this latter point, the Court invokes the prosecutor's argument in this case that youth is aggravating.[55] While acknowledging that these problems could be corrected by a rule requiring juries to attend to the mitigating force of youth, the Court mysteriously asserts that this would not address the "larger concerns."[56] The Court then cites the Diagnostic and Statistical Manual's (DSM-IV-TR) ban on diagnoses of antisocial personality disorders before age eighteen as evidence that even experts cannot reliably pick out the truly rotten individuals among those under age eighteen.[57] Thus, "[w]hen a juvenile offender commits a heinous crime, the State can exact forfeiture of some of the most basic liberties, but the State cannot extinguish his life and his potential to attain a mature understanding of his own humanity."[58]

The Court acknowledges that eighteen is not a perfect line; it is merely a proxy.[59] The Court concludes, though, that the logic

---

[51] Id at 1197.

[52] Id.

[53] Id.

[54] Id.

[55] Id.

[56] Id.

[57] Id; see American Psychiatric Association, *Diagnostic and Statistical Manual of Mental Disorders* 687, 702–06 (4th ed, text rev 2000) (hereafter "DSM-IV-TR") (defining diagnostic criteria for antisocial personality disorder as including the following: "There is a pervasive pattern of disregard for and violation of the rights of others occurring since age 15 years, as indicated by three (or more) of the [listed criteria.] The individual is at least age 18 years").

[58] 125 S Ct at 1197.

[59] Id at 1197–98; see text accompanying note 107.

of *Thompson* extends to those up to age eighteen, the age at which society draws many key distinctions between children and adults.[60]

The Court then reviews two problems with *Stanford*. First, the Court in *Stanford* failed to count states with no death penalty as states against the juvenile death penalty. Second, *Stanford* mistakenly deemed irrelevant the Court's "independent judgment" on proportionality, in defiance of precedent.[61]

Finally, the Court dedicates a lengthy section to showing that the international community supports its conclusion. Most notably, the Court observes that the "United States is the only country in the world that continues to give official sanction to the juvenile death penalty."[62] The Court explains, though, that international sources do not drive the decision, but "confirm[] our own conclusions" about our Constitution.[63]

2. *"Indefensibly arbitrary": The lack of consensus and the need for individualized determinations.* In dissent, Justice O'Connor argues that there is not a "genuine national consensus," that the Court does not even purport to find one, and that the Court's decision therefore rests on its own moral-proportionality analysis.[64] Though she agrees that the Constitution evolves in this area and that the Court's own judgment matters, O'Connor disagrees with the Court's independent judgment.[65] Specifically, she objects to the Court's use of a categorical proxy when the jury could decide the relevance of youth on a case-by-case basis: "Adolescents *as a class* are undoubtedly less mature, and therefore less culpable for their misconduct, than adults. But the Court has adduced no evidence impeaching the seemingly reasonable conclusion reached by many state legislatures: that at least *some* 17-year-old murderers

---

[60] Id at 1198.

[61] Id at 1192.

[62] Id at 1198.

[63] Id at 1198, 1200. Oddly, the Court never addresses the other question on which it granted certiorari: whether the Missouri Supreme Court could treat *Atkins* as overruling *Stanford*. See id at 1229 (Scalia, J, dissenting).

Justice Stevens writes separately, joined by Ginsburg, to highlight the principle that "our understanding of the Constitution does change from time to time," to observe that that principle "has been settled since John Marshall breathed life into its text," and to note that if we followed the original meaning only, then states could execute seven-year-olds. Id at 1205 (Stevens, J, concurring). (More on the last from Scalia, but with less apparent disapproval. See note 82 and accompanying text.)

[64] Id at 1206 (O'Connor, J, dissenting).

[65] Id at 1206–07 (O'Connor, J, dissenting).

are sufficiently mature to deserve the death penalty in an appropriate case."[66] O'Connor focuses on the differences she sees between mental retardation and juvenile delinquency. In addition to
the difference in the state trends, she views mental retardation as
a perfect proxy for reduced culpability and deterrability, and youth
as only an imperfect one.[67] And, she asserts, the Court has provided
no evidence that juries are incapable of assessing immaturity or
treating youth as mitigating.[68]

O'Connor gives several reasons for rejecting the Court's claim
that the differences between juveniles and adults support a categorical ban. First, the fact that juveniles are less culpable or deterrable does not mean that they are not *sufficiently* culpable or
deterrable to warrant the death penalty.[69] There is an age that is
always too young in cognitive capacities, but that age is not the
cusp of adulthood.[70] She invokes specific facts of the case, including
Simmons's reported comment that they could get away with the
crime because of their youth, to show that a juvenile offender may
be more "depraved" than the average murderer and may have the
capacity for at least an informal cost-benefit analysis.[71]

Second, relying on age is "indefensibly arbitrary" because there
is so much variation on both sides of the line.[72] In contrast, the
category of mental retardation is "*defined* by precisely the characteristics which render death an excessive punishment."[73] Moreover, the Court in *Atkins* could and did "le[ave] to the State[s] the
task of developing appropriate ways to enforce the constitutional
restriction upon [their] execution of sentences."[74] The failure of
the categorical rule, on this account, makes youth a perfect case
for the jury.

O'Connor concedes that the prosecutor's attempt to use Simmons's youth as an aggravating circumstance is "troubling," but

---

[66] Id at 1206 (O'Connor, J, dissenting).

[67] Id at 1214 (O'Connor, J, dissenting).

[68] Id at 1215 (O'Connor, J, dissenting).

[69] Id at 1212–13 (O'Connor, J, dissenting).

[70] Id at 1213 (O'Connor, J, dissenting).

[71] Id (O'Connor, J, dissenting).

[72] Id at 1214 (O'Connor, J, dissenting).

[73] Id (O'Connor, J, dissenting).

[74] Id at 1209 (O'Connor, J, dissenting) (quoting *Atkins v Virginia*, 536 US 304, 317
(2002) (internal quotation marks omitted)).

notes that, first, the prosecutor's statement wasn't "challenged with specificity in the lower courts and is not directly at issue here"; second, the Court presents no evidence for its claim that juries cannot weigh evidence of youth properly; and, third, the Court "fails to explain why" youth is different from other qualitative capital sentencing factors.[75] Ultimately, she thinks youth is mitigating, and as a legislator she would be inclined to set the age at eighteen, but thinks that inclination does not justify a categorical ban under the Constitution.[76]

3. *"Subjective views . . . and like minded foreigners": To the contrary.* Justice Scalia, joined in dissent by Rehnquist and Thomas, is predictably unimpressed by the argument that the Constitution's requirements can evolve within fifteen years, and also by the notion that the Court may rely on its own judgment rather than waiting for a firmer national consensus: "Because I do not believe that the meaning of our Eighth Amendment, any more than the meaning of other provisions of our Constitution, should be determined by the subjective views of five Members of this Court and like-minded foreigners, I dissent."[77]

Scalia makes three main points: (1) there is no national consensus;[78] (2) juvenile offenders sometimes warrant the death penalty;[79] and (3) international law and norms should not matter.[80]

First, he begins his discussion of the national-consensus issue by acknowledging, but disparaging as mistaken, the modern Eighth Amendment jurisprudence of looking to evolving standards.[81] (He drops a footnote to mention that the Court skipped the first step of the proper modern jurisprudence—i.e., whether this was a mode of punishment considered cruel and unusual at the nation's founding—and observes that at common law a seven-

---

[75] Id at 1215 (O'Connor, J, dissenting).

[76] Id at 1217. O'Connor, like Scalia after her, actually addresses the other question for certiorari, and devotes a short section to her indignation at Missouri's having taken upon itself to overrule *Stanford*. Id at 1209–10. Unlike Scalia, she agrees with the Court that international law can be relevant, though it cannot play a confirmatory role for her here because she doesn't think there's a national consensus or a convincing moral-proportionality argument. Id at 1215–16.

[77] Id at 1217 (Scalia, J, dissenting).

[78] Id at 1217–21 (Scalia, J, dissenting).

[79] Id at 1221–25 (Scalia, J, dissenting).

[80] Id at 1225–29 (Scalia, J, dissenting).

[81] Id at 1217 (Scalia, J, dissenting).

year-old could be executed, and there was a rebuttable presumption of incapacity to commit a capital or other felony until age fourteen.[82]) Then he contests the evidence of an adequate consensus here, highlighting (with O'Connor) that a few states that had no age limit before *Stanford* expressly adopted sixteen as their age limit since that case, and that Florida voters changed their constitution to override their court's decision that executing juvenile offenders violated that constitution.[83] He objects not only to the specific numbers cited by the Court, but also to treating states that lack the death penalty altogether as if they also must think an exception should be made for juveniles where the death penalty exists.[84]

In Scalia's view, a useful factor might instead be those states' laws about treating juveniles as adults for noncapital crimes: All those states without the death penalty at all (but for D.C. on life imprisonment) permit juveniles to be tried as adults. Indeed, some states actually require it for certain crimes. Thus, Scalia argues, these states do not believe that juveniles should be exempted from regular laws, or that they cannot be culpable in the way that adults can.[85] In general, since attitudes to the death penalty fluctuate over time, Scalia perceives a real harm from the Court's fixing in place one moment's view.[86]

Second, Scalia interprets the Court as implicitly saying that no juvenile could ever be culpable and deterrable enough to deserve the death penalty.[87] He disparages both the Court's reliance on its own view and the view itself, noting that the data on juvenile capacity and development are contradictory (and weren't put to the test of an adversarial process), and so evaluating these data is a task for legislatures, not courts.[88] He notes that in the context of abortion, psychological data about the cognitive maturity of juveniles have been offered to the Court as evidence that juveniles

---

[82] Id at 1218 n 1 (Scalia, J, dissenting).

[83] Id at 1220, 1220 n 6 (Scalia, J, dissenting); id at 1211 (O'Connor, J, dissenting).

[84] Id at 1218–19 (Scalia, J, dissenting).

[85] Id at 1219 (Scalia, J, dissenting).

[86] Id at 1220 (Scalia, J, dissenting).

[87] Id at 1221 (Scalia, J, dissenting).

[88] Id at 1222–23 (Scalia, J, dissenting).

should be treated like adults.[89] "In other words, all the Court has done today, to borrow from another context, is to look over the heads of the crowd and pick out its friends."[90] Rejecting the analogy to marriage, jury service, or abortion, Scalia asserts that decisions such as these are surely more complicated than the decision not to take a human life.[91] And he details the facts of this case and one of the terrible rape/murders described in Alabama's amicus brief to make the point that young people clearly can do terrible things.[92]

No constitutional rule, he thus concludes, should prevent "legislatures and juries from treating exceptional cases in an exceptional way—by determining that some murders are not just the acts of happy-go-lucky teenagers, but heinous crimes deserving of death."[93] Like O'Connor, Scalia is concerned about the Court's distrust of juries and ponders the slippery slope: Why, for instance, should juries be any better at properly considering the relevance of child abuse as a mitigating factor?[94] In addition, he finds no reason to think that no juveniles are susceptible to deterrence, and thus the Court's argument here must again depend on some mistaken absolute rule. Also like O'Connor, he cites the facts of this case to show that some youths do consider deterrence-like factors, and notes that the jury in this case may have considered Simmons's calculation that he could get away with murder relevant to its decision to impose the death penalty.[95]

Third, he believes that the Court must have taken "the so-called international community" into account in its decision, or the Court wouldn't have mentioned it at all.[96] He cites the United States's express reservation from the International Covenant on Civil and Political Rights as evidence that either the United States hasn't reached a national consensus, or it has reached the opposite

---

[89] Id (Scalia, J, dissenting) (citing Brief for American Psychological Association as Amici Curiae, *Hodgson v Minnesota*, 497 US 417 (1990) (Nos 88-805, 88-1125, 88-1309), 1989 WL 1127529).

[90] Id at 1223 (Scalia, J, dissenting).

[91] Id at 1224 (Scalia, J, dissenting).

[92] Id at 1223–24 (Scalia, J, dissenting) (citing Brief for Alabama, et al, as Amici Curiae, at 9–10, 2004 WL 865268).

[93] Id at 1224 (Scalia, J, dissenting).

[94] Id at 1225 (Scalia, J, dissenting).

[95] Id (Scalia, J, dissenting).

[96] Id at 1225, 1229 (Scalia, J, dissenting).

consensus as the international community.[97] He also criticizes the Court's apparent presumption that other countries, even horrible dictatorships, really behave as they say.[98] Here again he invokes the slippery slope, asking whether we must also adopt other international norms. Should life imprisonment without parole not be permitted for juveniles? Should there be less separation of church and state?[99]

II. "Seventeen Years Old. Isn't That Scary?": The Proportionality Analysis

The crux of the Court's decision must be its proportionality analysis, in particular, the diminished culpability discussion. Standing by itself, the less-than-"telling" trend among states cannot easily support the Court's conclusion. Even though Kennedy resolves the Denominator Dispute in favor of counting anti-death-penalty states as anti-juvenile-death-penalty (of which more later), the trend is hard to characterize as proving a "genuine national consensus."[100] Hence the Court's decision cannot plausibly turn on this part of the analysis. And, rightly or wrongly, the assertion that the death penalty could not possibly deter sixteen- and seventeen-year-olds falls a bit flat in a case in which the defendant reportedly urged his friends to commit murder by telling them they could get away with it because they were juveniles.[101] Finally, while international and comparative law may have played a role in the Court's assessment of "evolving standards of decency that mark the progress of a maturing society,"[102] that role was most plausibly to bolster rather than to supplant the Court's "own judgment."[103]

---

[97] Id at 1225–26 (Scalia, J, dissenting).

[98] Id at 1226 (Scalia, J, dissenting).

[99] Id at 1226–27. Scalia also notes his frustration that the Court did not admonish Missouri for purporting to overrule *Stanford*. Presumably with more sarcasm than sympathy, he concludes, however, that the Missouri Supreme Court's decision was somewhat understandable given that the Court's jurisprudence in this area makes it no longer the expert on the Constitution. Id at 1229.

[100] Id at 1206 (O'Connor, J, dissenting) ("Although the Court finds support for its decision in the fact that a majority of the States now disallow capital punishment of 17-year-old offenders, it refrains from asserting that its holding is compelled by a genuine national consensus.").

[101] See note 10.

[102] *Trop v Dulles*, 356 US 86, 100–01 (1958) (plurality opinion).

[103] *Roper v Simmons*, 125 S Ct at 1191. The Court's recent invocations of international and comparative law have received a great deal of attention. See, e.g., Sarah H. Cleveland,

A. AN ABSOLUTE DIFFERENCE?

While the dissenters agree that the crux of Kennedy's opinion is the Court's own proportionality analysis, they overread that opinion, disregarding both its opacity and its subtlety. Both O'Connor and Scalia seem to read the majority as concluding that *all* juveniles are insufficiently culpable to merit the death penalty. O'Connor writes: "[T]he rule decreed by the Court rests, ultimately, on its independent moral judgment that death is a disproportionately severe punishment for any 17-year-old offender."[104] Similarly, Scalia observes: "Of course, the real force driving today's decision is not the actions of four state legislatures, but the Court's 'own judgment' that murderers younger than 18 can never be as morally culpable as older counterparts."[105]

To be sure, this reading of the Court's opinion is not without foundation. The opinion is evasive on whether juveniles are categorically different from adults and thus universally less culpable. The best support for the dissenters' reading is this observation of Kennedy's: "Certainly it can be argued, although we by no means concede the point, that a rare case might arise in which a juvenile offender has sufficient psychological maturity, and at the same time

---

Our International Constitution, 31 Yale J Int'l L 1 (2005) (examining the recent controversy over the Court's use of international law in light of an extensive analysis of the Court's long-standing practice of invoking international law). Though not a focus of my article, a few words follow on the subject. The phrase "*evolving* standards of decency that mark the progress of a *maturing* society" seems to embrace a kind of Whiggish progress narrative in which we are becoming ever more decent over time. And while the question of which way progress lies seems indeterminate, discussions of the juvenile death penalty often seem to assume we know what progress looks like. Rather tellingly, the brief on behalf of Missouri—whose task is of course to convince the Court that evolving standards of decency do not preclude the juvenile death penalty—asserts that we do not "yet" have a national consensus on this point. Brief for Petitioner at *21–*22, *Roper v Simmons*, 125 S Ct 1183 (2005) (No 03-633), 2004 WL 903158; see notes 197–98 and accompanying text (quoting and discussing the relevant passage). The doctrinal metaphors of that progress narrative— evolution and maturation—may help to explain why international standards might seem relevant to the determination of our national standards of decency. Constructivist work by historians of age and of science notwithstanding, see notes 168–69 and accompanying text, we tend to think of evolution and maturation as natural processes. These metaphors therefore naturalize the progress narrative, helping to remove it from the realm of cultural difference and specificity, into a realm of inevitable and universal progress or growing up. Under this account, the "progress" of other nations toward a near-consensus on the juvenile death penalty must help to demonstrate, or to confirm (to take Kennedy at his word), that the Court's own judgment is right, that the states that have moved in this direction are right, and that the states that haven't outlawed the juvenile death penalty just haven't quite gotten there *yet* and need to be nudged along.

[104] 125 S Ct at 1206 (O'Connor, J, dissenting).

[105] Id at 1221 (Scalia, J, dissenting) (internal quotation marks omitted).

demonstrates sufficient depravity, to merit a sentence of death."[106] Kennedy refuses to concede that an individual juvenile might deserve the death penalty, but this is not an argument against the proposition.

Moreover, Kennedy later seems to admit the point:

> Drawing the line at 18 years of age is subject, of course, to the objections always raised against categorical rules. The qualities that distinguish juveniles from adults do not disappear when an individual turns 18. By the same token, some under 18 have already attained a level of maturity some adults will never reach. For the reasons we have discussed, however, a line must be drawn.[107]

Kennedy here seems to acknowledge that youth is an imperfect proxy for diminished culpability, suggesting that his earlier comment may simply reflect an unwillingness to concede expressly a quasi-empirical point that makes his conclusion harder to defend.

B. OF STEREOTYPES AND INDIVIDUALIZED ASSESSMENTS

Kennedy's opinion consists of a batch of generalizations—of stereotypes, in the pejorative language of antidiscrimination law—about juveniles. O'Connor's argument, perhaps unsurprisingly in light of her particularistic approach to constitutional law, instead emphasizes the need for case-by-case assessment:[108] Because youth is an imperfect proxy for diminished culpability, she reasons, the jury should determine in each case whether a particular individual's age mitigates his culpability. Unlike, for example, voting, where the alternatives to a blanket age-based rule would be costly and possibly invidious, death-penalty sentencing determinations always already demand individualized inquiries.[109] Declining the proxy in favor of an inquiry into the thing itself should therefore create little additional cost and no new harms in criminal sentencing. At first glance, then, O'Connor reasonably argues that the question of diminished culpability on account of youth should be answered by juries in individual cases.

---

[106] Id at 1197.

[107] Id at 1197–98.

[108] Cf., e.g., *Gratz v Bollinger*, 539 US 244, 280 (2003) (O'Connor, J, concurring); *Grutter v Bollinger*, 539 US 306, 335–37 (2003) (O'Connor, J).

[109] 125 S Ct at 1216.

Kennedy's generalizations about youth have also been criticized by a surprising source: proponents of youth liberation.[110] Advocates of children's rights split into two main camps: protectionists and liberationists.[111] Protectionists emphasize the special vulnerability of minors in order to argue for a solicitous state; liberationists, who trace their roots to mid-twentieth-century civil rights movements centered upon race and sex, seek autonomy and self-determination for young people.[112] Though at times adopting more familiar terms like *ageism* and *age discrimination*, which tend to evoke the struggles of older people, youth libbers have also coined more colorful terms like *ephebiphobia*—fear of youth—and *adultism* or *adultocracy*.[113] Though their normative goals are unlikely to capture the imagination of many adults,[114] youth liber-

---

[110] See, e.g., Mike Males, *Statistical Bigotry*, available at http://www.youthtoday.org/youthtoday/Apr05/males.html (Apr 5, 2005); Alex Koroknay-Palicz, Supreme Court Strikes Down Juvenile Death Penalty, available at http://www.oneandfour.org/archives/youth_rights/ (Mar 1, 2005); id (posted comments).

[111] Rosalind Ekman Ladd, *Introduction*, in Rosalind Ekman Ladd, ed, *Children's Rights Re-visioned: Philosophical Readings* 1, 2 (1996).

[112] See, e.g., id; Martha Minow, *Rights for the Next Generation: A Feminist Approach to Children's Rights*, in *Children's Rights Re-visioned* at 42, 48 (cited in note 111).

[113] For example, National Youth Rights Association, *Ephebiphobia*, in The Freechild Project's Survey of North American Youth Rights, available at http://www.freechild.org/SNAYR/Ephebiphobia.htm. ("Ephebiphobia is defined as the fear of youth. This fear is generally based in negative stereotypes of youth, and is perpetuated by popular media (news, tv, movies) around the world. Ephebiphobia often leads to Adultism, at its worst perpetuating the alienation of young people from society."); Mike Males, *The New Demons: Ordinary Teens*, LA Times (Apr 21, 2002) ("Ephebiphobia—extreme fear of youth—is a full-blown media panic. Images of 'ordinary' teenagers besieging grown-up havens are everywhere. . . . Today's ephebiphobia is the latest installment of a history of bogus moral panics targeting unpopular subgroups to obscure an unsettling reality: Our worst social crisis is middle-Americans['] own misdirected fear."); Brian A. Dominick, *Revolution Kid Style*, in *Liberating Youth* (2d ed 1997) (with Sara Zia), available at http://www.zmag.org/0009.htm ("[Y]oung people must learn that adults are not what is to be fought. Instead, the ideological construct that is adultocracy must be contended with. . . . For the youth liberation movement, adultocracy is the chief adversary. Its agents, we must remember, are not only adults but also other young people who have internalized notions of the adult/child dichotomy and thus perpetuate disruption of class consciousness. . . . How often do we see kids who feel worthless because they are kids? And who abuse those kids who do not feel worthless as such? If we did not oppress ourselves so efficiently, we would be able to rise up and fight in unity. But alas, we cannot, because we are too busy incorporating ageism into our daily lives.").

[114] See, e.g., John Holt, *Escape from Childhood* 18–19 (1974) (proposing that "the rights, privileges, duties, and responsibilities of adult citizens be made *available* to any young person, of whatever age, who wants to make use of them" and expressly "not say[ing] that these rights and duties should be tied into one package, that if a young person wants to assume any of them he must assume them all. He should be able to pick and choose . . . ."); John Harris, *The Political Status of Children*, in Keith Graham, ed, *Contemporary Political Philosophy: Radical Studies* 35, 49–51 (1982) (suggesting that we should move toward granting children "full political status"

ation arguments—whether academic philosophy or weblog posts—make some insightful points about the status of young people and draw intriguing parallels to subordination based on other traits. No less than Justice O'Connor, liberationists oppose generalizations about youth and plead for individualized judgments.

A rallying cry of this work is that stereotyping about youth artificially distinguishes individuals based on age and hinders the development and autonomy of young people.[115] Some youth liberation writing takes the point a step further, arguing that age-based classifications limit young people *and* adults, by pressing conformity and lifelessness on adults in the name of being "grown up."[116] Reminiscent of radical strands of feminist and queer politics, this form of youth liberation argument rallies around youthfulness, which it attempts to denaturalize, rather than around chronologically young age.[117]

But the central youth liberation critique focuses on the subordination of young people by adults, who control and stereotype them, in part through overbroad generalizations. In the words of a youth liberation classic, "By now I have come to feel that the fact of being a 'child,' of being wholly subservient and dependent,

---

from the age of ten); Dominick (cited in note 113) (arguing for youth liberation as a means to egalitarian anarchy); see also Judith Hughes, *The Philosopher's Child*, in *Children's Rights Revisioned* at 15, 20–22 (cited in note 111) (noting that Holt and Harris do not adequately address the practical challenges of their proposals).

[115] See, e.g., Holt at 25–26 (cited in note 114) (describing "the institution of childhood" as "a Great Divide in human life" that has "made us think that the people on opposite sides of this divide, the Children and the Adults, are very different. Thus we *act* as if the differences between any sixteen-year-old and any twenty-two-year-old were far greater and more important than the differences between someone aged two and someone aged sixteen, or between someone aged twenty-two and someone aged seventy. . . . In short, by the institution of childhood I mean all those attitudes and feelings, and also customs and laws, that . . . make it difficult or impossible for young people to make contact with the larger society around them, and, even more, to play any kind of active, responsible, useful part in it . . . .").

[116] See, e.g., Brian A. Dominick and Sara Zia, *Young and Oppressed*, in *Liberating Youth* (Behind Enemy Lines Publications, 1996), available at http://www.zmag.org/0009.htm ("Adults are expected to act 'grown up.' As their youth has been all but entirely eradicated, this is not a very high expectation. Being 'grown up' means discarding all curiosity, creativity and sense of adventure.").

[117] Dominick and Zia (cited in note 116) ("*Youth* is not necessarily possessed only by those who are young in age. It is a state of mind which can be attained by anyone, was once possessed by everyone, but is rarely present in anyone beyond adolescence."); see also Brian A. Dominick, *Introduction*, in *Liberating Youth* (cited in note 113) (explaining, in a new introduction to the pamphlet containing the Dominick and Zia article, that the article was originally written when the authors were seventeen and twenty, and that although the authors are now twenty and twenty-three, and "getting older all the time, . . . we both attest to feeling youthful, which is what counts. . . .").

of being seen by older people as a mixture of expensive nuisance, slave, and super-pet, does most young people more harm than good."[118] It is in this vein that youth libbers such as Alex Koroknay-Palicz criticize Kennedy's opinion in *Simmons* for "the argument that youth are mentally deficient and cannot be compared to adults."[119] More dramatically, Mike Males accuses Kennedy of "endors[ing] ugly, long-debunked 'biodeterminism' prejudices against adolescents that menace the fundamental rights of young people."[120]

C. AGE-BASED DISCRIMINATION? SIMMONS AS A PROPHYLACTIC RULE

The youth libbers' criticism, like O'Connor's, fails to recognize the curious antidiscrimination rationale that underlies Kennedy's reasoning, a rationale that comes in several steps. First, Kennedy is indeed saying that age-based classifications are rational, that is, they track certain traits relevant to culpability. On Kennedy's account, juveniles as a class are less responsible and more reckless, more susceptible to influence,[121] and less formed in their characters. Kennedy's account of how these characteristics of juveniles mitigate their culpability is skeletal, but the article from which Kennedy apparently draws this tripartite structure pairs each ju-

---

[118] Holt at 18 (cited in note 114).

[119] Koroknay-Palicz (cited in note 110); see also id (criticizing Kennedy's first point about juveniles as reckless as follows: "This argument enshrined in a SCOTUS decision is a dangerous foe of any possible judicial progress for youth rights. I dispute the validity of the scientific evidence cited, and am bothered by the casual 'as any parent knows' language. No doubt Justice Kennedy draws upon the long standing prec[e]dents of 'as every husband knows' and 'as every white person knows' to build this particular case against youth. . . .").

[120] Males, *Statistical Bigotry* (cited in note 110).

[121] Interestingly, this point brings together two quite different contributing factors to vulnerability: juveniles' being easily influenced because they are constrained by their environment and lack of societal autonomy, and their being so influenced because of the impressionability of this developmental stage. The Court quotes a sentence from Laurence Steinberg and Elizabeth Scott on this point—"[A]s legal minors, [juveniles] lack the freedom that adults have to extricate themselves from a criminogenic setting" (see note 122, at 1014)—for which Steinberg and Scott in turn cite Jeffrey Fagan, *Contexts of Choice by Adolescents in Criminal Events*, in Thomas Grisso and Robert G. Schwartz, eds, *Youth on Trial: A Developmental Perspective on Juvenile Justice* 371 (2000). 125 S Ct at 1195. Rather than discussing the constraining role of law, however, Fagan may best be read to be discussing the ways that the real threat of violence for "adolescents in dangerous, potentially lethal contexts" may constrain choices by making violence rational. Fagan at 389. Regardless of source, Koroknay-Palicz notes with some optimism the Court's seeming reference to the coercive circumstances of law as a youth rights argument. See Koroknay-Palicz (cited in note 110).

venile trait with traditional bases for mitigation: (1) diminished capacity (paired with lesser decision-making abilities); (2) duress, provocation, or coercion (greater vulnerability to coercive circumstances); and (3) the lack of bad character (juveniles' unformed character).[122]

Second, Kennedy asserts that, despite being "marked and well understood," these differences between juveniles and adults cannot be left to juries to discern and take into account.[123] This objection lies at the heart of his opinion. O'Connor responds that Kennedy does not sufficiently explain why juries cannot be trusted with these decisions.[124] But Kennedy's reasoning supplies an answer, one both fascinating and subtle.

Kennedy suggests that juries are too likely to get it wrong, for reasons similar to those that prompt prophylactic antidiscrimination rules in other contexts. His answer to O'Connor's question—Why not let juries make individualized determinations about the mitigating effect of age?—is more illustrative than deductive, and requires some elaboration. Kennedy presents two reasons why the risk is too great that juries will fail properly to treat youth as mitigating: one more cognitive, and one more emotional, though the distinction is of course inexact. (This distinction might be analogized to the distinction in social psychology between stereotypes and attitudes.[125]) In other words, Kennedy is concerned that jurors will err because identifying accurately the cases in which youth mitigates an individual's culpability is such a difficult cognitive task. He also fears that jurors' emotions may prevent them from properly exercising their rational capacities and at times cause them to disfavor those whom they should favor.

The cognitive reason is embedded in Kennedy's discussion of antisocial personality disorder, which, according to the DSM-IV-

---

[122] Laurence Steinberg and Elizabeth S. Scott, *Less Guilty by Reason of Adolescence: Developmental Immaturity, Diminished Responsibility, and the Juvenile Death Penalty*, 58 Am Psychologist 1009, 1016 (2003); see 125 S Ct at 1195–97.

[123] 125 S Ct at 1197 (noting "[a]n unacceptable likelihood" that the jury would err).

[124] Id at 1212 (O'Connor, J, concurring) ("[T]he Court adduces no evidence whatsoever in support of its sweeping conclusion.").

[125] For example, Becca R. Levy and Mahzarin R. Banaji, *Implicit Ageism*, in Todd D. Nelson, ed, *Ageism: Stereotyping and Prejudice Against Older Persons* 49, 51 (MIT Press, 2002) (distinguishing, in a discussion of implicit attitudes toward old age, "implicit age stereotypes (also called automatic or unconscious stereotypes)" from "implicit age attitudes (also called automatic or unconscious prejudice)").

TR, psychiatrists may not diagnose in those under age eighteen.[126] The reason, Kennedy observes, is that it is too difficult to figure out which young people are bad to the core and which are still changing and could improve. In Kennedy's words, "It is difficult even for expert psychologists to differentiate between the juvenile offender whose crime reflects unfortunate yet transient immaturity, and the rare juvenile offender whose crime reflects irreparable corruption."[127]

The meaning here is not entirely clear, but Kennedy seems to suggest two overlapping possibilities: (1) it is hard to tell which young people will not be bad forever because they will improve as they grow older; and (2) it is hard to tell which young people will not be bad forever because their youth itself causes them to commit bad acts. I will return to these points shortly, but for now it is worth noting that Kennedy's observation seems to implicate both ideas. The key point here is that if experts do not have the ability to determine accurately whether a juvenile offender is among the worst of the worst, then surely juries will not be able to draw the distinctions O'Connor wants them to make.

This explanation seems unsatisfying, though, in light of Kennedy's earlier assertion that the characteristics that mitigate youths' culpability are "marked and well understood"; if this is so, why not trust juries to err on the side of mitigating? This question brings me to Kennedy's other and more fundamental reason for rejecting O'Connor's individualized approach.

Features of juvenile death penalty cases in general, and this case in particular, Kennedy reasons, suggest that jurors' feelings about the crime and the criminal may render them incapable of properly making these individualized determinations of the mitigating force of age. This argument comes in two parts. First, the vicious nature of the crimes that render someone eligible for the death penalty may cause jurors to underestimate the mitigating force of youth.[128] Kennedy may be thinking of his own reaction to the Alabama amicus brief, which describes in excruciating detail several hor-

---

[126] See note 57 and accompanying text.

[127] 125 S Ct at 1197 (citing DSM-IV-TR at 701–06 (cited in note 57)); Steinberg and Scott at 1014–16 (cited in note 122).

[128] 125 S Ct at 1197 ("An unacceptable likelihood exists that the brutality or cold-blooded nature of any particular crime would overpower mitigating arguments based on youth as a matter of course, even where the juvenile offender's objective immaturity, vulnerability, and lack of true depravity should require a sentence less severe than death.").

rendous crimes committed by juveniles, and which he described at oral argument as "chilling."[129] But this fails to explain why juries would be any worse at making determinations of the mitigating force of *youth* than of any other mitigating factor in heinous death penalty cases. Perhaps Kennedy thinks that it is particularly difficult for juries to see the perpetrator of heinous acts as *young*, because, for instance, juries expect youth to be a time of innocence.[130] Although this might distinguish youth from other mitigating factors that juries must consider, and thus may respond to Scalia's and O'Connor's criticism, Kennedy does not directly suggest that this is his reasoning. More is needed, and this brings us to a crucial moment.

Kennedy tells us that juries may consider youth as the opposite of mitigating: as aggravating. "In some cases a defendant's youth may even be counted against him. In this very case, . . . the prosecutor argued Simmons' youth was aggravating rather than mitigating."[131] As noted earlier, at the penalty phase, the prosecutor argued,[132]

> Let's look at the mitigating circumstances. . . . Age, he says. Think about age. Seventeen years old. Isn't that scary? Doesn't that scare you? Mitigating? Quite the contrary I submit. Quite the contrary.[133]

This argument was not unique to *Simmons*; an article cited in Simmons's brief catalogues similar prosecutorial rhetoric in trials in other jurisdictions.[134]

---

[129] Oral Argument at *33 (cited in note 3) ("Well, there were a number—a number of cases in the Alabama amicus brief, which is chilling reading—and I wish that all the people that sign on to the amicus briefs had at least read that before they sign on to them— indicates that often the 17-year-old is the ringleader." (quoting Kennedy, J)).

[130] A prosecutorial argument from another case, the trial of Scott Hain, seems to rely on this logic. See text accompanying note 166.

[131] 125 S Ct at 1197.

[132] At oral argument Scalia proposed that these lines did not amount to an argument that youth was aggravating, only that it was not mitigating; he criticized the Missouri solicitor for "giv[ing] that one away." Oral Argument at *10–*11 (cited in note 3). But Kennedy at oral argument and in the opinion, as well as the others who spoke on the matter at oral argument, clearly reads this as a suggestion that youth is aggravating, and prosecutors in other jurisdictions have made the point even more plainly. See, e.g., Ashley Dobbs, *The Use of Youth as an Aggravating Factor in Death Penalty Cases Involving Minors*, 10 Juvenile Justice Update (June/July 2004), at 1, 15; note 138 and accompanying text.

[133] TT at 1156–57.

[134] Dobbs at 15 (cited in note 132) (cataloguing seven other such instances, the trial transcripts of which are quoted below); Brief for Respondent at *30 (cited in note 3).

Why would prosecutors think—and why would Kennedy agree—that this argument could persuade jurors? And so much so that even a rule requiring juries to consider youth as mitigating would not address Kennedy's "larger concerns"?[135] Something in this argument extends beyond its articulation by any particular prosecutor. That is, the argument has force because its underlying logic already exists in the public consciousness and therefore resonates with jurors; it is available to jurors whether a prosecutor argues it or not. And something in it threatens to derail a juror's impartial and appropriate *individualized* consideration of youth in the death penalty context.

One might think the prosecutor means that youth is scary because the juvenile offender will be alive longer and therefore have more time to commit future crimes, even if only in prison. This sort of argument—that youth allows more time for future dangerousness—seems to drive the youth-as-aggravating argument made by a Texas prosecutor in another recent juvenile death penalty case: "Just shows he's got that much longer to be bad and prey on others who are weak, who are helpless, who are alone."[136] Relatedly, prosecutors may present young offenders as especially dangerous by implying that they will be even larger, stronger, and scarier in the future. For example, another Texas prosecutor argued, "He's got a[n] onset of violence at 17 years of age. He's just now going into the violent period. You want to talk about a future forecast of dangerousness? What is the highest risk—what is the highest risk in terms of a time period? Where is it? 17 to 26. . . . What do you think we've got to look forward to in the next eight years?"[137] Another prosecutor, after reciting the horrific things done in prison by a defendant who was seventeen at the time of his crime, said, "And they want to tell you that because of his age that's mitigating? Ladies and gentlemen of the jury, if he's this mean at age 18, he's going to be something in a couple of years.

---

[135] 125 S Ct at 1197.

[136] Closing argument transcript at 32–92, *Guillen v State*, No 73,491 (Tex Crim App 2003) (quoting Mr. Barnes); see also Dobbs at 15 (cited in note 132) (noting the name and geographic location of the prosecutor).

[137] Closing argument transcript at 931–32, *Beazley v State*, No 72,101 (Tex Crim App 1997) (quoting Jack Skeen, Jr., Smith County District Attorney); see also Dobbs at 15 (cited in note 132) (reporting the name of the prosecutor and the fact that Napoleon Beazley was executed on May 28, 2002).

That's not mitigating at all. If[] anything it's aggravating."[138]

This idea of future dangerousness might be present in Simmons's case, as the court below observed.[139] But the prosecutor's invitation to the jury to "think about age" and his comment, "Seventeen years old. Isn't that scary?" seem not only to suggest prediction, but to imply that Simmons's youth made him more culpable.[140]

The prosecutor seems to be intimating that for a person to do such bad things when young must mean the person is *really* bad. That is, a youth who is capable of committing such horrific acts must be monstrous, or evil, or genetically defective.[141] Such a person must be off the charts of humanity, such that society is absolved of responsibility for either creating him or reforming him—indeed, even for allowing him to live. This argument appeals to a prosecutor, because it may help jurors wash their hands of this defendant and help them overcome any feeling of human sympathy, any sense of collective responsibility, for such a person. Moreover, it supplies a reason to view this individual as among the worst of the worst and therefore deserving of society's worst punishment.[142] To draw on language from another context, we might call this a *minoritizing* view of aggravating youth.[143]

On the other hand, the prosecutor's words may evoke something broader about teenagers. Taken alone, the words "Think about age. Seventeen years old. Isn't that scary?" resonate more generally. There is something scary about adolescents.[144] The qualities

---

[138] Closing argument transcript at 118–19, *Jones v State*, No 72,500 (Tex Crim App 1999) (quoting Assistant County Attorney Kerye Ashmore); see also Dobbs at 15 (cited in note 132) (providing the prosecutor's name and reporting Jones's age).

[139] *State ex rel Simmons v Roper*, 112 SW3d 397, 413 (Mo 2003) (en banc) ("Thus, Mr. Simmons' youth was used to suggest greater immorality and *future dangerousness* and so to provide a further reason to impose the death penalty." (emphasis added)).

[140] Cf. also id ("Thus, Mr. Simmons' youth was used to suggest *greater immorality* and future dangerousness and so to provide a further reason to impose the death penalty." (emphasis added)).

[141] Cf., e.g., Joe L. Kincheloe, *The New Childhood: Home Alone as a Way of Life*, in Henry Jenkins, ed, *The Children's Culture Reader* 159, 164 (1998) ("[T]he appearance of evil so close to goodness and innocence [makes] the child monster that much more horrible").

[142] Cf. note 163 (quoting from work representative of the superpredator panic of the 1990s).

[143] Cf. Eve Kosofsky Sedgwick, *Epistemology of the Closet* 85 (1990) (defining a minoritizing view of homosexuality as the view that "there is a distinct population of persons who 'really are' gay").

[144] Stanley Hall, author of a historic two-volume work on the subject, is typically credited

of youth Kennedy describes—immature and reckless, easily influenced, and lacking in determinate character—can be frightening. Moreover, sixteen- and seventeen-year-olds—the group at issue in this case—present a special threat: they are on the verge of adulthood, with physical strength and other capacities that approximate adults', but, by most accounts, they lack adults' self-control or other-regardingness.[145] As Kennedy has implied by suggesting that some juvenile offenders will grow out of their criminality because adolescence itself causes their criminal behavior,[146] seventeen is a scary age. Indeed, more than one psychological tradition characterizes adolescence as akin to mental illness.[147] This we might call a *universalizing* view of youth as aggravating.[148]

These notions of youth as aggravating may shape jurors' willingness—indeed, their ability—to identify with an offender, di-

with the popularization, if not the invention, of the concept of adolescence as a distinct period between puberty and adulthood. See generally G. Stanley Hall, *Adolescence* (1924); see also, e.g., Arlene Skolnick, *The Limits of Childhood: Conceptions of Child Development and Social Context*, 39 L & Contemp Probs 38, 62 (1975).

[145] See Skolnick at 62 (cited in note 144).

[146] See text accompanying note 127; see also Steinberg and Scott at 1015 (cited in note 122) ("Adolescent traits that contribute to criminal conduct are normative in adolescence, but they are not typical of adulthood."); cf. Males, *Statistical Bigotry* (cited in note 110) (arguing that the arguments on both sides in *Simmons* "could be summed up as, 'Our teens: willfully cold-blooded killers, or helplessly deranged psychopaths?'").

[147] See, e.g., Leslie A. Zebrowitz and Joann M. Montepare, *"Too Young, Too Old": Stigmatizing Adolescents and Elders*, in Todd F. Heatherton, et al, eds, *The Social Psychology of Stigma* 334, 340–41 (2000) (quoting Anna Freud as claiming that "[t]he adolescent manifestations come close to symptom formation of the neurotic, psychotic or dissocial disorder"). Childhood, with its unmediated expression of feeling and desire, also bears a long tradition of analogies to madness. See, e.g., Adam Phillips, *Going Sane* 93 (2005) ("Our earliest lives are lived in a state of sane madness—of intense feelings and fearfully acute sensations."). The analogy to mental illness is an interesting one, particularly in light of current efforts by some death penalty advocates to press for a rule prohibiting the death penalty for people who were "insane" at the time of their crimes. (The Court has already held that people cannot be executed when they are insane. *Ford v Wainwright*, 477 US 399, 401 (1986).) I do not develop the analogy here, but one interesting point of contrast concerns the complexity of attitudes in each area. As I discuss, part of what makes youth complicated is the combination of pervasive positive and negative attitudes. The reason that a prosecutor could say that a young person who commits terrible acts isn't really "childlike," see text accompanying note 166, is the background set of assumed characteristics of youth that are highly favorable, such as innocence and vulnerability. By contrast, though attitudes to mental illness are complicated, there is no compensating set of favorable attitudes that would make cognizable the statement by a prosecutor that a mentally ill person who does something bad couldn't possibly be mentally ill because mentally ill people are too good for such things. There may be some competing idea that mentally ill people are vulnerable and deserve state solicitude, but no highly positive set of ascriptions akin to those about youth.

[148] Cf. Sedgwick at 85 (cited in note 143) (defining a universalizing view of homosexuality as the view "that apparently heterosexual persons and object choices are strongly marked by same-sex influences and desires, and vice versa for apparently homosexual ones").

rectly or indirectly. In Simmons's trial, as in any other, there is more than one possible point of identification. One might identify with the victim, seeing the story through her eyes, as O'Connor seems to do, when she writes of "the terror that this woman must have suffered throughout the ordeal leading to her death."[149] Though jurors might be unlikely to identify with Simmons, they might identify with him indirectly, seeing the event through his parents' eyes. This was certainly true for some of the prospective jurors who never made it onto the jury. Most notable among these was venireman Dombrowski, who had a son the age of Chris Simmons, and who thought it would be hard to consider the death penalty in the abstract after seeing Simmons and thinking of his own son.[150] In his words, "The only uncomfortable feeling I have presently is looking at the young man, and perhaps blinking once or twice, and perhaps seeing your son's face there."[151] His image of blinking and seeing his own child was echoed by another prospective juror, who said she had "grand kids that age, and like one gentleman said, yesterday, you bat your eyes a couple times, and open them and see your grandson sitting there."[152]

This kind of familial identification with youth is a reason that youth might seem not to need special protection, just as old age might seem not to need protecting.[153] This distinguishes age-based differences from racial differences, for instance. In addition to having been that age once, we all, or most all of us, have relatives that age. Many of us have children that age. We can therefore in theory empathize with a young defendant's position.

Of course, similar arguments have been made about women, and there we have seen that familial identification and an associated desire to protect do not necessarily lead to fair treatment. Moreover, parental identification can cut both ways. Just as parents can adore, admire, and identify with their children, they can also

---

[149] 125 S Ct at 1213 (O'Connor, J, dissenting).

[150] TT at 216 ("I have a son approximately his age, and earlier we were asked to render our attitude, and I would think it would be difficult knowing his parents were somewhere waiting for us to make a decision, and trying to equate that with my son in perhaps a similar situation. I agree it would be difficult. It could be done, but that would be my attitude."); id at 292 ("Sitting here and seeing the young man there brings out our—whatever deeper biases, or unbiases we may have.").

[151] Id at 293.

[152] Id at 472 (quoting venireman Wright).

[153] But see text Part IV.

resent, envy, and isolate them.[154] And now, when children are typically a financial drain on the family, Viviana Zelizer has argued, their value to a family is principally emotional.[155] If children are expected to give back, in exchange for years of financial support, emotional benefits, what happens when they do not supply that value in exchange?

As the prosecutor stated to the jury, echoing his question about the scariness of Simmons's youth, "Look at what his friends and family told you. Isn't that scary? Look at how he repaid their love. . . . Show some mercy to his family, give him death."[156] That is, isn't it scary that Simmons could repay his family for their generosity by committing this heinous crime, putting them through this horrible ordeal, and making them a part of such an atrocity?

Similarly, outrage at the betrayal of parental goodwill seems to fuel the anger inspired by statements, in this case and others, that the young offender thought age would let him off the hook: for instance, Simmons's supposedly telling his friends that they could get away with the crime because they are juveniles,[157] or a seventeen-year-old offender in Texas who announced when he was caught, "I'm a juvenile, you can't do anything to me."[158] Prosecutors relish

---

[154] Cf., e.g., Eve Kosofsky Sedgwick, *A Poem Is Being Written*, in *Tendencies* 177, 198–99 (1993) ("There is always a potential for a terrifying involuntarity of meaning, in the body of a child."); Steven Mintz, *Huck's Raft: A History of American Childhood* 2–3 (2004) ("Americans are deeply ambivalent about children. Adults envy young people their youth, vitality, and physical attractiveness. But they also resent children's intrusions on their time and resources and frequently fear their passions and drives. Many of the reforms that nominally have been designed to protect and assist the young were also instituted to insulate adults from children.").

[155] See Viviana A. Zelizer, *Pricing the Priceless Child* passim, 11 (1985) (arguing that the children's expulsion from the market at the turn of the last century was coupled with a "sacralization" of children's lives centered on their sentimental value). Zelizer concludes the study by considering whether 1980s America was witnessing a return to any greater interest in the economic usefulness of children to their families; noting the need for more research, she observes, "The notion, inherited from the early part of this century, that there is a necessarily negative correlation between the emotional and utilitarian value of children is being revised." Id at 227. As Zelizer describes it, though, any such shift seems to involve adding a financial element to the familial expectations of children's emotional contributions, rather than reducing their expected emotional contribution: "The sentimental value of children may now include a new appreciation of their instrumental worth." Id (noting the need, however, for more research on the lives of children, particularly those living in poverty and in single-parent families).

[156] TT at 1157. Cf. text accompanying note 133 (quoting the longer passage containing the words, "Think about age. Seventeen years old. Isn't that scary?").

[157] See note 10 and accompanying text.

[158] Closing argument transcript, *Guillen* at 32–92 (cited in note 136) (quoting Mr. Barnes) (raising this quotation in the same paragraph in which he argued that Guillen's youth should be aggravating rather than mitigating, see text accompanying note 136).

the chance to remind juries of such quotes at the sentencing phase, perhaps because they strike a particular chord for adults. By arrogantly invoking their youth, these young offenders seem to pay back our generosity, our willingness to come down easy on them, by turning our generosity into an excuse for their mistreatment of us. (Curiously, the arguments of the young offenders—that they will be protected by their youth from punishment—sound rather like the pro-youth-punishment arguments that conflate mitigation and excuse.[159]) The double-edged nature of parent-child reciprocity may further explain how youth could be understood as aggravating.

Kennedy finds this sort of prosecutorial argument or juror reasoning unacceptable. He worries that jurors will be inflamed against young offenders, will use their youth in exactly the wrong way (against them rather than for them), and will therefore fail at the difficult task of reliably distinguishing the truly incorrigible from the reparable teenagers. To avoid these errors, we must instantiate into law one generalization—of teens as less mature and therefore less culpable—to combat the potential use of another, less acceptable generalization—of teen offenders as particularly scary predators deserving of harsher punishment on account of their adolescence.

D. THE SOURCE OF THE PROBLEM

But why does Kennedy—and O'Connor and apparently others at oral argument—deem the treatment of youth as aggravating to be patently unacceptable (and perhaps even shocking)? One wonders why such treatment is illicit. Indeed, the constitutional status of such arguments is unclear: In a series of decisions since the early '80s, the Court has drifted toward and away (and back toward again) finding an Eighth Amendment or due process violation in the consideration of a mitigating factor as aggravating, but no holding conclusively resolves the issue.[160] (O'Connor may have

---

[159] Cf. Elizabeth S. Scott and Laurence Steinberg, *Blaming Youth*, 81 Tex L Rev 799, 800 (2003) (criticizing the common conflation of excuse and mitigation and arguing that youth should be mitigating but not a basis for excuse).

[160] See, e.g., *Penry v Lynaugh*, 492 US 302, 328 (1989); *Johnson v Texas*, 509 US 350, 372–73 (1993); *Graham v Collins*, 506 US 461, 475–76 (1993); *Penry v Johnson*, 532 US 782, 804 (2001) ("Penry II"); *Tennard v Dretke*, 542 US 274, 288–89 (2004); see also *Zant v Stephens*, 462 US 862, 885 (1983) (stating in dicta that if the state had "attached the 'aggravating' label to factors that are constitutionally impermissible or totally irrelevant to the sentencing process, such as for example the race, religion, or political affiliation of the defendant, or to conduct that actually should militate in favor of a lesser penalty, such

cause for frustration with Kennedy here, since they have been on opposite sides of this issue in a number of cases, most notably in *Johnson v Texas*.[161])

1. *Race.* One cause for concern—though there is no indication that this was Kennedy's concern—might be the potential role of race in determining whether youth is deemed aggravating rather than mitigating. Some research suggests that race influences whether probation officers attribute juvenile criminality to internal factors such as attitude and personality rather than to external factors such as social environment, and race affects their predictions of future dangerousness and sentence recommendations.[162] If criminality is more likely to be deemed a personality trait of African-American juvenile offenders, then their youth would be less likely to be deemed mitigating. Indeed, the intense fears of dangerous youth typified by the superpredator panic of the '90s bore clear racial overtones.[163]

---

as perhaps the defendant's mental illness[, then] due process of law would require that the jury's decision to impose death be set aside" (internal citations omitted)).

[161] In *Johnson*, Kennedy and O'Connor were similarly situated as majority and dissent in a case that deemed youth adequately available to the jury to consider as mitigating even if the evidence of it came in only under a future dangerousness query. Compare *Johnson v Texas*, 509 US 350, 367, 368 (1993) (Kennedy, J) ("There is no dispute that a defendant's youth is a relevant mitigating circumstance that must be within the effective reach of a capital sentencing jury if a death sentence is to meet the requirements of *Lockett* and *Eddings*. . . . The relevance of youth as a mitigating factor derives from the fact that the signature qualities of youth are transient; as individuals mature, the impetuousness and recklessness that may dominate in younger years can subside. We believe that there is ample room in the assessment of future dangerousness for a juror to take account of the difficulties of youth as a mitigating force in the sentencing determination. As we recognized in *Graham*, the fact that a juror might view the evidence of youth as aggravating, as opposed to mitigating, does not mean that the rule of *Lockett* is violated. As long as the mitigating evidence is within 'the effective reach of the sentencer,' the requirements of the Eighth Amendment are satisfied." (citations omitted)); with id at 388 (O'Connor, J, dissenting) ("'[Y]outh is more than a chronological fact.' The emotional and mental immaturity of young people may cause them to respond to events in ways that an adult would not. Because the jurors in Johnson's case could not give effect to this aspect of Johnson's youth, I would vacate Johnson's sentence and remand for resentencing." (quoting *Eddings v Oklahoma*, 455 US 104, 115 (1982)).

[162] See George S. Bridges and Sara Steen, *Racial Disparities in Official Assessments of Juvenile Offenders: Attributional Stereotypes as Mediating Mechanisms*, 63 Amer Soc Rev 554, 567 (1998).

[163] See, e.g., John J. Dilulio, Jr., *The Coming of the Super-Predators*, Weekly Standard (Nov 27, 1995) at 23, 25 ("While the trouble will be greatest in black inner-city neighborhoods, other places are also certain to have burgeoning youth-crime problems that will spill over into upscale central-city districts, inner-ring suburbs, and even the rural heartland. . . . In the extreme, moral poverty is the poverty of growing up surrounded by deviant, delinquent, and criminal adults in abusive, violence-ridden, fatherless, Godless, and jobless settings."); William J. Bennett, John J. Dilulio, and John P. Walters, *Body Count: Moral Poverty . . . and How to Win America's War Against Crime and Drugs* 28 (1996)

Simmons is white, so it is not clear whether or how race affects an argument that youth is aggravating in his case. The opinion makes no mention of race, but some of the briefs discuss it, and the role of racism could be part of the subtext in *Simmons*.[164] Alternatively, or additionally, Simmons's identity as a white, blond boy from the Midwest might strengthen the minoritizing vision of him as a demon child. If his life was relatively easy, if he was the boy next door, then his "badness" must come from inside rather than from his surroundings, and thus he must be monstrous or inherently evil.[165]

2. *Teen criminality and romantic childhood.* Relatedly, the fact that a young person has committed a serious crime may in itself cause people to view his youth as aggravating. That is, to the extent we see or want to see childhood as a time of innocence, cognitive dissonance may prompt us to reconceive a child who does terrible things as an adult. The following prosecutorial argument from another case seems to rely on this logic:

> Scott Hain made the choices that took him down. He tried to claim that he was functioning like a child. . . . What about his conduct is child-like? Children don't commit rapes, assaults,

("[M]any of these super-predators grow up in places that may best be called criminogenic communities . . . . At core, the problem is that most inner-city children grow up surrounded by teenagers and adults who are themselves deviant, delinquent, or criminal. . . . The problem is not merely that so many inner-city children grow up insufficiently socialized to the norms and values of a civilized, noncriminal way of life, but that they grow up almost completely unmoralized and develop character traits that are more likely to lead them into a life of illiteracy, illicit drugs, and violent crime than into a life of literacy, intact families, and steady jobs."); see also id at 14 (arguing that "the nation's drug and crime problem is fueled largely by moral poverty, and put[ting] question marks over both some of the liberal litany of 'root causes' (economic poverty, lack of government-funded social programs, racism) and over some of the conservative catechism of toughness (resortlike prisons, too few executions, too much gun control)").

[164] See, e.g., Brief for NAACP Legal Defense Fund, et al (cited in note 3); Brief for Respondent at *31 (cited in note 3). Cf. *Coker v Georgia*, 433 US 584, 598 (1977) (holding, without expressly mentioning race, that the Eighth Amendment prohibits the death penalty for rape of an adult woman); Jack Greenberg, *Crusaders in the Courts* 440 (1994) (explaining that efforts to combat the death penalty for rape were launched "because almost 90 percent of the 455 defendants executed for rape since 1930 were blacks convicted of raping white women" and that these efforts ultimately translated "into a full-scale attack on capital punishment, as arbitrary, cruel and unusual, and racist").

[165] Cf. Mike Males, *Framing Youth: Ten Myths About the Next Generation* 292–94 (1998); Kincheloe at 164 (cited in note 141). The notion of the demonic child has historic roots in, among other sources, the Calvinist doctrine of "infant depravity," which deemed the newborn doomed to sin unless the parents intervened to control him. See Skolnick at 44 (cited in note 144). Golding's *Lord of the Flies* supplies a contemporary analogue. William Golding, *Lord of the Flies* 185–87 (1959).

murder. That is not child-like. . . . . In what way is he child-like?

. . . . What he is is what the evidence shows. He's vicious and sadistic. That's not child-like.[166]

Moreover, as noted earlier, young people at the brink of adulthood may be particularly susceptible to at least the universalizing idea of youth as aggravating. This is a period in the life span characterized by increased criminality, which is part of what makes it hard to identify those juvenile offenders whose criminal behavior reflects deeply antisocial character as opposed to something more transient.[167] The particularly negative associations with juveniles on the cusp of adulthood may help explain why Kennedy tends to speak of juveniles in general, rather than sixteen- and seventeen-year-olds, although no one was arguing that *Thompson* should be overturned or reinterpreted to mean that states could execute people who committed their crime at *any* age up to eighteen.

None of this squarely answers the question, though, of why Kennedy would deem the possibility of juries treating youth as aggravating as so obviously wrong as to justify a constitutional

---

[166] Closing argument transcript at 916, *Hain v State of Oklahoma*, Creek County Court; see also Dobbs at 15 (cited in note 132) (stating Scott Hain's date of execution and age at time of offense). In what seems to be similar rhetoric, at Michael Lopez's sentencing for murdering a police officer when he was seventeen, the prosecutor argued:

> At the age of 17, this man, instead of going to jail, chose and wanted to put a bullet into the body of a police officer. What does that say about the capacity and the mentality and the mind of this man at the age of 17? And he ain't a boy and he ain't a child, he's a grown man, and he's been a grown man for a lot longer than some of you were. He carried a weapon with him everywhere he went. You know that. He wasn't afraid to use it that night when called upon.

Closing argument transcript at 28, *Lopez v State*, No 72,536 (Tex Crim App 2002) (quoting the prosecutor, Kelly Siegler, of Harris County); see also Dobbs at 15 (cited in note 132) (providing the prosecutor's name and reporting that Michael Lopez was sentenced to death on May 25, 1999, and listing the docket number as No 73,356). Similarly, the prosecutor of Dwayne Allen Wright argued, "This Defendant may have been seventeen years old when he was involved in all these crimes, but he was seventeen years old going on twenty seven. He has a streak of meanness that far exceeds the chronological age that he has today." Closing argument transcript at 144, *Virginia v Wright*, No 70648 (Fairfax Cty Circuit Ct, Nov 16, 1991).

[167] See, e.g., Terrie E. Moffitt, *Adolescent-Limited and Life-Course-Persistent Antisocial Behavior: A Developmental Taxonomy*, 100 Psychol Rev 674, 675–79 (1993) (reviewing data on the increased prevalence and incidence of illegal behavior during adolescence, with offending rates peaking around age seventeen, and theorizing a nonobvious distinction between individuals whose antisocial behavior is limited to their adolescent years and those whose antisocial behavior is persistent over their lives); see also note 57 and accompanying text (discussing the DSM-IV-TR's limitation on diagnosis of antisocial personality disorder to those who are at least eighteen).

ban. Perhaps he simply embraces the romantic notion of childhood as a special time of innocence and vulnerability, which, as a set of historians since Philippe Ariès has been telling us in increasingly refined ways, emerged in the mid-eighteenth century, largely displacing an idea that children were just smaller, and less able, adults.[168] As Steven Mintz has recently argued, this romantic notion of childhood—what Mintz calls the modern view—now exists uneasily alongside a postmodern view of childhood, in which children are not seen merely as little adults, but are nonetheless deemed to have adult-like knowledge and experience and buying power.[169] Perhaps Kennedy clings to the modern view and wants to instantiate it into law.

3. *Inflamed jurors.* But this possible reading of Kennedy's opinion goes too far. Kennedy does present an account of three relevant differences between adults and juveniles, and uses these to create a rule under law that removes them from the individualized consideration of the jury. Ultimately, however, I think his reasoning turns at least as much on concerns about the potentially inflamed, misguided, and mistaken "discriminator"—the juror—as on the mind and emotions of the juvenile.

In particular, Kennedy is troubled by the prospect that jurors will get it wrong and, particularly, for the wrong reasons. Our ideas about youth are complicated. We think we favor youth, we think we should favor youth, but in fact we may, in some circumstances, not only not favor them but actually disfavor them. Our beliefs about how we do and should feel may not always track how we actually feel. Jurors may, of course, err by failing to treat youth (or any other mitigating factor) as appropriately mitigating. But a tendency to do the *opposite* of what is expected—to treat youth as aggravating—may inflict a harm that goes beyond the mere error. To execute a juvenile because jurors treat him *worse* on the basis of a trait that should make them treat him *better* may be perverse, or irrational, to the point of unconstitutionality.

---

[168] See, e.g., Mintz at 3–4 (cited in note 154); Hugh Cunningham, *Histories of Childhood*, 103 Am Hist Rev 1195, 1197–99, 1203–07 (1998); Harvey J. Graff, *Interdisciplinary Explorations in the History of Children, Adolescents, and Youth—for the Past, Present, and Future*, 85 J Am Hist 1538, 1539 (1999); see generally Philippe Ariès, *Centuries of Childhood: A Social History of Family Life* 411–13 (Robert Baldick transcript, 1962); cf. also note 155 and accompanying text (discussing Viviana Zelizer's thesis about recent changes in the understandings of childhood).

[169] Mintz at 3–4 (cited in not 154).

To the extent that we limit young people's rights and responsibilities, we justify these limitations in part by saying that youth are particularly vulnerable. To treat youth worse on the basis of their special vulnerability—a vulnerability arguably increased by the legal limitations imposed by the state[170]—partially undermines the justifications for treating them differently in the first place. And a jury that treats youth as aggravating enacts persecution in place of protection. In this way, the rule of *Simmons* is a prophylactic rule that aligns our treatment of this group with our expectations, that is, with how we think we feel, and how we think we should feel, about the group.[171]

Kennedy suggests further that a prophylactic rule is required because of the seriousness of executing a young person. At the close of his discussion of why we cannot trust juries to get it right, Kennedy tells us: "When a juvenile offender commits a heinous crime, the State can exact forfeiture of some of the most basic liberties, but the State cannot extinguish his life and his potential to attain a mature understanding of his own humanity."[172] The irreversibility of any erroneous execution is of course a common thread in arguments against the death penalty. But Kennedy is making a more particular point. *Young* people should not be prevented by execution from growing up. They cannot be prevented from growing up by negative attitudes and stereotypes against them.[173] This reasoning implicates another basis for society's treating youth differently from adults, a kind of rough justice rationale: Young people will all be adults some day, and so the limitations placed on them are temporary and common to everyone. Additionally, eighteen is the typical age demarcation for those legal limitations, as Kennedy's appendices show. In this light, Kennedy

---

[170] Cf. note 121.

[171] Cf. David A. Strauss, *The Ubiquity of Prophylactic Rules*, 55 U Chi L Rev 190 (1988).

[172] 125 S Ct at 1197.

[173] An oddity here is that he speaks almost as if juveniles are being executed, despite the fact that the pace of death penalty proceedings and appeals means no juveniles are in fact being executed. See, e.g., Victor L. Streib, *Death Penalty for Children: The American Experience with Capital Punishment for Crimes Committed While Under Age Eighteen*, 36 Okla L Rev 613, 631 (1983) (noting that "[n]o children have been executed since 1964"). We may perhaps understand Kennedy to see executing juvenile offenders for acts committed when they were young as similar to stopping time for them at that younger age, making them no longer recognizable by the state after that point, since they are then condemned to die for their actions at that time. Alternatively, his point may simply be animated by the mere theoretical possibility of executing a minor.

may be read to say that it is perversely unjust to let some of our negative attitudes toward this class that we have partially created prevent them from graduating into the dominant group. For these reasons, among the others discussed, the risks of error are too great—both in frequency and severity—for a standard rather than a rule.

This brings me back to O'Connor's and Scalia's claims that Kennedy is saying that juveniles are categorically different, rather than saying that youth is a good proxy for certain differences. As noted earlier, Kennedy seems somewhat inconsistent, saying at one point that he will not concede that any youth is sufficiently mature and culpable to deserve death, and at another point that this categorical rule is imperfect, because of course some juveniles are more mature than adults and vice versa.[174] But in light of the foregoing, it seems that the different language of those two passages may be significant. In the first, Kennedy says that he won't concede that there are juveniles who are sufficiently mature *and* sufficiently depraved, and in the second, he says that only some juveniles are (at least) sufficiently mature.

At the risk of overreading, the two statements may perhaps be reconciled if we take Kennedy to be saying that even if a juvenile were mature enough to be like an adult in all respects, a juvenile simply cannot be depraved enough to warrant the death penalty, because depravity is in the mind of the judge or juror. That is, when speaking of depravity, Kennedy may be making a normative, rather than an empirical, claim: Rather than saying that no child could—as a matter of fact—ever be as mature as an adult, Kennedy is saying that no one of us should—as a matter of law—fatally judge a child to be as depraved as an adult. Even if there are a few juveniles who could be among the worst of society's offenders, jurors will make errors of unacceptable frequency and magnitude. For this reason, we cannot trust ourselves to decide that a child is culpable enough to be punished as an adult in an irreversible way that fails to permit that child ever to become an adult.

Ultimately, Kennedy is saying that youth are categorically less culpable than adults—not in the sense that they could not be as bad or as guilty, but in the sense that we are too flawed to permit ourselves to deem them to be so. We hold prejudicial stereotypes

---

[174] See text accompanying notes 106–07.

and attitudes that run directly counter to our expectations of ourselves and our proper treatment of young people, and the weighty context of ending a young life requires a prophylactic rule to align our expectations with our actions under law.

III. "An Act of Nomological Desperation": The Denominator Dispute

Kennedy's conclusion that a prophylactic rule is necessary to guard against disfavoring youth also plays a subtle role in his discussion of the national consensus. Though apparently neither compelling nor dispositive, evidence of a national consensus against the juvenile death penalty must play some role in the Court's decision. For instance, had there been no shift at all since *Stanford*, or had the current spread of the states differed significantly from that in *Atkins*, or had the Court not found a majority of states to be opposed, it seems unlikely that the Court would have reached the same conclusion.[175] In this light the Denominator Dispute becomes important, as it determines whether even a majority of states opposes the juvenile death penalty.[176] As noted, this term refers to the disagreement between Kennedy and Scalia over whether to count states that ban the death penalty altogether as opposing the juvenile death penalty.

Kennedy counts states with no death penalty within the denominator, a departure from *Stanford* that Scalia calls "an act of nomological desperation."[177] In Scalia's view, the denominator should include only those states that permit the death penalty, because the fact that twelve states prohibit the death penalty for everyone says "nothing—absolutely nothing—about consensus that offenders under 18 deserve special immunity from such a penalty."[178] Kennedy, by contrast, reasons that "a State's decision

---

[175] Although the Court found a "national consensus" in *Atkins* without counting the no-death-penalty states as among the states opposed to executing people with mental retardation, the Court in *Atkins* faced a much more dramatic shift in relevant state enactments since the time of *Penry*, as the Court noted when distinguishing *Stanford*. *Atkins v Virginia*, 536 US 304, 315 n 18 (2002) ("A comparison to [*Stanford*], in which we held that there was no national consensus prohibiting the execution of juvenile offenders over age 15, is telling. Although we decided *Stanford* on the same day as *Penry*, apparently only two state legislatures have raised the threshold age for imposition of the death penalty.").

[176] Cf. Norman J. Finkel, *Prestidigitation, Statistical Magic, and Supreme Court Numerology in Juvenile Death Penalty Cases*, 1 Psychol Pub Pol'y & L 612, 614 (1995).

[177] 125 S Ct at 1219 (Scalia, J, dissenting).

[178] Id (Scalia, J, dissenting).

to bar the death penalty altogether of necessity demonstrates a judgment that the death penalty is inappropriate for all offenders, including juveniles."[179]

This is a puzzle, and one not much illuminated by Scalia's analogies. Writing for the majority in *Stanford*, Scalia criticized similar reasoning by the dissent by comparing it to "discerning a national consensus that wagering on cockfights is inhumane by counting within that consensus those States that bar all wagering."[180] He is, of course, right in his narrower point, but the analogy is flawed. A more pertinent analogy would be to counting states that ban wagering on animal fighting as opposing as inhumane wagering on cockfighting.[181]

In dissent in *Simmons*, Scalia's new analogy is to "including old-order Amishmen in a consumer-preference poll on the electric car."[182] Like the cockfighting analogy, Scalia's invocation of

---

[179] Id at 1198.

[180] *Stanford v Kentucky*, 492 US 361, 370 n 2 (1989) ("The dissent takes issue with our failure to include, among those States evidencing a consensus against executing 16- and 17-year-old offenders, the District of Columbia and the 14 States that do not authorize capital punishment. It seems to us, however, that while the number of those jurisdictions bears upon the question whether there is a consensus against capital punishment altogether, it is quite irrelevant to the specific inquiry in this case: whether there is a settled consensus in favor of punishing offenders under 18 differently from those over 18 insofar as capital punishment is concerned. The dissent's position is rather like discerning a national consensus that wagering on cockfights is inhumane by counting within that consensus those States that bar all wagering. The issue in the present case is not whether capital punishment is thought to be desirable but whether persons under 18 are thought to be specially exempt from it. With respect to that inquiry, it is no more logical to say that the capital-punishment laws of those States which prohibit capital punishment (and thus do not address age) support the dissent's position, than it would be to say that the age-of-adult-criminal-responsibility laws of those same States (which do not address capital punishment) support our position.").

[181] Cf. *Sanders v State*, 585 A2d 117, 138–39 (Del 1990) (describing Scalia's reasoning by analogy in *Stanford* as "opaque," and proposing that "[i]f one sought to discern a national consensus that cockfighting is inhumane, one would certainly look to States that outlaw cruelty to animals").

[182] 125 S Ct at 1219 (Scalia, J, dissenting) ("Consulting States that bar the death penalty concerning the necessity of making an exception to the penalty for offenders under 18 is rather like including old-order Amishmen in a consumer-preference poll on the electric car. Of *course* they don't like it, but that sheds no light whatever on the point at issue. . . . In repealing the death penalty, those 12 States considered *none* of the factors that the Court puts forth as determinative of the issue before us today—lower culpability of the young, inherent recklessness, lack of capacity for considered judgment, etc. What might be relevant, perhaps, is how many of those States permit 16- and 17-year-old offenders to be treated as adults with respect to noncapital offenses. (They all do; indeed, some even require that juveniles as young as 14 be tried as adults if they are charged with murder.) The attempt by the Court to turn its remarkable minority consensus into a faux majority by counting Amishmen is an act of nomological desperation.").

Amishmen is more amusing than illuminating. Indeed, this analogy is so far from helpful that it is quite difficult to rephrase it to parallel the question in *Simmons*. The problem with Scalia's analogies is that he posits situations in which the underlying motivations are unrelated. But that is not the case in *Simmons*. Those who oppose the death penalty always or nearly always oppose its application to juveniles, if that is the best they can get.

One way to see the problem in Scalia's approach is to consider a (hypothetical) national landscape in which nearly all states outlaw the death penalty altogether. That is, if forty-two states prohibit the death penalty, would Scalia say that the views of only the remaining eight states would determine whether there was a national consensus against the juvenile death penalty? If only two of the eight states that permitted the death penalty outlawed the juvenile death penalty, would Scalia really say that the relevant denominator is the eight states, and no national consensus opposes the juvenile death penalty because 75 percent of the *states that count* do not oppose it? This seems absurd, and I will return to it.

With regard to age-based distinctions, the Denominator Dispute, at first glance, appears to have inverted Scalia and Kennedy. Scalia, discussing moral proportionality, dismisses as irrelevant age-based distinctions in other contexts (e.g., in the majority's appendices on voting, jury service, and marriage), whereas in the Denominator Dispute he finds other contexts of age-based distinctions relevant. Specifically, he believes that knowing how legislatures have made age distinctions in criminal punishment more generally will help resolve the Dispute.[183] In contrast, Kennedy looks to the difference between juveniles and adults intrinsically and legally in a range of contexts to help make his proportionality argument, but in the Denominator Dispute wants to take society's views about how to treat people in general as representative of their views on how to treat juveniles.

But on closer look, Kennedy's reasoning about youth here does in fact track his reasoning in the proportionality analysis. Juveniles are a lesser included group.[184] That is, in a way that again elides

---

[183] This is a departure from his position in *Stanford* where he presented as comparably worthless the endeavors of looking at age in other criminal contexts and of looking at the death penalty in general. See note 180.

[184] 125 S Ct at 1198 ("[A] State's decision to bar the death penalty altogether of necessity demonstrates a judgment that the death penalty is inappropriate for all offenders, including juveniles.").

the distinction between the descriptive and the normative, Kennedy seems to argue that we *should* treat juveniles as less culpable than adults. States could not possibly—or rather, if they could, they shouldn't—think adults should not be given the death penalty but juveniles could. If members of any states think that people in general must not be given the death penalty, then only (descriptively or normatively) unacceptable views could lead them to say that they would permit juveniles to be executed.

To make this more vivid, imagine a state that banned the death penalty for adults, but permitted it for juveniles. (While the Court "has said repeatedly that age is not a suspect classification,"[185] it has reached this conclusion only in the context of cases involving old age,[186] and such a statute might encounter Equal Protection problems,[187] but this is not the question here.) Intuitively it seems unacceptable, and perhaps constitutionally so under the Eighth Amendment, to mete out the ultimate punishment to juveniles and not to adults. Fantastical as such a statutory scheme may seem, one can imagine how a state might reach that point: for example, through the kind of superpredator hype of the '90s,[188] combined

---

[185] *Gregory v Ashcroft*, 501 US 452, 470 (1991) (citing *Massachusetts Bd. of Retirement v Murgia*, 427 US 307, 313–14 (1976); *Vance v Bradley*, 440 US 93, 96–97 (1979); *Cleburne v Cleburne Living Center, Inc.*, 473 US 432, 441 (1985)).

[186] Cf. *Hedgepeth v Washington Metro. Area Transit Authority*, 386 F3d 1148, 1154 (DC Cir 2004) (Roberts, J) (noting that "the Supreme Court cases applying rational basis review to classifications based on age all involved classifications burdening the elderly" and then rejecting the argument that youth is different from old age in ways that merit granting it heightened scrutiny).

[187] *Ramos v Town of Vernon*, 353 F3d 171, 187 (2d Cir 2003) (striking down under the Equal Protection Clause a juvenile curfew ordinance based in part on the reasoning that restrictions on the constitutional rights of youth must aim to protect minors, to wit, "if a municipality wishes to single out minors as a group to curtail a constitutional freedom, which the minors have absent parental prohibition, then the municipality must satisfy constitutional requirements by tying their policies to the special traits, vulnerabilities, and needs of minors. . . ."); see also *Bellotti v Baird*, 443 US 622, 635 (1979) ("[A]lthough children generally are protected by the same constitutional guarantees against governmental deprivations as are adults, the State is entitled to adjust its legal system to account for children's vulnerability and their [other] needs.").

[188] Cf. Dilulio, Jr., *The Coming of the Super-Predators* (cited in note 163); note 163 and accompanying text; see also U.S. Department of Health and Human Services, *Youth Violence: A Report of the Surgeon General* 5 (2001) (listing among the "myths about youth violence" the idea that "[a] new violent breed of young superpredators threatens the United States," and explaining that "[t]here is no evidence that young people involved in violence during the peak years of the early 1990s were more frequent or more vicious offenders than youths in earlier years. The increased lethality resulted from gun use, which has since increased dramatically. There is no scientific evidence to document the claim of increased seriousness or callousness . . . .").

with several high-profile cases of terrible juvenile offenders,[189] and some social science literature arguing that young criminals will commit the worst crimes or that greater penalties are necessary to deter young offenders because they are more criminally prone.[190] Indeed, the practice of worse treatment for juveniles is not historically unprecedented, but has been the basis for reforms of the juvenile justice system over the past century.[191]

Such an upside-down scheme is simultaneously unimaginable and comprehensible for the same reasons that the prosecutor's youth-as-aggravating argument shocks and disturbs most who hear it, including Kennedy and, it seems, O'Connor.[192] That is, we think we treat youth more favorably, and think that we should so treat them in general, but we also have an inkling that the reality of adult stereotypes about and attitudes toward youth does not always track these expectations. The upside-down statute may or may not have a rational justification; the problem, as in *Simmons*, is that it might stem from some combination of false stereotyping and sheer prejudice.

My imaginary state statute is a categorical rule, but it need not be framed that way. What if instead the death penalty applied on its face to everyone, but only juveniles ever ended up being executed? Here we have disparate impact, coupled with the "inexorable zero" that may permit us to assume disparate treatment in administration.[193] And what if juvenile offenders in this imaginary state get the death penalty disproportionately (instead of exclusively)? The conceivable disparate impact would raise a serious question for the same reasons as the youth-as-aggravating argument.

---

[189] See generally Males at 294 (cited in note 165).

[190] Cf., e.g., Moin A. Yahya, *Deterring Roper's Juveniles: Why Immature Criminal Youth Require the Death Penalty More Than Adults—A Law & Economics Approach* 2 (ExpressO Preprint Series Working Paper 761), available at http://law.bepress.com/expresso/eps/761 (arguing that, if youth are present-oriented risk-lovers who cannot engage in proper cost-benefit analysis, then law and economics methodology shows that youth can still be deterred but the penalties need to be greater than for adults, and thus that the Supreme Court in *Roper* deprived the states of a valuable tool in combating juvenile crime).

[191] See, e.g., Minow at 54–55 (cited in note 112); Elizabeth F. Emens, Nancy W. Hall, Catherine Ross, and Edward F. Zigler, *Preventing Juvenile Delinquency: An Ecological, Developmental Approach*, in Edward F. Zigler, et al, eds, *Children, Families, and Government: Preparing for the Twenty-First Century* 308, 311 (1996).

[192] See note 3 and accompanying text.

[193] See *Yick Wo v Hopkins*, 118 US 1064 (1886); see also *Int'l Brotherhood of Teamsters v United States*, 431 US 324, 342 n 23 (1977) (quoting *United States v T.I.M.E.-D.C., Inc.*, 517 F2d 299, 315 (5th Cir 1975) (coining the phrase "inexorable zero")).

Scalia thinks juveniles can be as bad as adults in some cases, so society can reasonably think them so. Kennedy thinks they are rarely as bad, and cannot possibly be worse, on the basis of youth itself, so he imposes a rule to prevent jurors from thinking otherwise.[194] That rule may be the logical principle underpinning Kennedy's position in the Denominator Dispute.

By way of postscript, let me return briefly to the hypothetical in which a state allows the death penalty only for juveniles. Curiously, part of what makes Scalia's position on the Denominator Dispute implausible, particularly in that hypothetical, is that it is hard to imagine a person who cares enough about treating young people the same as adults that her views on age parity would trump her views on the death penalty. But, as we've seen, some youth libbers suggest just that possibility when they critique *Simmons* for insidious generalizing about youth.[195] As youth libbers are not only marginal but are generally not old enough to vote, though, a state's laws presumably do not reflect such views.

Rather, it is easier to imagine a hypothetical state with the death penalty only for juveniles because of popular opinion fueled by negative attitudes to youth, than it is to imagine a state with the death penalty for deserving individuals of all ages, based in a popular embrace of youth liberation views. Though the "national consensus" inquiry into the implications of legislative action is at best complicated and at worst deeply flawed,[196] Kennedy's resolution of the Denominator Dispute has the virtue of consistency with the logic of his reasoning elsewhere in the opinion. As noted, it seems almost inconceivable to think, in a scenario in which only a tiny fraction of states still permitted the death penalty at all, that the question of whether the states had reached a consensus on the juvenile death penalty would turn on what percentage of the tiny remaining states still executed juveniles.

The reason for this lies in part in Kennedy's alignment rule from the proportionality analysis: That is, in imagining the scenario of widespread opposition to the death penalty, we cannot help but read into those many states Kennedy's presumption of youth as an included group—to be treated at least as favorably as adults if not

---

[194] See text Part II.

[195] See notes 119–20 and accompanying text.

[196] See Tonja Jacobi, *The Subtle Unraveling of Federalism: The Illogic of Using State Legislation as Evidence of an Evolving National Consensus*, 84 NC L Rev (forthcoming, 2006).

more so—and to read out the alternative possibility that the citizens of these many states oppose the death penalty for adults but not for minors. So widespread is the assumption that progress lies in the direction of abolishing the juvenile death penalty that the Missouri brief in *Simmons* even asserted that there is not "yet" a consensus among states against the juvenile death penalty.[197] If the party with the most interest in resisting the notion that progress means not executing juvenile offenders assumed, in its brief before the Court, that that point on the progress narrative will eventually arrive, then the idea of treating youth favorably presumably has wide appeal to our better selves.[198] In his resolution of the Denominator Dispute, Kennedy makes a judgment about acceptable views of youth by aligning our reasoning under law with how we think we do, and should, treat young people.

IV. "The Enemy of Forty": Negative Attitudes Under the ADEA

Kennedy's concern about negative attitudes toward youth in *Simmons* has links to other areas of law in which age discrimination is expressly forbidden. Kennedy's opinion suggests that attitudes to age are complicated, and that we need to look closely not only for stereotypes but also for prejudice, even in areas where individualized treatment might generally be expected to lead to fair outcomes. In this way, *Simmons* has implications for the Court's conclusions this Term about a different group in a different area of law: older Americans under the ADEA.[199]

Consider through an antidiscrimination lens Kennedy's conclusion that the Eighth Amendment requires in the death penalty context a

---

[197] Brief of Petitioner at *21–*22 (cited in note 103) ("In *Stanford*, this Court identified twelve states, out of thirty-seven that had capital punishment, that expressly excluded that penalty as an option for the seventeen-year-old offender. Today, the situation is not appreciably different. We do not *yet* have a pattern of lawmaking sufficient to establish a national consensus that capital punishment is 'cruel and unusual' when imposed on anyone 'so much as one day under' eighteen." (emphasis added) (citations omitted)); see also discussion in note 103.

[198] Whether the word was a slip revealing underlying attitudes about progress, or an intentional attempt not to sound so out of step with contemporary attitudes, the use of "yet" here reflects something of the pervasiveness of the attitude that the abolition of the juvenile death penalty lies on the road to progress. The fact that not-"yet" would seem more surprising in an argument about attitudes to the death penalty for adults supports the idea that the juvenile death penalty is widely considered a lesser included category.

[199] 29 USC §§ 621–34 (2000).

rule based on a rational and acceptable proxy—under eighteen as mitigating—in order to preclude the possible use of an irrational or at least unacceptable proxy—under eighteen as aggravating. At one level, Kennedy's reasoning might seem to resemble the reasoning supporting affirmative action. In both contexts, the state uses a prophylactic rule that favors a particular group in order to combat unfavorable stereotypes and attitudes. But on closer examination, two key differences distinguish *Simmons*'s age-based rule from typical affirmative action. First, affirmative action is usually based on concerns about a history of discrimination or pervasive negative attitudes that require rectification. By contrast, in *Simmons*, individual jurors are imagined to hold both positive and negative attitudes toward youth. Kennedy's concern is that jurors will use the negative rather than the positive, and so he imposes a rule to take the decision out of jurors' hands and thus compel the favorable view of youth.

Second, the *Simmons* rule forbids individualized decisions, whereas affirmative action requires them. The state, not the individual, acts affirmatively to protect the group. The state must adopt a rule to implement the favorable stereotypes and oust the unfavorable ones. Rather than being like affirmative action, the *Simmons* rule replaces an affirmative-action-type rule—the thumb-on-the-scale individualized treatment of youth as mitigating—with a categorical rule.

Perhaps the *Simmons* rule looks more like the ADEA. An age-aware statute—which prohibits discrimination against people over the age of forty[200] and proscribes only discrimination in favor of younger over older[201]—tries to prevent people from taking age into account. To prevent people from using age negatively, the statute prevents people from using age at all (subject to certain exceptions).

But the ADEA allows individual decision makers to fire individual workers, so long as they do not do so on the basis of age. Indeed, individual treatment is a core aim of the statute—to try to prevent negative age-based stereotyping from preventing accurate assessment of individual skills and abilities. This clearly distinguishes the statute from the rule in *Simmons*, which replaces individualized assessments with a categorical rule. A recent development in the Court's interpretation of the ADEA, however, may have inched the

---

[200] 29 USC § 631(a) (2000).

[201] See *General Dynamics Land Systems v Cline*, 540 US 581, 584 (2004).

statute closer to a group-based rule, rather than a rule that promotes individualized consideration. In the same month that the Court handed down *Simmons*, it ruled in *Smith v City of Jackson* that plaintiffs can bring disparate-impact suits under the statute.[202]

The case involved a disparate-impact challenge to a police department pay plan that gave larger raises to officers with less seniority. The plan was "motivated, at least in part, by the City's desire to bring the starting salaries of police officers up to the regional average."[203] Most of the officers over forty had greater seniority and therefore received smaller pay raises, forming the basis of the disparate-impact claim.[204] The Fifth Circuit rejected the claim, holding that disparate-impact suits are categorically unavailable under the ADEA.[205] Responding to a circuit split on the question, the Supreme Court granted certiorari.[206] The Court concluded that disparate-impact suits are available under the ADEA, but that the plaintiffs' claim nonetheless failed.[207]

Smith finds O'Connor once again in dissent, though here Kennedy joins her. Stevens writes for a plurality, with Scalia concurring. The opinions in *Smith* speak principally to questions of statutory interpretation and agency deference, and I do not aim here to resolve the merits of these disputes or to assert that some hidden logic drove the result. Instead, I want to use *Simmons* to highlight an overlooked normative rationale for *Smith* and a way that the decision in *Smith* might be used to combat a less obvious form of age discrimination.

The *Smith* plurality and the dissent seem to agree more than disagree. First, they agree that age-based discrimination has little or nothing to do with animus or dislike. Writing for a plurality that includes Souter, Ginsburg, and Breyer, Justice Stevens reviews the legislative history of the ADEA and notes the conclusion of the Wirtz Report that "there was little discrimination arising from dislike or intolerance of older people, but that 'arbitrary' discrimination did

---

[202] *Smith v City of Jackson*, 125 S Ct 1536, 1540 (2005) (plurality opinion) (Stevens, J); id at 1546 (Scalia, J, concurring in the judgment and concurring in the conclusion that the ADEA permits disparate-impact claims).

[203] Id at 1539.

[204] Id.

[205] *Smith v City of Jackson*, 351 F3d 183, 187 (5th Cir 2003).

[206] *Smith*, 125 S Ct at 1543 (citing cases).

[207] Id at 1540 (plurality opinion); id at 1546 (Scalia, J, concurring).

result from certain age limits."[208] Similarly, O'Connor, in a dissent joined by Kennedy and Thomas, reads the Wirtz Report as finding no evidence of animus.[209] (Scalia, whose concurrence is grounded in an argument for agency deference, does not directly address the issue.[210]) The report itself seems implicitly to acknowledge some role for feelings and attitudes in age discrimination, as when it calls this "a Nation which . . . worships the whole idea of youth."[211] But parts of the report support O'Connor's more absolute assessment of its conclusions: "[In contrast to e]mployment discrimination because of race [which] is identified, in the general understanding of it, with non-employment resulting from feelings about people entirely un-related to their ability to do the job[,[212] t]here is *no* significant dis-

---

[208] Id at 1540 (citing Report of the Secretary of Labor, *The Older American Worker: Age Discrimination in Employment* 22 (June 1965), reprinted in U.S. Equal Employment Opportunity Commission, *Legislative History of the Age Discrimination in Employment Act* (1981) (hereafter "Wirtz Report")).

[209] She writes,

> [T]he Report emphasized that age discrimination is qualitatively different from the types of discrimination prohibited by Title VII of the Civil Rights Act of 1964 (i.e., race, color, religion, sex, and national origin discrimination). Most importantly—in stark contrast to the types of discrimination addressed by Title VII—the Report found no evidence that age discrimination resulted from intolerance or animus towards older workers. Rather, age discrimination was based primarily upon unfounded assumptions about the relationship between an individual's age and her ability to perform a job. Wirtz Report 2. In addition, whereas ability is nearly always completely unrelated to the characteristics protected by Title VII, the Report found that, in some cases, "there is in fact a relationship between [an individual's] age and his ability to perform the job."

125 S Ct at 1553 (O'Connor, J, dissenting).

[210] Id at 1546–49 (Scalia, J, concurring). His concurrence in the relevant part of Stevens's opinion, the part that mentions the Wirtz Report's findings discussed here, suggests he agrees with this account.

[211] Wirtz Report at 3 (cited in note 208) ("[T]he median age of the population in the United States is going down. . . . What this means is that a Nation which already worships the whole idea of youth must approach any problem involving older people with conscious realization of the special obligation a majority assumes with respect to 'minority group' interests. This is, to be sure, one minority group in which we all seek, sometimes desperately, eventual membership. Discrimination against older workers remains, nevertheless, a problem which must be met by a majority who are not themselves adversely affected by it and may even be its temporary beneficiaries. The 'discrimination' older workers have most to fear, however, is not from any employer malice, or unthinking majority, but from the ruthless play of wholly impersonal forces—most of them part of what is properly, if sometimes too casually, called 'progress.'").

[212] Of course, this "general understanding" does not comprise all of race discrimination's many forms. Cf., e.g., Charles R. Lawrence III, *The Id, the Ego, and Equal Protection: Reckoning with Unconscious Racism*, 39 Stan L Rev 317, 322 (1987) ("Traditional notions of intent do not reflect the fact that decisions about racial matters are influenced in large part by factors that can be characterized as neither intentional . . . nor unintentional.").

crimination of this kind so far as older workers are concerned."[213]

Second, the Justices agree that age often tracks many job-related qualities and that the ADEA's reasonable factors other than age (RFOA) defense is therefore much broader than the bona fide occupational qualification (BFOQ) defense under Title VII.[214] Thus, while concluding that the statute provides for disparate-impact suits, the Court finds that the RFOA defense applies in this case, and implies that it would apply in many cases under the statute.[215]

Contrary to the Wirtz Report's conclusions, recent work in social psychology suggests that we do experience age-based dislike, but that we are unaware of it—that is, it is implicit rather than explicit. And, in fact, even as we grow older and our explicit attitudes to old age become more favorable, the line representing our implicit attitudes remains basically flat: Our implicit negativity does not decrease with age.[216] Whether we call this animus—a term often reserved for conscious dislike—these findings on implicit responses to older people involve negative *attitudes* and not just false beliefs.

While we do not know for certain that these implicit negative attitudes translate into discriminatory workplace behavior, research indicates that older job applicants receive less favorable responses than younger applicants,[217] and it seems plausible that negative at-

---

[213] Wirtz Report at 2 (cited in note 208) (emphasis in original). The Report identified three other types of discrimination that do affect older people: (1) rejection of older people based on "assumptions about the effect of age on their ability to do a job *when there is in fact no basis for these assumptions*" (in the Report's terminology, "'arbitrary discrimination'"); (2) "decisions not to employ a person for a particular job because of his age *when there is in fact a relationship between his age and his ability to perform his job*" (which "does not exist" in the context of race or religion and which should perhaps be called "something else entirely" rather than discrimination); and (3) rejection of older persons "because of programs and practices actually designed to *protect* the employment of older workers while they remain in the work force, and to provide support when they leave or are ill." Id.

[214] *Smith*, 125 S Ct at 1545.

[215] Id at 1546 (holding that granting larger raises to more junior employees was based on a reasonable factor other than age, in that it furthered the legitimate goal of retaining employees by raising salaries to match those in surrounding communities).

[216] Levy and Banaji at 49, 54–55 (cited in note 125) (reporting that implicit negativity remains constant while negative attitudes diminish until by age seventy-one respondents think that they hold positive attitudes to older people); Brian A. Nosek, Mahzarin R. Banaji, and Anthony G. Greenwald, *Harvesting Implicit Group Attitudes and Beliefs from a Demonstration Web Site*, 6 Group Dynamics 101, 108 (2002) (same). These studies are comparing implicit attitudes to "young" versus "old," and thus showing a strong preference for "young." This is consistent with the general feeling of favoring youth; it does not undermine the likelihood that certain subgroups of young people—affected by criminality, or race, or the cusp of adulthood—could prompt an unfavorable response. Research focused on implicit attitudes in these areas would be very useful.

[217] See, e.g., Mark Bendick, Jr., Charles W. Jackson, and J. Horacio Romero, *Employment*

titudes of which we are unaware could affect our decision making in ways that would be hard to anticipate, notice, or control.[218] At the least, these data suggest that we should be suspicious of age-based classifications, and even age-based effects, despite the apparent rationality of age-based classifications and effects.[219]

That is, age may track many employment-related characteristics and therefore be a rational proxy, but age-based distinctions (whether intentional or unintentional) are nonetheless not necessarily rational—rather than based in negative stereotypes or attitudes—in any given case. Likewise, if older people don't realize that or how much they disfavor their own group, then this calls into doubt the argument made by Richard Posner (among others) that employment discrimination laws on the basis of age are akin to the "mad" idea of protecting black people from employment discrimination in a society run by a dominant majority of black people.[220] The data on implicit attitudes trouble Posner's charges of madness. His argument assumes in-group favoritism, or at least in-group accurate individualized treatment. But, as noted, data suggest that older people's negative implicit attitudes toward older people are as strong as those held by younger people, and that these implicit attitudes remain negative even after the bearer of the attitudes turns seventy-one, the age at which our explicit attitudes to old age finally

---

Discrimination Against Older Workers, 8 J Aging & Soc Policy 25, 33–34 (1996) (reporting that in pairs of resumés with equal qualifications, resumés implying that the applicant is thirty-two received significantly more favorable responses than resumés implying that the applicant is fifty-seven); Mark Bendick, Jr., Lauren E. Brown, and Kennington Wall, *No Foot in the Door: An Experimental Study of Employment Discrimination Against Older Workers*, 10 J Aging & Soc Policy 5, 10–11 (1999) (extending the previous study beyond the initial contact stage, and finding again that pairs of younger and older applicants to the same jobs showed the younger applicants receiving more favorable responses).

[218] Cf. Lawrence at 349 (cited in note 212) ("[W]hen the discriminator is not aware of his prejudice . . . neither reason nor moral persuasion is likely to succeed.").

[219] See also Brief for AARP, et al, as Amici Curiae Supporting Petitioners at *23–*24, *Smith v City of Jackson*, 125 S Ct 1536 (2005) (No 03-1160), 2004 WL 1356592 (citing Levy and Banaji) (cited in note 125).

[220] See, e.g., Richard A. Posner, *Aging and Old Age* 320 (1995) ("It is as if the vast majority of persons who established employment policies and who made employment decisions were black, federal legislation mandated huge transfer payments from whites to blacks, and blacks occupied most high political offices in the nation. It would be mad in those circumstances to think the nation needed a law that would protect blacks from discrimination in employment. Employers—who have a direct financial stake in correctly evaluating the abilities of their employees and who for the most part are not young themselves—are unlikely to harbor either serious misconceptions about the vocational capacities of the old (so it is odd that employment should be the main area in which age discrimination is forbidden) or a generalized antipathy toward old people.").

turn from negative or neutral to mildly positive.[221] (Moreover, the implicit-attitude studies also call into question Posner's conclusion with regard to race, as the studies suggest that blacks show slightly negative implicit in-group attitudes.[222])

These empirical findings have implications for the Court's decision in *Smith*. First, though the Court's decision was a matter of statutory interpretation, to which my discussion does not speak, these findings suggest that the conclusion the Court reached on the statutory merits—that disparate-impact suits are available under the ADEA—may also be sound as a matter of policy, at least to the extent that we think the statute should attempt to root out negative attitudes to old age.[223] Second, and relatedly, these data suggest that courts should be more circumspect than the Court's decision might imply when concluding that employers have satisfied the RFOA defense.

This circumspection in some way resembles the concern about age-based attitudes in *Simmons*: We may think we like children,[224] and we may think that our treatment of them will be fair and rational, even where it differs from our treatment of adults, but negative stereotyping and, more surprisingly, negative attitudes can enter the mix and create a need for prophylactic rules. Similarly, we might think that we like and respect older people, or at least empathize with them through contact with our parents and other relatives or through our own experiences as we grow older. But even as we age, our implicit attitudes toward old age fail to improve, suggesting a need for careful evaluation of workplace policies creating a disparate impact on older workers.

V. Conclusion

In *Simmons*, Justice Kennedy confronts a difficult question: Given that being younger than eighteen is merely a proxy for diminished culpability, why not let jurors decide whether youth mit-

---

[221] Levy and Banaji at 55 (cited in note 125).

[222] Nozek, Banaji, and Greenwald at 106 (cited in note 216).

[223] This brief discussion of *Smith* does not attempt to resolve the larger normative question of the merits of the ADEA, a subject of provocative and important debate. See, e.g., Samuel Issacharoff and Erica Worth Harris, *Is Age Discrimination Really Age Discrimination? The ADEA's Unnatural Solution*, 72 NYU L Rev 780 (1997); Christine Jolls, *Hands-Tying and the Age Discrimination in Employment Act*, 74 Tex L Rev 1813 (1996).

[224] We may even think we "worship" them. Cf. Wirtz Report at 3 (cited in note 208); note 211 (quoting relevant passage).

igates the culpability of an individual sixteen- or seventeen-year-old offender? His subtle answer draws on psychological literature about the differences between juveniles and adults, but turns as much on concerns about the mind of the adult juror as on the distinctive traits of juveniles.

In short, the argument has three steps. First, youth is a rational proxy for diminished culpability. Second, jurors will sometimes fail to consider youth as mitigating because they may have negative stereotypes and, worse yet, negative attitudes toward youth. Indeed, they may treat youth as aggravating, thus creating a peculiarly troubling type of error: treating an individual *less favorably* on the basis of the trait, youth, that should prompt *more favorable* treatment. Third, such errors are sufficiently weighty that the Eighth Amendment requires a prophylactic rule that removes such decisions from the jury.

A concern about negative attitudes to youth also supports Kennedy's resolution of the Denominator Dispute, because Kennedy's view could not countenance a state that applied the death penalty only to juveniles; such a position would be akin to treating youth as aggravating.

This understanding of *Simmons* does not establish the rightness of Kennedy's opinion. But it does suggest that the opinion is supported by a stronger rationale than it fully articulates, a rationale that has implications for other areas of law involving the irrationality of apparently rational categories. Another case from last term, *Smith v City of Jackson*,[225] which held that disparate-impact claims are available under the ADEA, provides an example of a context in which negative attitudes that may corrupt individualized determinations warrant further attention.

As Kennedy's *Simmons* opinion suggests, that age is a rational proxy does not mean that people will apply that proxy rationally. The legislative history of the ADEA discussed in *Smith* highlights stereotyping to the exclusion of animus and implies that negative attitudes toward older people are not a problem. But, as *Simmons* shows, negative attitudes can arise in unexpected contexts, and recent work in social psychology supports the conclusion that we tend to dislike older people more than we think we do. Thus, courts should be on the alert for policies and decisions apparently based

---

[225] *Smith v City of Jackson*, 125 S Ct 1536 (2005).

on factors other than age that may nonetheless stem from unacknowledged negative attitudes about age.

A rhetorical flourish in the preceding Term's most significant ADEA case, *General Dynamics Land Systems v Cline*,[226] curiously brings together the language of dislike with the idea that youth can sometimes be the object of dislike: As Justice Souter put it, "The enemy of 40 is 30, not 50."[227] Of course the idea that age-based dislike can be directed at younger as well as older—or at least the idea that such dislike is a cause for concern—cuts against the holding of *Cline* that the ADEA recognizes as discrimination on the basis of age only actions favoring younger employees over their elders. But Souter's language outruns his meaning: Youth, at least to those who are no longer young, can indeed be aggravating.

---

[226] *General Dynamics Land Systems v Cline*, 540 US 581 (2004).
[227] Id at 591.

JULIA D. MAHONEY

KELO'S LEGACY: EMINENT DOMAIN AND THE FUTURE OF PROPERTY RIGHTS

The most striking thing about *Kelo v New London*,[1] which held that the condemnation of fifteen homes pursuant to an economic development plan qualifies as a "public use" under the Fifth Amendment's Takings Clause,[2] is that there was significant public surprise and outcry at the outcome. For decades conventional wisdom had held that the phrase "public use" in the Takings Clause placed little, if any, constraint on exercises of the eminent domain power,[3] and that any acquisition of property undertaken to further a legitimate public purpose was almost certain to be judged lawful. To be sure,

Julia D. Mahoney is Professor of Law and David H. Ibbeken Research Professor, University of Virginia School of Law.

AUTHOR'S NOTE: I thank Lillian BeVier, James DeLong, Kim Forde-Mazrui, Paul Mahoney, G. Edward White, and Ann Woolhandler for helpful comments and conversations. Matt Watson and Rachale Miller provided excellent research assistance.

[1] 125 S Ct 2655 (2005).

[2] US Const, Amend V: "[N]or shall private property be taken for public use, without just compensation." The Takings Clause was held applicable to the states by the Fourteenth Amendment in *Chicago, B. & Q.R. Co. v Chicago*, 166 US 226 (1897).

[3] See Bruce Ackerman, *Private Property and the Constitution* 190 n 5 (1977) ("[T]he modern understanding of 'public use' holds that any state purpose otherwise constitutional should qualify as sufficiently 'public' to justify a taking"); Laurence H. Tribe, 1 *American Constitutional Law* 837 (3d ed 2000) (noting "the Court's refusal in modern times to give teeth to the 'public use' requirement"); Thomas W. Merrill, *The Economics of Public Use*, 72 Cornell L Rev 61 (1986) ("[M]ost observers today think the public use limitation is a dead letter"). But see Richard A. Epstein, *Takings: Private Property and the Power of Eminent Domain* (1985).

it was not wholly implausible to believe that the complaining land-owners could prevail, and the Institute for Justice, a prominent libertarian public interest law firm, vigorously promoted the land-owners' cause.[4] But expansive language in *Hawaii Housing Authority v Midkiff*[5] and *Berman v Parker*,[6] the two leading precedents ad-dressing the meaning of "public use" under the Fifth Amendment, pointed to the conclusion that the "Property Rights" movement was on the verge of suffering its third straight defeat of the October 2004 Term.[7]

That defeat did come, in a 5–4 decision handed down in late June. The loss, though, was hardly a resounding one. Not only did the city of New London prevail by only the slimmest of margins, but the majority opinion implied, and the one concurring opinion—written by a member of the majority—underscored, that the "public use" limitation constitutes a real check on exercises of governmental power.

Notwithstanding the predictability of the result or the indications that the Court had in fact tightened its standard of review for de-termining when a taking is for "public use," *Kelo* sparked a confla-gration of outrage that even months later showed no sign of abating.[8] *Kelo*'s detractors expressed fury that moderate-income res-idents could be forced out of their homes to make way for more upscale development, as well as disbelief that the nation's highest court would permit such a gross abuse of power. The volume and

---

[4] See discussion in Part I.B.

[5] 467 US 229, 241 (1984) ("[W]here the exercise of the eminent domain power is rationally related to a conceivable public purpose, the Court has never held a compensated taking to be proscribed by the Public Use Clause").

[6] 348 US 26, 32 (1954) ("[T]he legislature, not the judiciary, is the main guardian of the public needs to be served by social legislation. . . . This principle admits of no ex-ception merely because the power of eminent domain is involved").

[7] The first two were *Lingle v Chevron*, 125 S Ct 2074 (2005) (rejecting a claim that a Hawaii rent control statute was invalid under the Takings Clause because it failed to substantially advance a legitimate state interest), and *San Remo Hotel L.P. v City and County of San Francisco*, 125 S Ct 2491 (2005) (holding that federal courts are precluded from adjudicating takings claims that have already been adjudicated in state court).

[8] See *Hands Off Our Homes: Property Rights and Eminent Domain*, Economist (Aug 20, 2005) (reporting that "a Supreme Court ruling that allows the government to seize private property has set off a fierce backlash that may yet be as potent as the anti-abortion movement"); The Kelo Decision: Investigating Takings of Homes and Other Private Prop-erty: Hearing Before the United States Senate Committee on the Judiciary (Sept 20, 2005) (testimony of Thomas W. Merrill, Charles Keller Beekman Professor of Law, Columbia University) (observing that Kelo "is unique in modern annals of law in terms of the negative response it has evoked").

ferocity of these objections provoked a swift and sustained response from politicians. Within three weeks of the decision, the United States House of Representatives had agreed (by a vote of 365 to 33) to a nonbinding resolution expressing "grave disapproval" of the majority opinion,"[9] and by early 2006, legislation designed to curb governmental condemnation powers was under consideration in almost every state.[10]

The closeness of the *Kelo* vote, the content of the opinions produced, the fierce tenor of the public criticism, and the quickness of politicians across the ideological spectrum to criticize the outcome all suggest that the law of eminent domain could be on the cusp of a transformation. Neither *Kelo* itself nor the prescriptions offered in response, however, provide a coherent framework for limiting the excesses of eminent domain while facilitating socially beneficial condemnations. As a result, at a time of focused attention on the potential importance of secure property rights for both individual dignity[11] and economic growth,[12] the legacy of *Kelo* could be inadequate or even counterproductive protections of property rights.

The costs of nonoptimal legal regimes may be high. The failure to constrain eminent domain leaves the less politically powerful members of society exposed to the autonomy injuries that involuntary transfers of property—particularly transfers for purposes not regarded as legitimate—can entail. Eminent domain can also impose economic losses on owners of condemned properties, because the "just compensation" to which they are constitutionally entitled is generally limited to fair market value, as distinct from the value that the owner would demand to part willingly with her property.[13]

---

[9] H Res 340 (2005). In addition, the following November the House passed the Private Property Rights Protection Act of 2005, HR 4128, 109th Cong (2005), prohibiting federal agencies from using, and restricting federal economic development assistance to state and local entities that use, eminent domain powers for economic development.

[10] See John M. Broder, *States Curbing Right to Seize Private Homes*, NY Times (Feb 21, 2006), at A1 ("In a rare display of unanimity that cuts across partisan and geographic lines, lawmakers in virtually every statehouse across the country are advancing bills and constitutional amendments to limit use of the government's power of eminent domain to seize private property for economic development purposes").

[11] See, e.g., Nicole Stelle Garnett, *The Neglected Political Economy of Eminent Domain* 52–58 (Notre Dame Law School Legal Studies Research Paper No 06-01, 2006), available at http://ssrn.com/abstract=785425.

[12] See, e.g., Ines Lindner and Holger Strulik, *Why Not Africa?—Growth and Welfare Effects of Secure Property Rights*, 120 Public Choice 143 (2004).

[13] See Richard A. Posner, *Economic Analysis of Law* 55–60 (6th ed 2003); Richard A. Epstein, *A Clear View of the Cathedral: The Dominance of Property Rules*, 106 Yale L J 2091, 2093 (1997).

In short, when the government has broad eminent domain powers that can be "lent" to commercial actors, property is no longer protected by a "property rule" requiring voluntary transactions, but instead by a "liability rule" that permits nonconsensual transfers at judicially determined prices.

To protect themselves against forced sales, property owners may divert resources from investment and other constructive activities to monitoring and influencing government in order to protect the security of their property. In addition, broad eminent domain powers may encourage individuals and firms to pursue their financial self-interest through persuading the government to reconfigure property rights.[14] This danger may be especially acute in settings where the acquired property is to be transferred to developers or other commercial interests, thereby creating an opportunity for profit-seeking firms to acquire property for less than they would have to pay in negotiated purchases. On the other side of the ledger, overly stringent limitations on eminent domain can impede the ability of governments to solve holdout and other market failure problems, as well as to regulate industries through the reassignment of property rights.

This article begins by describing the background of *Kelo*. Part I describes the New London redevelopment plan and explains why, notwithstanding the very serious doctrinal weaknesses of the homeowners' case, victory was not inconceivable. Part II analyzes the decision in *Kelo* and details how each of the four opinions produced by the Court—the majority by Justice Stevens (joined by Justices Kennedy, Souter, Ginsburg, and Breyer), a concurrence by Justice Kennedy, a dissent by Justice O'Connor (joined by Justices Rehnquist, Scalia, and Thomas), and a dissent by Justice Thomas for himself alone—marks a retreat from the constitutional vision expressed in earlier cases, which in essence held that any but the most casual judicial scrutiny of property condemnations was unwarranted and imprudent. In contrast, the *Kelo* opinions all exhibit some recognition of the harms that eminent domain projects can inflict, particularly on vulnerable populations. Each also contemplates, albeit to varying degrees, a meaningful role for the judiciary in policing the security of property rights. None of the opinions, however, provides a workable template for distinguishing constitutional

---

[14] Cf. William J. Baumol, *Entrepreneurship: Productive, Unproductive and Destructive*, 98 J Pol Econ 893 (1990).

exercises of the eminent domain power from unconstitutional ones.

Part III turns to the question of whether the infirmities of *Kelo* matter much, given the groundswell of political activity the decision has engendered. From one perspective, the spectacle of a highly unpopular Supreme Court decision followed by a rush of reform proposals is a sign that the system is functioning smoothly, and is thus reason for celebration rather than concern. I argue that there is sound reason to fear the political activity the decision has incited will not resolve the controversies surrounding eminent domain, in part because the proposals that have to date garnered the greatest support—most notably restricting the use of eminent domain for "economic development"—threaten to be both overinclusive and underinclusive. The strong possibility that eminent domain controversies will not be settled in the political sphere suggests that pressure on the judiciary to find instances of eminent domain unconstitutional will persist. In Part IV, I examine the ramifications of continued judicial involvement and discuss the potential benefits of multiple vetoes over exercises of the eminent domain power.

I. Eminent Domain in New London

A. THE REDEVELOPMENT PLAN

The dispute in *Kelo* arose from efforts to revitalize New London, a small Connecticut city that had suffered a steep decline since its nineteenth-century glory days as a thriving commercial seaport. The city's falling population, high unemployment rate, and lack of industry led a state agency to designate it a "distressed municipality," and in the late 1990s state and local officials targeted it for economic revival.[15] To assist in the rehabilitation project, the New London Development Corporation (the NLDC), a private, nonstock, nonprofit organization established in 1978 to promote economic development, was reactivated, and Claire Gaudiani, the civically prominent president of Connecticut College, was recruited to serve as the organization's head.[16] The newly energized NLDC moved quickly, and by February 1998 had helped persuade the Pfizer Corporation, one of the world's largest pharmaceutical firms (and the employer of Gaudiani's spouse), to agree to build

---

[15] 125 S Ct at 2658–59.

[16] *Urban Development: Putting the New Back in New London*, Economist (June 13, 1998), at 27.

a research facility on the New London waterfront, on a site adjacent to the Fort Trumbull peninsula.[17] As part of the drive to attract the company, the city and the state of Connecticut pledged to invest over $50 million in the Fort Trumbull neighborhood.[18]

Soon after Pfizer's announcement, New London's city council authorized the NLDC to begin work on an economic development plan for a 90-acre portion of the Fort Trumbull area.[19] As part of its planning process, the NLDC conducted a series of neighborhood meetings to educate the public and formulated and submitted plans to a number of state agencies for review.[20] After obtaining the necessary state regulatory approvals, the NLDC finalized its redevelopment plan, which called for the transformation of the 90-acre tract from a neighborhood of small businesses and lower-middle-class residences into a mix of office, retail, recreational, and upscale residential space. New London's city council adopted the plan in January 2000. Pursuant to state law, it designated the NLDC to act as the city's agent and to acquire the property needed for the development project through negotiated purchases or eminent domain.

Under the plan, some of the land acquired was to be leased to a private developer to be selected at a later date, which would in turn transfer leasehold interests to other business enterprises. The proposed project generated heated controversy, including accusations that the politically powerless were being forced out in order to create opportunities for the better connected. Residents' bruised feelings were hardly assuaged by reports that the impolitic Ms. Gaudiani had defended the planned displacements with the statement: "Anything that's working in our great nation is working because somebody left skin on the sidewalk."[21]

Most owners of parcels in the redevelopment area agreed to sell, but nine, who owned a total of fifteen residential properties, refused. In late 2000 the NLDC initiated condemnation proceedings. The NLDC elected to bring its condemnation actions

---

[17] Id.

[18] Robert A. Hamilton, *Pfizer Reaches Across the Thames for More Space*, NY Times (Feb 22, 1998), Sect 11, at 7.

[19] 125 S Ct at 2671 (O'Connor, J, dissenting).

[20] 125 S Ct at 2659.

[21] Laura Mansnerus, *All Politics Is Local, and Sadly, Sometimes Personal*, NY Times (July 3, 2005), Sect 14CN, at 1.

pursuant to a Connecticut statute expressly authorizing eminent
domain to meet industry and business needs. The resisting property owners, including an octogenarian who had lived in one of
the condemned properties since birth and a newcomer to Fort
Trumbull who had invested substantial amounts of money and
time in improving her home, brought suit in New London Superior Court. The homeowners argued, among other things, that
the proposed acquisitions were not for a "public use" and would
thus violate the Fifth Amendment. Although the plaintiffs achieved
a partial victory at the trial court level, they met with defeat before
the Supreme Court of Connecticut. In ruling that none of the
challenged condemnations contravened the Fifth Amendment or
Connecticut law, the court concluded that "an economic development plan that the appropriate legislative authority rationally
has determined will promote significant municipal economic development constitutes a valid public use for the exercise of the
eminent domain power."[22] Three justices concurred in part and
dissented in part. While agreeing with the majority's determination that economic development qualified as a public use, the
dissenters argued that the court should "grant the legislature no
deference on this issue and place the burden on the taking authority to establish by clear and convincing evidence that the public benefit anticipated in the economic development agreement is
reasonably ensured."[23] The landowners appealed, and in September 2004 the Supreme Court granted certiorari to determine
"whether a city's decision to take property for the purpose of
economic development satisfies the 'public use' requirement of
the Fifth Amendment."[24]

B. THE LEGAL BACKGROUND

Convincing the Supreme Court even to hear the case represented something of a coup for the Institute for Justice. For half
a century, the Court had vigorously and consistently rejected any
suggestion that the Public Use Clause substantially constrained
exercises of the eminent domain power. In the 1954 case *Berman*

[22] *Kelo v New London*, 843 A2d 500, 528 (Conn 2004).
[23] Id at 602.
[24] 125 S Ct at 2661.

v Parker,[25] a unanimous Court had upheld the constitutionality of the District of Columbia Redevelopment Act of 1945, an Act of Congress empowering the District of Columbia Redevelopment Land Agency to acquire property for the prevention, reduction, or elimination of blight and its causes, and to transfer the properties obtained to private firms and individuals as well as to public agencies.[26] Wrote Justice William O. Douglas:

> Public safety, public health, morality, peace and quiet, law and order—these are some of the more conspicuous examples of the traditional application of the police power to municipal affairs. . . . In the present case, the Congress and its authorized agencies have made determinations that take into account a wide variety of values. It is not for us to reappraise them. If those who govern the District of Columbia decide that the Nation's Capital should be beautiful as well as sanitary, there is nothing in the Fifth Amendment that stands in the way. Once the object is within the authority of Congress, the right to realize it through the exercise of eminent domain is clear. For the power of eminent domain is merely the means to the end.[27]

In interpreting the public use requirement, then, the *Berman* Court concluded that courts should display an extraordinary level of deference to legislative and agency determinations. As Cass Sunstein has observed, the test outlined in *Berman* "is even more deferential than the rationality requirements of the due process and equal protection clauses, for the legislative judgment on the point is accepted as nearly conclusive."[28] In staking out this bold position, the Court departed from a number of earlier decisions and opinions that had stressed that the determination of what constitutes a "public use" was a matter for judicial consideration.[29]

---

[25] 348 US 26 (1954)

[26] Id at 29–30.

[27] Id at 32–33.

[28] Cass R. Sunstein, *Naked Preferences and the Constitution*, 84 Colum L Rev 1689, 1725 (1984).

[29] See, e.g., *Cincinnati v Vester*, 281 US 439, 446 (1930) ("[T]he question of what is a public use is a judicial one"); *Rindge Co. v County of Los Angeles*, 262 US 700, 705 (1923) ("The nature of a use, whether public or private, is ultimately a judicial question"). See also *U.S. ex rel Welch*, 327 US 546, 556 (Reed, J, concurring) ("This taking is for a public purpose but whether it is or is not is a judicial question"); *U.S. ex rel Welch v TVA*, 327 US 546, 557 (1946) (Frankfurter, J, concurring) ("This Court has never deviated from the view that under the Constitution a claim that a taking is not 'for public use' is open for judicial consideration, ultimately by this Court"); Philip Nichols, Jr., *The Meaning of Public*

To be sure, the Court's opinion in *Berman* was in keeping with the highly deferential posture toward governmental measures affecting property and other "economic" rights that was firmly in place by the middle of the twentieth century.[30] In addition, it bears emphasis that in both outcome and reasoning *Berman* marked the extension of trends already well underway in the area of eminent domain law. For decades, the idea that legislative determinations concerning what types of takings constituted public uses should be regarded as conclusive, or nearly so, had been ascendant.[31] Indeed, Justice Black's opinion for the Court eight years earlier in *U.S. ex rel Welch v TVA*[32] approached *Berman* in its deference. The notion that deference to legislative determinations was nearly always warranted had evolved roughly in tandem with the related idea that the term "public use" could be construed to encompass a wide range of public benefits. Thus by the middle of the century many argued that the so-called "public use doctrine," that is, the construct that governments could expropriate private property only for a limited set of otherwise lawful purposes, had outlived whatever utility it may once have had.[33]

Nevertheless, the Court's decision to abjure any serious role in interpreting "public use" proved fateful. While the precise meaning of "public use" had frequently been in doubt—with various courts at various times construing the phrase to denote public ownership, actual use by the public, or the generation of particular kinds of public benefits[34]—and in practice courts had often hesitated to invalidate condemnations on public use grounds, the threat of judicial action had imposed a certain discipline on the exercise of condemnation powers.[35] By embracing near conclusive

---

Use in the Law of Eminent Domain, 20 BU L Rev 615 (1940) ("[W]hat constitutes a public use, although in the first instance a legislative question, is in the last analysis a question of Constitutional Law to be determined by the courts").

[30] See generally, Robert G. McCloskey, *Economic Due Process and the Supreme Court: An Exhumation and Reburial*, 1962 Supreme Court Review 34.

[31] See Eric R. Claeys, *Public Use Limitations and Natural Property Rights*, 2004 Mich St L Rev 877, 905–09.

[32] 327 US 546 (1946).

[33] See, e.g., Note, *The Public Use Limitation on Eminent Domain: An Advance Requiem*, 58 Yale L J 599, 614 (1949) (concluding that "doubtless the doctrine will continue to be evoked nostalgically in dicta. . . . Kinder hands, however, would accord it the permanent interment in the digests that is so long overdue").

[34] See Harry N. Scheiber, *Property Law, Expropriation, and Resource Allocation by Government: The United States 1789–1910*, 33 J Econ Hist 232 (1973).

[35] See Nichols, 20 BU L Rev at 624 (cited in note 29).

deference, the Court exposed not only the welfare of property owners but its own reputation to the vagaries of government action. In essence, the Court held, without troubling to provide any convincing justification, that judicial oversight was all but unnecessary to protect the security of property rights against government action.[36]

Thirty years after *Berman*, the Court declined to reevaluate its interpretation of "public use." In *Hawaii Housing Authority v Midkiff*,[37] also a unanimous decision, the Court held that the Fifth Amendment did not prohibit the state of Hawaii from implementing a land reform program that transferred property from lessors to tenants for the stated purpose of reducing the concentration of land ownership. In an opinion that hewed closely to *Berman*, Justice O'Connor (who, interestingly, would later dissent in *Kelo*), wrote that the public use requirement is "coterminous with the scope of a sovereign's police powers," and while courts do have some role to play "in reviewing a legislature's judgment of what constitutes a public use," it is an "extremely narrow" one.[38] Consequently, the Court accepted without analysis the state legislature's determination that Hawaii's small number of landowners constituted a "land oligopoly" that had caused the market for land to malfunction, and agreed that redistribution of land "to correct deficiencies in the market determined by the state legislature to be attributable to land oligopoly is a rational exercise of the eminent domain power."[39] In O'Connor's formulation, the Court had no viable choice but to go along with the legislative program: "[I]n our system of government, legislatures are better able to assess what public purposes should be advanced by an exercise of the taking power. . . . *Thus, if a legislature, state or federal, determines there are substantial reasons for an exercise of the taking power, courts must defer to its determination that the taking will serve a public use.*"[40]

To make matters even less auspicious for the *Kelo* plaintiffs,

---

[36] Cf. McCloskey, 1962 Supreme Court Review at 40 (cited in note 30) (concluding that members of the Court never provided a full public explanation of "the basis for their abnegation" of economic substantive due process and arguing that this omission "leaves, to say the least, a large gap in the rationale that underlies the structure of modern constitutional law").

[37] 467 US 229 (1984).

[38] Id at 240

[39] Id at 243.

[40] Id at 244 (emphasis added).

Berman and *Midkiff* were by no means the only Supreme Court
precedents that contained reasoning highly damaging to their
cause. In *Ruckelshaus v Monsanto*,[41] decided just one month after
Midkiff, the Court had found that any taking that might occur of
a pesticide manufacturer's trade secrets, disclosed to the Environmental Protection Agency and made available to competing firms
pursuant to federal law, would be for public use, despite the fact
that the most obvious and direct beneficiaries of any condemnation
would be competitors. Congress's determination that furnishing
the information to other private entities would "eliminate costly
duplication of research" and thus promote healthy competition in
the market for pesticides, the Court had agreed, was "well within
the police power of Congress."[42] And in the 1992 decision *National
Railroad Passenger Corp. v Boston & Maine Corp.*, the Court had, in
the course of upholding a government-orchestrated condemnation
that resulted in the transfer of property from one private rail
concern to another, emphasized that "the public use requirement
of the Takings Clause is coterminous with the regulatory power."[43]
There were even decisions from the early twentieth century that,
although old and of uncertain value as precedents, contained language that lent support to the proposition that at least some condemnations whose "public use" was the promotion of economic
development were constitutional.[44]

Yet despite the grave doctrinal weaknesses of the landowners'
case, it was not beyond imagination that they could win. For one
thing, public attitudes toward eminent domain programs had
cooled over the years. There was growing recognition that the
large-scale urban renewal projects of the 1950s and 1960s had
exacted a terrible toll on poor and minority populations,[45] and

---

[41] 467 US 986 (1984).

[42] Id at 1015.

[43] 503 US 407, 422 (1992).

[44] See, e.g., *Strickley v Highland Boy Gold Mining Co.*, 200 US 527 (1906); *Clark v Nash*,
198 US 361 (1905).

[45] See Wendell E. Pritchett, *The "Public Menace" of Blight: Urban Renewal and the Private
Uses of Eminent Domain*, 21 Yale L & Policy Rev 1 (2003); Brief for NAACP, et al, as
Amici Curiae Supporting Petitioners, *Kelo v New London*, 125 S Ct 2655 (2005) (No 04-
108). See also Patricia Munch, *An Economic Analysis of Eminent Domain*, 84 J Pol Econ
473 (1976) (concluding, based on an analysis of land acquisitions by the Chicago Department of Urban Renewal for three large projects during the years 1962–70, that evidence supports the hypothesis that "high-valued parcels receive more than market value
and low-valued parcels receive less than market value").

articles sympathetic to property holders injured by eminent domain programs—particularly owners of homes and small businesses—were appearing with regularity in the mainstream press. Exercises of eminent domain that transferred property from one private party to another, better politically connected one drew especially harsh criticism.[46] Accompanying this shift in popular sentiment were several high-profile decisions in which courts had ruled that particular "economic development" condemnations were not in accord with the "public use" clause of the federal constitution[47] or similar provisions of state constitutions.[48] Although these decisions did not of course carry any formal authority with the Court, they had the potential to influence its deliberations, if only as indications of shifting societal attitudes.

In addition, since 1987 the Court had manifested, albeit intermittently, greater concern about government infringements of property rights, most notably in the area of regulatory takings.[49] The Court's decisions were often puzzling, and the "Property Rights" movement had sustained more losses than victories. Nevertheless, the Court's greater solicitude for property rights fit uncomfortably with the untempered deference prescribed in *Berman* and applied in rote fashion in *Midkiff* and other cases. Since the time of *Berman*, the Court had become far more willing to engage in the practice of defending constitutional rights from government intrusions.[50] Once property rights were placed—even in a sporadic and inchoate way—in the category of rights potentially worthy of such protection, the judicial practice of giving only cursory examination to an entire category of state action involving property rights appeared less robust.

Finally, *Berman*'s extreme deference looked outdated for another reason. As a product of its time, *Berman* manifested great faith in

---

[46] See, e.g., Gary Greenberg, *The Condemned*, Mother Jones (Jan/Feb 2005); Jonathan Rauch, *Bush's Landgrab—and the New York Times*, National Journal (July 27, 2002); Sam Staley, *Wrecking Property Rights*, Reason (Feb 2003).

[47] See, e.g., *Daniels v Area Plan Comm'n*, 306 F3d 445 (7th Cir 2002); *99 Cents Only Stores v Lancaster Redevelopment Agency*, 237 F Supp 2d 1123 (CD Cal 2001).

[48] See, e.g., *Southwestern Ill. Dev. Auth. v Nat'l City Envtl.*, 768 NE2d 1 (Ill 2002); *Wayne v Hathcock*, 684 NW2d 765 (Mich 2004).

[49] See *Eastern Enterprises v Apfel*, 524 US 498 (1998); *Dolan v City of Tigard*, 512 US 374 (1994); *Lucas v S.C. Coastal Council*, 505 US 1003 (1992); *Nollan v Cal. Coastal Comm'n*, 483 US 825 (1987).

[50] See David A. Strauss, *Why Was Lochner Wrong?* 70 U Chi L Rev 373 (2003); G. Edward White, *Historicizing Judicial Scrutiny*, 57 SC L Rev 1 (2005).

the merits of bypassing the market through central planning, as well as in the legislature's proclivity to promote the public interest rather than the agendas of politically influential groups. At the beginning of the twenty-first century, both these suppositions were regarded as highly questionable in a way they had not been fifty (or even twenty) years earlier. And although the Court cannot be said to have systematically incorporated either confidence in market mechanisms or the insights of public choice theory into its jurisprudence,[51] it was not beyond imagining that this profound shift in outlook could have an impact on the Court's analysis.

II. THE DECISION IN KELO

In the end, the city of New London prevailed as expected. But even before it became apparent that *Kelo* would gain a place of honor in the pantheon of highly unpopular Supreme Court decisions, it was clear the case had important ramifications. Gone, even from the majority opinion, was the robotic deference that had been the hallmark of the Court's eminent domain jurisprudence for over fifty years. The difficulty is that it is not at all clear what has replaced it. All the opinions manifest an awareness of the damage that expropriations can inflict on individual lives. And all display at least some grasp of the potentially huge social costs of untrammeled government power to reconfigure property rights. At the same time, none offers a well thought out framework of constitutional interpretation that addresses these issues.

A. THE MAJORITY OPINION

Justice Stevens, writing for the five Justices in the majority, produced an opinion replete with tension, one that claims to be bound by precedent even as it distances itself from it. Justice Stevens quotes liberally from *Berman* and *Midkiff* and details at length the Court's history of "affording legislatures broad latitude in determining what public needs justify the use of the takings power."[52] The opinion concludes by acknowledging the "hardship that condemnations may entail, notwithstanding the payment of just com-

---

[51] Cf. Stephen Breyer, Economic Reasoning and Judicial Review: AEI-Brookings Joint Center 2003 Distinguished Lecture Presented at the American Enterprise Institute, Dec 4, 2003 (AEI-Brookings Joint Ctr. for Reg. Studies ed, 2004).

[52] 125 S Ct at 2664.

pensation," but insisting that a long line of precedent leaves the Court with no option but to rule against the property owners.[53] Perhaps anticipating that public displeasure is in store, the majority opinion is quick to point to the individual states as a potential source of protection from eminent domain abuse: "We emphasize that nothing in our opinion precludes any State from placing further restrictions on its exercise of the takings power."[54]

At the same time, the majority opinion does not assert that the Court must defer to legislative determinations that an exercise of the takings power will serve a public use. Nor does the majority specify that rational basis review applies to such determinations. Instead, the Court's opinion examines in detail both the content of the redevelopment plan and the circumstances of its creation. The condemnations at issue, it emphasizes, were undertaken pursuant to a comprehensive plan that was carefully formulated to bring about the rejuvenation of a distressed municipality. This plan provided not only for the transfer of property rights from one set of private owners to another, but also for the provision of public spaces, including marinas, pedestrian walkways, and a museum. The majority further notes that the New London plan was the product of "thorough deliberation" involving local government, state agencies, and even the affected neighborhood, whose residents were given the opportunity to attend informational meetings about the planning process. Justice Stevens also takes pains to report that not only the trial judge but also "all the members of the Supreme Court of Connecticut agreed that there was no evidence of an illegitimate purpose in this case."[55] The goal of the plan, the majority pronounces itself satisfied, was to "provide appreciable benefits to the community, including—but by no means limited to—new jobs and increased tax revenue," not to further the interests of Pfizer or other businesses.[56]

---

[53] Id at 2668.

[54] Id.

[55] Id at 2661.

[56] Id at 2665. Some of the Court's stated reasons for concluding that the development plan's goal was not to promote private interests are unconvincing. The most glaring example is the Court's statement: "[W]hile the City intends to transfer certain of the parcels to a private developer in a long-term lease—which developer, in turn, is expected to lease the office space and so forth to other private tenants—the identities of those private parties were not known when the plan was adopted. It is, of course, difficult to accuse the government of having taken A's property to benefit the private interests of B when the identity of B was unknown." Id at 2661–62 n 6. It is obvious that even if a

Absent from the majority opinion, however, is any serious analysis of why the considerations it discusses matter, the weights they carry, or what other sorts of information might be relevant to an assessment of constitutionality. Consequently, it is unclear precisely what will insulate exercises of the eminent domain power from invalidation, or, conversely, what condemnation practices will likely be held unlawful. The greatest puzzle is the Court's stance toward condemnations that provide clear benefits to private parties and can be justified as constituting a public use only on the grounds they increase tax revenues, provide employment, or in some other respect promote economic flourishing. In rejecting the home owners' arguments that the Court should draw a bright line prohibiting the use of the eminent domain power for economic development (or, in the alternate, require a showing of "reasonable certainty" that public benefits will in fact accrue before upholding economic development takings), the majority opinion stresses that "promoting economic development is a traditional and long accepted function of government" and asserts that there is "no principled way of distinguishing economic development from the other public purposes that we have recognized."[57] But that broad language, although suggestive, is a far cry from a guarantee that future condemnations for economic development purposes will meet with a favorable reception. In fact, the majority opinion is careful to warn that a taking of one private owner's property followed by transfer to a second private party "executed outside the confines of an integrated development plan" for the sole reason that the new owner will use the property in a more productive way, thus generating more tax revenue, would be an "unusual exercise of government power" that would "certainly raise a suspicion that a private purpose was afoot."[58]

This last statement—expressing confidence that courts will be able to readily identify takings that have no conceivable public purpose other than to generate additional taxes—to some degree undermines the earlier claim that there is no practicable way to distinguish economic development takings from other exercises of

---

government has not publicly identified private beneficiaries, there might nonetheless exist informal understandings with private parties. Also, even if the identities of private beneficiaries are in fact unknown at the time a plan is formulated or approved, governments can use redevelopment programs to enrich favorites selected later.

[57] Id at 2665.

[58] Id at 2667.

the eminent domain power. At the very least, it indicates that there is a subset of economic development takings that perceptibly differs from other sorts of takings and ought to incite greater judicial attention than the average condemnation.

In essence, then, the majority opinion intimates that the extraordinary deference standard is a thing of the past, and that some takings—particularly ones similar to those in *Kelo* but perhaps not so carefully planned or documented—might very well not survive judicial review. But left unexplained is precisely why and to what degree the Court is prepared to retreat from the precedents that it insists render it unable to offer relief to the New London home owners. Clearly, the Court is convinced that the security of property rights is important, for it emphasizes that the Constitution imposes restrictions on the use of state power to deliberately advance the interests of one private entity at the expense of another through the reconfiguration of property rights.[59] Yet the majority does not address the issue of what ends are served by this limitation, and without knowing more about what the Court understands to be the dangers of eminent domain—infringements of fundamental human rights, for example, or distortions of the political process wrought by would-be beneficiaries of condemnations—it is hard to predict what sort of alternative to the "super deference" model the Court might be prepared to construct.

B. JUSTICE KENNEDY'S CONCURRENCE

Because Justice Kennedy provided the crucial fifth vote for the majority opinion, his concurring opinion demands particularly careful analysis.[60] Kennedy begins by declaring that governmental takings are permissible so long as they bear a rational relationship to a public purpose. In practice, explains Kennedy, this entails applying a form of the rational basis test normally used in reviewing economic regulation under the Due Process and Equal Protection Clauses. He cites as an example of this sort of review

---

[59] Id at 2661.

[60] See Richard A. Posner, *The Supreme Court, 2004 Term—Foreword: A Political Court*, 119 Harv L Rev 31, 95 (2005) (noting that when a Justice casts the "essential fifth vote for the 'majority' opinion while also writing a separate opinion" it creates uncertainty "whether the majority opinion or the concurring opinion should be regarded as the best predictor of how the Court would decide a similar case in the future").

the Court's 1955 decision in *Williamson v Lee Optical*,[61] a curious choice given that in that case the Court pointedly refused to invalidate a statute that had the obvious purpose and effect of protecting ophthalmologists and optometrists from competition from opticians.[62] Justice Kennedy thus expresses confidence that rational basis style review in the context of eminent domain will succeed where other instances of rational basis review have often failed—that is, that it will provide courts with an effective tool with which to stop government actions intended to "favor a particular private party, with only incidental or pretextual public benefits."[63] In the context of the Public Use Clause, states Justice Kennedy, courts can accomplish this by engaging in "meaningful" rational basis review: Faced with a "plausible accusation of impermissible favoritism," courts should take the allegations seriously and "review the record," albeit with the "presumption that the government's actions were reasonable and intended to serve a public purpose."[64] Because in Justice Kennedy's assessment the trial court engaged in this type of respectful but not supine oversight, he agrees that the condemnations in *Kelo* survive constitutional challenge.

But Justice Kennedy's faith in the power of rational basis review—even in its brawnier "meaningful" incarnation—to rein in unconstitutional exercises of the eminent domain power is not absolute. While rejecting the idea that all condemnations justified on economic development grounds should be adjudged or presumed unlawful, Kennedy declines to rule out the possibility that a "more narrowly drawn category" of such takings might merit a "more stringent standard of review."[65] A delineation of what would cause a condemnation of property to fall into this category, however, is left for another day, for Justice Kennedy refuses to engage in "conjecture as to what sort of cases might justify a more de-

---

[61] 348 US 483 (1955).

[62] See J. M. Balkin, *The Footnote*, 83 Nw U L Rev 275, 315 n 96 (1989): "In *Williamson*, a case about the protection of vision, we witness the virtual *elimination* of vision (scrutiny). Not only does Justice Douglas [the author of *Williamson* as well as the nearly contemporaneous *Berman* decision] not scrutinize the statute closely, he deliberately looks the other way. He refuses to see what is obvious on the face of the statute—that this regulation was designed to favor ophthalmologists and optometrists over opticians, and in particular, to curtail the growth of cut-rate volume optical services in department stores."

[63] 125 S Ct at 2669 (Kennedy, J, concurring).

[64] Id (Kennedy, J, concurring).

[65] Id at 2670 (Kennedy, J, concurring).

manding standard."[66] He does list four factors that persuaded him that rational basis style review sufficed in *Kelo*: the condemnations were accomplished pursuant to a comprehensive plan designed to alleviate a "serious city-wide depression"; the economic benefits of the project "cannot be characterized as *de minimis*"; at the time the comprehensive plan was crafted, it was not yet known who most of the private beneficiaries would be;[67] and New London's compliance with "elaborate procedural requirements" that made easier judicial review of the city's motivations for the condemnations.[68] These enumerated factors, however, raise more questions than they answer about when departure from the rational basis framework might be warranted. Justice Kennedy's discussion suggests he harbors profound anxieties about the prospect of private entities being singled out for overly harsh or generous governmental treatment.[69] But lacking in his opinion is any algorithm for determining when the institutional structures that normally inhibit such abusive governmental conduct are likely to malfunction, thus justifying more intense judicial oversight. As with the majority opinion, Justice Kennedy's concurrence does not so much set out an alternative to the highly deferential approach as imply one might be forthcoming.

C. JUSTICE O'CONNOR'S DISSENT

Of all the opinion writers, Justice O'Connor, in whose dissent Rehnquist, Scalia, and Thomas joined, had the hardest task. O'Connor forthrightly admits that the "troubling result" in *Kelo* follows from what she terms "errant language" in *Berman* and *Midkiff*.[70] As the author of *Midkiff*, Justice O'Connor is determined

---

[66] Id (Kennedy, J, concurring).

[67] Kennedy's concurrence, like the majority opinion, interprets the failure to identify beneficiaries at the time of the adoption of the development plan as evidence that the motivations of the legislature were to promote the public interest, not to create opportunities for favored private entities to profit at the expense of others.

[68] 125 S Ct at 2670 (Kennedy, J, concurring).

[69] Cf. *Eastern Enterprises v Apfel*, 524 US 498, 547–48 (1998) (Kennedy, J, concurring in the judgment and dissenting in part) (noting with approval that although the Court has "been hesitant to subject economic legislation to due process scrutiny as a general matter, the Court has given careful consideration to due process challenges to legislation with retroactive effects" in large part because of the "legislative 'temptation to use retroactive legislation as a means of retribution against unpopular groups or individuals.'"). (Citations omitted.)

[70] 125 S Ct at 2675 (O'Connor, J, dissenting).

to distinguish its facts and articulate grounds on which the New London condemnations are unconstitutional, for she regards the majority opinion as nothing short of a disaster. By failing to lay out clear rules about what takings are permissible, she charges, the Court renders all private property subject to "being taken and transferred to another private owner, so long as it might be upgraded."[71] After *Kelo*, "the specter of condemnation" will haunt every property owner, for nothing "is to prevent the State from replacing any Motel 6 with a Ritz-Carlton, any home with a shopping mall, or any farm with a factory."[72] Those with the fewest resources, she predicts, will suffer most.

Justice O'Connor locates the grounds she seeks for differentiating the takings in *Kelo* in the concepts of harm and benefit. She notes that the Court's precedents have identified three categories of lawful takings, the first two of which she characterizes as "relatively straightforward and uncontroversial."[73] The three categories are transfers to public ownership; transfers to private entities, including common carriers, that will permit members of the public to make actual use of the condemned property; and transfers to private entities in situations in which the use of the targeted property is causing societal harm.[74] O'Connor asserts that in both *Midkiff* and *Berman* the "extraordinary, precondemnation use of the targeted property inflicted affirmative harm on society" and that because the takings in those cases "*directly* achieved a public benefit," the fact that the condemned properties were turned over to private holders is irrelevant.[75] The "well-maintained" homes at issue in *Kelo* are different, argues O'Connor, in that no one can claim they are the "source of any social harm."[76]

There are two problems with this attempt to distinguish *Kelo* from earlier cases. First, the uses of the properties condemned in *Berman* and *Midkiff* were harmful only in the sense that they were part of larger social problems of, respectively, urban blight and land oligopoly. But if the concept of "harm" is that broad, then it is hard to see why it does not also cover general economic distress, the

---

[71] Id at 2671 (O'Connor, J, dissenting).

[72] Id at 2676 (O'Connor, J, dissenting).

[73] Id at 2673 (O'Connor, J, dissenting).

[74] Id at 2673–74 (O'Connor, J, dissenting).

[75] Id at 2674 (O'Connor, J, dissenting).

[76] Id at 2675 (O'Connor, J, dissenting).

situation that New London identified as motivation for the condemnations in *Kelo*. Second, the Court's public use precedents extend beyond *Berman* and *Midkiff*. O'Connor's dissent neglects to address them, possibly because the argument that the precondemnation uses of property in those cases were more harmful than the precondemnation uses of the New London home owners is even harder to make than the analogous argument about the land uses in *Berman* and *Midkiff*.[77] This omission underscores that O'Connor's taxonomy of lawful takings is in tension with the realities of the modern administrative state, with its regulatory schemes that entail reassignments of property rights in circumstances where it would be puzzling to characterize the original owner's use of the property as "harmful."

Most important, Justice O'Connor's harm/benefit framework fails to provide either the clear guidance she faults the majority opinion for omitting or much in the way of protection for the nonaffluent property owners she identifies as eminent domain's most likely victims. If concentrated land ownership in Hawaii counts as a harm to be remedied through eminent domain because it distorts the local real estate market, the category of harm is so large as to be close to useless for the purpose of restricting condemnations. And O'Connor and the other dissenters surely realize that many of the less prosperous individuals they worry about live in neighborhoods that meet almost any definition of "blight," and that a framework under which the condemnations in *Berman* are unproblematic is unlikely to shield them from displacement.

One other feature of Justice O'Connor's opinion bears mention. In labeling as "relatively straightforward and uncontroversial" condemnations for transfer to government entities or common carriers and the like, O'Connor implies that the only problematic condemnations—at least for purposes of the Public Use Clause—are those that result in transfers to private owners who will refuse the public access as of right. Yet Justice O'Connor's chief concern is that condemnations will enrich the already prosperous and influential at the expense of the poorer and less well connected, and it is clear that many of the condemnations she labels "uncontroversial" could have that precise effect. One need not own property in order to

---

[77] See, e.g., *Ruckelshaus v Monsanto*, 467 US 986 (1984).

capture its benefits,[78] and property acquisitions the government claims are in the general interest may instead further private interests.

Justice O'Connor's posture is particularly curious given the obvious possibility that the restrictions she advocates could lead to increased public ownership, as governments circumvent constitutional limitations by opting to retain title to condemned properties. The interpretation of the Public Use Clause O'Connor endorses, in short, could have the perverse consequence of increasing government involvement in redevelopment schemes. It is true that a practice of keeping condemned properties in public ownership can decrease the returns to private parties from lobbying governments for the chance to acquire property at favorable prices. But encouraging public ownership can introduce another variety of social cost, as government proprietors will often fail to manage properties as well as their counterparts in the private sector.

D. JUSTICE THOMAS'S DISSENT

Justice Thomas's separate dissent is the most poignant of the four opinions, for it goes into the greatest detail about those whose "skin was left on the sidewalk" by eminent domain programs. As he observes, over 97 percent of the thousands of people uprooted from their homes by the urban renewal projects undertaken by the District of Columbia Redevelopment Land Agency in the wake of the *Berman* decision were African-Americans, and similar programs in Baltimore and St. Paul demolished minority communities. Along with the other dissenters, Justice Thomas is convinced *Kelo* could portend similarly disastrous consequences for the least well off: "Allowing the government to take property solely for public purposes is bad enough, but extending the concept of public purpose to encompass any economically beneficial goal guarantees that these losses will fall disproportionately on poor communities. Those communities are not only systematically less likely to put their lands to the highest and best social use, but are also the least politically powerful."[79]

In his search for limitations on the eminent domain power,

---

[78] See, e.g., Karen R. Merrill, *Public Lands and Political Meaning: Ranchers, the Government, and the Property Between Them* (2002) (describing the benefits that ranching interests have derived from publicly owned lands).

[79] 125 S Ct at 2686–87 (Thomas, J, dissenting).

Justice Thomas, not surprisingly, turns to constitutional text and history. Unfortunately for Thomas, there is not much material for him to work with. After consulting late-eighteenth-century dictionaries, analyzing the text of the Public Use Clause against the backdrop of other constitutional provisions, and surveying early American eminent domain practices, Justice Thomas concludes that the "most natural reading of the Clause is that it allows the government to take property only if the government owns, or the public has a right to use, the property," as distinct from taking it for any plausible public purpose.[80]

Still, Thomas draws back from arguing that all exercises of the eminent domain power that do not meet these criteria are unconstitutional. Rather, he is willing to go only so far as to recommend that the Court "revisit" its eminent domain cases and "consider" returning to what he regards as the Fifth Amendment's original meaning.[81] Thomas does not explain whether or how his favored interpretation would protect those imperiled by eminent domain. It may be that whether property ends up in government ownership or is open to use by the public is a reliable—or at least, within the strictures of Thomas's interpretive commitments, the best attainable—proxy for the threat a condemnation poses to the weak, but Thomas does not argue this. Nor does he explain why he is willing to sign onto Justice O'Connor's dissent, with its conclusion that condemnations to alleviate "harms" such as "blight" are constitutional.

Whatever construction the Court puts on the term "public use," maintains Justice Thomas, there is no justification for "affording almost insurmountable deference to legislative conclusions" about which uses are public.[82] Courts do not accord similar obeisance to legislative judgments in other contexts involving constitutional rights, including determinations about when the police may carry out searches of homes. This discrepancy convinces Thomas that "something has gone seriously awry with this Court's interpretation of the Constitution," for "though citizens are safe from the government in their homes, the homes themselves are not."[83] Justice Thomas does not, however, provide any detail regarding what

---

[80] Id at 2679 (Thomas, J, dissenting).

[81] Id at 2686 (Thomas, J, dissenting).

[82] Id at 2684 (Thomas, J, dissenting).

[83] Id at 2685 (Thomas, J, dissenting).

sort of judicial oversight should replace the "almost insurmountable deference" approach he objects to so strongly.

III. The Political Response

For all that the opinions in *Kelo* both manifest and sow confusion about the meaning of "public use" and the role of the judiciary in securing property rights, these conceptual struggles may be unimportant if the boundaries of the eminent domain power are refined in the political arena. This seemed plausible in the immediate aftermath of *Kelo*, for within days of the decision it was clear that public opinion ran strongly against the outcome and that political actors were mobilizing in response. Indeed, Justice Stevens, in a widely reported speech in August 2005 defending the Court's ruling, expressed the belief that the clamor "that greeted *Kelo* is some evidence that the political process is up to the task of addressing" eminent domain issues.[84]

If Stevens is correct, that would be good news for the Supreme Court, battered from charges that its decision in *Kelo* amounts to an abdication of its institutional responsibilities. Political resolution of eminent domain controversies could recast the Court's opinion in *Kelo* as a prudent act of restraint that served as a catalyst for popular deliberation.[85] In refusing to venture into a potential property rights quagmire, the argument might go, the Court recognized the limits of its own capacities and ensured that decisions about the limits of the eminent domain power would be made by the institutions best suited to grappling with the complex economic and moral issues involved. After all, the legislative and constitutional amendment processes are, at least in theory, highly responsive to and thus well equipped to balance the competing interests of a broad set of individuals and institutions. Moreover, the political process is, again in theory, better able to effect rapid reform. This is not to say that decisions by the Court cannot and

---

[84] Justice John Paul Stevens, Judicial Predilections, Address to the Clark County Bar Association (Aug 18, 2005).

[85] Cf. Posner, 119 Harv L Rev at 98 (cited in note 60): "Paradoxically, the strong adverse public and legislative reactions to the *Kelo* decision are evidence of its pragmatic soundness. When the Court declines to invalidate an unpopular government power, it tosses the issue back into the democratic arena. The opponents of a broad interpretation of 'public use' now know that the Court will not give them the victory they seek. They will have to roll up their sleeves and fight the battle in Congress and state legislatures—where they may well succeed."

have not brought about radical transformations—the huge shifts in Contract, Commerce, and Due Process Clause doctrine in the first decade of the New Deal attest to that[86]—but only that the methodology of constitutional interpretation tends to produce incremental rather than discontinuous change. If the current regime of eminent domain is seriously deficient—as the furor triggered by *Kelo* suggests it may be—then it seems reasonable to look to statutes and constitutional amendments for relief.

Nevertheless, there is reason for skepticism that the political sphere will satisfactorily resolve eminent domain controversies. For one thing, while the political process responds to popular concerns, it also responds to organized interest groups.[87] Consequently, the same forces that lead to dubious eminent domain practices in the first place may impede efforts to curb them.[88] If a significant portion of redevelopment schemes result from questionable dealings between government and business interests, as many are convinced could be the case,[89] then there exist highly motivated and organized constituencies with a strong interest in maintaining the present system. Another reason to question the capacity of the political arena to settle eminent domain controversies is that much of whatever reform occurs will likely take place at the state and local level.[90] Since it is highly improbable that all jurisdictions will be covered, then to the extent that the interests of property owners are insufficiently safeguarded under the present system, some portion of the population will be left without adequate security. This same concern holds with respect to suggestions that judicial interpretations of state constitutional provisions will provide a bulwark against abusive eminent domain practices.

An examination of the substance of the most prominent reform

---

[86] See G. Edward White, *The Constitution and the New Deal* 198–200 (2000).

[87] See James M. Buchanan and Gordon Tullock, *The Calculus of Consent* (1962); Jerry L. Mashaw, *Greed, Chaos and Governance: Using Public Choice to Improve Public Law* 15–21 (1997).

[88] See William A. Fischel, *Regulatory Takings: Law, Economics and Politics* 100–140 (1995).

[89] See, e.g., Posner, 119 Harv L Rev at 97 (cited in note 60) (concluding that while it is uncertain whether examples of "what appear to be foolish, wasteful, and exploitive redevelopment plans" are representative, it "would not be surprising to discover that redevelopment plans are for the most part unholy collusions between the real estate industry and local politicians").

[90] See Broder, NY Times (cited in note 10).

proposals furnishes still more cause for doubt. Many of these proposals seek to restrict or prohibit condemnations for "economic
development."[91] Although definitions of "economic development"
vary—indeed, it is sometimes left undefined—the term is generally
understood to cover those property transfers from one private
entity to another that are intended to increase tax revenue or
employment or to promote economic growth rather than to eliminate some existing harm.[92] In essence, these proposals attempt to
codify some of the restrictions on eminent domain urged in Justice
O'Connor's dissent.[93] As such, they suffer from the same defects
as the O'Connor opinion, and threaten to frustrate a number of
socially useful exercises of the condemnation power while offering
only incomplete protection against its dangers. Restricting the
government's power to reallocate property among private entities
can impair its ability to regulate commerce and industry. While
it is incontrovertible that not all such reconfigurations of property
rights will promote the general welfare, the social costs of erring
too far on the side of interdiction can be high. In addition, restrictions on transfers to private firms can inhibit the formation
of public-private partnerships to carry out innovative land use
planning, thus encouraging governments to undertake projects
designed to promote economic growth themselves instead of drawing on the expertise of the private sector. The focus on transfers
to private firms has the additional drawback of providing no measure of protection for those whose property is taken for transfer
to government or common carriers and the like.

It is also important to recognize that forbidding condemnations
for "economic development" will not relieve the judiciary of any
obligation to police the boundaries of the eminent domain power.
"Economic development" is not a self-executing concept, but one
that will require substantial judicial interpretation. Inevitably,
judges will be called on to decide whether a particular project
involving condemnations serves some higher public purpose or is
simply an "economic development" project motivated "only" by
the desire to increase overall wealth. Should widespread restrictions on eminent domain for "economic development" be adopted,

---

[91] Id.

[92] See, e.g., Private Property Rights Protection Act of 2005, HR 4128, 109th Cong
(2005).

[93] See discussion in Part II.C.

continual judicial scrutiny of condemnations will be necessary.

Other widely heralded reforms are also likely to prove of limited value. Two in particular merit discussion: changing eminent domain procedures to provide for more and better process, including increased public participation, and granting condemnees who suffer consequential damages and subjective losses compensation in excess of the constitutionally mandated "fair market value." These measures have garnered the endorsement of several prominent organizations, including the American Planning Association.[94] Both process and compensation reforms are justified on the grounds that they will raise the costs associated with eminent domain, thereby encouraging governments to negotiate with property owners rather than condemn. Increased process is said to have the additional benefit of furnishing useful information to decision makers, especially about the magnitude and intensity of opposition to proposed exercises of eminent domain.

With respect to process reforms, it is hard to argue with the proposition that many eminent domain procedures are antiquated and could stand improvement.[95] It is important to recognize, though, that many highly controversial exercises of eminent domain—including the one in New London—had no dearth of process, and that there is no clear reason to believe that improved process will yield benefits that justify the costs of reform. As for providing greater compensation, unless the total amount proffered equals or exceeds the price at which an owner becomes a willing seller, it is unlikely that those who lose their property will be satisfied with the outcome. That figure is, of course, known only to the owner and hard—in fact, in some instances impossible—for a third party to determine absent a consensual transaction. The formidable difficulties inherent in the valuation of property, particularly property with hard to measure attributes, mean that even under a supercompensatory regime many owners of condemned properties will believe themselves inadequately compensated.[96] At the same time, if the amounts paid out exceed the prices that property holders would require to consummate voluntary sales, then another problem

---

[94] See Brief for American Planning Association, et al, as Amici Curiae Supporting Respondents, *Kelo v New London*, 125 S Ct 2655 (2005) (No 04-108).

[95] See Merrill (cited in note 8) (observing that "as an administrative law professor I am struck by how outmoded eminent domain processes appear to be. . . . Eminent domain procedures were developed in the nineteenth century, and have scarcely been modified since").

[96] Cf. Henry E. Smith, *Property and Property Rules*, 79 NYU L Rev 1719 (2004).

will surface: Owners will have incentives to devote resources to *trying* to get their properties condemned.[97] In short, compensation reforms are unlikely to provide a satisfactory solution, but instead to lead to overcompensation in some instances while failing to quell controversy in others.

IV. JUDICIAL PROTECTION OF PROPERTY RIGHTS

Should the political process fail to defuse public anger over condemnations, there will likely continue to be pressure on the Court to subject exercises of eminent domain power to meaningful judicial review. The Court may well accede to this pressure, for if history is any guide it will be responsive to the popular will.[98] Such a development could be a positive one. For although judges may not have superior capabilities when it comes to making complicated assessments of economic and moral issues, the imposition of multiple vetoes over condemnations of property can serve as a powerful deterrent to socially undesirable behavior.

A. THE BENEFITS OF MULTIPLE VETOES

Defenders of judicial deference to determinations of what constitutes "public use" often bolster their position by arguing that courts are less skilled than legislatures, agencies, and private entities that exercise eminent domain powers at figuring out whether transfers of property rights will produce social benefits. Indeed, in its eminent domain jurisprudence the Court has sounded this theme on a number of occasions. The comparative incompetence of judges, or so the argument goes, means that courts should shrink from second-guessing decisions to condemn properties for purported public uses. In support of this claim, many proponents point to the doctrinal confusion that sometimes reigned in the nineteenth and early twentieth centuries, when courts on occasion engaged in protracted inquiries into the precise meaning of "public use." As Thomas W. Merrill puts it, history suggests that "lawyers and judges are not particularly good at anticipating the ways in

---

[97] See Lee Anne Fennell, *Taking Eminent Domain Apart*, 2004 Mich St L Rev 957, 993–94.

[98] See Michael J. Klarman, *From Jim Crow to Civil Rights: The Supreme Court and the Struggle for Racial Equality* 449 (2004) ("Constitutional law generally has sufficient flexibility to accommodate dominant public opinion, which the justices have little inclination, and limited power, to resist"). See also Barry Friedman, *The Politics of Judicial Review*, 84 Tex L Rev 257 (2005).

which reconfigurations of ownership rights may produce significant public benefits," nor do they excel at "articulating abstractions that will capture a high percentage of the situations in which reconfiguration would be desirable."[99]

What this argument fails to recognize is that judicial oversight can add value even if judges have inferior ability to calculate the social costs and benefits of eminent domain. This is because the existence of multiple veto points in rearranging property rights addresses what Barry Weingast has characterized as "the fundamental political dilemma of an economic system."[100] Governments that are strong enough to create property rights are also capable of expropriating the wealth of their citizenry.[101] Thus a well functioning society requires not just the establishment of property rights and an adequate law of contracts, but also a secure political foundation that restricts the state's capacity to alter these rights and legal regimes.[102] One way in which constitutions restrict public interference with private rights is to establish multiple veto points by requiring multiple actors within the government to agree before the government can act.

In the context of property condemnations, the mere fact that there is some probability that a taking will be enjoined will make eminent domain a less promising prospect for extracting wealth through influencing the government. As a result, would-be beneficiaries of eminent domain will have incentives to devote their resources to activities other than lobbying governments to condemn the property of others. In turn, the knowledge that their property rights are secured by more than one branch of the government will spur property owners to devote more resources to investment and innovation, instead of monitoring the political process and seeking to protect themselves.[103] This knowledge will also

---

[99] Merrill (cited in note 8).

[100] Barry R. Weingast, *Constitutions as Governance Structures: The Political Foundations of Secure Markets*, 149 J Institutional & Theoretical Econ 286, 287 (1993).

[101] Id.

[102] Id.

[103] See Douglass C. North and Barry R. Weingast, *Constitutions and Commitment: The Evolution of Institutions Governing Public Choice in Seventeenth-Century England*, 49 J Econ Hist 803, 829 (1989) (concluding that "an explicit set of multiple veto points along with the primacy of the common law courts over economic affairs" worked to secure property rights and fuel economic growth in late-seventeenth-century England).

make property owners feel less vulnerable to dislocations and more in control of their destinies.

Whether judges are skilled at distinguishing reconfigurations of property rights that increase overall welfare from those that decrease it, in sum, may be of secondary importance. What matters is not that their doctrinal formulations invariably separate the socially beneficial from the socially harmful, but that judicial involvement increases the number of government actors who have to agree in order for rearrangements of property rights to occur. In short, one cannot justify putting the scope of eminent domain into the hands of the other branches merely by arguing that they have an advantage over courts in making determinations about the merits of proposed condemnations.

B. THE MERITS OF JUDICIAL OVERSIGHT

By telling property owners to look almost wholly to the non-judicial branches for limitations on eminent domain, the near total deference standard protected only against the most obvious and egregious abuses. As a result, judicial review of condemnations provided little protection, and the potential benefits of judicial involvement went unrealized. By contrast, the sort of oversight hinted at in the *Kelo* majority opinion—and espoused more explicitly in Kennedy's concurrence—promises to invalidate a larger set of condemnations. Taken together, the majority opinion and the concurrence can be read as signaling a willingness to enjoin condemnations in situations where there is convincing evidence of government favoritism or animus, or where there is no plausible claim that the overall public interest is being served. If that is correct, then the legacy of *Kelo* may be to lay the foundation for the adoption of a form of genuine rational basis review—as distinct from the Potemkin rational basis scrutiny typified by *Midkiff*—of exercises of the eminent domain power, with perhaps even the prospect of more searching review in selected instances.

Such an approach could have significant benefits. It would prevent some, although admittedly not all, condemnations that stem from questionable relationships between government and business. It might even stop some eminent domain practices that are well intentioned but ill-advised and cruelly disruptive, as was the case with many of the urban renewal programs of the 1950s and 1960s. The strongest argument for this approach, however, is one of elimination, for none of the alternatives is as attractive. The near abdication of judicial oversight contained in *Berman* and *Midkiff* is all but unthinkable in the wake of the public response to *Kelo*, and in any event every Justice has rejected it outright or retreated from it. The approaches of both *Kelo* dissents threaten to frustrate legitimate government aims while failing to protect the vulnerable. And varieties of heightened scrutiny have the drawback of asking courts to engage in the sorts of cost-benefit and moral analysis normally left to the other branches.

V. Conclusion

In retrospect, the Court's decision to apply near total deference to legislative and agency determinations of "public use" was a risky move. After decades of insisting that judicial oversight was for all practical purposes unnecessary for guaranteeing the adequate security of property rights, the Court found itself with little room to maneuver in the face of burgeoning public ire regarding condemnation practices. When confronted with *Kelo*, with its obvious implications for the property rights of millions of Americans, all the Justices retreated from the near total deference model. But the sweeping character of the Court's own precedents, together with the formidable challenge of reining in eminent domain's excesses without quashing its benefits, hampered their ability to devise alternatives.

The result was a majority opinion that suggests that courts examine carefully the circumstances of condemnations while failing to provide guidance on how this inquiry should proceed. The concurrence by Justice Kennedy is more explicit in its vision of a substantial judicial role for preventing condemnations designed to promote private interests rather than the public welfare, expressing confidence that the rational basis standard will provide a vigorous check in most situations and leaving open the possibility of more stringent review for particularly suspicious transactions. But as with the majority opinion, the concurrence offers little in the way of analysis regarding under what circumstances and in what ways eminent domain abuses are likely to occur, thus creating a need for judicial oversight. Not surprisingly, these efforts were insufficient to stem public fury at the Court's perceived failure to vindicate its role of defender of constitutional rights.

These failures may not matter if the uproar over *Kelo* leads to a quick resolution in the political arena. But although predictions are of course fallible, it is hard to imagine that political fixes will dissipate the controversy over eminent domain anytime soon. This means the Court may again be called upon to confront questions about the meaning of public use and the role of the judiciary in securing property rights. Indeed, given the public reaction to *Kelo*, the Court may welcome the opportunity. If it does so, it will be confronted with the task that it so studiously avoided in *Kelo*, namely, to begin the work of constructing an alternative to the near total deference framework that it embraced so fully and declined to reexamine for so long.

ADAM M. SAMAHA

ENDORSEMENT RETIRES: FROM RELIGIOUS SYMBOLS TO ANTI-SORTING PRINCIPLES

Our constitutional law respecting religious establishments has nearly nothing to do with the federal government. Putting aside the best reading of constitutional text and constitutional law outside the courts, the central government has little to fear from the Establishment Clause.[1] In fact, the Supreme Court has almost never invalidated federal action on Establishment Clause grounds.[2] Maybe this is because national political institutions generate results that are less often troubling to the Court, or because it holds such action to a less demanding standard, or both. Regardless of the best explanation, the law's bite is at the state and local levels.

Adam M. Samaha is Assistant Professor, University of Chicago Law School.

AUTHOR'S NOTE: Thanks to Christopher Berry, Emily Buss, Mary Anne Case, Mark Chavez, Adam Cox, Jake Gersen, Philip Hamburger, Bernard Harcourt, Saul Levmore, Tracey Meares, Tom Miles, Martha Nussbaum, Michael Stokes Paulsen, Julie Roin, Geof Stone, Lior Strahilevitz, David Strauss, Cass Sunstein, Adrian Vermeule, and Jay Wexler for their comments and suggestions. Shane Davis provided excellent research assistance.

[1] "*Congress* shall make no law respecting an establishment of religion . . . ." US Const, Amend I (emphasis added).

[2] The partial exception is *Tilton v Richardson*, 403 US 672 (1971), which largely upheld a federal construction-grant program that included religious colleges, but which invalidated and severed a provision that would have allowed non-secular use of the funded facilities after twenty years. *Aguilar v Felton*, 473 US 402 (1985), which invalidated New York's attempt to implement a federal special-education funding program, see id at 404–07, turned on choices made by the locals and was overruled in *Agostini v Felton*, 521 US 203, 235 (1997).

Knowing this helps account for an overlooked and yet revealing quirk of the endorsement test for Establishment Clause violations: the question is for judges, not juries.[3] The reason for this allocation of power is not evident from the nature of the test. Roughly speaking, the query is whether a reasonable observer would think that the government sent a message favoring religion over non-religion.[4] Context matters, including the community setting.[5] Juries regularly answer questions like this. Negligence cases call for somewhat similar judgment.[6] Even better, juries may determine whether speech is so offensive to community standards that it qualifies as obscenity.[7]

There is a plausible reason why judges, particularly federal judges, retain control over the endorsement question. Preventing government endorsement of religion can be a shield for minorities within a community against majority orthodoxy. The archetypal endorsement problem is state-orchestrated prayer in public schools. In this scenario, government is *proselytizing*. It becomes an instrument for propagating mainstream religion, with dissidents either persuaded, submissive, or publicly identified and exposed to ostracism.[8] Federal courts, which are theoretically more insulated from ordinary political pressure, are then called on to comfort these minorities. But on this account, impaneling a local jury drawn from a fair cross-section of the community would be, to put it politely, counterproductive. The endorsement test was written for and by "outsiders."

The test does more than protect impressionable children, however, and powerful criticisms have been leveled at it. One is that judges manipulate the test to reflect their own tastes for religion, and in a way that provides insufficient warning of what will prompt judicial rebuke. This objection might gain ammunition from the

---

[3] See *Lynch v Donnelly*, 465 US 668, 694 (1984) (O'Connor, J, concurring); *Joki v Board of Educ. of Schuylerville Cent. Sch. Dist.*, 745 F Supp 823, 829–30 (NDNY 1990).

[4] Or vice versa. See generally Part II.A.

[5] See, e.g., *Capitol Sq. Rev. & Advisory Bd. v Pinette*, 515 US 753, 779–80 (1995) (O'Connor, J, concurring) (likening the reasonable observer to the reasonable person in tort law).

[6] See Restatement (Third) of Torts: Liability for Physical Harm § 8, cmt b (Proposed Final Draft, 2005).

[7] See, e.g., *Jenkins v Georgia*, 418 US 153, 157 (1974). One might guess that courts do not trust the average non-judge to decide matters touching on religion. But jury participation in employment-discrimination cases is to the contrary. See, e.g., *Johnson v Spencer Press of Maine, Inc.*, 364 F3d 368, 372–75 (1st Cir 2004).

[8] See *Abington Sch. Dist. v Schempp*, 374 US 203, 224 (1963).

split decisions in last Term's Ten Commandments cases.[9] Much doctrine is subject to similar assault, but the endorsement test is especially vulnerable. It seems focused on relatively minor injuries, like offensiveness to adult sensibility, and it is often difficult to predict whether judicial intervention will cause more outrage than it remedies. With the departure of Justice O'Connor—the author and most committed supporter of the endorsement notion—there is a good chance that the test will retire along with her. In fact, because the test is so keyed to judicial perception, a change in personnel almost necessarily changes the rule.

There is another perspective by which a version of the endorsement test might be salvaged—an *anti-sorting* perspective. Religious messages can be used not only to persuade or ostracize existing community members, they can also signal the community's character to non-members. Depending on the preferences of these outsiders, the message might be either enticing or repugnant. Hurt feelings and inculcation are not the immediate problems, however. The issue is government amplifying a cultural facet of the community and recipients of the message sorting themselves accordingly.[10] A political community's religious character and power structure are not transparent at a glance. Government-approved religious symbols can speak to those matters, thereby helping to achieve a preferred religious composition for the polity. And this is true even if no one changes their religious identity or feels pressure to do so. Proselytizing is not required to prompt sorting. Conceptually the difference is between a sign inside the local schoolhouse reading "Come to Jesus," and a sign at the town border reading, "Come to Corpus Christi, Population 98% Christian."[11] The first sign clearly proselytizes but both could encourage sorting.

Government messages about religion might therefore be assessed under two principles: anti-proselytism and anti-sorting. These principles can coexist but they are not redundant. Government officials could maximize religious homogeneity across political jurisdictions

---

[9] See *McCreary County v ACLU of Ky.*, 125 S Ct 2722 (2005); *Van Orden v Perry*, 125 S Ct 2854 (2005); Parts I & II.A.

[10] Compare Charles M. Tiebout, *A Pure Theory of Local Expenditures*, 64 J Pol Econ 416, 418 & n 12 (1956) (modeling local government competition for mobile citizens). I use the terms "symbols" and "messages" interchangeably.

[11] See Part II.B. For use of signaling theory in support of anti-proselytism rather than anti-sorting principles, see Richard H. McAdams, *An Attitudinal Theory of Expressive Law*, 79 Or L Rev 339, 383–89 (2000) (bolstering an anti-caste mission).

without overtly proselytizing (e.g., by gerrymandering municipal boundaries), and they might proselytize without prompting inter-local sorting (e.g., by promoting monotheism through federal government mouthpieces). The implications of an anti-sorting principle, moreover, stretch well beyond religious symbols.[12] First, an anti-sorting perspective deepens our understanding of founding era religious establishments. They might be better characterized as efforts to sort rather than inculcate. Second, the principle can be attached to the nationalizing spirit of the Reconstruction Amendments, along with subsequent judicial and theoretical suggestions that religious faiths should not be divided by political boundaries. Such division risks group polarization across jurisdictions, as well as traditional non-establishment and free-exercise violations within those jurisdictions. Third, an anti-sorting principle recommends a slant in other constitutional doctrine drafted by courts. For example, national standards for religious liberty would be better than local political discretion and the resulting policy variance. In any case, an anti-sorting principle is linked to deep questions about cultural pluralism and government institutions.[13] Whatever are its imperfections, triviality is not one.

But any anti-sorting principle must meet a new set of challenges.[14]

---

[12] See Part III.A.–B.

[13] See generally Peter H. Schuck, *Diversity in America: Keeping Government at a Safe Distance* (2003); Will Kymlicka and Wayne Norman, *Citizenship in Culturally Diverse Societies: Issues, Contexts, Concepts*, in Will Kymlicka and Wayne Norman, eds, *Citizenship in Diverse Societies* 1 (2000). Occasionally these discussions reach religion and the law literature—which has been heavy on political theory and selected precedent, but lighter on history, sociology, and empirical knowledge. See, e.g., Thomas C. Berg, *Religion, Race, Segregation, and Districting: Comparing Kiryas Joel with Shaw/Miller*, 26 Cumb L Rev 365 (1996); Robert M. Cover, *The Supreme Court, 1982 Term—Forward: Nomos and Narrative*, 97 Harv L Rev 4, 26–33 (1983); Christopher L. Eisgruber, *The Constitutional Value of Assimilation*, 96 Colum L Rev 87 (1996) (hereafter Eisgruber, *Assimilation*); Christopher L. Eisgruber, *Madison's Wager: Religious Liberty in the Constitutional Order*, 89 Nw U L Rev 347 (1995) (hereafter Eisgruber, *Madison*); Judith Lynn Failer, *The Draw and Drawbacks of Religious Enclaves in a Constitutional Democracy: Hasidic Public Schools in Kiryas Joel*, 72 Ind L J 383 (1997); Abner S. Greene, *Kiryas Joel and Two Mistakes About Equality*, 96 Colum L Rev 1 (1996); Sanford Levinson, *On Political Boundary Lines, Multiculturalism, and the Liberal State*, 72 Ind L J 403 (1997); Sanford Levinson, *Some Reflections on Multiculturalism, "Equal Concern and Respect," and the Establishment Clause of the First Amendment*, 27 U Richmond L Rev 989 (1993); Ira C. Lupu, *Uncovering the Village of Kiryas Joel*, 96 Colum L Rev 104 (1996); see also Schuck, *Diversity in America*, ch 7; Richard C. Schrager, *The Role of the Local in the Doctrine and Discourse of Religious Liberty*, 117 Harv L Rev 1810 (2004) (arguing that local-government action should be another factor in Establishment Clause doctrine); Steven H. Shiffrin, *The Pluralistic Foundations of the Religion Clauses*, 90 Cornell L Rev 9, 89–90 (2004) (discussing religious instruction).

[14] See Part III.B.–C.

One task is practical. The principle must be elaborated in a way that is concrete, coherent, and administrable, especially if courts will be involved. Options range from modest versions that prohibit government action only if it purposely pushes citizens to separate along political boundaries, to more assertive versions that inhibit less intentional facilitation of religious sorting, or that demand affirmative government action to achieve religious "diversity." A possible legal analogue is racial segregation, but the constitutional arguments play out differently with respect to religion. A related problem for any anti-sorting principle is normative. A mixture of religious views within each political jurisdiction is a contentious mission. Local homogeneity can be a virtue, as Charles Tiebout and his followers have tried to demonstrate. Religious symbols could be roughly accurate representations of community character and therefore helpful warnings or welcome signs. As well, much about the sociology of religious sorting in America is unknown.

In some ways, the endorsement test is caught between a marginal goal that produces as much animosity as reconciliation, and a monumental goal that is encumbered with normative, positive, and practical difficulties. Not every relevant question can be answered here; and I will conclude that current knowledge supports only a modest anti-sorting principle that is judicially enforceable.[15] This is nevertheless an important supplement to present understandings of constitutionally problematic religious establishments. Without preempting the field, an anti-sorting perspective exposes unrecognized features of old and new controversies, it fits with judicial skepticism about local treatment of religion, and it gives reason to pay attention to symbolic battles.[16]

I. DECALOGUES

Last Term, the Supreme Court decided two cases involving Ten Commandments renderings. In a practical sense, however, a third display was under consideration: the Court's own frieze of lawgivers.[17] One of them is located in the courtroom, above and to

---

[15] See text accompanying notes 199–204, 252.

[16] Religious sorting in state and local governments is the concern. I set aside religiously homogenous electoral districts, which raise distinct issues. See Part III.B.1. Nor do I discuss sorting across national boundaries.

[17] See Office of the Curator, Supreme Court of the United States, *Information Sheet: Courtroom Friezes: North and South Walls* (2000), online at http://www.supremecourtus.gov/about/north&southwalls.pdf.

the left of the bench from the Justices' perspective. In this rendering, Moses is holding two tablets representing the Commandments. But only the second half of the Decalogue is visible at all; that portion is written in Hebrew and mostly obscured by Moses's body. He is squeezed between Hammurabi and Solomon, not far from Menes of Egypt and Lycurgus of Sparta—thus set within a line of a dozen other figures, like a Metro car full of lawgivers at rush hour. Whatever one's aesthetic tastes, the frieze is an impressive enough achievement as a matter of craft, which should be no surprise. Its specific content and shape were delegated to a skilled architectural sculptor who was responsible for other pieces of national culture, like the design of the dime.[18]

Uncertainty surrounded the outcome of the two docketed cases, but the Court's own use of religion-connected imagery was not at risk. The aesthetic character of Washington, D.C., is a safe harbor. Even Justice Brennan's dissent in *Lynch v Donnelly*[19]—which opposed seasonal municipal displays of a Nativity scene accompanied by less religious symbols—made an effort to preserve "In God We Trust" on the national coinage and "under God" in the Pledge of Allegiance.[20] When a challenge to voluntary recitation of the Pledge reached the Court, a majority dodged the merits on a novel standing theory and the rest proclaimed their support for such nationalistic references to monotheism.[21] These messages are not inclusive enough to reach several prominent religions in the United States, and calling them "nondenominational" is a bit of unearned self-congratulation. If there were 20 million Hindus and 20 million Buddhists in this country the judiciary and Congress might think differently.[22] But maybe current practice is close enough for con-

---

[18] See Sydney P. Noe, *The Medallic Work of A. A. Weinman*, 7 Numismatic Notes & Monographs 1, 8 (1921).

[19] 465 US 668 (1984).

[20] Id at 716–17 (Brennan, J, dissenting) (expressing uncertainty but offering arguments).

[21] See *Elk Grove Unified Sch. Dist. v Newdow*, 124 S Ct 2301, 2305 (2004); id at 2316–20 (Rehnquist, CJ, concurring) (reaching the merits); id at 2323–27 (O'Connor, J, concurring) (same, listing factors for a ceremonial-deism safe harbor); id at 2327, 2330 (Thomas, J, concurring) (same, relying on a modest anti-coercion rule and resistance to incorporation).

[22] See Ariela Keysar, Barry A. Kosmin, and Egon Mayer, *American Religious Identification Survey* 6, 13 (2001) (hereafter ARIS Survey) (reporting results of a national telephone survey of 50,000 adults and estimating that, in 2001, there were 1,182,000 self-identified Buddhists and 766,000 Hindus—numbers more than double the results in a similar 1990 study); see also Roger Finke and Rodney Stark, *The Churching of America, 1776–2005: Winners and Losers in Our Religious Economy* 241 (2d ed 2005) (reporting larger numbers).

stitutional work, and in any event the ceremonial deism that Washington ordinarily produces is protected from judicial interference.

The two cases on the docket presented questions about state and local displays. The state-sanctioned display was, almost literally, a fifty-year-old version of the Commandments. Among English-speaking adherents to the Hebrew Bible, there is no "the" Ten Commandments. Different Bibles differently translate the Book of Exodus from Hebrew to English. Some of the differences are organizational or structural (like numbering and therefore grouping); others are textual. One potentially important choice is between an injunction against "kill[ing]" or "murder[ing]."[23] Those who created the monument at issue in *Van Orden v Perry*[24] understood this. Ultimately working with a private civic association, a committee representing Protestants, Catholics, and Jews selected the wording for a Ten Commandments monument.[25] It is not a transcription from any Bible of which I am aware. The structure looks Lutheran while the text seems to be an excerpt from the Protestant King James version.[26] Perhaps hundreds of such monuments were distributed throughout the country, at least ostensibly in an effort to reduce juvenile delinquency.[27] One six-foot-high monument ended up on the capitol grounds in Austin, Texas:

> I AM the LORD thy God.
> Thou shalt have no other gods before me.
> Thou shalt not make to thyself any graven images.
> Thou shalt not take the Name of the Lord thy God in vain.
> Remember the Sabbath day, to keep it holy.
> Honor thy father and thy mother, that thy days may be long
>   upon the land which the Lord thy God giveth thee.
> Thou shalt not kill.
> Thou shalt not commit adultery.
> Thou shalt not steal.

---

[23] Compare *The Holy Bible: Authorized King James Version* 72 (World Publishing Co., 1972) ("Thou shalt not kill.") and *The Holy Bible: Confraternity-Douay Version* 98 (Catholic Book Publishing Co., 1961) ("You shall not kill."), with *Tanakh: The Holy Scriptures* 116 (Jewish Publication Soc., 1985) ("You shall not murder.") and *The Access Bible: New Revised Standard Version* 96 (Oxford, 1999) (same); id at 96 n c ("Or *kill*"). An accessible discussion that emphasizes the textual and possible substantive differences is Paul Finkelman, *The Ten Commandments on the Courthouse Lawn and Elsewhere*, 73 Fordham L Rev 1477 (2005).

[24] 125 S Ct 2854 (2005).

[25] See *Books v City of Elkhart*, 235 F3d 292, 294 (7th Cir 2000).

[26] See Finkelman, 73 Fordham L Rev at 1492 (cited in note 23).

[27] See *Van Orden*, 125 S Ct at 2878 (Stevens, J, dissenting).

Thou shalt not bear false witness against thy neighbor.
Thou shalt not covet thy neighbor's house.
Thou shalt not covet thy neighbor's wife, nor his manservant, nor his maidservant, nor his cattle, nor anything that is thy neighbor's.

PRESENTED TO THE PEOPLE AND YOUTH OF TEXAS
BY THE FRATERNAL ORDER OF EAGLES OF TEXAS 1961[28]

If one takes the capitol grounds as the frame, the Eagle's monument is not alone. It was placed among several others dedicated to historical events and good deeds of factions within the state.[29] In a sense, the Texas display is more reflective of private social movements, but its surroundings have an ecumenical quality similar to the Court's frieze.

The county-level display in *McCreary County v ACLU of Kentucky*[30] was the least cosmopolitan of the three. The Ten Commandments element consisted of a framed sheet of paper. It was surrounded by other documents, such as the Declaration of Independence, which have at best a tangential historical relationship to the Decalogue. County officials chose to transcribe in more detail the King James version from its Book of Exodus and, unlike the Texas monument, the document was so labeled.[31] As such the remainder of the text and structure was similar to the Eagles's choices forty years earlier yet distinct.[32] The warning about graven images was reprinted in full, closing with a penalty clause: "for I the LORD thy God am a jealous God, visiting the iniquity of the fathers upon the children unto the third and fourth generation of them that hate me." Taking the Lord's name in vain was supplemented with a second caution: "for the LORD will not hold him guiltless that taketh his name in vain." And the final clauses on coveting are grouped together, altering the implied numbering of the Commandments.[33] No outside organization appears to have motivated the display, although a county resolution indicates officials wanted

---

[28] See id at 2873–74, 2891.

[29] See id at 2858 (plurality opinion of Rehnquist, CJ).

[30] 125 S Ct 2722 (2005). In the text, I am referring to the third and final version.

[31] See id at 2730.

[32] See id at 2730–31; Letter from Nancy Rankin, ACLU of Ky, to Adam Samaha, University of Chicago Law School 2 (Oct 24, 2005) (on file with the author) (reproducing the display).

[33] McCreary's document also referred to coveting "ox" and "ass" rather than "cattle."

to show support for Roy Moore,[34] and the county was working around federal court supervision.[35] Residents took up a collection for litigation expenses.[36] So the local version was more home-grown, sectarian, and contemporary than its state and national counterparts.

Perhaps the results should have been predicted. The Court permitted the state's display and prohibited the county's. The former was closer to the frieze and the Pledge. Although the Court was divided and relied on the county's alleged purpose of endorsing religion,[37] the differences in content among the displays are notable. Not every locality would produce a display like McCreary's, of course. One would expect Chicago's population and politics to differ from those of Kentucky coal country. The point is that decentralizing religious symbolism produces messages often different from comparable national efforts, and with meaningful variance among localities. Judged by self-identification, no religion exceeds 25 percent of the national population;[38] but localizing decisions changes the mixture of religious values.

II. Missions

The question is whether anyone, especially courts, should care about the way government is decorated. The textual hooks are of course the First and Fourteenth Amendments.[39] But conventional sources of interpretation leave important questions open. So courts select particular problems for attention, which begs the question about religious symbolism cases. Nobody is losing the right to vote, or speak, or receive tangible government benefits; nobody is formally compelled to attend or not attend religious ceremonies; nobody is taxed to pay for substantial material benefits to religious causes. And yet Supreme Court majorities have supported an en-

---

[34] See *McCreary*, 125 S Ct at 2729. Moore ultimately lost his well-publicized effort to maintain a Ten Commandments monument at the Alabama State Judicial Building. See, e.g., *Glassroth v Moore*, 335 F3d 1282 (11th Cir), cert denied, 540 US 1000 (2003).

[35] See, e.g., *ACLU of Ky. v Pulaski County*, 96 F Supp 2d 691, 702 (ED Ky 2000).

[36] See Letter from Jimmie W. Greene, McCreary County, to Adam Samaha, University of Chicago Law School 1 (Oct 21, 2005) (on file with the author) (recollecting that little money was collected in the defense fund and that the money was spent on radio and newspaper advertisements).

[37] See text accompanying note 74.

[38] See ARIS Survey at 12–13 (cited in note 22).

[39] See *Everson v Board of Educ. of Ewing Township*, 330 US 1, 14–15 (1947).

dorsement test that sometimes prohibits government affiliation with religious messages.

This section offers two possible justifications. The first is conventional wisdom: courts are enforcing a principle against state proselytizing, which attends to direct psychic and cultural impact within a static community membership. On its own, that principle probably cannot sustain the endorsement test in its current form. The second justification has not been noticed but its objective is far from trivial. It can be expressed as an anti-sorting principle, which is generally opposed to religiously monolithic localities. As applied to religious symbols, the concern is people judging the religious character of a community and then sorting themselves accordingly. Unlike anti-proselytism, an anti-sorting principle may apply even if nobody is offended, convinced, or ostracized.

A. ORTHODOXY: GOVERNMENT PROSELYTIZING

In 1984, Justice O'Connor suggested a refashioning of Establishment Clause doctrine around the idea of non-endorsement. Attempting to capture the essence of the clause, she asserted that government must not act with the purpose or effect of endorsing religion over non-religion, or one religion over another.[40] More generally, religion should not be relevant to anyone's "standing in the political community."[41] "In" has unappreciated significance. It indicates that the test targets localities that treat some of their current members *as if* they were outsiders. Prohibited endorsement informs religious nonadherents that they are "outsiders, not full members of the political community," and it conveys to adherents that they are "insiders, favored members of the political community."[42]

The endorsement test became popular with some, but it failed to unify the field. Justices most skeptical of government benefits flowing to religion embraced the test, sometimes forging major-

---

[40] See *Lynch v Donnelly*, 465 US 668, 688, 690 (1984) (O'Connor, J, concurring) (stating that government may not disapprove of religion, either); cf. *Lemon v Kurtzman*, 403 US 602, 612–13 (1970) (referring to secular purpose, religious effect, and excessive entanglement).

[41] *Lynch*, 465 US at 687 (O'Connor, J, concurring).

[42] Id at 688 ("Disapproval sends the opposite message.").

ities.[43] In addition, some commentators were excited. A strong form of the test fit with certain "neutrality" theories of the religion clauses,[44] and some scholars saw an opportunity to merge race issues under the Equal Protection Clause.[45] But the test never fulfilled these hopes. Endorsement did not become the sole touchstone for Establishment Clause claims; the Supreme Court did not adopt neutrality toward religion as a guiding principle in any strong form;[46] and unsuccessful challenges to displays of the Confederate battle flag[47] suggested the idea of non-endorsement might be an orphan in constitutional law.

Moreover, the endorsement test prompts strange questions. It might make a difference whether the government mails checks to religious organizations according to the number of people they serve, or instead sends the checks to individuals who will then sign them over to those same organizations.[48] Such inquiries seem unhelpful at best. It might be important that individual beneficiaries choose whether their religious service providers receive state funding, but that does not depend on the immediate recipient of the funds. And it is hard to see the good use for such perception-

---

[43] See, e.g., *Santa Fe Indep. Sch. Dist. v Doe*, 530 US 290, 308 (2000) (addressing a system facilitating prayer before high school football games); *County of Allegheny v ACLU Greater Pittsburgh Ch.*, 492 US 573, 593 (1989) (addressing a Nativity scene in a county courthouse).

[44] See, e.g., Douglas Laycock, *Theology Scholarships, the Pledge of Allegiance, and Religious Liberty: Avoiding the Extremes but Missing the Liberty*, 118 Harv L Rev 155, 177, 223 (2004); Arnold H. Loewy, *Rethinking Government Neutrality Toward Religion Under the Establishment Clause: The Untapped Potential of Justice O'Connor's Thought*, 64 NC L Rev 1049, 1055–59, 1069 (1986).

[45] See Kenneth L. Karst, *The First Amendment, the Politics of Religion and the Symbols of Government*, 27 Harv CR-CL L Rev 503, 512–25 (1992).

[46] See, e.g., *Zelman v Simmons-Harris*, 536 US 639 (2002); *Mitchell v Helms*, 530 US 793 (2000). In fact, Justice O'Connor initially promoted her test as a way to *preserve* some state action benefiting religion, such as exemptions from secular regulation and mere "acknowledgment" of American religious heritage. See *Lynch*, 465 US at 691–93 (O'Connor, J, concurring).

[47] See *Coleman v Miller*, 117 F3d 527, 530–31 (11th Cir 1997) (per curiam), cert denied, 523 US 1011 (1998); *NAACP v Hunt*, 891 F2d 1555, 1565 (11th Cir 1990) ("The federal judiciary is not empowered to make decisions based on social sensitivity."); *Mississippi Div. of United Sons of Confederate Veterans v Mississippi State Conf. of NAACP Branches*, 774 So2d 388, 389–90 (Miss 2000); *Daniels v Harrison County Bd. of Supervisors*, 722 So2d 136, 137 (Miss 1998); cf. *Briggs v Mississippi*, 331 F3d 499, 502, 508 (5th Cir 2003) (rejecting an Establishment Clause attack on the St. Andrews-cross-like element of the Confederate battle flag, which is incorporated into the Mississippi state flag), cert denied, 540 US 1108 (2004).

[48] See *Mitchell*, 530 US at 842–43 (O'Connor, J, concurring) (referring to public perceptions).

centered questions in adjudicating emerging controversies, like exemptions from conditions on government subsidies for religious recipients. Before she retired, Justice O'Connor herself openly doubted that the Establishment Clause could be sensibly implemented in one test.[49]

Non-endorsement is now restricted in scope but it remains vital in the government-speech context.[50] One reason is heritage. It is an extension of the school prayer cases decided in the 1960s.[51] They dealt with government officials delivering religious messages to children in public schools, which were provided at no extra charge to parents who were legally obligated to educate their children somewhere. The exact effect of these religious exercises is not really known. Some children surely accepted the content already, or were deaf to it; others might have been inculcated, or identified themselves as dissenters by not participating.[52] In any case, the Court held government proselytizing intolerable in this setting—even if students were formally permitted to opt out.[53] Although the Court sought to prohibit more than conventional coercion,[54] there was unmistakable attention to circumstances of persuasion. The gist of the endorsement test in its present form is not far removed from anti-proselytism. It is supposed to shield community members from government-backed messages that make them feel like outsiders.[55]

---

[49] See *Board of Educ. of Kiryas Joel Vill. Sch. Dist. v Grumet*, 512 US 722, 718–21 (1994) (O'Connor, J, concurring).

[50] See id at 720 (suggesting this application).

[51] The word was even used. See *Engel v Vitale*, 370 US 421, 436 (1962) (acknowledging that the "governmental endorsement" of a prayer might seem insignificant); *Abington Sch. Dist. v Schempp*, 374 US 203, 257 n 23 (1963) (Brennan, J, concurring), quoting Letter of Dec 7, 1871, to Rev D. McAlister, in Charles Bradley, ed, *Miscellaneous Writings of the Late Hon. Joseph P. Bradley* 357–58 (1901) ("The Constitution was evidently framed and adopted . . . to avoid all appearance even of a State religion, or a State endorsement of any particular creed or religious sect."); see also, e.g., *Lowe v City of Eugene*, 463 P2d 360, 363 (Or 1969) (addressing a publicly displayed religious symbol), cert denied, 397 US 1042 (1970).

[52] See *Schempp*, 374 US at 205–12 (noting opt-out rights and describing trial testimony).

[53] Contrast *West Va. Bd. of Educ. v Barnette*, 319 US 624, 642 (1943), which thundered, "no official, high or petty, can prescribe what shall be orthodox in politics, nationalism, religion, or other matters of opinion," yet allowed flag-salute ceremonies to go on with formal opt-out rights.

[54] See *Schempp*, 374 US at 223; *Engel*, 370 US at 431; accord *Lee v Weisman*, 505 US 577, 587 (1992).

[55] See *Wallace v Jaffree*, 472 US 38, 70 (1985) (O'Connor, J, concurring) (worrying about pressure on non-adherents and quoting *Engel*, 370 US at 431).

Criticism of the test has not been so much about its origins as its alleged extravagance and self-reference.[56] Judicial proponents of the test seem fixated on stand-alone psychological injuries that might not be judicially cognizable in other fields of constitutional law.[57] There is a long distance between feelings of alienation produced by government symbols and those produced by more severe manifestations of second-class citizenship, such as the inability to receive cash benefits, to vote, or to hold office. This is not to dismiss emotional injury as beneath concern.[58] The doctrine, moreover, might be defended as prophylactic. Perhaps fearing manipulation of religious culture by the state, courts intervene at the threat's outer boundaries. But the intervention is not cost-free. Soothing secular and religious minorities in this way can incite the hostility of local majorities. Even if locals are not apoplectic about having to modify a religious display (the stakes might be judged equally low for supporters of these messages), national interest groups are sometimes happy to bear litigation costs. In fact, these groups might gain by *losing* on the merits.[59] And at least equally important problems—public symbols associated with racism—were left unaddressed.[60]

Furthermore, a test that is too restrictive will prevent real gains

---

[56] Especially helpful critiques are Jesse H. Choper, *The Endorsement Test: Its Status and Desirability*, 18 J L & Pol 499 (2002), and Steven D. Smith, *Symbols, Perceptions, and Doctrinal Illusions: Establishment Neutrality and the "No Endorsement" Test*, 86 Mich L Rev 266 (1987).

[57] See *Allen v Wright*, 468 US 737, 755 (1984) (recognizing racial stigma as a cognizable injury *if* the litigant was personally denied equal treatment); cf. *United States v Hays*, 515 US 737, 744–45 (1995) (denying standing to *non*-residents of a congressional district allegedly gerrymandered by race, yet indicating residents have standing because of the *risks* of representational harm).

[58] Converting emotional harm into a damages figure is challenging but this does not mean there is *no* harm. Nor are religious symbolism cases get-rich-quick schemes. Damages are rarely at issue.

[59] Compare Alan Cooperman, *Christian Groups Plan More Monuments*, Washington Post (June 28, 2005) A6 (reporting that both sides "said the displays are now the frontline of a proxy war, standing in for the bigger issue of the place of religion in public life").

[60] Compare Jesse H. Choper, *Securing Religious Liberty: Principles for Judicial Interpretation of the Religion Clauses* 101–02 (1996) (arguing that racially stigmatizing messages are the greater concern). But cf. *Virginia v Black*, 538 US 343, 361–63 (2003) (permitting states to punish cross burning with intent to intimidate, given certain safeguards). For a nuanced account of Confederate monuments, see Sanford Levinson, *Written in Stone: Public Monuments in Changing Societies* 76–77, 104–10 (1998) (indicating some government use of religious symbols should be judicially policed, but not existing Confederate battle flags). For other views on flags, see Bennett Capers, *Flags*, 48 Howard L J 121 (2004), and James Foreman, Jr., Note, *Driving Dixie Down: Removing the Confederate Flag from Southern State Capitols*, 101 Yale L J 505 (1991).

toward *secular* goals. Cobb County, Georgia's, stickers for biology textbooks ("Evolution is a theory, not a fact . . . .") were crudely phrased, but they were apparently bundled with the decision to make instruction on evolution mandatory instead of optional.[61] If religious opposition to such instruction was widespread and if the participants were acting in good faith, it might have made sense to exchange a sign of respect for a broader education in mainstream science. Probably no other scientific theory is so accepted within the discipline and so openly doubted in public opinion.[62] Compromise on educational method is a delicate matter, but a judicial bar on negotiation might hinder a comprehensive science curriculum.[63]

Then there are issues of vagueness and perspective. Constitutional violations based on religious offense to any one observer would multiply beyond control, so a "reasonable" observer's perspective was adopted.[64] This led to debate about the characteristics of the construct.[65] Perhaps not surprisingly, Justice O'Connor's reasonable observer came to look more and more like the judge who was operating the test: striving for some kind of objectivity, familiar with the history and context of the state action at issue, perhaps misperceiving the government's intended message.[66]

---

[61] See *Selman v Cobb County Sch. Dist.*, 390 F Supp 2d 1286, 1289–97, 1313 (ND Ga 2005) (enjoining use of the stickers). The full text of the sticker is, "This textbook contains material on evolution[.] Evolution is a theory, not a fact, regarding the origin of living things[.] This material should be approached with an open mind, studied carefully, and critically considered." Id at *5. Evolution *is* a theory (regarding species diversity)—but so is gravity, and thus the issue is the district's decision to single out evolution in this way.

[62] See, e.g., Lisa Anderson, *Museums Take Up Evolution Challenge*, Chi Trib (Oct 16, 2005) (reporting results of a 2005 Gallup Poll in which 53 percent of respondents indicated a belief that "God created humans in their present form exactly the way the Bible describes it," 31 percent indicated that God guided a process whereby humans evolved over millions of years from other life forms, and 12 percent indicated that humans evolved but God played no part in the process).

[63] See also Tracey Meares and Kelsi Brown Corkran, *When 2 or 3 Come Together*, University of Chicago Public Law Working Paper No. 107 (Oct 2005) (discussing police use of a religious message to help organize church leaders).

[64] See, e.g., *McCreary County v ACLU of Ky.*, 125 S Ct 2722, 2737 (2005); *Elk Grove Unified Sch. Dist. v Newdow*, 124 S Ct 2301, 2321 (2004) (O'Connor, J, concurring); see also *Santa Fe Indep. Sch. Dist. v Doe*, 530 US 290, 308 (2000) (assuming the perspective of an objective high school student at a football game).

[65] Compare *Capitol Sq. Rev. & Advisory Bd. v Pinette*, 515 US 753, 780–82 (1995) (O'Connor, J, concurring) (assuming more knowledge), with id at 807–08 & n 14 (Stevens, J, dissenting) (assuming less knowledge).

[66] See id at 776–77, 780–82 (O'Connor, J, concurring) (intimating that the reasonable observer can be reasonably confused); *Wallace v Jaffree*, 472 US 38, 70 (1985) (O'Connor, J, concurring).

Some of these problems are reparable matters of detail, but the endorsement test is problematic even for those committed to an anti-proselytism principle.

All of which leaves endorsement in a precarious state. In last Term's cases, the fissures were obvious. Although the Court is essentially unanimous on some kind of anti-proselytism principle,[67] several Justices oppose the non-endorsement concept as too stringent, while the test's adherents disagree on its precise content. Thus the Texas monument was left standing by a plurality basically unconcerned with "passive" and non-"coercive" displays of monotheism,[68] plus Justice Breyer, whose pragmatism counseled against sending forklifts to remove this and perhaps hundreds of other decades-old monuments.[69] His opinion was overtly anti-doctrine, claiming to find no guidance in tests and instead pointing to vague principles and a bundle of facts.[70] For example, taking the capitol grounds as the denominator and considering the civic and ecumenical features of the donor, one might see a reflection of several influential components of state heritage without an obtrusive effort to promote religious faith per se. The case did involve government's connection to religious symbols, but not a very effective form of proselytism.

McCreary County's conduct was judged differently. Justice Breyer seemed to revert to a presumption against government attachment to religious content,[71] and he must have guessed that in this instance judicial intervention was worth the resulting local friction. A municipality was changing the aesthetic status quo,

---

[67] Justice Kennedy has written that the government should not proselytize and that a Latin cross on the top of city hall would be unconstitutional. See *County of Allegheny v ACLU Greater Pittsburgh Cb.*, 492 US 573, 661 (1989) (Kennedy, J, concurring in part and dissenting in part). Justice Scalia's dissent in *McCreary County* suggests that government cannot take official positions on live controversies over religious doctrine, see 125 S Ct at 2762 n 12—which presumably would foreclose a national Book of Common Prayer or an official translation of the Hebrew Bible. Justice Thomas is a partial exception because he would not apply Establishment Clause norms to the states, see, e.g., *Newdow*, 124 S Ct at 2328 (Thomas, J, concurring), but he *would* so apply anti-coercion norms from the Free Exercise Clause, see id at 2330, 2333 n 5.

[68] See *Van Orden*, 125 S Ct at 2861 (plurality opinion of Rehnquist, CJ).

[69] Compare id at 2870 (Breyer, J, concurring) (stressing the absence of strife surrounding the monument until this suit, and lack of evidence that the placidity was due to oppression).

[70] See id at 2871.

[71] He joined Justice Souter's majority opinion. To confirm a strong preference for only secular government symbols, we would need to know whether Justice Breyer would invalidate a municipal choice to *remove* a religious symbol from government property despite risks of strife.

partial to the King James Decalogue, and associating itself with Roy Moore's challenge to federal authority. A majority was achieved with three other Justices who strongly prefer government abstention from religious messages, and Justice O'Connor, who connected the issue to freedom of conscience[72] and therefore proselytism. Distinguishing the county's final display from the Texas version was tricky, though. Its Decalogue was joined with several documents lacking religious content.[73] So the majority concentrated on the legislative and litigation history, condemning what it took to be the county's purpose of highlighting religious messages.[74] This strategy is telling, and not only because this purpose suggests a future threat of proselytizing. It indicates concern with how municipalities operate, not just how they look.

But appearances do matter for endorsement purposes and many observers cannot identify a sufficiently important mission for the test. It is a step removed from government proselytizing. It comes with the risk of populist backlash. And it seems to incorporate a self-referential and D.C.-centric religious aesthetic that is foreign to many localities.

B.   REFORMULATION: RELIGIOUS SORTING

There might be another way to justify something like a non-endorsement rule, but it requires a departure from the anti-proselytism perspective. Instead, an anti-sorting principle would animate judicial intervention and oppose the coincidence of political and religious boundaries. There is a connection between anti-sorting and anti-proselytism principles, which will be apparent in the discussion below. For instance, a public school district's decision to promote a literal reading of the Book of Genesis as contradicting and superior to any scientific theory of evolution would be a basis for sorting into and out of that jurisdiction. Anti-proselytism and anti-sorting have different legal implications, however, and they require different justifications.[75] But for all its problems—and they are serious—an anti-sorting principle extends

---

[72] See *McCreary County*, 125 S Ct at 2746 (O'Connor, J, concurring).

[73] See id at 2731 (opinion of the Court).

[74] See id at 2737–41 (noting one display that posted a version of the Decalogue essentially alone and a second that added other texts but emphasized their religious content).

[75] See Part III.A.–B.

the mission of non-endorsement beyond prevention of offense.

To get the gist of how interlocal sorting might work, Charles Tiebout's well-known model is a good place to start. Different people have different preferences for government services and taxation, as well as matters of lifestyle. If we permit state and local governments to offer different policy packages, and if we permit mobile citizens to select among these governments, then (given some additional assumptions) government offerings will better match preset citizen preferences and implementation of these policies should be easier. Voting and other forms of voice might be far less significant than the dynamic created by citizens with an exit option. In fact, a big selling point for the model was that, through migration, citizen preferences for public goods would be credibly revealed to government officials.[76]

But the model then adds a strong assumption about the knowledge of *citizens*. It assumes consumer-voters have perfect information about the available policy packages.[77] Certain municipal features, like property taxes or road conditions, are easy to ascertain. Others are not. How people interact, their preferences beyond policy, the set of informal associations, the social hierarchy, the political power structure, and other elements of "community character" are difficult to grasp at a glance—at least in the absence of an effort by insiders to signal outsiders. Whether deciding on where to reside, recreate, retire, or work, outsiders will often care about these intangible features of a community.

A community's religious character may fall into the second category. Unlike race,[78] one's religion is not necessarily a visible feature. Looking at people is a low-probability tool for an outsider seeking knowledge about neighborhood religion. And reliable demographic data on religion are surprisingly difficult to obtain. Again unlike race, for which statistics are available decennially at the micro-levels of census tract and block,[79] religious-affiliation data are no longer collected by the federal government.[80] County-

---

[76] See Tiebout, 64 J Pol Econ at 418–19 (cited in note 10).

[77] See id at 419 (assumption 2 regarding "full knowledge").

[78] In its socially defined sense. See Pierre L. Van den Berghe, *Race and Racism: A Comparative Perspective* 9 (1967) (incorporating physical criteria into the definition).

[79] The data are available at http://www.census.gov. For census purposes, "race" is self-reported and so responses will not necessarily track social definitions of race.

[80] Between 1850 and 1936, the Census Bureau collected membership data from religious organizations. See 1 U.S. Bureau of the Census, *Historical Statistics of the United States:*

level data are assembled by private parties,[81] but even these numbers are not entirely dependable. Because the survey depends on reporting by participating religious organizations, sometimes total reported religious membership will exceed the best estimate of the total population; on other occasions the "unclaimed" population is implausibly high.[82] Thus we can conclude with reasonable confidence—and from any personal computer with Internet access—that in the year 2000 there were approximately 17,080 McCreary County residents, of whom 108 identified themselves as African American or black, nearly all of whom lived in the Pine Knot area. But the fraction of the county's 2000 population unclaimed by any participating religious organization is 76 percent.[83] This number cannot say anything meaningful about religious life and power in the county, given a local government that defended multiple Ten Commandments displays against costly ACLU-backed litigation.[84]

Even if demographic data on religion were perfect, sorting would still be more difficult than a Tiebout enthusiast would prefer. Aside from speech restrictions on real estate agents inspired by the Fair Housing Act,[85] there is the question of local political power. This will never be transparent from demographic information. More is needed, and a government's chosen symbols can

---

Colonial Times to 1970 at 389 (1975); Finke and Stark, *The Churching of America* at 16, 295 n 4 (cited in note 22). Although no religion data were collected by the Bureau after the 1940s, in 1976 Congress prohibited the Bureau from making religion-related questions mandatory. See Pub L No 94-521, § 13(3), 90 Stat 2459 (1976) (codified at 13 USC § 221(c)).

[81] See *Religious Congregations and Membership in the United States 2000: An Enumeration by Region, State and County Based on Data Reported for 149 Religious Bodies* (Dale E. Jones et al, eds, 2001) (hereafter ASARB Data).

[82] See generally id at xv–xvi (listing 39 counties where claimed adherents exceeded census population figures and offering possible explanations); id at xiii–xiv (noting that none of the historically African-American denominations participated in the 2000 survey).

[83] See id at 209.

[84] Among reported adherents, however, there is significant agreement: the Southern Baptist Convention claims 83 percent (3,368) of all adherents (4,068); the next most numerous are United Methodists who claim 8 percent (330). See id (listing seven other groups, including one member of Baha'i).

[85] See notes 206–08 and accompanying text. Whatever is the correct statutory interpretation, real estate agents are sometimes trained to avoid discussing demographics. See Rhonda L. Daniels, *Fair Housing Compliance Guide* 15–16 (1990) (regarding ethnic composition); *Hannah v Sibcy Cline Realtors*, 147 Ohio App 3d 198, 205, 769 NE2d 876, 881 (Ohio Ct App 2001) (describing an agent's practice of referring questions about religion to, for example, the Jewish Federation). But cf. Lior J. Strahilevitz, *Exclusionary Amenities in Residential Communities*, 92 Va L Rev n 17 (forthcoming 2006) (noting that racial steering seems to persist).

help fill the gap. Like a Confederate battle flag hoisted above a public beach[86] or a black-fist sculpture at a city's center,[87] symbols can speak to the mix of decision makers on public questions along with the groups most likely to feel welcome.

The concept is readily extended to religion. As a start, signaling might be done by naming new cities after religious figures—Corpus Christi, Kiryas Joel, Rajneeshpuram, Saint Paul, San Diego.[88] Demographics may change over the decades and renaming municipalities is disruptive, however. Today signaling might be accomplished by placing a large Latin cross at the center of town;[89] depicting religious symbols on city signs, vehicles, and offices;[90] carving religious messages into key government buildings;[91] or zoning a church into a place of pride.[92] In these ways, a political community can inform outsiders or remind insiders of the dominant local culture, and thus help maintain preferred spiritual demographics.

A modern example is the City of Republic in southwestern Mis-

---

[86] Compare *Daniels v Harrison County Bd. of Supervisors*, 722 So2d 136 (Miss 1998) (permitting the flag to stay, along with seven flags that formerly flew over what is now Mississippi).

[87] Compare Pat Zacharias, *The Monuments of Detroit*, Detroit News (2002) (describing and depicting a 24-foot-long, ungloved, horizontal, forearm-and-fist memorial dedicated to boxer Joe Louis).

[88] Compare *Oregon v City of Rajneeshpuram*, 598 F Supp 1208 (D Or 1984) (involving Oregon's refusal to recognize a city in territory developed by followers of the Bhagwan Rajneesh).

[89] Compare *Paulson v City of San Diego*, 294 F3d 1124, 1125–28 (9th Cir 2002) (en banc) (involving a mountaintop plot with a 43-foot-tall cross), cert denied, 538 US 978 (2003).

[90] Compare *Robinson v City of Edmond*, 68 F3d 1226, 1228 (10th Cir 1995) (invalidating a seal that incorporated a cross), cert denied, 517 US 1201 (1996); *Harris v City of Zion*, 927 F2d 1401, 1412–15 (7th Cir 1991) (similar), cert denied, 505 US 1229 (1992); *Friedman v Board of County Comm'rs of Bernalillo*, 781 F2d 777, 782 (10th Cir 1985) (en banc) (similar), cert denied, 476 US 1169 (1986); *ACLU v City of Stow*, 29 F Supp 2d 845, 851–52 (ND Ohio 1998) (similar). But cf. *Murray v City of Austin*, 947 F2d 147, 149, 155 (5th Cir 1991) (permitting a seal in light of its connection to Stephen Austin's coat of arms), cert denied, 505 US 1219 (1992).

[91] Compare *Lambeth v Board of Comm'rs of Davidson County*, 407 F3d 266, 267–68 (4th Cir 2005) (upholding dismissal of a challenge to a decision to inscribe "In God We Trust" in 18-inch block letters on the facade of the County Government Center).

[92] Compare Dianna Smith, *Landmark Church Slated for Ave Maria Development*, Naples Daily News (Mar 25, 2004) (describing plans for a town including Ave Maria University and a 150-foot-tall church with a 40-foot-tall body of Christ). According to one report, the founder of the university indicated the church "is there to remind the people 'what we're about.'" Id. For lists of intentional communities with spiritual missions, see http://directory.ic.org. For a network of Christian real estate agents, see http://www.hismove.com/about_us.htm.

FIG. 1.—Official flag of the City of Republic, Missouri (1991–99). Source: "Flags of the World," http://www.crwflags.com/fotw/flags/us-morep.html.

souri.[93] After running a contest for a city flag and seal, the local government chose an elliptical shape with symbols in four quadrants. On the bottom half were images of a traditional nuclear family and a fish, or *ichthys*, commonly associated with Christianity (see fig. 1). The seal was displayed on city buildings, city vehicles, city stationery, and city-limit signs.[94] A local minister declared that the ACLU had correctly associated the *ichthys* with Jesus Christ, adding, "I say the line is drawn. Stay out of Republic. We're going to stand for Christian principles."[95] Municipalities with exclusively secular missions could send messages equally overt.[96]

One feature of religious faith, moreover, makes public symbols especially useful devices for sorting. Individual religious commitments are relatively opaque. So even if municipalities had constitutional authority to exclude newcomers on the basis of religion—and they do not[97]—signaling community character might still be valuable. It empowers outsiders to *sort themselves* based on

[93] See *Webb v City of Republic*, 55 F Supp 2d 994 (WD Mo 1999).

[94] See id at 995; id at 996 (quoting plaintiff's deposition testimony).

[95] Id at 999 (quoting comments at a board of aldermen meeting, and noting statements of two residents who claimed to have moved into the city because of the *ichthys*); see also id at 996 (explaining that plaintiff and her children moved out). The court enjoined use of the *ichthys*, but on anti-proselytism grounds and without confronting sorting arguments. See id at 1000–01.

[96] See text at note 166 (discussing the southwest Missouri town of Liberal in the late 1800s).

[97] See Part III.A.1.

privately held beliefs.[98] In addition, subsets of outsiders will have greater difficulty clueing in on local religious culture and power. Such information is less easily available to secularists and non-denominational religionists. For members of religious groups, finding co-adherents is usually easy. If organized, these associations often advertise themselves, and might offer information about their comfort within a locality. Perhaps yet again unlike race, shared religious faith usually comes with a social network for adherents.

The endorsement test, however unwittingly, already inhibits such efforts to encourage sorting. Though formulated in the tradition of anti-proselytism, the test's outcomes are not sufficiently predictable to work around with certainty. And supporting religious symbols can be costly, aside from foregone residents. Organizations like the ACLU sometimes sue, attorney's fees are available if a lawsuit is successful,[99] some municipalities are not wealthy, and those with only weak preferences for religious homogeneity are not likely to spend much to fight about it.[100] The costs do cut both ways. Costly signals are credible signals,[101] so current doctrine may facilitate signaling—maybe especially if the government loses in litigation. What better sign of loyalty to religious referents than a bull-headed defense of the state's commitment to religious symbols? On the other hand, there are Rule 11 risks for government lawyers, and few officials are both dedicated to uniformity in religious faith and as confrontational as Roy Moore, in light of the alternatives.

The point about alternatives is worth emphasizing. The case for outsider ignorance is easy to overstate. A variety of *non*-government conduct indicates local religious character: the number, denomination, and location of visibly religious structures (churches, synagogues, mosques, and so forth); Christmas lights on houses; fishlike emblems on cars; "WWJD" pendants on peo-

---

[98] A similar argument is elaborated with respect to private property rights in Lior J. Strahilevitz, *Information Asymmetries and the Rights to Exclude*, 104 Mich L Rev (forthcoming 2006) (discussing "exclusionary vibes").

[99] See 42 USC § 1988.

[100] See John Witte, Jr., *Religion and the American Constitutional Experiment: Essential Rights and Liberties* 173 (2000).

[101] See generally Eric A. Posner, *Law and Social Norms* 18–27 (2000).

ple.[102] Residents were already using the *ichthys* in southwest Missouri when Republic appropriated it;[103] indeed, popular use made it possible for the symbol to serve a sorting function. Furthermore, unavailable information on religious demographics might be dependably correlated with available information, like voting patterns, race, and urban/rural setting.[104] With effort, intelligent people can understand how a locality functions. That said, gradations of difficulty can make a difference in the extent of religious sorting, especially if it is a soft preference for substantial numbers of people.[105] Accurate information about religion and local power, moreover, is especially challenging for an outsider to obtain.

III. ANTI-SORTING PRINCIPLES

The foregoing explains how religious symbols can be used to match a community-preferred character with individual religious identities. This is not a reason to interfere with the sorting process, however, least of all by constitutional law. Remember that Tiebout and his followers built a theory to justify intramunicipal uniformity of preferences, intermunicipal diversity in policy, and competition for residents. So geographic clustering by religion might be welfare enhancing, at least in the short run.

On the other hand, Tiebout sorting is not obviously entrenched in constitutional law. Although courts recognize a constitutional right of interstate migration[106] and a qualified right of private associations to exclude people on some criteria,[107] otherwise the Tiebout model is largely a question of subconstitutional policy.

---

[102] Compare William A. Fischel, *The Homevoter Hypothesis: How Home Values Influence Local Government Taxation, School Finance, and Land-Use Policies* 60–61 (2001) (canvassing studies regarding the likelihood and impact of Tiebout sorting on public school quality).

[103] See *Webb v City of Republic*, 55 F Supp 2d 994, 999 (WD Mo 1999).

[104] Compare Larry L. Hunt and Matthew O. Hunt, *Race, Region, and Religious Involvement: A Comparative Study of Whites and African Americans*, 80 Social Forces 605, 615, 622 (2001) (reporting higher religious participation by African Americans than whites in the urban South).

[105] Compare Darren E. Sherkat, *Religious Intermarriage in the United States: Trends, Patterns, and Predictors*, 33 Social Sci Res 606, 611–13, 619 (2004) (reporting that more than half of surveyed Caucasian marriages were interfaith).

[106] See *Saenz v Roe*, 526 US 489, 500 (1999).

[107] See, e.g., *Boy Scouts of Am. v Dale*, 530 US 640, 659 (2000) (relying on interference with expressive mission). But cf. *Roberts v United States Jaycees*, 468 US 609, 626–27 (1984) (finding insufficient burden on expressive interests to justify gender discrimination in voting).

Neither persons nor groups are constitutionally entitled to a government that mirrors their policy preferences. Furthermore, constitutional case law plainly rejects state-facilitated sorting in some circumstances. Race is the familiar example. Today a city is constitutionally barred from designating residential space for whites only, even if every current resident supports the regulation and regardless of housing opportunities elsewhere.[108] It is easy for us to see government-backed racial separation as part of a caste system, inhibiting individual liberty while reinforcing categorical distinctions between people that now seem irrational at best. Judicial concern with racial sorting, moreover, goes beyond officials outright forcing people to physically separate along racial lines. More subtle forms of encouragement or facilitation sometimes prompt judicial intervention.[109]

Is the Constitution a like impediment to separation along *religious* lines? May government officials intentionally encourage religious sorting across political boundaries? Knowingly facilitate such sorting? Decline to inhibit or remedy such sorting? Perhaps not, but these questions should not be answered by lockstep analogy to race cases. Religion and race are different phenomena. Decades of debating, litigating, legislating, politicking, and theorizing about sorting by race will not simply carry over to religion. For example: (1) our national experience and constitutional traditions differ with respect to religion and race; (2) race, as socially defined, is visible in a way that religion need not be; (3) religion, according to some conceptions, is connected to value systems and organization in ways that race need not be; (4) the number of religions in America is almost countless, whereas the concept of race might produce fewer salient divisions; (5) the desire or impetus for sorting may differ with respect to race and religion. These distinctions indicate the possibility of justifiably different treatment.

Without pretending to offer comprehensive solutions, the rest of this article digs into the constitutional law of religious sorting. It focuses on aspects of the problem that have been underappre-

---

[108] See also *Runyon v McCrary*, 427 US 160, 175–76 (1976) (permitting application of a civil rights statute to private schools with admissions policies that excluded racial minorities).

[109] See *Anderson v Martin*, 375 US 399, 402 (1964) (invalidating a requirement that candidate race be noted on ballots); Part III.B.1. (exploring possible versions of anti-sorting principles).

ciated, including legal history, demographics, and doctrinal implications. Only a humble constitutional rule seems defensible at this time. But to understand the choice set, I will push the anti-sorting arguments much further. For example, an entirely plausible distinction between intentional government mandates and unwitting government facilitation of religious sorting will not be imposed at the outset. Accordingly, the discussion starts with precedent and the best justifications for an anti-sorting principle of any dimension, then turns to more concrete versions and possible implications, and closes with powerful objections to ambitious anti-sorting rules enforced by courts.[110]

A. JUSTIFICATIONS

1. *Sorting precedent.* There are two key building blocks in Supreme Court precedent for an anti-sorting principle. The first is a case about exclusion. Upon learning that a Santeria church was planned for construction within the City of Hialeah, a series of ordinances was adopted.[111] Part of the Santeria faith calls for animal sacrifice, and the practical effect of the ordinances was to outlaw "ritual" animal sacrifice without threatening kosher butchers.[112] The Court unanimously held the ordinances invalid. Going out of its way to teach the locals a lesson, the majority explained that Santeria is a religion for First Amendment purposes even though the city did not argue otherwise.[113] The opinion opened with the observation that local officials "did not understand, failed to perceive, or chose to ignore the fact that their official actions

---

[110] Religious sorting is also a pure policy question, and there are familiar objections to the Tiebout model in any case. Critics argue that, for example: (1) the original model needs a political system, and its assumptions—such as perfect information, no externalities, and dividends providing all income for the citizenry—must be loosened; (2) subsequent empirical work suggests that residential choices are primarily driven by factors other than government services and taxes, like family and employment needs; and (3) Tiebout sorting is normatively controversial if one is committed to certain notions of social equality, voice-based democracy, and public-spirited citizenship. See, e.g., Gerald E. Frug, *City Making: Building Cities Without Walls* 168–73 (1999); Paul W. Rhode and Koleman S. Strumpf, *Assessing the Importance of Tiebout Sorting: Local Heterogeneity from 1850 to 1990*, 93 Am Econ Rev 1648 (2003); Susan Rose-Ackerman, *Beyond Tiebout: Modeling the Political Economy of Local Government*, in George R. Zodrow, ed, *Local Provision of Public Services: The Tiebout Model After Twenty-five Years* 56–57 (1983). But only some of the standard objections are relevant here. They must plausibly relate to constitutional law.

[111] See *Church of the Lukumi Babalu Aye, Inc. v City of Hialeah*, 508 US 520, 526 (1993).

[112] See id at 535–36.

[113] See id at 531; see also id at 541–42 (opinion of Kennedy, J, joined by Stevens, J).

violated the Nation's essential commitment to religious free-dom."[114]

Commentators discuss the Santeria case as a matter of free ex-ercise,[115] and it is surely that. Presumably the same result would obtain if the state of Florida or the federal government adopted the same rules for animal sacrifice. But in the spirit of Tiebout, the Court might have told the newcomers to sort themselves into a more accepting municipality.[116] Or, recognizing that the City of Hialeah could not have guaranteed Santeria space in any other jurisdiction, the Court might have distinguished a hypothetical statewide program that achieved such a guarantee. But nothing in the Court's decision is so pro-sorting. It does not suggest that a municipality may expel a disfavored religion from its territory as long as another municipality stays open. To the contrary, the opin-ion—protecting "the *Nation's* essential commitment" to religious liberty[117]—indicates opposition to sect-targeted and government-backed efforts to achieve local homogeneity. For federal consti-tutional purposes, then, religion looks more like race than wealth: localities may more or less explicitly zone for homogeneity in the latter but not the former.[118] The Court would blanch at overt government efforts to restrict migration of African-Americans to select communities even if 99 percent of residential property within the region remained open. A different result seems unlikely for denominations like Santeria.[119]

---

[114] Id at 524.

[115] See, e.g., Schragger, 117 Harv L Rev at 1852 (cited in note 13).

[116] Compare *City of Renton v Playtime Theatres, Inc.*, 475 US 41, 53–54 (1986) (munic-ipality could isolate sexually explicit movie theaters to 5 percent of the city's total area, even if that left no commercially viable locations); *Miller v California*, 413 US 15, 24 (1973) (permitting community standards to help define obscenity); see also *City of Erie v Pap's A.M.*, 529 US 277, 301–02 (2000) (plurality opinion) (municipality could apply a public nudity ban to nude dancing in strip clubs). But cf. *Schad v Borough of Mt. Ephraim*, 452 US 61, 76 (1981) (municipality violated speech rights by zoning out live entertainment, including nude dancing at an adult bookstore—at least in the absence of evidence that "the kind of entertainment appellants wish to provide is available in reasonably nearby areas"); Mary Anne Case, *Community Standards and the Margin of Appreciation*, 25 Human Rts L J 10, 10–11 (2005) (noting that obscenity law seems to be an outlier).

[117] *Lukumi*, 508 US at 524 (emphasis added).

[118] See *Village of Arlington Heights v Metropolitan Housing Dev. Corp.*, 429 US 252 (1977); *Buchanan v Warley*, 245 US 60, 70–71, 81–82 (1917).

[119] The Court stressed that Santeria had been purposefully and effectively singled out by the city for disfavor, see *Lukumi*, 508 US at 534, 545–46, thereby distinguishing broader legislation with an equally burdensome impact when applied to ritual sacrifice. But this problem of effective substitutes for overt discrimination is not special to anti-sorting principles.

Even so, the Hialeah decision is not entirely anti-sorting. In fact it might be read as *pro*-sorting but anti-*subordination*. In the spirit of *Carolene Products*[120] rather than Charles Tiebout, the Court might have been protecting the interests of non-mainstream religions to sort themselves however they wish. Perhaps Santeria's victory means that the local political unpopularity of a migrant's religion, like her race, is not something she should have to worry about while sorting. But even with a useful concept of "minority religion" within a multitude of faiths, this reading is not quite right. The Court's concern goes beyond empowering minorities to join a locality that prefers to maintain its religious composition.

The point is made by a second and more controversial case. A year after the Hialeah decision, the New York legislature was rebuked for drawing a new public school district at the request of the Satmar Hasidim.[121] The district's boundaries would have matched the Satmars' residential enclave in the Village of Kiryas Joel, and the Court balked at officials consciously aligning political institutions with religious geography.[122] This was true even though both the Satmars and the adjacent community were probably grateful for the partition. The former wanted the new district to provide special education services apart from non-Satmar students, who were a source of discomfort and humiliation for their children.[123]

The ramifications of the case are unclear, however. The decision did not entail invalidation of the Satmars' *village*, for example, even though it was religiously homogenous by any standard.[124]

---

[120] See *United States v Carolene Products Co.*, 304 US 144, 153 n 4 (1938).

[121] See *Board of Educ. of Kiryas Joel Vill. Sch. Dist. v Grumet*, 512 US 687, 690 (1994).

[122] See id at 698–702 & n 6 (plurality opinion) (condemning the act for districting by religious criterion); id at 711 (Stevens, J, concurring) (asserting that the act "affirmatively supports a religious sect's interest in segregating itself"); id at 728 (Kennedy, J, concurring) ("[G]overnment may not use religion as a criterion to draw political or electoral lines."); see also *Larkin v Grendel's Den, Inc.*, 459 US 116 (1982) (invalidating a delegation to churches of veto power over liquor licenses); cf. *Lynch*, 465 US at 687–88 (O'Connor, J, concurring) (condemning "excessive entanglement with religious institutions, which may . . . foster the creation of political constituencies defined along religious lines"); Lupu, 96 Colum L Rev at 108–09 (cited in note 13) (noting residency incentives for Satmars arguably created by the special district).

[123] See *Kiryas Joel*, 512 US at 692; see also id at 691–93 (noting earlier conflicts over zoning and special education at an off-site location); note 2 above (noting *Aguilar* was later overruled).

[124] See *Kiryas Joel*, 512 US at 703 n 7 (distinguishing the village); id at 729–30 (Kennedy, J, concurring) (same).

Why not? The majority's worry was that state officials purpose-fully singled out the Satmars for special treatment in creating the school district; but that problem does not apply to the village.[125] "State action" was needed to get either one, of course. But the state might have been too conscious of sectarian beneficiaries in dealing with the school district, and failed adequately to assure empathy for similarly situated communities. By contrast, the vil-lage's boundaries were generated by a process facially neutral with respect to religion. Any group could seek municipal status by that process.[126] If we assume the Satmar village is constitutionally per-missible, perhaps the state may facilitate sorting by all groups, as long as it does not purposefully facilitate *religious* sorting. On the other hand, an anti-subordination principle might reenter the pic-ture here; it could restrict the benefits of municipal status for religiously monolithic communities to systematic losers in the po-litical process. After all, the Satmars traveled a long way before reaching Kiryas Joel, ultimately seeking village status to escape restrictive zoning ordinances burdening their way of life. The character of any principle underlying the case is thus undefined.

One limit to the Court's opposition to religious sorting should be emphasized here. The attention is on religious cleavages that match political boundaries, but not all boundaries will be policed. This is a fair inference from race cases. A majority of the Court has been concerned when officials draw legislative districts to match racial demographics.[127] Yet dissenters in those cases—all of whom voted to *invalidate* the Satmars' special school district— indicated that religion is a presumptively valid basis on which to draw legislative districts.[128] The majority did not disagree on the

---

[125] See id at 690; id at 717 (O'Connor, J, concurring) (indicating a preference for ac-commodations that benefit both religious *and* secular groups); see also *Grumet v Pataki*, 720 NE2d 66 (NY 1999) (striking a subsequent, nominally neutral statute), cert denied, 528 US 946 (1999).

[126] But cf. *Oregon v City of Rajneeshpuram*, 598 F Supp 1208 (D Or 1984) (refusing to dismiss a state's constitutional objection to the formation of a city by followers of the Bhagwan Rajneesh, which would have been solely composed of a county road and church-owned property).

[127] See, e.g., *Miller v Johnson*, 515 US 900, 910–11 (1995).

[128] See id at 944–45 (Ginsburg, J, dissenting) ("Our Nation's cities are full of districts identified by their ethnic character—Chinese, Irish, Italian, Jewish, Polish, Russian, for example."); *Shaw v Reno*, 509 US 630, 679 (1993) (Stevens, J, dissenting) ("If it is per-missible to draw boundaries to provide adequate representation for rural voters, for union members, for Hasidic Jews, for Polish Americans, or for Republicans, it necessarily follows that it is permissible to do the same thing for members of the very minority group whose

religion point,[129] and nobody contended that such districting needed to relieve religious subordination. Why the free pass on legislative districts?

A simple explanation turns on the different functions served by jurisdictional boundaries. In legislative districting, officials mold the membership of a decision-making body drawn from a given citizenry. Those representatives later assemble and make policy. District lines no doubt affect the legislature's composition, but homogeneity within districts will not necessarily have a serious impact on influence within the assembly. In drawing state and municipal boundaries, however, the citizenry itself is defined. This is important as long as state and local governments retain significant decision-making authority of their own.[130] And homogeneity within such polities is undeniably connected to influence over what is taught in public schools, who enjoys exemptions from regulation, which books show up in public libraries, who runs the local courts, and so on. Religious anti-sorting principles are aimed at the manufacture of such polities.

2. *Sorting experiments and legal change.* Details aside, the Satmar and Santeria decisions indicate that special government efforts to promote religious homogeneity are sometimes invalid. But can we justify, or at least account for, the precedent? Is there a legitimate constitutional foundation for anti-sorting principles?

Arguments from plain text or original meaning at the founding are unlikely suspects. The First Amendment's religion clauses were drafted as restraints on "Congress" and, by logical extension, the rest of the federal government.[131] The posture of state and local governments toward religion was an issue for them to resolve.[132] As such, the Federal Constitution of 1791 was at most agnostic

history in the United States gave birth to the Equal Protection Clause."); Mary Anne Case, *Lessons for the Future of Affirmative Action from the Past of the Religion Clauses?* 2000 Supreme Court Review 325, 340–41.

[129] See *Miller*, 515 US at 918 (indicating that respect for "communities defined by actual shared interests" helps defeat race-based equal protection attacks on legislative districts).

[130] Compare Richard Thompson Ford, *Geography and Sovereignty: Jurisdictional Formation and Racial Segregation*, 49 Stan L Rev 1365 (1997) (arguing that racial segregation at the municipal level is more troubling than in the electoral districting context). Constituent services do connect the function of electoral districts with municipalities, however.

[131] The guarantee might be a dead-letter otherwise, or the conduct of other branches might be traced back to congressional authorization. See also US Const, Art VI, cl 3 (barring religious tests for federal office).

[132] See generally Akhil Reed Amar, *The Bill of Rights: Creation and Reconstruction* 32–34, 41 (1998).

about religious sorting. And the explicit promise that Congress would make no law "respecting" an establishment of religion made the document arguably *pro*-sorting.[133] Whatever else the clause meant when ratified, it indicated restraints on the ability of the federal government to interfere with state religious "establishments." So a constitutional anti-sorting norm depends on movement since 1791. The importance of the Fourteenth Amendment and subsequent constitutional theory is examined below. However, the argument should begin with government policy predating the Constitution and the dramatic legal change thereafter. This history is sufficiently intriguing that countless scholars have traced and retraced it. But major developments that are crucial from a sorting perspective are not highlighted in contemporary legal scholarship.

The fact is that our country ran an extended experiment with religious sorting policies at the state and local level. These experiments were intimately associated with official religious "establishments," and they did not survive. This history is commonly seen as a regrettable episode of intolerant deprivations of religious liberty and equality—a misstep to be forgiven in light of a population so much less diverse than today's.[134] But that homogeneity was partly the *result* of purposeful official efforts to sculpt religious demographics in the New World. Religious establishments were part of a dynamic migration system. Less welcoming atmospheres tend to ward off the less welcome, while attracting the favored class. A religious-sorting perspective on American history emphasizes these dynamics.

The British colonies provided havens for Protestants, who had strong incentives to sort themselves out of Europe, and for those who thought the Church of England was corrupt.[135] The colonies were sometimes advertised as such.[136] At the same time, these

---

[133] Compare US Const, Art I, § 9, cl 1 (barring Congress from prohibiting migration of persons that existing States thought proper to admit, until 1808).

[134] Compare, e.g., Leonard W. Levy, *The Establishment Clause: Religion and the First Amendment* 9, 27 (1986) (missing the sorting dynamic when asserting that a State establishment of Christianity or Protestantism in 1790 would have been "for practical purposes, a comprehensive or non-preferential establishment).

[135] See Thomas J. Curry, *The First Freedoms: Church and State in America to the Passage of the First Amendment* 3 (1986); 1 Anson P. Stokes, *Church and State in the United States* 227 (1950).

[136] See, e.g., Walter A. Knittle, *Early Eighteenth Century Palatine Emigration* 12, 22–31 (1937); id at 20 ("[In Germany,] Pennsylvania was the best advertised province and it was mainly due to the liberal use of printer's ink.").

outposts executed the most severe forms of intolerance against other faiths. Certainly part of the story is about religious liberty simpliciter. Regulation of religious practices, such as rules limiting who could preach or perform legally recognized marriage ceremonies,[137] were obviously impositions on minorities within a given colony. But such regulation and promotion also were mechanisms that encouraged sorting during periods of mass migration.[138] For a time, some colonies even adopted immigration laws to exclude or deport those of the wrong religion.[139] A Virginia policy excluded Catholics and Puritans; Massachusetts Bay Colony banished Quakers and others.[140] In the latter case, Quakers faced the death penalty for *returning* to Massachusetts, not simply for their heresy.[141] The colony preferred conformity, to be sure, but the primary tool seems to have been population control rather than conversion.

These formal exclusions were abandoned before separation from the Crown, but efforts to shape the religious population continued. Several early state governments officially preferred sets of religious beliefs and practices. For example, South Carolina's 1778 Constitution declared Protestantism the state's established religion.[142] To achieve incorporated status, religious societies would have to agree that Christianity is the "true religion," the New Testament is "of divine inspiration," and there is a "future state of rewards

---

[137] See Michael W. McConnell, *Establishment and Disestablishment at the Founding, Part I: Establishment of Religion*, 44 Wm & Mary L Rev 2105, 2162, 2165–67, 2175 (2003).

[138] See Stokes, 1 *Church and State* at 227–28 (cited in note 135) ("From the British government's standpoint an object always in mind was a desire to prevent Roman Catholicism . . . from getting the upper hand in North America."); McConnell, 44 Wm & Mary L Rev at 2161–62 (cited in note 137) (discussing Massachusetts Bay Colony).

[139] See Edward P. Hutchinson, *Legislative History of American Immigration Policy 1798–1965* at 389–90 (1981); Emberson E. Proper, *Colonial Immigration Laws: A Study of the Regulation of Immigration by the English Colonies in America* 17–18, 26–27, 58–61 (1900) (finding a general tendency to deny or discourage Catholic immigration).

[140] See John T. Noonan, Jr., *The Lustre of Our Country: The American Experience of Religious Freedom* 51–53 (describing Massachusetts's policy from 1656 to 1681); McConnell, 44 Wm & Mary L Rev at 2117, 2119 (cited in note 137) (describing Virginia's policy and its apparent success regarding Catholics).

[141] See Richard P. Hallowell, *The Quaker Invasion of Massachusetts* 139–43 (3d ed 1884) (reproducing laws from 1658 and 1661); Noonan, *The Lustre of Our Country* at 52–53 (cited in note 140); see also Curry, *The First Freedoms* at 20–21 (cited in note 135) (noting regional opposition to Quaker presence).

[142] See SC Const, Art XXXVIII (1778), reprinted in 6 *The Federal and State Constitutions: Colonial Charters, And Other Organic Laws of the States, Territories, And Colonies Now or Heretofore Forming the United States of America* 3255–57 (Francis N. Thorpe ed., 1909) (hereafter Thorpe).

and punishments."[143] Such provisions were liberal compared to colonial policy, but they still made statements about the religious commitment expected of inhabitants.[144]

More important, some colonies and states taxed people for the specific purpose of funding preferred churches or ministers. Virginia famously ran such a system for a time. Massachusetts, Connecticut, and New Hampshire authorized municipalities to select a minister for tax-and-transfer, thereby further decentralizing without rejecting religious establishments.[145] From a sorting perspective, these programs might be superior to immigration laws. The latter must have been difficult to enforce insofar as religious commitments can be sustained without social visibility—a fact that helps explain severe penalties for return after banishment. A tax, in contrast, can be levied on all or many residents and the proceeds then directed to an identifiable religious organization or figure.[146] In other words, officially preferred beneficiaries were probably easier to identify than disfavored religionists. In addition, financing schemes that allowed people to opt out, or to direct their tax contribution to minority religions,[147] can also facilitate sorting. To choose one of these options is to identify oneself as a dissident. Adherents to minority religions might well prefer to remain anonymous, and so either conform or go elsewhere.

Not all states aimed to be narrowly sectarian enclaves. One could avoid the Congregational influence in New England and the Anglican establishments of some southern states by settling in Delaware, Pennsylvania, New Jersey, or Rhode Island. They billed themselves as relatively open political societies.[148] The variance in

---

[143] Id.

[144] See also, e.g., Mass Declaration of Rights, Art II (1780) ("It is the right as well as the duty of all men in society, publicly, and at stated seasons, to worship the Supreme Being . . . ."), reprinted in 3 Thorpe at 1889 (cited in note 142); cf. Va Declaration of Rights § 16 (June 12, 1776) ("[I]t is the mutual duty of all to practise Christian forbearance, love, and charity towards each other."), reprinted in 7 Thorpe at 3814 (cited in note 142); Proper, *Colonial Immigration Laws* at 27 (cited in note 139) (noting voting rights restrictions).

[145] See generally Gerard V. Bradley, *Church-State Relationships in America* ch 2 (1987); Levy, *The Establishment Clause* at 15–24 (cited in note 134) (noting exemptions for certain sects at certain times).

[146] Not that tax collection was easy in that era. See Robert A. Becker, *Revolution, Reform, and the Politics of American Taxation, 1763–1783* at 7, 116 (1980).

[147] See Levy, *The Establishment Clause* at 27–28 (cited in note 134) (describing Massachusetts law in 1780).

[148] See generally id at 1, 5, 9–10, 25–26.

church-state policies offered choices of politico-religious culture. Many people must have made decisions accordingly.[149] Forced to characterize the early American law of religion as anti-liberty or pro-sorting, one could easily favor the latter.

Either way, the formal establishments soon collapsed. Any Anglican establishment was poorly situated to outlive the Revolution. Other schemes failed as well. For instance, South Carolina's pro-establishment clauses were repealed in 1790.[150] Massachusetts' system of locally established faiths, which outlasted all the other formal establishments, was abolished in 1833.[151] Buffeted by immigration, additional sources of religious diversity, and competing economic interests,[152] the impulse for religiously closed states softened. Interfaith animosity was not eliminated, of course. If nothing else, the experience of Catholics in the nineteenth century defeats that claim.[153] And religiously restrictive covenants were used to shape local demographics long after the original establishments were discontinued.[154] Yet the idea of state-orchestrated partition of religious groups seems to have lost legitimacy in relatively short order.

In fact, a sign of the change can be found in a passage of Justice Harlan's dissent in *Plessey v Ferguson*. It put state-mandated *religious* segregation on a list of shocking hypotheticals that the supporters of *racial* segregation were challenged to distinguish:

> [I]f this statute of Louisiana is consistent with the personal liberty of citizens, why may not the state require the separation

---

[149] See Finke and Stark, *The Churching of America* at 27–33, 285–89 (cited in note 22) (extrapolating from data on the number and location of congregations and showing regional variation).

[150] See SC Const, Art I, §§ 4, 6, 8, 23, Art II, §§ 2–3, Art VIII (1790), reprinted in 6 Thorpe at 3258–62, 3264 (cited in note 142); Levy, *The Establishment Clause* at 51 (cited in note 134).

[151] See Mass. Articles of Amend. XI (1833), reprinted in 3 Thorpe at 1914 (cited in note 142); see generally Douglas Laycock, *"Nonpreferential" Aid to Religion: A False Claim About Original Intent*, 27 Wm & Mary L Rev 899–901 (1986).

[152] See Schuck, *Diversity in America* at 261 (cited in note 13); Steven D. Smith, *Getting Over Equality* 21 (2001) (asserting that pluralism, not doctrine, produced religious freedom).

[153] See, e.g., Philip Hamburger, *Separation of Church and State* ch 8 (2002); Kurt T. Lash, *The Second Adoption of the Establishment Clause: The Rise of the Nonestablishment Principle*, 27 Ariz St L J 1085, 1119–20 (1995).

[154] See William E. Nelson and Norman R. Williams, *Suburbanization and Market Failure: An Analysis of Government Policies Promoting Suburban Growth and Ethnic Assimilation*, 27 Fordham Urban L J 197, 215 (1999).

> in railroad coaches of native and naturalized citizens of the
> United States, or of Protestants and Roman Catholics?[155]

This statement might support only a narrow anti-sorting rule, involving legally coerced segregation by religion. But it's a start.

3. *Anti-sorting in theory.* Entrenching every perceived resolution of political conflict is no way to do constitutional law, of course. Anti-sorting principles need arguments to distinguish them from other trends. As a matter of constitutional text, the critical sources are the state-restraining provisions of the Fourteenth Amendment. But because that text is so underspecified, and because its inspiration was chattel slavery, a religion-oriented anti-sorting norm must be reinforced with a broader or different constitutional theory. This is not the place for a fully articulated sorting theory or an end to the "incorporation" debate. Normative and empirical uncertainties strongly caution against a robust anti-sorting principle, anyway. Yet with a little effort, we can see the structure of the argument. And this structure will further the equally challenging task of grinding out concrete versions of the principle.

There are two promising routes to a constitutional anti-sorting principle. Both rely on implications of the Fourteenth Amendment and Reconstruction.[156] The first route is conventional yet synergistic. The concept of "law respecting an establishment of religion" would be borrowed from the First Amendment and converted into a prohibition on state action by one or more clauses in the Fourteenth. The second route does not directly rely on First Amendment concepts. Instead, the Fourteenth Amendment itself underwrites an anti-sorting norm. Either way, the argument is above and beyond the particularities of Establishment Clause interpretation. These two lines of the argument can then be joined with modern political theory, concern for consequences, and empirical data.[157]

---

[155] *Plessy v Ferguson*, 163 US 537, 558 (1896) (Harlan, J, dissenting).

[156] These arguments are heavily influenced by the work of Akhil Amar, Christopher Eisgruber, and Kenneth Karst. See Amar, *The Bill of Rights* at 248–57 (cited in note 132); Eisgruber, *Madison* at 351–355, 371–78, 381–88 (cited in note 13); Christopher L. Eisgruber, *Ethnic Segregation by Religion and Race: Reflections on Kiryas Joel and Shaw v. Reno*, 26 Cumb L Rev 515, 515–22 (1996); Eisgruber, *Assimilation* at 92 (cited in note 13); Christopher L. Eisgruber, *Political Unity and the Powers of Government*, 41 UCLA L Rev 1297, 1323–28 (1994); Kenneth L. Karst, *Justice O'Connor and the Substance of Equal Citizenship*, 2003 Supreme Court Review 357; Karst, 27 Harv CR-CL L Rev at 512–25 (cited in note 45).

[157] Conventional Religion Clause theories are not terribly useful here. See Hugh Baxter, *Managing Legal Change: The Transformation of Establishment Clause Law*, 46 UCLA L Rev

a) The first path depends on certain understandings of both the First and Fourteenth Amendments. The latter explicitly restrains state action in multiple ways that might be relevant: protecting privileges or immunities, guaranteeing liberty with due process, demanding equal protection of the laws; even the grants of national and state citizenship can be relied on. A free-exercise norm, moreover, fits easily within these concepts. There is even Fourteenth Amendment drafting history to that effect.[158] Excluding people or organizations from states or municipalities, such as Hialeah's attempt to prevent Santeria's immigration, is thus relatively easy to prohibit under the Fourteenth Amendment. The result in the Santeria case shielded a sect from a ritual-targeting government prohibition. But for discretionary benefits like a school district for the Satmars, the constitutional problem is harder to see (at least if equal protection norms are satisfied). In some ways the new district *promoted* religious liberty—perhaps not a system of liberty in which multiple sects thrive and interact, but surely the religious autonomy of the Satmars was served. It is not even clear that the new district would have required substantial additional tax dollars from outsiders who might object. This suggests that more must be done to articulate a non-establishment norm that plausibly can be appropriated by the Fourteenth Amendment. After all, the Establishment Clause of the First Amendment was a federalism-promoting concession to the states that resists an easy transplant into the Fourteenth.

The best argument on this track is that the American view of religious establishments changed between 1791 and 1868. Perhaps it moved from local option to liberty killer. Even ignoring stare decisis, there is material to support this thesis. However disconnected disestablishment was from the notion of religious liberty at the founding, these ideas were sometimes coupled by the time the

343, 351 n 32 (1998) (collecting theories). "Substantive neutrality," which prefers to minimize the impact of state action on religious choices, always has a difficult time selecting a subset of government conduct to monitor, and it is not immediately clear what baseline is best for sorting purposes. More important, a simple neutrality theory—whether "substantive" or "formal"—will not explain why federal action seems to be treated more leniently than analogous state and local action. Theorists seeking to maximize religious liberty (e.g., those who are pro-"accommodation" plus anti-"coercion") cannot be sure whether sorting across political boundaries diminishes religiosity or alters its mix in a problematic way. Finally, "strict separation" would be highly concerned with overt state efforts to build religion-sustaining political enclaves. But not much is clear beyond that and, in any event, the theory is infeasible in its strong forms and not particularly popular in the courts, anyway.

[158] See Amar, *The Bill of Rights* at 253 (cited in note 132).

Fourteenth Amendment was ratified.[159] In fact, a few state and territorial constitutions even mimicked the federal Establishment
Clause and its "law respecting" language.[160] Thomas Cooley's 1868
treatise summarized state constitutions in just those terms.[161] It is
extremely unlikely that these clauses reflected yet another structural
decision to decentralize religious questions to municipalities, and
they were certainly not cross-jurisdictional protection for other
states. A better explanation lies in the shift away from formal establishments among the original states, along with changing political values in the West.[162] Government was by no means disconnected from religion in the 1800s; part of the allergy to
"church"-state connection, moreover, was anti-Catholicism that accompanied new waves of international immigration.[163] But subnational "establishments" became incompatible with prevailing notions of the proper relationship between government and religion.
And we now know that sorting accompanied state and colonial
programs regarding religion, we might conclude that government-
propelled religious messages are a component of any "establishment" worthy of the name, and we are in any case much closer to
placing an anti-sorting norm within the Fourteenth Amendment.[164]

Once the values of deregulated religious liberty and non-establishment are imported, anti-sorting is not only a matter of historical
analogy. The principle may be prophylactic, and here there is a
connection with anti-proselytism. Monitoring the conduct of officials within local religious enclaves can be difficult. Without ef-

---

[159] See Lash, 27 Ariz St L J at 1133 (cited in note 153) (asserting that "by Reconstruction,
northern state courts had translated the prohibition of the original Establishment Clause
to be an expression of fundamental religious liberty"); see also id at 1130.

[160] See id at 1133 & n 224.

[161] See Thomas M. Cooley, *A Treatise on the Constitutional Limitations Which Rest Upon
the Legislative Power of the States of the American Union* 469–71 (1868) (distinguishing
"solemn recognition of a super-intending Providence in public transactions and exercises
as the general religious sentiment requires"—at least to meet secular goals of public
morality and order).

[162] See Amar, *The Bill of Rights* at 248–52 (cited in note 132).

[163] See generally Hamburger, *Separation of Church and State*, ch 8 (cited in note 153);
see also Adam M. Samaha, *Separation Rhetoric and Its Relevance*, 19 Const Comm 713,
728–30 (2002) (book review) (analyzing the muted relevance of the failed Blaine
Amendment).

[164] Compare McConnell, 44 Wm & Mary L Rev at 2131 (cited in note 137) (asserting
that "establishment" means "the promotion and inculcation of a common set of beliefs
through governmental authority" and noting variations in coerciveness). The best definition of "establishment" and the propriety of prophylactic measures beyond it are controversial questions, but no less difficult for anti-proselytism principles.

fective monitoring, however, these enclaves can disrupt political choices at the state and national levels. Furthermore, sorting will often be imperfect. This was true even under colonial regimes.[165] Religious faith can be relatively invisible if an individual so chooses, while non-religious reasons plainly affect location decisions. Thus a municipality dominated by one sect might still have non-conformists to deal with. Leaving the law to such imperfectly sorted religious enclaves can therefore threaten social policy. Nor is the threat restricted to sectarian proselytizing and ostracism. There is likewise reason to worry that imperfectly sorted secular enclaves will disregard constitutional guarantees of religious liberty. And the more generous one is with free exercise rights, the more worried one should be about secular dominance within a political community. As such the sectarian vision of Republic, Missouri, in the 1990s was not categorically different from the atheistic aspiration of Liberal, Missouri, in the 1880s—a town more than happy to declare its official opinion that "MAN'S SAVIOR MUST BE MAN ALONE."[166]

Fears persist, moreover, even when sorting is complete. A nightmare scenario is suggested by charges against the Fundamentalist Church of Jesus Christ of Latter Day Saints in Colorado City, Arizona. Members allegedly sorted themselves into relative isolation, minimized access to communications technology, taught theories of racial superiority, subordinated girls to patriarchal domination, banished hundreds of teenage boys to maintain a gender imbalance for polygyny, used government officials to further Church diktats concerning romantic relationships, and diverted tax dollars intended for public schools to Church operations.[167] In fact,

---

[165] See Part III.A.2.; cf. Lee Anne Fennell, *Revealing Options*, 118 Harv L Rev 1399, 1456–57 (2005) (noting the constraints of bundled choices, change of preferences over time, and transition costs of sorting and re-sorting if local legal rules are flat and fixed).

[166] Philip Hamburger, *Illiberal Liberalism: Liberal Theology, Anti-Catholicism, and Church Property*, 12 J Contemp Legal Issues 693, 702 n 29 (2002) (citation omitted) (adding that "the happiest and best community is that one which is the freest from the dogmas of religion"). Séances were popular in the town, however. See J. P. Moore, *This Strange Town—Liberal, Missouri* 74 (1963).

[167] See David Kelly, *Lost to the Only Life They Knew*, L.A. Times (June 13, 2005) at A1; Petition for Appointment of Receiver, In re Colorado City Unified Sch. Dist. No. 14, Case No. 2005-001, at 8–10 (Aug 12, 2005) (filed with the Arizona State Board of Education) (noting that all school board members and administrators are FLDS members, and charging them with mismanaging district property to the benefit of FLDS). The Attorney General's petition alleges, for example, that the district purchased an airplane and later was unable to pay teachers' salaries. See id at 4, 8.

"diversion" loses meaning in this context. If critics are correct about Colorado City, local government authority is now an arm of the Church and wielded to achieve religious goals. This fits any plausible definition of religious establishment. Separation of church and state might be a poor slogan for the Establishment Clause, but church-state *integration* is certainly not the vision. Anyway, the important argument for anti-sorting principles is that religious homogeneity makes such constitutional violations more likely. And in an interconnected society with a substantial welfare state, "complete exit" of religious groups is more difficult to achieve.[168]

Religious sorting therefore should be most distressing to those who support robust versions of anti-establishment norms. However appealing one might think it to rope off "the government" from religious symbols, religious justifications for public policy, and subsidies benefiting religious institutions, those goals will be harder to obtain if the community is monolithically dedicated to one version of religious faith.[169] All the more so at the local level where the public/private line, often by design, is faintest.

b) The argument for a principle disfavoring religious sorting is bolstered by an alternative path. Post-Reconstruction ideals of citizenship and nationalism may support it. Kenneth Karst is a leader here. He forged a theoretical connection between race and religion through the concept of equal citizenship.[170] He did so in service of nationalism—some bare minimum of national identity and civic unity in a multicultural country,[171] which stands against exclusionary or polarizing use of race and religion in politics. Race might be more salient in America, but religion is another tool with which politicians and officials can divide the country. Engineering a desired composition of religion within a political boundary is a literal example of this feared partition. And one can reach these conclusions without specifying the best interpretation of the First Amendment.[172]

---

[168] Compare Greene, 96 Colum L Rev at 8, 17 (cited in note 13) (discussing complete exit and partial exit).

[169] An attempt to hold all of these positions, and grant legislatures the option to authorize political enclaves for "minority" religions, is id at 24–26, 83 n 329, 85 n 335, 86.

[170] See Karst, 27 Harv CR-CL L Rev at 512–25 (cited in note 45).

[171] See Kenneth L. Karst, *Belonging to America: Equal Citizenship and the Constitution* 101, 173 (1989).

[172] Compare Amar, *The Bill of Rights* at 254 (cited in note 132) (concluding that Alabama could not declare itself "the White Supremacy State" and suggesting the same for Utah declaring itself "the Mormon State").

Yet insofar as racial sorting implicates fears of perpetual subordination, religious sorting is distinct. Perhaps few believe that race is a normatively defensible category for many purposes and all else equal, instead of a social fact or a tool for organizing disadvantaged groups. But religion is another story. It is far more difficult to demonstrate that society would be better off with the extermination of religion as a category. Furthermore, free-exercise values suggest that the Constitution prefers liberated religiosity. The Reconstruction Amendments, in contrast, are tough to read as promoting racial identity for its own sake or even for instrumental purposes. Anti-sorting would get more mileage out of a theory treating religion as constitutionally valued and religious divisions as indissoluble.

The conventional legal logic begins to stretch thin, but perhaps the nationalizing influence of the Civil War's resolution supports a neo-Madisonian theory of religious faction. Madison's now-hackneyed insight was that the collection of interests into a single political institution could facilitate reasoned compromise[173] or at least prevent factional domination. He applied the theory to religious sects in *The Federalist*.[174] But he did not touch state and local affairs. While Madison promoted federal constitutional guarantees of religious liberty against the states, he could not achieve it in the Bill of Rights.[175] Yet the point is useful for an anti-sorting principle, because it sees religion as politically powerful rather than habitually subordinated. It recommends integrating multiple denominations within political institutions. And it limits the principle to groups dominating political jurisdictions, not simple geographic clumping. Christopher Eisgruber pushes similar arguments, singling out organized religion from other interests. Although critical to healthy societal diversity, he contends, religious groups are often cohesive, impervious to ordinary rational argument, and uncompromising because organized on matters of principle.[176] These characteristics

---

[173] See Cass R. Sunstein, *The Partial Constitution* 19–20, 133–34, 347 (1993) (observing a general structural tendency in the Constitution to promote reasoned deliberation).

[174] See Federalist 10 in Clinton Rossiter, ed, *The Federalist Papers* 84 (1961) ("A religious sect may degenerate into a political faction in a part of the Confederacy; but the variety of sects dispersed over the entire face of it must secure the national councils against any danger from that source."); Federalist 51 at 324.

[175] Compare US Const, Amend I (singling out Congress), with Bernard Schwartz, *The Great Rights of Mankind: A History of the American Bill of Rights* 177, 233 (1977) (noting Madison's support for an amendment protecting "the equal rights of conscience" from state action).

[176] See Eisgruber, *Madison* at 372–73 (cited in note 13).

might be accentuated when reinforced with a matching political boundary. Those lines can bolster group loyalty, and the use of government machinery may help solve any remaining collective action problems.

Such theories might leave little for a local government to decide, though. Before we take constitutional law to nationalize the primary school curriculum, it is worth recalling the virtues of decentralized democracy. Aside from the hoped-for benefits of Tiebout sorting, some democrats prefer a measure of decentralized government power because it creates locations for citizen participation.[177] The wish is that people develop public-regarding arguments and interests, rather than simply presenting individual preferences for aggregation.[178] In addition, interaction might produce cross-cultural knowledge and cooperation skills, which could themselves qualify as public goods. Other democrats are not interested in or oppose the goal of molding citizen interests through local politics, yet encourage decentralization for other reasons. Even representative forms of local government can be superior to wholly centralized power. Local officials might be better informed about local values and conditions, and local residents might be better informed about official conduct. If so, public policy can be more efficiently implemented and officials can be better monitored.

Neither theory for decentralized democracy is seriously assisted by religious homogeneity. This is clearer for participatory democrats. Many of them want citizens to confront and understand differences, not eliminate them by political boundaries or social pressure to conform.[179] Representative democrats also have something to fear from religious sorting, even if preference homogeneity has upsides. One problem is group polarization.[180] Given certain conditions, a group of individuals predisposed toward one position will end up supporting more extreme policies after deliberation than

---

[177] See, e.g., Frug, *City Making* at 20–24 (cited in note 110); Benjamin R. Barber, *Strong Democracy: Participatory Politics for a New Age* xiv–xv, 117 (1984).

[178] See Iris M. Young, *Inclusion and Democracy* 108–20, 188–89 (2000); Iris M. Young, *Justice and the Politics of Difference* 234–41 (1990); accord Diana L. Eck, *A New Religious America: How a "Christian Country" Has Now Become the World's Most Religiously Diverse Nation* 69–70 (2001).

[179] See, e.g., Young, *Justice* at 237–38 (cited in note 178); cf. Lee C. Bollinger, *The Tolerant Society* 9–10, 140–44 (1986) (justifying free speech as a method for developing tolerance).

[180] See, e.g., Cass R. Sunstein, *Deliberative Trouble? Why Groups Go to Extremes*, 110 Yale L J 71, 74–75 (2000).

would have been predicted by their predeliberation preferences. In addition, too few dissenters can lead to no disagreement being voiced at all. And similar imbalances can generate cascades, as subsequent evaluations are skewed by prior political victories.[181] Sometimes these syndromes might happily produce exciting social experiments. On other occasions the results might be disastrous, without a guarantee that the effects will be wholly localized or that participants will learn much from mistakes. Representative democracy might dampen the risks, but this seems less likely at the local level. As political boundaries encompass smaller populations, representatives and constituents begin to mirror a single social group. In this sense, secular enclaves are no different from their religious counterparts.

Lastly, social trends might make an anti-sorting norm attractive to many integrationists and nationalists. The country includes undeniably deep cultural divisions and religion plays a part. Few can believe that the United States will fit strong versions of the secularization thesis anytime soon,[182] while empirical work suggests:

- co-religionists are clumped regionally and sometimes locally[183]—at the county level, perhaps to a degree now similar to segregation scores for African Americans;[184]
- foreign immigration trends may be contributing to religious separation, as newcomers sometimes bring shared religious commitments to geographically distinct communities;[185]
- fundamentalist denominations are gaining proportionally to

---

[181] See Cass R. Sunstein, *Why Societies Need Dissent* 5–13 (2003).

[182] The expectation, shared by intellectuals from Marx to Mill to Durkheim, was that modernity would diminish religiosity. See Jose Casanova, *Public Religions in the Modern World* 17–20, 211–12 (1994). Trends in some of Europe fit the thesis; but U.S. data are more difficult to square. See Pippa Norris and Ronald Inglehart, *The Sacred and the Secular: Religion and Politics Worldwide* 5, 84–85, 94 (2004); Laurence R. Iannoccone, *Introduction to the Economics of Religion*, 36 J Econ Lit 1465, 1468–72 (1998).

[183] See ARIS Survey at 39–42 (cited in note 22) (exhibit 15) (breaking down responses by state); Norris and Inglehart, *The Sacred and the Secular* at 94 (cited in note 182) (noting regional and urban/rural differences).

[184] See Rhode and Strumpf, 93 Am Econ Rev at 1670–71 (figures 5 and 6) (cited in note 110).

[185] See, e.g., Norris and Inglehart, *The Sacred and the Secular* at 93–94 (cited in note 182) (noting that proportional shifts away from "mainline" Protestant growth can be partly accounted for by immigration patterns); Rhode and Strumpf, 93 Am Econ Rev at 1672 (figure 7) (cited in note 110) (showing an increase in segregation by foreign birth, measured by Gini and dissimilarity indices, from 1960 to 1990).

other sects;[186]
- yet the percentage of the population unaffiliated with any religious institution is substantial, if not growing.[187]

Religious segregation scores are worth pausing over. The calculations of Professors Rhode and Strumpf suggest that, between 1890 and 1990, the nation became equally segregated at the county level with respect to religions, African Americans, and the foreign born—with the first score falling slightly, the second falling substantially, and the third recently increasing.[188] A single nationwide number for "religion" is not undoubtedly comparable to that for other social categories. The spatial distribution of many small sects must be aggregated to get a single segregation score,[189] a handful of larger sects predominate in respective regions of the country, and our normative commitments are likely distinct in the religion context. But segregation indices are not the only relevant data point. With year 2000 county-level numbers, we can see that a single denominational family exceeds 50 percent of claimed adherents in a large number of counties.[190] Although the percentage of residents who are claimed varies significantly across counties, the numbers may understate geographic unevenness in terms of anti-sorting con-

---

[186] See Finke and Stark, *The Churching of America* at 244–48 (cited in note 22); Norris and Inglehart, *The Sacred and the Secular* at 94 (cited in note 182); Iannoccone, 36 J Econ Lit at 1471–72 (cited in note 182).

[187] See ARIS Survey at 10 & n 5, 13 (cited in note 22) (stating that in 2001, 14 percent responded "no religion" to the question "What is your religion, if any?" compared to 8 percent in 1990, when the question was "What is your religion?"); Norris and Inglehart, *The Sacred and the Secular* at 93 (figure 4.5) (cited in note 182) (showing a similar shift from 1991 to 2002 in responses to a General Social Survey question). Other polling indicates that about 94 percent of respondents will say they believe in some kind of god, however, with results fairly steady since 1947. See Norris and Inglehart, *The Sacred and the Secular* at 90 (table 4.1) (cited in note 182).

[188] See Rhode and Strumpf, 93 Am Econ Rev at 1670–72 (figures 5–7) (cited in note 110) (showing scores from somewhat below 0.50 to about 0.60). Rhode and Strumpf's trendlines for "religion" in figure 6 are Gini and dissimilarity scores. Those scores are designed for a single group (see note 202)—not a single number for the 27 religion categories used by the authors. The formula they used to aggregate the scores is reproduced id at 1660–61; it is a population-weighted average for each category, modified with a denominator that seems to further reduce the influence of small-group scores.

[189] Compare Alberto Alesina, Reza Baqir, and Caroline Hoxby, *Political Jurisdictions in Heterogeneous Communities*, 112 J Pol Econ 348, 361 (2004) (table 1) (showing an average county-level "heterogeneity" score of 0.631 for 17 Judeo-Christian groupings in 1990—that is, there was a 63.1 percent probability that two randomly selected residents would *not* be members of the same grouping).

[190] See ASARB Data (cited in note 81) (fold-out map) (grouping all Baptists and Lutherans).

cerns. A county that is relatively "diverse" as a whole might be divided at a more local level. Cook County, Illinois, to take a fairly extreme example, includes over 100 cities, villages, and towns, not to mention dozens more special purpose districts for education, parks, libraries, and so on. Strong anti-sorters might care about each of these divisions.

As discussed below, some of these trends are untroubling or even thrilling. Anti-sorting is not anti-diversity; indeed, it could be quite the opposite. The principle is concerned with how social divisions are institutionalized. When multiple social cleavages are piled upon each other, and then reinforced by coinciding political boundaries, there is cause to fear an overly fractionated country operating more as a confederation of monolithic associations than a nation of people sharing any fundamental commitment.

Likewise, it should be clear that anti-sorting principles are not anti-religion in a strong sense. Dispersing fellow believers is not the objective; the worry is alignment of religious and political borders. A denomination's geographic concentration is not problematic under the theory unless, for example, it falls within and dominates a single political jurisdiction. Furthermore, religious clumping within a political jurisdiction is not facially problematic if the jurisdiction as a whole is religiously diverse.[191] The theory is concerned with monolithic local democracies, not neighborhoods lacking governmental authority.[192] Second, the principle does not entail opposition to religion in politics. One can object to the coincidence of government institutions and uniform beliefs about religion without fearing the effects of religiosity on politics.[193] In fact, anti-sorting is compatible with *support* for religious argument within democratic institutions. Yet it does imply qualms about organized

---

[191] What constitutes acceptable or optimal religious diversity is an enormous question for anti-sorting proponents. See note 202; Part III.C.

[192] Insofar as a "neighborhood" is a unit of local government under relevant law, anti-sorting theories apply with similar force. As for families, presumably they would be distinguished on the same public/private line that differentiates religions themselves, or by rights of intimate association and child-rearing. See, e.g., *Roberts v United States Jaycees*, 468 US 609, 618–19 (1984); *Pierce v Society of Sisters*, 268 US 510 (1925).

[193] Accord *McDaniel v Paty*, 435 US 618 (1978) (invalidating a ministerial exception). Contrast, for example, Vincent Blasi, *Vouchers and Steering*, 18 J L & Pol 607, 613 (2002) ("[R]eligion remains a distinctively dangerous political force."), Abner S. Greene, *The Political Balance of the Religion Clauses*, 102 Yale L J 1611, 1614 (1993), and Kathleen M. Sullivan, *Religion and Liberal Democracy*, 59 U Chi L Rev 195, 197 (1992).

religious factions, which ought to be accounted for by institutional choice and design.

A preference for mixing cannot achieve universal support, of course. Religious separatists dedicated to avoiding communities of sin, secularists convinced that religion is an infectious fraud, and still others will not be satisfied. Anti-sorting principles cannot be any more neutral than, say, basic commitments to liberal democracy.[194] But unmitigated tolerance seems inconceivable for a functioning nation, and anti-sorting is consistent with a liberal goal of relative inclusion.

B. APPLICATIONS

If an anti-sorting principle is rightly planted in constitutional law, what form should it take in live controversies? Facets of the question track the debates about segregation by race.[195] Should the Constitution be invoked only to prevent or remedy de jure state action that separates people or encourages them to separate among political subdivisions, or also to more affirmatively strive for *integration* as a matter of social fact? Or is religion-blindness the appropriate norm, such that conscious official efforts to integrate are forbidden by the Constitution? Before presenting a critique of anti-sorting principles, this section explores the options. It demonstrates that the idea, however controversial, can do lots of work.

1. *Versions.* Because the concern is political boundaries aligning with religious divisions, and assuming state and local governments retain significant authority and that their political community is importantly defined by physical territory, then there are two targets for anti-sorting principles: (1) the geographic distribution of people and (2) the physical location of political borders. Anti-sorting principles might affect either one, but parts of both targets are practically immobile. First, people have already sorted themselves to some degree and, although the U.S. population is fairly transient today, not everyone is interested in a change of scenery. Second, changing political boundaries is disruptive, administra-

---

[194] See John Rawls, *Political Liberalism* 199–200 (1996) (discussing education requirements).

[195] See generally David A. Strauss, *Discriminatory Intent and the Taming of Brown*, 56 U Chi L Rev 935, 949 (1989); Greene, 96 Colum L Rev at 28–29 (cited in note 13) (analogizing racial segregation).

tively and conceptually. It is theoretically possible intermittently to redraw municipal boundaries, as we do legislative districts, and local government lines already change through state-law mechanisms of incorporation and annexation. But the Constitution's text addresses boundary adjustments to one state that involve the territory of another state;[196] almost any boundary change is costly as people adjust to a new polity and territorial unit; and some boundaries are so conceptually hardened that they are not going anywhere in the near term.

In the same spirit, certain extreme anti-sorting norms can be ruled out. The Constitution will not be read to mandate, and no court will order, the forced relocation of people to achieve an equal distribution by religion across municipalities. Compelled displacement for reasons related to religion is a liberty and property intrusion conceivable for settlers in Gaza but not for residents of the United States today; and equal distribution, even with an adequate measure, is just a bad idea in no way dictated by constitutional logic. Geographic quotas for every religious denomination and secular theory would be almost impossible to administer and normatively wrongheaded. Harmless or innovative sects with small memberships might not survive as their numbers are spread thin throughout a state or the nation. This is particularly true in the United States, where there are almost countless religions, from Druid to nondenominational Christian to Foursquare Gospel.[197] And there is good reason to accept diverse versions of diverse localities.[198]

But anti-sorting law can be equally *un*controversial. At a minimum, subnational political boundaries could not be drawn by government officials to separate religious sects and/or the nonreligious against their will. The same can be said for coercive relocation of people to maintain separation across political boundaries. Both would be pure forms of mandatory segregation. They produce the threats associated with religious sorting without cap-

---

[196] See US Const, Art IV, § 3, cl 1 ("[Not] any State [shall] be formed by . . . Parts of States, without the Consent of the Legislatures of the States concerned as well as of the Congress."); cf. *United States v Louisiana*, 363 US 1, 35 (1960) (indicating congressional control over state boundaries, at least at the point of admission to the Union).

[197] See ARIS Survey at 10, 12–13 (cited in note 22) (relying on self-identification).

[198] See Part III.C.

turing the upside of unregulated private choice.[199] Neither Karst nor Tiebout would be pleased. We might imagine two or more groups intensely opposed to each other's religious values, verging on violence and seeking each other's elimination, yet committed to ongoing confrontation within the same local political institution. At that point, government might produce adequately compelling reasons for separation. Otherwise, it is safe to assume that a plausible anti-sorting principle bars government officials from either drawing political boundaries or moving people to ensure religious segregation against (or regardless of) private party wishes. At the least, the principle reaches officials *pushing people apart* on religious criteria without compelling reason.

   The short logical extension is to state action beyond forced relocation or strategic boundary drawing, but which serves the same function. A useful analogy is to certain race-based equal protection claims under the Fourteenth Amendment. For facially race-neutral state action, the generic test requires more than disparate impact on a minority group; it demands discriminatory purpose.[200] For religion at least, the issue is not only minority subordination but also other risks posed by homogeneity like group polarization, conformity, cascades, and the threat to non-establishment and free-exercise norms. So the ideas of disparate impact and discrimination can be supplemented with a concern for religious separation per se, as long as it takes place across political boundaries. A fairly minimal anti-sorting principle could therefore prohibit government action that is both (1) done for the purpose[201] of achieving religious homogeneity[202] within a political

---

[199] See *Board of Educ. of Kiryas Joel Vill. Sch. Dist. v Grumet*, 512 US 687, 690 (1994) (invalidating special legislation creating a school district at the *request* of a religious sect); cf. *Gomillian v Lightfoot*, 364 US 339, 341 (1960) (refusing to dismiss a challenge to new municipal boundaries that excluded almost all African-American voters who were part of the old jurisdiction).

[200] See *Village of Arlington Heights v Metropolitan Housing Dev. Corp.*, 429 US 252, 265 (1977).

[201] A satisfying test for official purpose is hard to find, particularly as applied to collectives. But we are not limited to direct inquiries into historical fact. Purpose can be checked by post hoc justifications and their fit with observable state action. See *Republican Party of Minn. v White*, 536 US 765, 779–80 (2002); *Greater New Orleans Broad. Ass'n, Inc. v United States*, 527 US 173, 187 (1999) (distinguishing asserted government interests from enacted legislative policy).

[202] This is a key clause for anti-sorting proponents to define and I do not offer a precise formula here. An indisputable example is a plan to achieve 100 percent adherence to a single church by 100 percent of the polity. But dangers of sorting will arise before then. Republic, Missouri's, vision of a Christian city seems sufficiently exclusionary, for example.

jurisdiction[203] and (2) does or is likely to either (*a*) cause greater religious homogeneity within that jurisdiction or (*b*) prevent reduction of such homogeneity—at least without a compelling justification.

This kind of "hold harmless" orientation is inelegant yet relatively manageable. It resists all calculated state action that risks pushing people in the direction of religious homogeneity. Once a court detects a purpose incompatible with any anti-sorting principle—achieving a religiously uniform citizenry through sorting— then the challenged state action cannot be carried out if it threatens to move the population toward that goal. Furthermore, a variety of conduct could violate the rule. It is not restricted to the construction of political boundaries or the physical relocation of people. On the other hand, the test does not make courts responsible for halting privately instigated religious sorting. It demands problematic government objectives, it is keyed to officials promoting a religious demography potentially at odds with disaggregated private choice, and it concentrates on homogeneity within a polity rather than trying to pick a version of "adequate religious diversity."[204] Assuming a homogenous status quo, then, the town of Liberal, Missouri, could not use government resources to provide free land or down payments on houses for atheists alone.

In this vein, it is worth noting the many statistical measures of "segregation." See Douglas S. Massey and Nancy A. Denton, *The Dimensions of Residential Segregation*, 67 Social Forces 281, 282–83 (1988) (grouping 20 indices into categories of evenness, exposure, concentration, centralization, and clustering). "Evenness" is a candidate for anti-sorting purposes; it measures distribution of a given group's population across geographic subunits. See id at 283–84, 308 (recommending the dissimilarity index). Roughly speaking, the dissimilarity index is the proportion of a particular subpopulation that would have to move from their current subunit(s) to other(s) in order for each subunit to have the same percentage of that subpopulation. See Douglas S. Massey and Nancy A. Denton, *American Apartheid: Segregation and the Making of the Underclass* 20 (1993); Karl E. Taeuber and Alma F. Taeuber, *Negroes in Cities: Residential Segregation and Neighborhood Change* 203–04 (1965). Evenness is not a very good measure of political power, however. A faith can be perfectly spread throughout all subunits and be a powerless minority, an ineffectual majority, or a commanding monolith in every one.

[203] The suggested test would not look for system-wide effects from state-encouraged sorting. This limit is intended as a sacrifice of ideal form in return for a test courts can more easily operate.

[204] Compare Samuel Issacharoff, *Gerrymandering and Political Cartels*, 116 Harv L Rev 593, 627 (2002) (distinguishing the optimal number of firms in a competitive market from the identification of anticompetitive behavior); Richard H. Pildes, *A Theory of Political Competition*, 85 Va L Rev 1605, 1612 (1999) ("In theory and in doctrine, we can often identify what is troublingly unfair, unequal, or wrong without a precise standard of what is optimally fair, equal, or right.").

Nor could Republic, Missouri, do the same for members of the Southern Baptist Convention.

Another type of state action is not so purposeful or assertive yet it *facilitates* religious sorting. Illustrations are facially neutral procedures for incorporating new municipalities and state efforts to make publicly available accurate demographic data, including religious affiliation. Such action might be taken without any purpose that sorting will be increased or maintained. At this point, committed integrationists and Tiebout enthusiasts begin rapidly to diverge. The former will remain dedicated to preventing separation, regardless of official motives. As an analogy, some state action has been condemned for encouraging or facilitating racism or racial separation. The classic example is *Shelley v Kraemer*.[205] Case law under the Fair Housing Act might be an even better model, since it directly regulates communication.[206] Some courts bar real estate advertisers from consciously picturing people of only one race,[207] or real estate agents from supplying information on racial demographics.[208] Such propositions could be exported to the religion context—the Act probably should be read to treat race and religion similarly, anyway—and then enforced as constitutional law against state action not expressly speaking to real estate transactions.[209] Under this version of the anti-sorting principle,

---

[205] 334 US 1 (1948); cf. *Norwood v Harrison*, 413 US 455, 466–67 (1973) (involving state aid to segregated schools); *Reitman v Mulkey*, 387 US 369, 381 (1967) (involving an attempt to entrench the absence of antidiscrimination laws).

[206] 42 USC § 3604(c) (making it unlawful to "publish . . . any notice, statement, or advertisement, with respect to the sale or rental of a dwelling that indicates any preference, limitation, or discrimination based on race, color, religion, sex, handicap, familial status, or national origin").

[207] See *Ragin v New York Times Co.*, 923 F2d 995, 1001–02 (2nd Cir) (affirming the denial of a publisher's motion to dismiss), cert denied, 502 US 821 (1991).

[208] See 42 USC § 3604(a), (b), & (d); 24 CFR § 100.70. There is disagreement over what constitutes unlawful "steering," however. Compare *Village of Bellwood v Dwivedi*, 895 F2d 1521, 1530–31 (7th Cir 1990) (demanding disparate treatment of customers because of race to make out a racial steering claim, such that accurately responding to customer requests about racial demographics apparently would not violate the Act) and *Leadership Council for Metro. Open Communities, Inc. v Rossi Realty, Inc.*, No 98 C 7852, 2001 WL 289870, at *5 (ND Ill 2001) (unpublished) (granting summary judgment for defendants on a religious-steering claim under the rule of *Dwivedi*), with *Heights Community Congress v Hilltop Realty Inc.*, 774 F2d 135, 140 (6th Cir 1985) (condemning conduct with the intent and effect of "steering," and suggesting that the Act can be violated by "truthful informational statements with racial content" or "failure to show homes in a particular location absent a specific request"), cert denied, 475 US 1019 (1986).

[209] There is no strong reason to think that rules first authored or suggested by Congress are unavailable for use by courts as constitutional law. In some instances Congress might

and without an anti-subordination override of some variety, creating the Village of Kiryas Joel was constitutionally forbidden. Similarly, Congress's refusal to admit the Mormon-designed State of Deseret in the mid-1800s[210] was constitutionally compelled. This certainly would be an aggressive constitutional rule. But recall that some Establishment Clause precedent, including the endorsement test, polices both government purpose and effect.

A difficult issue is then the official promotion of a jurisdiction as a haven for a particular denomination. This conduct might be painted as either an improper government effort to shape demographics or a justifiable provision of accurate information. Strong integrationists cannot accept such facilitation of sorting but Tiebout followers certainly might. Promotion of community character could be a municipal service that the model suggests people should sort over—a public good hindered by collective action problems, at least in localities filled with unorganized secularists or nondenominational Christians. For some uses of religious messages, the disagreement can be overcome. An official purpose to alter religious sorting patterns in a particular direction without residents' consent seems problematic, and officials might select crude or otherwise misleading messages for just that reason.[211] Moving constitutional law much further, however, depends on a choice between fundamental commitments.

Some of these outcomes might be implausible, but there are even bolder strokes to be considered. One is whether governments may or must take *affirmative action* to create or maintain some kind of religious diversity—through promotional efforts or otherwise.[212] Similar issues have been difficult to settle in the race context, and Justice Kennedy has suggested that the government has

---

be the first institution to articulate a rule that comports with a sound elaboration of the Constitution, but that does not mean that those rules cannot be mimicked or built on in court doctrine.

[210] See Dale L. Morgan, *The State of Deseret* 2–3, 9 (1987).

[211] But cf. *Meese v Keene*, 481 US 465, 467–69, 478–85 (1987) (rejecting a Speech Clause challenge to the federal government labeling certain foreign films "political propaganda," at least without evidence that the public was actually influenced or misled).

[212] Compare Kenneth T. Jackson, *Crabgrass Frontier: The Suburbanization of the United States* 138–55 (1985) (describing a trend roughly opposite: the rise of incorporation for suburban municipalities and the decline of annexation and consolidation for many large, older, central cities); Ankur J. Goel, *Maintaining Integration Against Minority Interests: An Anti-Subjugation Theory for Equality in Housing*, 22 Urban Law 369 (1990) (critically reviewing racial integration-maintenance measures, including ceiling quotas on minorities, steering, and equity insurance).

a constitutional obligation to be religion-blind when choosing political boundaries. In his *Kiryas Joel* concurrence he flatly stated, "government may not use religion as a criterion to draw political or electoral lines,"[213] although he also referenced religious segregation as the problem at hand.[214] But if the constitutional objective is preventing the social fact of religious segregation, then "diversity" efforts should be either presumptively valid or constitutionally mandated. This ambitious goal might not otherwise be achieved.

2. *Implications.* Legislative and executive action are not the only government influences on religious sorting. Court decisions also can play a role. An anti-sorting principle should prompt judiciaries to think about the consequences of their constitutional decisions for religious clumping across political boundaries. This might not entail massive doctrinal revision, but it would slant judicial choices in at least three ways.

First, a premium would be placed on *uniformity* in the treatment of religion by government across jurisdictions, to avoid incentives to sort. It follows that national decision making on issues of religious freedom would be preferred to local decision making. The former increases the likelihood that many religious and secular values are incorporated into the process for generating a national rule.[215] In fact, this preference for centralized solutions is not a departure from current judicial practice. Last Term was an excellent illustration. At the same time the Justices divided over state and local Ten Commandments displays, they voted unanimously to reject an Establishment Clause challenge to a federal statute that required religious accommodations for prison inmates.[216] The next most recent unanimous decision involving the Establishment Clause was nearly twenty years ago—and it likewise upheld a federal legislative accommodation.[217]

---

[213] *Board of Educ. of Kiryas Joel Vill. Sch. Dist. v Grumet*, 512 US 687, 728 (1994) (Kennedy, J, concurring).

[214] See id; cf. *United States v Hays*, 515 US 737, 739, 744–46 (1995) ("We have never held that the racial composition of a particular voting district, without more, can violate the Constitution.").

[215] Not to say that the mix at the federal level is all-inclusive. Some sects may be without political leverage. This concern can be addressed, however, with a sect-neutrality principle. Accommodations for any religion or comparable secular interest would have to reach all "religions."

[216] See *Cutter v Wilkinson*, 125 S Ct 2113, 2117–18 (2005).

[217] See *Corporation of Presiding Bishop of Church of Jesus Christ of Latter-Day Saints v Amos*, 483 US 327, 329–30 (1987).

On the other hand, invalidation of the Religious Freedom Restoration Act as applied to state and local action in *City of Boerne v Flores*[218] looks inconsistent with a strong anti-sorting principle. The Act provided a uniform standard for mandatory government accommodation of religion.[219] The Court's preferred test set out in *Employment Division v Smith*,[220] which nearly forecloses required accommodation,[221] might appear equally uniform. But the upshot of *Smith* empowered state politics to grant or withhold dispensations from secular burdens.[222] Likewise is *Locke v Davey*,[223] which permitted the State of Washington to exclude devotional theology majors from a college scholarship program. Each of these decisions would be suspect at best. They open the possibility of substantial policy diversity across jurisdictions on the sensitive issue of religious accommodations, and therefore create incentives for religious sorting. It is possible, of course, that every jurisdiction will provide the same set of accommodations as they compete for religious residents. But this is quite improbable given variable local preferences. In this regard, the tension between the Court's pre-*Smith* Free Exercise and Establishment Clause decisions on religious exemptions[224] no longer seems so bad. No one wants doctrine that simultaneously requires and forbids the same religious exemption. But narrowing the area of political discretion over exemptions should diminish incentives to sort.[225]

Second, a strong anti-sorting principle has a substantive bias beyond uniformity. More specifically, a *liberty-based* conception of religious freedom might be preferred to equality-based notions. The former is sensitive to government-imposed burdens on religion regardless of how the state treats anyone else. Outcomes do not nec-

---

[218] 521 US 507 (1997).

[219] 42 USC § 2000bb-1(a)–(b) (prohibiting government from substantially burdening religious exercise unless it demonstrates that the burden serves a compelling governmental interest by the least restrictive means).

[220] 494 US 872 (1990).

[221] See id at 879; Adam M. Samaha, *Litigant Sensitivity in First Amendment Law*, 98 Nw U L Rev 1291, 1336–37 n 238 (2004) (listing *Smith*'s possible limits).

[222] See *Smith*, 494 US at 890.

[223] 540 US 712 (2004).

[224] See, e.g., Suzanna Sherry, *Lee v Weisman: Paradox Redux*, 1992 Supreme Court Review 123.

[225] Perhaps Congress rather than the Supreme Court should be setting national rules for religious exemptions. But an anti-sorting theory probably has little to say about that institutional choice.

essarily depend on whether religion is being singled out, or whether a comparable group is receiving favorable treatment. An equality-based conception is pegged to just such facts. This means that successful claims are contingent on the features of a particular legal regime. That is unfortunate from the anti-sorting perspective. Variance should be minimized, even if it cannot be eliminated over a series of applications.

Thus the outcomes might be the same in cases like *Church of the Lukumi Babalu Aye v City of Hialeah*[226]—striking down local ordinances that singled out certain types of religiously motivated animal sacrifice[227]—and *Tenafly Eruv Association v Borough of Tenafly*[228]— holding that a municipality likely violated the Free Exercise Clause by prohibiting use of utility poles to demarcate an *eruv*.[229] But the rationales would be rewritten to stress the burden on religious practice from the challenged regulation, instead of intentionally disparate government treatment compared to some other conduct. A similar objection might be lodged against some federal statutes. Legislation akin to the Equal Access Act of 1984[230] might become problematic, although that particular statute's broad base of protected activities does relieve sorting fears, and the central source of decision making should be comforting.

Third, an anti-sorting orientation might *define "religion."* This is a notoriously difficult issue,[231] but guidance is provided by the objective. The problem with which anti-sorting is concerned involves uniformity of values or worldview. This is the condition that arguably produces threats of group polarization, monitoring difficulties, risks of government-facilitated proselytizing or ostracism. Accordingly, the anti-sorting principle suggests definitions of religion focusing on a shared belief system about good and evil, the purpose and origins of life, the relationship of human beings to a

---

[226] 508 US 520 (1993).

[227] See id at 524.

[228] 309 F3d 144 (3d Cir 2002), cert denied, 539 US 942 (2003).

[229] See id at 167–68 (relying on lack of executive enforcement against similar conduct).

[230] 20 USC § 4071(a)–(b) (prohibiting public secondary schools that receive federal funding and that choose to create a "limited open forum" from denying student access to the forum on the basis of the "religious, political, philosophical, or other content of the speech at such meetings"); *Board of Educ. of Westside Community Schs v Mergens*, 496 US 226, 253 (1990) (rejecting a facial challenge to the Act under the Establishment Clause).

[231] For helpful analysis, see Choper, *Securing Religious Liberty* at 64–86 (cited in note 60); Laurence H. Tribe, *American Constitutional Law* § 14-6 (2d ed 1988); and Kent Greenawalt, *Religion as a Concept in Constitutional Law*, 72 Cal L Rev 753 (1984).

higher power, and so forth. For anti-sorting claims, the concept of religion would come close to Paul Tillich's description of "ultimate concern"[232] and "deeply held" belief systems that guide human conduct, which were the target of Vietnam era conscientious objector cases.[233] Second, an organization and an interactive community also seem relevant—the types of features stressed by *Wisconsin v Yoder*,[234] albeit in a case of near-complete exit. But longevity, rituals, belief in a personified god or gods, and written scripture would be far less important in and of themselves. This time, a broad belief-oriented concept of religion would not be used to liberate individuals from secular power, but the concept nevertheless fits the aspirations of anti-sorting.

C.   RESERVATIONS

Having pushed the anti-sorting idea about as far as it might go, we should conclude with some hardheaded skepticism. The last implication regarding the definition of religion is a useful starting point. It suggests monumental difficulties with strong versions of an anti-sorting principle, at least when enforced by courts as constitutional law. Once elaborated, the principle becomes hard to confine to "religion"; and if it is so confined, the principle will disadvantage co-religionists seeking political power through sorting. More concretely, if shared ideology is basically what makes religious homogeneity within political communities problematic, then conventional definitions of religion do not capture the threat. They are underinclusive. Geographic separation by partisan affiliation, for example, could produce the same dynamic.[235] We might distinguish religious groups by their average commitment, cohesion, and unwillingness to compromise.[236] But surely that characterization is a crude one. Conventional notions of religion are

---

[232] Paul Tillich, *Dynamics of Faith* 1–12 (1957).

[233] *Welsh v United States*, 398 US 333, 344 (1970) (exempting "those whose consciences, spurred by deeply held moral, ethical, or religious beliefs, would give them no rest or peace"); id at 344–45 (Harlan, J, concurring); see *United States v Seeger*, 380 US 163, 180–83 (1965).

[234] 406 US 205, 216 (1972) (distinguishing the Amish and their "deep religious conviction, shared by an organized group, and intimately related to daily living").

[235] Compare *Vieth v Jubelierer*, 124 S Ct 1769, 1799 (2004) (Kennedy, J, concurring) (refusing, at least for the time being, to impose federal constitutional restraints on partisan gerrymandering).

[236] See note 176 and accompanying text.

also *over*inclusive for anti-sorting purposes. It is not clear that a monolithic community of, for example, nondenominational Christians presents the same risks of group polarization, lack of dissent, cascades, government proselytizing, and so on.

A lawyer's response—that religion must be treated differently because of constitutional text—is probably unavailable. It is not as if judicial suspicion of local action regarding religion was ever firmly guided by textualism. The judiciary certainly could have done a better job defending its application of non-establishment norms through the Fourteenth Amendment. Anyway, to be logically satisfying, anti-sorting principles might have to expand beyond religious separation, unless religion can be meaningfully distinguished in this context from other group characteristics. An argument, grounded in empirical fact, is needed to contrast religion from partisanship, race, gender, age, class, national origin, sexual orientation, and other concepts on which individuals might sort themselves. We can start by emphasizing shared values and organization, but that is just a beginning.

If religion is special, there are other powerful objections to strong anti-sorting principles. *Normative* complaints have been touched on above. We should not want a perfect distribution of religious and secular affiliates, even if we could get it. Particularly for groups posing no law-enforcement concerns and habitually losing political battles, a separate local government might do them and society much good.[237] Some social experiments require uniformity of purpose before they can be evaluated; and allowing them to play out reflects a healthy skepticism about perfection in mainstream culture.[238] Better that not every state and municipality end up like the Federal Election Commission: balanced and feckless.

A price of religious integration, furthermore, can be minority humiliation and unwanted assimilation.[239] At least sometimes, sep-

---

[237] Compare Heather K. Gerken, *Second-Order Diversity*, 118 Harv L Rev 1099 (2005) (drawing from scholarship in local government law and using juries and districting as examples); Ankur J. Goel et al., Comment, *Black Neighborhoods Becoming Black Cities: Group Empowerment, Local Control, and the Implications of Being Darker Than Brown*, 24 Harv CR-CL L Rev 415 (1988) (describing efforts to secede and incorporate East Palo Alto and Mandela as separate municipalities, and defending such a strategy for disadvantaged racial minorities).

[238] Accord Greene, 96 Colum L Rev at 8 (cited in note 13).

[239] Compare *Board of Educ. of Kiryas Joel Vill. Sch. Dist. v Grumet*, 512 US 687, 692

aration defuses enough social friction to make up for losses in empathy, learning, and the hope for intergroup cooperation. As well, religiosity seems to correlate with desperate conditions. Often religion thrives where people are at the brink of elimination.[240] Breaking up co-religionists into separate local democracies could dissipate solidarity that is useful for overcoming existential challenges. Perhaps there is no constitutional right to associate within a preferred government institution; but threats to disadvantaged communities ought to check any impulse favoring ambitious versions of an anti-sorting principle. In addition, religion has the potential of softening other problematic social divisions, like race. There is a long history of racial homogeneity in many U.S. churches,[241] but not all.[242] And there is always the draw of Tiebout, aggregated private choice, and interlocal competition.

Speaking of "diversity" raises a *conceptual* problem for an ambitious principle. What does it mean for a local political community to be sufficiently diverse when there are hundreds of recognized religions? "One of each" is not possible in a nation so vast without killing off countless sects.[243] The hard job, therefore, would be to articulate a minimum requirement for religious diversity within all or some types of local government.[244] Which religious "minorities" are substitutes for others? Should the law prioritize mainline mixing with the least powerful denominations, following a kind of anti-subordination value? Should it prize integration of denominations most in need of reconciliation, on the theory that social contact diminishes animosity? There are answers to these questions but it is tough to find them in conventional

---

(1994) (recounting social troubles of disabled Satmar children in the existing public schools).

[240] See Norris and Inglehart, *The Sacred and the Secular* at 240–41 (cited in note 182).

[241] See Kevin D. Dougherty, *How Monochromatic Is Church Membership? Racial-Ethnic Diversity in Religious Community*, 64 Soc of Relig 65, 74 (2003) (scoring a sample of congregations with the entropy index and noting that 42.9 percent were 100 percent racially homogenous).

[242] See ARIS Survey at 35 (cited in note 22) (exhibit 13); Howard Elinson, *The Implications of Pentecostal Religion for Intellectualism, Politics, and Race Relations*, 70 Am J Soc 403, 406, 414–15 & n 34 (1965); see also John Burdick, *What Is the Color of the Holy Spirit? Pentecostalism and Black Identity in Brazil*, 109 Latin Am Res Rev 109, 124 (1999).

[243] See also Michael Lewyn, *Suburban Sprawl, Jewish Law, and Jewish Values*, 13 Southeastern Envt'l L J 1, 23 (2004) (arguing that "sprawl is to some extent a Jewish issue").

[244] For an attempt to define a "racially balanced" public school, see *Comfort v Lynn Sch. Comm.*, 418 F3d 1, 6–9 & n 4 (1st Cir 2005) (en banc) (describing and upholding a local policy regulating the interschool transfer of pupils).

constitutional sources. It is far easier to identify religious homogeneity than to agree on the appropriate concept for diversity.

A softer cautionary note arises from uncertainty about the *extent* of religious sorting in America. Empirical data on religious segregation are less reliable and precise than is standard for other divisions like race and income. True, and as noted above, a trend-line of intercounty segregation scores can be calculated for religion.[245] On the other hand, county-level numbers are probably too general and there are weaknesses in the underlying data.[246] At least we can say that religiously homogenous counties are reason for integrationist worries, understanding that numbers alone will not depict political influence.

A related uncertainty is more important. Assuming there are troubling levels of religious separation—and that current separation is not so entrenched as to be irremediable—we lack a firm understanding of the *mechanisms* for religious sorting.[247] Why and how deeply do people prefer to stick with fellow believers in a state or municipal setting? It is not difficult to imagine that many people feel most comfortable, or are only comfortable, when their values and morality are reflected in those around them. This is true for denominations like the Old Order Amish and many Orthodox Jews. Yet we also know that people choose living, work, and recreational places for several reasons. Surveys indicate that residential location choices are often prompted by housing, family, or employment needs that are not necessarily related to religion.[248]

---

[245] See Rhode and Strumpf, 93 Am Econ Rev at 1671 (table 6) (cited in note 110).

[246] See note 82 and accompanying text.

[247] Compare Taeuber and Taeuber, *Negroes in Cities* at 28 (cited in note 202) (distinguishing processes from patterns of residential racial segregation). There are case studies from which lessons might be drawn. See Gerald Gamm, *Urban Exodus: Why the Jews Left Boston and the Catholics Stayed* 15–24 & n 10 (1999) (claiming that Jewish and Protestant congregations tend to be less territory-oriented than Catholic parishes, at least before Vatican II).

[248] See U.S. Census Bureau, *American Housing Survey for the United States* (2003) (table 2-11) (displaying results of survey questions on reasons/the main reason for choosing present neighborhood; reporting significant numbers under "looks/design" and "other"); U.S. Census Bureau, *Why People Move: Exploring the March 2000 Current Population Survey* 2 (2001).

The relative paucity of data on religious sorting in the United States might reflect relative calm among religions and secularists. Contrast research in countries with recent histories of serious interfaith battles, like Israel and Northern Ireland. See, e.g., A. S. Adair et al., *The Local Housing System in Craigavon, N. Ireland: Ethno-religious Residential Segregation, Socio-tenurial Polarisation and Sub-markets*, 37 Urban Studies 1079 (2000); John McPeake, *Religion and Residential Search Behaviour in the Belfast Urban Area*, 13 Housing

Religious demographics might play a role within the set of choices bounded by other necessities; but there seems to be no good formula for now. Furthermore, there is reason to believe that race and income are, on the whole, more powerful drivers of jurisdictional separation. Unlike religious heterogeneity scores, racial and income heterogeneity recently have been connected to the number of municipalities within U.S. counties.[249] On a related note, it is likely that some religious sorting is an artifact of other social divisions. Perhaps much religious separation is a consequence of racial separation. If so, attacking the former would not relieve sorting pressures generated by the latter.

Furthermore, it is not clear that tipping models for neighborhood changes in racial composition[250] work the same way for religion. Again, religion is less visible than race; and it might well be that fewer Americans feel strongly about the addition of new religions to their localities. Perhaps this bodes well for integration efforts, but it also suggests that any preferences for religious homogeneity will often be overrun by other factors. To the extent that the urge to sort religiously remains salient, we cannot be certain of the degree to which state action is implicated. With respect to government signaling, sometimes messages about demographics and power can be credibly delivered by private parties.[251] Organized religious groups have, by definition, overcome collective action problems. Uncertainty about the system of religious sorting in the United States today makes it hard to defend ambitious anti-sorting principles.

Studies 527 (1998); Itzhak Omer and Itzhak Benenson, *Investigating Fine-Scale Residential Segregation, by Means of Local Spatial Statistics*, 12 Geographical Res F 41 (2002).

[249] See Alesina et al, 112 J Pol Econ at 360–63, 387–91 (cited in note 189) (concentrating on 1960 and 1990, using 17 Judeo-Christian groupings, and calculating "heterogeneity" by the probability that two randomly selected residents will be members of the same group). The authors did, however, find a statistically significant relationship between the number of school attendance districts (in contrast to school districts) and religious heterogeneity at the county level, and which was stronger than that for such racial or income heterogeneity. See id at 368 (reporting that a two-standard-deviation increase in religious heterogeneity is associated with a 15 percent increase in school attendance areas).

[250] See generally Thomas C. Schelling, *Micromotives and Macrobehavior* 140–55 (1978); Abraham Bell and Gideon Parchomovsky, *The Integration Game*, 100 Colum L Rev 1965 (2000).

[251] After the Seventh Circuit barred a Ten Commandments monument from the lawn in front of the Elkhart municipal building, see *Books v City of Elkhart*, 235 F3d 292, 295 (7th Cir 2000), cert denied, 532 US 1058 (2001), it was relocated to a plot owned by a lumber company along the Riverwalk, see *Indiana Ten Commandments Case Won't Be Reopened*, AP, Aug 15, 2002.

These reservations do not mean that an anti-sorting principle is worthless or that courts should never intervene to prevent religious separation. Total judicial abstention and unyielding judicial enforcement of aggressive anti-sorting rules are equally extravagant positions. Yet current constitutional law has the advantage of flexibility; anti-sorting ideas are present but not fully articulated. We can therefore advocate small steps without disrupting settled law. Despite the uncertainties, courts have strong reason to enforce a rule along the lines of the one suggested above[252]—invalidating government action if it is both designed and likely to help achieve religious homogeneity within a political jurisdiction—at least absent a genuine purpose of accommodating a subordinated group in accord with free-exercise values. Furthermore, a modest anti-sorting principle should affect other constitutional doctrine drafted by courts. In situations of reasonable doubt, the judiciary should favor doctrine that is less likely to generate religious sorting across political boundaries. Even these cautious moves are subject to dispute, of course, for being too loose or too vague. But they are defensible guidelines for courts. Going much further would require knowledge and justification that we do not now have.

All of this indicates that the Supreme Court was correct to leave the Texas monument alone and perhaps wrong to order removal of the McCreary County display. Signaling a local religious character is within the concern of even modest anti-sorting principles. But those versions of the principle have little apprehension for a forty-year-old monument, sharing space with other sculpture on state capitol grounds, identified by date and private donor. It is hard to imagine this icon having much present effect on decisions of outsiders to locate or visit in Austin or the State of Texas, and the limited record provided no reason to believe that the politicians who accepted the gift intended otherwise. The anti-proselytism principle can complement anti-sorting arguments, but the former has little traction in this setting. McCreary County's promotional efforts are more troubling, but likely innocuous as a constitutional matter without additional information. Placing a Decalogue inside a building used for vehicle registration and trial court business is a poor strategy for attracting or repelling transients. A high-profile external display would be far more vulnerable

---

[252] See text accompanying notes 199–204.

to anti-sorting arguments.[253] This does not imply that anti-sorting principles will not invalidate state action that is likely to occur—which might be an unhealthy requirement for constitutional doctrine in any event. Republic, Missouri, is not the only contemporary American polity that has indicated a longing to manufacture religious homogeneity.[254]

Conclusions

The endorsement test is, like the rest of the doctrine surrounding religious establishments, primarily concerned with state and local misbehavior. There are historical, structural, and theoretical reasons for this. But taking away majority-supported symbols generates more resentment than one might anticipate. So it makes sense to have a strong reason for doing it. Anti-proselytism—preventing state power from joining or overrunning religious missions to inculcate citizens—is a defensible constitutional objective. However, this problem is not strongly implicated by many public religious messages. And supporters of the anti-proselytism principle seem to take community membership as unrealistically static. Adding an anti-sorting principle—which would cover state and local governments influencing their demographics by the strategic deployment of religious symbols—provides needed heft to the non-endorsement idea. Equally important, the principle understands political community membership as dynamic and shaped by state action.

At the same time, humility is in order. We do not know all that we reasonably might about the system of religious sorting in America. In addition, strong anti-sorting rules are understandably controversial. Nobody should want an even distribution of every identifiable denomination and secular philosophy across every political jurisdiction. A defensible measure of "religious diversity," moreover, is not readily available. Nor will the work done on race smoothly carry over into the religion context, where the historical, sociological, and normative differences fall somewhere between

---

[253] It is possible that a relatively poor area like McCreary meant to boost local loyalty to the County by reflecting community values as a way of retaining population. But without more evidence, this is speculation.

[254] See notes 89–95 and accompanying text (collecting examples that might constitute unconstitutional government encouragement of religious sorting by political jurisdiction, all of which took place during the development of the endorsement test).

significant and massive. Tempered measures are best, especially
with respect to constitutional law enforced by courts. For now the
judicial focus ought to be on religious homogeneity within political
jurisdictions, official action that consciously and effectively promotes or entrenches such sorting, and the sorting risks that ac-
company other doctrinal choices. Doing this much would be relatively unambitious yet meaningful.

Whatever are the appropriate doctrinal implications, an anti-
sorting perspective focuses on questions that matter. It pinpoints
live social phenomena in a modern, dynamic, and religiously diverse nation. This should be a welcome addition to our continuing
search for the proper relationship between religion and political
institutions. If remixing the Supreme Court's composition helps
us revisit this relationship, then the endorsement test's inevitable
retirement is also a hopeful beginning.

ROBERT POST

COMPELLED SUBSIDIZATION OF SPEECH: JOHANNS v LIVESTOCK MARKETING ASSOCIATION

In recent years the Supreme Court has decided a spate of cases about the compelled subsidization of speech.[1] All have involved federal statutes creating industry boards empowered to tax producers of specific agricultural products in order to promote and stabilize the market in those products. Some of these statutes were enacted during the New Deal era,[2] whereas others are quite recent.[3] In the past decade these statutes have been challenged on the ground that they compel producers to subsidize objectionable commercial advertisements. The resulting cases have raised conceptually difficult and complex First Amendment questions, which the Court has proved unable to master.

At first, in *Glickman v Wileman Bros. & Elliott*,[4] the Court upheld a federal marketing program for California summer fruits that required private parties to subsidize an advertising campaign. Dis-

---

Robert Post is David Boies Professor of Law, Yale Law School.

Author's note: I am grateful for the immensely helpful comments of Don Herzog, Fred Schauer, Reva Siegel, Geof Stone, and Jim Weinstein, as well as for the invaluable assistance of David Newman, Matt Spence, Robert Wiygul, and Mark Wu.

[1] *Glickman v Wileman Bros. & Elliott*, 521 US 457 (1997); *United States v United Foods, Inc.*, 533 US 405 (2001); *Johanns v Livestock Mktg Ass'n*, 125 S Ct 2055 (2005).

[2] *Glickman*, 521 US at 461.

[3] *United Foods*, 533 US at 408.

[4] 521 US 457 (1997).

missing claims that this mandated subsidization amounted to compelled speech in violation of the First Amendment, the Court in a narrow five-to-four opinion held that "our compelled speech case law . . . is clearly inapplicable to the regulatory scheme at issue here."[5] Four years later the Court reversed course, and in *United States v United Foods, Inc.*[6] struck down a program designed to promote and stabilize the market in fresh mushrooms. The opinion, joined by six Justices, announced that "First Amendment concerns apply" whenever the state requires persons to "subsidize speech with which they disagree."[7]

The Court's opinion in *United Foods* sparked a cascade of lower-court decisions that rapidly developed what may be called compelled subsidization of speech doctrine,[8] which in the remainder of this article I shall refer to as "CSSD." *United Foods* set forth the basic premise of CSSD: First Amendment scrutiny is triggered whenever someone is forced to pay for speech that she finds objectionable. Because taxation involves the compelled subsidization of government speech, an obvious difficulty with this premise is that it seems to imply that constitutional scrutiny is required every time a taxpayer disagrees with government messages supported by her tax dollars. This is plainly an untenable position, yet the seemingly inexorable pressure of CSSD led the Eighth Circuit in *Livestock Marketing Ass'n v Department of Agriculture*[9] to conclude that "a determination that the expression at issue is government speech

---

[5] Id at 470.

[6] 533 US 405 (2001).

[7] Id at 410–11. An important question, which I shall not discuss in this article, is whether and how compelled speech doctrine ought to apply to the kind of commercial speech that is at issue in these cases. See note 117 below.

[8] See, e.g., *Pelts & Skins, LLC v Landreneau*, 365 F3d 423 (5th Cir 2004) (Louisiana Alligator Resource Fund), vacated, 125 S Ct 2511 (2005); *Cochran v Veneman*, 359 F3d 263 (3d Cir 2004) (Dairy Promotion Stabilization Act of 1983), vacated sub nom, *Lovell v Cochran*, 125 S Ct 2511 (2005), and *Johanns v Cochran*, 125 S Ct 2512 (2005); *Mich. Pork Producers Ass'n v Veneman*, 348 F3d 157 (6th Cir 2003) (Pork Promotion, Research and Consumer Information Act), vacated sub nom, *Mich. Pork Producer Ass'n v Campaign for Family Farms*, 125 S Ct 2511 (2005), and *Johanns v Campaign for Family Farms*, 125 S Ct 2511 (2005); *Delano Farms Co. v Cal. Table Grape Comm'n*, 318 F3d 895 (9th Cir 2003) (California Table Grape Commission); *In re Wash. State Apple Adver. Comm'n*, 257 F Supp 2d 1290 (ED Wash 2003) (Washington State Apple Commission); *Charter v U.S. Dep't of Agr.*, 230 F Supp 2d 1121 (D Mont 2002), vacated, 412 F3d 1017 (9th Cir 2005); *Gerawan Farming, Inc. v Kawamura*, 90 P3d 1179 (Cal 2004); *Dep't of Citrus v Graves Bros. Co.*, 889 So2d 831 (Fla Dist Ct App 2004).

[9] 335 F3d 711 (8th Cir 2003), vacated sub nom, *Johanns v Livestock Mktg. Ass'n*, 125 S Ct 2055 (2005).

does not preclude First Amendment scrutiny in the compelled speech context."[10]

The Supreme Court acted swiftly to check this radical implication of its own doctrine. Last Term in *Johanns v Livestock Marketing Ass'n*[11] it reversed the Eighth Circuit to hold "that compelled funding of government speech does not alone raise First Amendment concerns."[12] Although *Johanns* is quite definite that citizens "have no First Amendment right not to fund government speech,"[13] it never offers a theoretical account of why taxation is an exception to the basic premise of CSSD. *Johanns* instead stresses the practical point that "it seems inevitable that funds raised by the government will be spent for speech and other expression to advocate and defend its own policies."[14] The exemption accorded by *Johanns* to government speech is thus a blunt *ipse dixit*; it does not prompt the Court to reconsider the basic framework of CSSD.

This is unfortunate, for CSSD's failure to explain why taxation should not prompt constitutional scrutiny is merely the surface manifestation of deep conceptual insufficiencies. Indeed, I shall argue in this article that the fundamental premise of CSSD is flawed, and that the premise has accordingly generated a dangerously unstable doctrinal structure which *Johanns* patched but did not repair. It is simply not true that First Amendment concerns are implicated whenever persons are required to subsidize speech with which they disagree. My thesis is that CSSD cannot be rebuilt along theoretically defensible lines until we have some better explanation of when

---

[10] *Livestock Mktg.*, 335 F3d at 723 n 9. The court explained, "appellees in the present case are challenging the government's authority to compel them to support speech with which they personally disagree; such compulsion is a form of 'government interference with private speech.' The two categories of First Amendment cases—government speech cases and compelled speech cases—are fundamentally different." Id at 720.

[11] 125 S Ct 2055 (2005).

[12] Id at 2062.

[13] Id at 2063.

[14] Id at 2062 (quoting *Bd. of Regents v Southworth*, 529 US 217, 229 (2000)). In *Keller v State Bar of California*, 496 US 112–13 (1990), the Court was more explicit about the practical impossibility of extending the doctrinal structure of CSSD to include government speech:

> Government officials are expected as a part of the democratic process to represent and to espouse the views of a majority of their constituents. . . . If every citizen were to have a right to insist that no one paid by public funds express a view with which he disagreed, debate over issues of great concern to the public would be limited to those in the private sector, and the process of government as we know it radically transformed.

First Amendment review should be triggered and when it should not. Without such an explanation, the Court stands at risk of the kind of untoward consequences and embarrassing pirouettes that have afflicted its recent forays into this area.

I. CSSD After Johanns

In 1985 Congress enacted the Beef Promotion and Research Act,[15] which announced that it was "in the public interest to authorize the establishment . . . of an orderly procedure for financing (through assessments on all cattle sold in the United States and on cattle, beef, and beef products imported into the United States) and [for] carrying out a coordinated program of promotion and research designed to strengthen the beef industry's position in the marketplace and to maintain and expand domestic and foreign markets and uses for beef and beef products."[16] The Act directed the Secretary of Agriculture to establish a "Cattlemen's Beef Promotion and Research Board,"[17] whose members would "be cattle producers and importers appointed by the Secretary,"[18] and in particular to establish a Beef Promotion Operating Committee, which would be composed of ten Board members elected by the Board "and ten producers elected by a federation that includes as members the qualified State beef councils."[19] The function of the Committee was to "develop plans or projects of promotion and advertising, research, consumer information, and industry information, which shall be paid for with assessments collected by the Board."[20]

The Act provided that the promotional campaigns of the Committee and the Board were to be subject to the approval of the Secretary of Agriculture, and that they were to be supported by an excise tax, or "checkoff," on the sale or importation of cattle or on the importation of beef products.[21] Since 1988, "more than $1 billion has been collected through the checkoff and a large fraction of that sum has been spent on promotional projects authorized by

---

[15] 7 USC §§ 2901–11 (2000).

[16] 7 USC § 2901(b).

[17] 7 USC § 2904(1).

[18] Id.

[19] 7 USC § 2904(4)(A).

[20] 7 USC § 2904(4)(B).

[21] *Johanns*, 125 S Ct at 2058.

the Beef Act—many using the familiar trademarked slogan 'Beef. It's What's for Dinner.'"[22]

Two associations whose members paid the checkoff and several individuals who raised and sold cattle brought suit objecting to various statutory and constitutional aspects of the promotional program sponsored by the Beef Board and its Operating Committee. While their suit was pending, the Supreme Court decided *United States v United Foods, Inc.,*[23] in which the Court, over the dissenting votes of Justices O'Connor, Ginsburg, and Breyer, upheld a challenge to the Mushroom Promotion, Research, and Consumer Information Act.[24] The Act authorized the Secretary of Agriculture to create a Mushroom Council empowered to impose mandatory assessments on handlers of fresh mushrooms in order to serve the statute's goals of advancing projects of mushroom promotion, research, consumer information, and industry information.[25] The Court concluded that requiring mushroom growers to subsidize a mushroom promotional campaign with which they disagreed violated their First Amendment rights.

The cattlemen amended their complaint to allege First Amendment violations of a similar nature. The Eighth Circuit concluded that "'[t]he beef checkoff program is, in all material respects, identical to the mushroom checkoff' at issue in *United Foods.*"[26] Although the Court in *United Foods* had pretermitted the claim that "the advertising here is government speech, and so immune from the scrutiny we would otherwise apply,"[27] the Eighth Circuit held that even on the assumption that the promotional programs sponsored by the Beef Board were government speech, compelled subsidization of the programs could be justified only if "the governmental interest in the commercial advertising under the Beef Act is sufficiently substantial to justify the infringement upon appellees' First Amendment right not to be compelled to subsidize that commercial

---

[22] Id at 2059 (citation omitted). The Eight Circuit found that at least 50% of the checkoff funds were used to support advertising planned by the Operating Committee. 335 F3d at 717.

[23] 533 US 405 (2001).

[24] 7 USC §§ 6101–12 (2000).

[25] 7 USC § 6104(c)(4).

[26] 335 F3d at 717 (quoting *Livestock Mktg. Ass'n v U.S. Dep't of Agric.*, 207 F Supp 2d 992, 1002 (DSD 2002)).

[27] *United Foods*, 533 US at 416. The reason offered by the Court was that "this argument was 'not raised or addressed' in the Court of Appeals." Id.

speech."[28] Answering that inquiry in the negative, the Eighth Circuit ruled that the beef checkoff program established by the Beef Promotion and Research Act was unconstitutional on its face.

The Supreme Court reversed the Eighth Circuit in *Johanns v Livestock Marketing Ass'n*.[29] The opinion for the Court was authored by Justice Scalia. It was joined by Chief Justice Rehnquist and by Justices O'Connor, Thomas, and Breyer. Scalia began his analysis by dividing "First Amendment challenges to allegedly compelled expression"[30] into two categories. He distinguished "true 'compelled speech' cases, in which an individual is obliged personally to express a message he disagrees with, imposed by the government,"[31] from "'compelled subsidy' cases, in which an individual is required by the government to subsidize a message he disagrees with, expressed by a private entity."[32]

Acknowledging that the Court in *United Foods* had struck down "an assessment very similar to the beef checkoff, imposed to fund mushroom advertising,"[33] Scalia noted that *United Foods* had nevertheless rested "on the assumption that the advertising was private speech, not government speech."[34] This assumption was decisive, because *Johanns* announced the categorical rule that individuals "have no First Amendment right not to fund government speech."[35] Scalia did not seek to explain this rule, except to observe that "[s]ome of our cases have justified compelled funding of government speech by pointing out that government speech is subject to democratic accountability."[36]

---

[28] 335 F3d at 723.

[29] 125 S Ct 2055 (2005).

[30] *Johanns*, 125 S Ct at 2060.

[31] Id.

[32] Id. In compelled subsidy cases "individuals are compelled not to speak, but to subsidize a private message with which they disagree." Id at 2060–61.

[33] Id at 2061.

[34] Id.

[35] Id at 2063.

[36] Id at 2064. Scalia also noted in a footnote that the compelled subsidization of private speech violates the First Amendment "because being forced to fund someone else's private speech unconnected to any legitimate government purpose violates personal autonomy." Id at 2065 n 8. "Such a violation does not occur," Scalia continued, "when the exaction funds government speech." Id. This reasoning does not distinguish *Johanns* from *United Foods*, because the "government purpose" in *United Foods* was exactly the same as its purpose in *Johanns*: the stabilization and promotion of a market for American agricultural produce. The categorical distinction between being compelled to subsidize private speech and being

The debate in *Johanns* was whether the advertisements sponsored by the beef checkoff program were in fact government speech. In the years after *United Foods*, lower courts had more or less come to the conclusion that the First Amendment did not prohibit the compulsory funding of government speech,[37] and they had articulated an intricate jurisprudence to distinguish government from private speech. This jurisprudence asked two questions. The first focused on whether "the government nominally controls the production of advertisements, but as a practical matter has delegated control over the speech to a particular group that represents only one segment of the population."[38] The second focused on whether persons were compelled to fund government speech through general taxation or instead through "assessments levied on a particular group."[39]

Johanns flatly rejects both these factors. Even though the promotional campaigns of the Beef Board and its Operating Committee

---

compelled to subsidize government speech thus cannot be explained by the presence or absence of a legitimate government purpose.

[37] Most courts differed in this regard from the Eighth Circuit decision in *Livestock Marketing*. See text at note 10. For a classic statement, see *R.J. Reynolds Tobacco Co. v Shewry*, 384 F3d 1126, 1136 (9th Cir 2004).

[38] *R.J. Reynolds*, 384 F3d at 1136. See, e.g., *Pelts & Skins, LLC v Landreneau*, 365 F3d 423, 431 (5th Cir 2004) (holding that generic advertising authorized by the Louisiana Fur and Alligator Advisory Council is not government speech in part because the Council "reflects private rather than government interests"), vacated, 125 S Ct 2511 (2005); *Cochran v Veneman*, 359 F3d 263, 279 (3d Cir 2004) (holding that government speech doctrine does not apply to generic advertising by the National Dairy Promotion and Research Board because the "promotional programs" created by the Dairy Promotion Stabilization Act of 1983 are "special interest legislation on behalf of the industry's interest more so than the government's"), vacated sub nom, *Lovell v Cochran*, 125 S Ct 2511 (2005), and *Johanns v Cochran*, 125 S Ct 2512 (2005); *Mich. Pork Producers Ass'n v Veneman*, 348 F3d 157, 161 (6th Cir 2003) ("[T]he pork industry's extensive control over the Pork Act's promotional activities prevents their attribution to the government."), vacated sub nom, *Mich. Pork Producers Ass'n v Campaign for Family Farms*, 125 S Ct 2511 (2005), and *Johanns v Campaign for Family Farms*, 125 S Ct 2511 (2005); *In re Wash. State Apple Adver. Comm'n*, 257 F Supp 2d 1274, 1281–82 (ED Wash 2003) (holding that government speech doctrine does not apply to generic advertising by the Washington State Apple Commission because "the Commission is not answerable to the State of Washington" and "the Government retains virtually no control over the Commission").

[39] *Pelts & Skins*, 365 F3d at 430. See *Mich. Pork Producers*, 348 F3d 157, 161–62 (6th Cir 2003) ("[T]he Pork Act's promotion activities" are not government speech in part because, "unlike the typical scenario in which speech is considered governmental in nature, the programs' funding does not come from general tax revenues. . . . The Pork Act's funding comes solely from mandatory assessments paid by pork producers . . . ."); *United States v Frame*, 885 F2d 1119, 1132 (3d Cir 1989) ("When the government allocates money from the general tax fund to controversial projects or expressive activities, the nexus between the message and the individual is attenuated. In contrast, where the government requires a publicly identified group to contribute to a fund earmarked for the dissemination of a particular message associated with that group, the government has directly focused its coercive power for expressive purposes").

were supported by assessments levied specifically on beef producers, *Johanns* holds that the "First Amendment does not confer a right to pay one's taxes into the general fund, because the injury of compelled funding (as opposed to the injury of compelled speech) does not stem from the Government's mode of accounting."[40] And even though as a practical matter the Beef Board and its Operating Committee were deliberately designed to include the interests of the beef industry, *Johanns* holds that "[w]hen, as here, the government sets the overall message to be communicated and approves every word that is disseminated, it is not precluded from relying on the government-speech doctrine merely because it solicits assistance from nongovernmental sources in developing specific messages."[41] *Johanns* also deems it irrelevant that the promotional campaign subsidized by the Beef Board and its Operating Committee never announced that it was sponsored by the government, and indeed that the campaign seemed to disguise that fact by producing advertisements which typically displayed "the attribution 'Funded by America's Beef Producers.'"[42]

Johanns holds that a First Amendment claim of compelled speech, as distinct from compelled subsidization of speech, would lie if the Beef Board's advertisements "were attributed" to individual plaintiffs.[43] But such a claim of compelled speech could not be used to attack the Beef Promotion and Research Act on its face. At most it could be used to invalidate those particular applications of the Act in which specific plaintiffs could produce credible evidence that

---

[40] 125 S Ct at 2063. "Apportioning the burden of funding government operations (including speech) through taxes and other levies does not violate autonomy simply because individual taxpayers feel 'singled out' or find the exaction 'galling.'" Id at 2065 n 8.

[41] Id at 2063. "Here, the beef advertisements are subject to political safeguards more than adequate to set them apart from private messages. The program is authorized and the basic message prescribed by federal statute, and specific requirements for the promotions' content are imposed by federal regulations promulgated after notice and comment. The Secretary of Agriculture, a politically accountable official, oversees the program, appoints and dismisses the key personnel, and retains absolute veto power over the advertisements' content, right down to the wording. And Congress, of course, retains oversight authority, not to mention the ability to reform the program at any time. No more is required." Id at 2064.

[42] Id at 2059 (citation omitted). "[T]he correct focus is not on whether the ads' audience realizes the government is speaking, but on the compelled assessment's purported interference with respondents' First Amendment rights. As we hold today, respondents enjoy no right not to fund government speech—whether by broad-based taxes or targeted assessments, and whether or not the reasonable viewer would identify the speech as the government's." Id at 2064 n 7.

[43] Id at 2065.

Beef Board advertisements were actually attributed to them. The Court could see no such evidence in the record.

Justice Thomas joined Scalia's opinion for the Court, but he wrote separately to emphasize his continuing allegiance to what he regarded as the fundamental premise of *United Foods*, which was "that '[a]ny regulation that compels the funding of advertising must be subjected to the most stringent First Amendment scrutiny.'"[44] Thomas, like Scalia, did not explain why this principle did not apply to compelled funding of government speech.[45] He pointed only to the brute practicalities of the situation: "I recognize that this principle must be qualified where the regulation compels the funding of speech that is the government's own. It cannot be that all taxpayers have a First Amendment objection to taxpayer-funded government speech, even if the funded speech is not 'germane' to some broader regulatory program."[46]

Justice Breyer also authored a separate opinion. He had dissented in *United Foods* on the grounds "that the challenged assessments involved a form of economic regulation, not speech."[47] Breyer joined the opinion of the Court in *Johanns* "[w]ith the caveat that I continue to believe that my dissent in *United Foods* offers a preferable approach."[48] Justice Ginsburg concurred in the judgment of the Court. Although she refused to credit that the advertisements funded by the checkoff program were "government speech," because they were not "attributed to the Government,"[49] she nevertheless continued to maintain, as she had in *United Foods*, that "the assessments in

---

[44] Id at 2066 (Thomas, J, concurring) (quoting *United Foods*, 533 US 405, 419 (2001) (Thomas, J, concurring)).

[45] Thomas did note that "[t]he payment of taxes to the government for purposes of supporting government speech is not nearly as intrusive as being forced to 'utter what is not in [one's] mind,' or to carry an unwanted message on one's property." Id at 2067 (quoting *W. Va. Bd. of Ed. v Barnette*, 319 US 624, 634 (1942)). But of course this line of thought would seem to suggest that in each case of subsidized speech, the presence or absence of First Amendment concerns would depend upon the extent of intrusion created by the precise method of subsidization. This would in turn undermine what Thomas evidently regarded as the fundamental premise of *United Foods*, which was that the compelled funding of speech *always* raised First Amendment concerns.

[46] Id at 2066. Thomas also stressed that "[t]he government may not, consistent with the First Amendment, associate individuals or organizations involuntarily with speech by attributing an unwanted message to them, whether or not those individuals fund the speech, and whether or not the message is under the government's control." Id.

[47] Id at 2067 (Breyer, J, concurring).

[48] Id.

[49] Id at 2067 (Ginsburg, J, concurring in the judgment).

these cases . . . qualify as permissible economic regulation."[50]

Justice Souter authored the principal dissent; he was joined by Stevens and Kennedy. He began with the premise that the facts of *Johanns* were "on all fours with *United Foods*,"[51] which had struck down the Mushroom Promotion, Research, and Consumer Information Act because it "violated the growers' First Amendment right to refuse to pay for expression when they object to its content."[52] Souter agreed with the Court that there was a "need to recognize the legitimacy of government's power to speak despite objections by dissenters whose taxes or other exactions necessarily go in some measure to putting the offensive message forward to be heard."[53] But he argued that on the facts of *Johanns* the advertisements of the Beef Board and its Operating Committee ought not to be considered government speech.

Souter's argument is complex and not entirely transparent, but its gist is that infringements of the "presumptive autonomy"[54] protected by the First Amendment against compelled subsidization of speech must be evaluated not only in light of the state's interest in requiring subsidization,[55] but also with an eye to the precise forms of subsidization exacted by the state and to the mechanisms that could potentially serve as "an effective political check on forced funding for speech."[56] Souter contrasted government speech supported by revenues secured through general taxation with government speech supported by revenues secured through narrowly targeted assessments, like those at issue in *Johanns*:

> [W]hen government funds its speech with general tax revenue, as it usually does, no individual taxpayer or group of taxpayers can lay claim to a special, or even a particularly strong, connection to the money spent (and hence to the speech funded). Outrage is likely to be rare, and disagreement tends to stay temperate.

---

[50] Id at 2068.

[51] Id at 2070 (Souter, J, dissenting).

[52] Id at 2069.

[53] Id at 2070. Souter, like the other Justices who considered the question, seemed to conceive the relationship between government speech and CSSD in terms of sheer practical necessity. "To govern, government has to say something, and a First Amendment heckler's veto of any forced contribution to raising the government's voice in the 'marketplace of ideas' would be out of the question." Id.

[54] Id at 2071.

[55] Souter interprets *United Foods* as prohibiting "compelled subsidy of speech . . . absent a comprehensive regulatory scheme to which the speech was incidental." Id at 2068.

[56] Id at 2073 n 8.

But the relative palatability of a remote subsidy shared by every taxpayer is not to be found when the speech is funded with targeted taxes. For then, as here, the particular interests of those singled out to pay the tax are closely linked with the expression, and taxpayers who disagree with it suffer a more acute limitation on their presumptive autonomy as speakers to decide what to say and what to pay for others to say.[57]

Souter's basic point is that the "autonomy" of persons to refuse to fund speech with which they disagree grows more compromised as the link between the subsidy and the speech becomes closer and more direct.[58] Speech supported by "a targeted assessment . . . makes the First Amendment affront more galling."[59] In such circumstances "greater care is required to assure that the political

---

[57] Id at 2071 (citation omitted).

[58] Seventeen years ago the Third Circuit, considering the same statute as that at issue in *Johanns*, articulated this basic idea in terms of what it called a "coerced nexus" test:

Both the right to be free from compelled expressive association and the right to be free from compelled affirmation of belief presuppose a coerced nexus between the individual and the specific expressive activity. When the government allocates money from the general tax fund to controversial projects or expressive activities, the nexus between the message and the individual is attenuated. In contrast, where the government requires a publicly identified group to contribute to a fund earmarked for the dissemination of a particular message associated with that group, the government has directly focused its coercive power for expressive purposes. This sort of funding scheme, with its close nexus between the individual and the message funded, more closely resembles the *Abood* situation, where the unions, as exclusive bargaining agents, served as the locutors for a distinguishable segment of the population, i.e., the employees, or the *Wooley* case, where the state "require[d] an individual to participate in the dissemination of an ideological message by displaying it on his property in a manner and for the express purpose that it be observed and read by the public," regardless of whether the state-issued license plates constituted "government speech."

United States v Frame, 885 F2d 1119, 1132–33 (3d Cir 1989) (citations omitted) (quoting *Wooley v Maynard*, 430 US 705, 713 (1977)). The coerced nexus test was influential among lower courts. See, e.g., *Pelts & Skins, LLC v Landreneau*, 365 F3d 423 (5th Cir 2004), vacated, 125 S Ct 2511 (2005); *Cal-Almond, Inc. v Calif. Dept. of Agric.*, 14 F3d 429, 435 (9th Cir 1993); *Summit Med. Ctr of Ala., Inc. v Riley*, 284 F Supp 2d 1350, 1360–61 (MD Ala 2003). See also *Forum for Academic and Institutional Rights v Rumsfeld*, 390 F3d 219, 259 (3d Cir 2004); *R.J. Reynolds Tobacco Co. v Shewry*, 384 F3d 1126, 1149 (9th Cir 2004) (Trott, J, dissenting).

[59] *Johanns*, 125 S Ct at 2071. Souter invokes "the commonsense notion that individuals feel a closer connection to speech that they are singled out to fund with targeted taxes than they do to expression paid for with general revenues. We recognized this in *Massachusetts v Mellon*, 262 US 447 (1923), where we noted that the individual taxpayer's 'interest in the moneys of the Treasury—partly realized from taxation and partly from other sources—is shared with millions of others [and] is comparatively minute and indeterminable.' Id. at 487. This commonsense notion, then, provides a 'principled way' to distinguish in this context between targeted and general taxes." Id at 2071 n 4.

process can practically respond to limit the compulsion . . . ."[60]

Souter conceives political accountability as ensuring "that government is not untouchable when its speech rubs against the First Amendment interests of those who object to supporting it; if enough voters disagree with what government says, the next election will cancel the message."[61] "[T]he requirement of effective public accountability" is not met in *Johanns,* Souter argues, because "the Beef Act does not establish an advertising scheme subject to effective democratic checks. . . . [T]he ads are not required to show any sign of being speech by the Government, and experience under the Act demonstrates how effectively the Government has masked its role in producing the ads."[62] Souter thus concludes that the government speech exception to CSSD ought not to apply in *Johanns*: "[E]xpression that is not ostensibly governmental, which government is not required to embrace as publicly as it speaks, cannot constitute government speech sufficient to justify enforcement of a targeted subsidy to broadcast it."[63]

The exact function of political accountability in Souter's dissent is obscure. Souter writes as if accountability were necessary to check government taxation from becoming too violently inconsistent with the First Amendment interests of those forced to subsidize government speech. But why political accountability would perform this function is never explained. It is true that we can expect voters to cancel messages that they dislike, but voters have no particular reason to cancel those messages that especially violate the autonomy of taxpayers. It may be that cattlemen deeply object to, and find

---

[60] Id at 2071–72 (Souter, J, dissenting). Such scrutiny would be practical, Souter argues, because "[w]hereas it would simply be unrealistic to think that every speech subsidy from general revenue could or should be scrutinized for its amenability to effective political response, the less-common targeted speech subsidies can be reviewed specifically for their susceptibility to response by the voters, and the intensity of the provocation experienced by the targeted group justifies just such scrutiny." Id at 2072.

[61] Id at 2071.

[62] Id at 2072. "It means nothing," Souter writes, "that Government officials control the message if that fact is never required to be made apparent to those who get the message, let alone if it is affirmatively concealed from them. The political accountability of the officials with control is insufficient, in other words, just because those officials are allowed to use their control (and in fact are deliberately using it) to conceal their role from the voters with the power to hold them accountable." Id at 2073.

[63] Id at 2073–74. Justice Kennedy in *Johanns* filed a short separate opinion to note that he would "reserve for another day the difficult First Amendment questions that would arise if the government were to target a discrete group of citizens to pay even for speech that the government does 'embrace as publicly as it speaks.'" Id at 2068 (Kennedy, J, dissenting).

especially galling, a message that is quite popular with voters. Public approval of a message does not seem a plausible candidate for a mechanism to prevent the abuse of the autonomy of targeted tax-payers.[64]

Souter proposes that the First Amendment interest protected by CSSD is the "autonomy"[65] not to be connected through the medium of money to speech to which one objects. Souter invokes the "commonsense notion" that this "connection" can be "closer" or less close,[66] depending upon the directness of the relationship between the subsidy and the speech it funds. As the connection grows closer, the violation of First Amendment autonomy grows greater; as the connection becomes more distant, the violation diminishes in significance. That is why for Souter the doctrinal notion of "government speech" is at most a label used to express the outcome of a detailed process of constitutional analysis and balancing. Souter's dissent is in fact carefully written to avoid the implication that "government speech" is a categorical exception to CSSD. Souter asks only whether the interests served by a particular instance of "government speech" are "sufficient to justify enforcement of a targeted subsidy to broadcast it."[67]

In contrast, Scalia's majority opinion conceives "government speech" as a distinct category of expression that obliterates whatever First Amendment interest persons may have in not being required to subsidize the speech of others. Although Scalia apparently agrees with Souter that the underlying constitutional interest at stake is

---

[64] I do not mean to deny, of course, that there may be circumstances in which First Amendment jurisprudence should care very deeply about political accountability. The Constitution ought to be concerned, for example, about the distortions potentially inflicted upon the marketplace of ideas whenever the government enters public debate by stealth, as apparently occurred when the Department of Health and Human Services packaged video segments promoting a Medicare bill to look like news reports and paid to broadcast them during local news telecasts, or when the Department of Education paid the columnist Armstrong Williams to promote the No Child Left Behind Act in his capacity as a television pundit. See generally Clay Calvert, *Payola, Pundits, and the Press: Weighing the Pros and Cons of FCC Regulation*, 13 Commlaw Conspectus 245 (2005); Gregory Klass, *The Very Idea of a First Amendment Right Against Compelled Subsidization*, 38 UC Davis L Rev 1087, 1128–29 (2005). But the constitutional issues raised by government stealth do not depend upon whether government speech is funded by a general tax or by targeted assessments. These issues are structural and do not involve the "autonomy" First Amendment rights of individual taxpayers.

[65] See text at note 57.

[66] See note 59 above.

[67] *Johanns*, 125 S Ct at 2073 (Souter, J, dissenting).

one of "personal autonomy,"[68] he conceptualizes the "government speech" exception to CSSD as categorical and without qualifications of degree.[69] A First Amendment question is presented if persons are compelled to support the speech of a private individual, but not if persons are taxed, whether by a general tax or by a targeted assessment, to support the speech of the government. Scalia's approach seems to advance a clear and forceful rule, but it actually renders quite mysterious the nature of the First Amendment interests that CSSD aspires to protect. Exactly what kind of interests would require stringent First Amendment scrutiny to prevent the compelled subsidization of the expression of private parties, but no scrutiny at all to prevent the compelled subsidization of government speech?

The strangely dichotomous character of the First Amendment interests presupposed by Scalia is especially puzzling because we know that the First Amendment interests of persons in what Scalia at the outset of his opinion calls "true 'compelled speech' cases"[70] do not disappear when persons are compelled to express the message of the government. Scalia cites two compelled speech cases: *West Virginia Board of Education v Barnette*,[71] in which schoolchildren were required to recite the Pledge of Allegiance, the text of which was set out by state regulation, and *Wooley v Maynard*,[72] in which George Maynard, a Jehovah's witness, was required to display the state motto of New Hampshire on the prefabricated license plate of his automobile. In each case the relevant message was composed by the government. In each case the First Amendment was interpreted to protect a right "to refrain from speaking at all,"[73] and in each case it did not matter whether the message whose utterance was compelled was that of the government or that of a private party.

Johanns itself establishes that there is no "government speech" exception to claims of compelled speech, for it holds that plaintiffs' allegation of compelled speech can succeed if they are able to prove

---

[68] See notes 36 and 40.

[69] Scalia never explains why autonomy interests cannot be more or less violated, depending upon the closeness of the connection between the subsidy and the speech.

[70] 125 S Ct at 2060.

[71] 319 US 624 (1943).

[72] 430 US 705 (1977).

[73] *Wooley*, 430 US at 714. See *Barnette*, 319 US at 634 ("[A] Bill of Rights which guards the individual's right to speak his own mind" does not leave it "open to public authorities to compel him to utter what is not in his mind.").

on remand that the Beef Board's advertisements were "attributed" to them individually.[74] Because *Johanns* holds that these advertisements are government speech, the Court necessarily concludes that plaintiffs have First Amendment interests in not being compelled to express government speech. But surely it is puzzling that First Amendment interests in not being compelled to speak are indifferent to whether the compelled speech is governmental or private, whereas First Amendment interests in not being compelled to subsidize speech depend entirely upon this distinction. Why should this be so?

What renders the question particularly disturbing is that Scalia's distinction between compelled speech cases and compelled subsidy cases is itself highly uncertain. In *Wooley*, for example, nobody could plausibly have imagined that George Maynard was actually speaking through the prefabricated license plate he was forced to display. Indeed (then) Justice Rehnquist dissented in *Wooley*, asking why there was "any 'speech' or 'speaking' in the context of this case. . . . The issue, unconfronted by the Court, is whether appellees, in displaying, as they are required to do, state license tags, the format of which is known to all as having been prescribed by the State, would be considered to be advocating political or ideological views."[75]

The Court could not respond to Rehnquist's challenge; it could only vaguely mutter that "compelling the affirmative act of a flag salute [in *Barnette*] involved a more serious infringement upon personal liberties than the passive act of carrying the state motto on a license plate, but the difference is essentially one of degree." *Wooley* tells us that:

> Here, as in *Barnette*, we are faced with a state measure which forces an individual, as part of his daily life indeed constantly while his automobile is in public view to be an instrument for fostering public adherence to an ideological point of view he finds unacceptable. . . . New Hampshire's statute in effect requires that appellees use their private property as a "mobile billboard" for the State's ideological message or suffer a penalty, as Maynard already has.[76]

Having one's car transformed into a "mobile billboard" for state

---

[74] *Johanns*, 125 S Ct at 2065.

[75] *Wooley*, 430 US at 720–21 (Rehnquist, J, dissenting).

[76] Id at 715.

messages is not precisely the same as being forced to speak. It is more like being forced to allow one's car to be used as a platform for the state to speak. This suggests that *Wooley* is not so much about George Maynard's First Amendment interest in not being forced to speak as it is about his First Amendment interest in not having his property appropriated to subsidize government speech. But *Johanns* seems to hold that this interest does not exist.

Souter's dissenting opinion is by contrast free from such internal tensions. He begins with the premise that a First Amendment autonomy interest is compromised whenever persons are required to subsidize speech with which they disagree, and he applies this premise to the context of government speech. Souter postulates that government speech subsidized by general taxation so minimally affects this autonomy interest as to be beyond judicial protection. But he concludes that this interest remains vivid and enforceable in the context of government speech supported by targeted assessments. This logic is faithful to the structure of CSSD as set forth in *United Foods*. The difficulty, however, is that Souter's dissent is based upon a false premise.

II. The Theoretical Foundations of CSSD

Consider the case of *Banning v Newdow*,[77] in which Michael Newdow, the same prickly pro se litigant who challenged the constitutionality of the Pledge of Allegiance,[78] was involved in an "ongoing child custody proceeding."[79] Newdow objected to an order "to pay a portion of the attorney's fees of the child's mother."[80] He advanced the argument, which no doubt would be unthinkable to a trained lawyer, that the order was unconstitutional because of CSSD. Newdow contended that requiring him to pay the attorneys' fees of his opponent was to compel him directly to subsidize expression with which he disagreed. Because the speech of the opposing attorney was private, Newdow's argument is not affected by the holding of *Johanns*, which purports to leave in place the doctrinal structure of CSSD that was established in *United Foods*.

Newdow's innovative argument should make us pause, because,

---

[77] 14 Cal Rptr 3d 447 (Ct App 2004).

[78] *Elk Grove Unified Sch. Dist. v Newdow*, 542 US 1 (2004).

[79] *Banning*, 14 Cal Rptr 3d at 449.

[80] Id.

in a literal sense, all statutes awarding attorneys' fees force "certain individuals to pay subsidies for speech to which they object."[81] Souter's dissent in *Johanns* postulates an intrinsic "autonomy" interest in not being forced to pay for the speech of another, and it conceptualizes the strength of this interest as dependent upon the closeness of the connection between the subsidy and the speech it supports. We should note, therefore, that in Newdow's case this connection is as close and as direct as it is possible to be. And of course Newdow vigorously disagrees with the speech that he is forced to subsidize, for it is the expression of his opponent in litigation.

The logic of CSSD would thus support Newdow's position. Although that logic does not establish whether any particular attorneys' fees statute is constitutional or unconstitutional, it does raise the question of whether all such statutes must be given careful First Amendment attention.[82] Newdow's argument forces us to ask whether we should regard all attorneys' fees statutes as raising constitutional concerns that need to be adjudicated on a statute-by-statute basis.[83]

The *Newdow* case is only the tip of the iceberg, for there are many ordinary situations in which government compels persons directly to pay for the speech of third parties. Consider, for example, the requirement that cars can be registered only if mechanics are

---

[81] *United States v United Foods, Inc.*, 533 US 405, 410 (2001).

[82] To invoke a distinction that is associated with the work of Frederick Schauer, we must in such cases distinguish between First Amendment "coverage," which requires "that the constitutionality of [a] regulation must be determined by reference to First Amendment doctrine and analysis," and First Amendment "protection," which implies that the First Amendment renders a particular regulation unconstitutional. Robert Post, *Encryption Source Code and the First Amendment*, 15 Berkeley Tech L J 713, 714 (2000). See Frederick Schauer, *The Boundaries of the First Amendment: A Preliminary Exploration of Constitutional Salience*, 117 Harv L Rev 1765, 1769–72 (2004). CSSD is above all a doctrine that is designed to define the scope of First Amendment coverage, as distinct from First Amendment protection. In fact both the Court and Souter have been notably reluctant to specify a test for First Amendment protection. See, e.g., *United Foods*, 533 US at 410; *Johanns*, 125 S Ct at 2074 n 10 (Souter, J, dissenting).

[83] The court in *Newdow* knew that it had to reject Newdow's claim, but it didn't know quite how to do so, and as a consequence it could only sputter that CSSD is not relevant unless the "only purpose" of "compelled assessments" is "to support the offensive speech. . . . Here the purpose of the fee award is to ensure that a child's best interests are represented." *Banning*, 14 Cal Rptr 3d at 449. The problem with this reasoning is that it misrepresents *United Foods*, in which the federal government had imposed targeted assessments in order to stabilize and promote the market for mushrooms, just as the targeted assessments in *Johanns* were for the purpose of stabilizing and promoting the market for beef. It will be a rare case indeed in which the state compels speech for no reason at all.

paid to certify that they meet smog emission standards.[84] Consider the requirement that children can be enrolled in public school only if physicians are paid to certify their immunization records.[85] Or consider the requirement that publicly owned businesses pay for the financial reports of independent accountants.[86] We must decide whether these everyday government regulations have all along posed deep, unrecognized First Amendment issues, or whether, like the government speech at issue in *Johanns*, they do not present any constitutional question at all.[87]

These examples suggest that there are strong reasons to conclude that First Amendment concerns are not always triggered whenever persons are forced to subsidize the speech of a third party. This conclusion would render CSSD consistent with First Amendment

---

[84] Forced to conduct emissions inspections by federal clean-air rules, many states have outsourced their inspection duties by relying on a "decentralized network [that] uses gasoline stations or repair facilities as test centers." See Arnold W. Reitze, Jr., *Air Quality Protection Using State Implementation Plans: Thirty-Seven Years of Increasing Complexity*, 15 Vill Envtl L J 209, 265 (2004).

[85] See, e.g., Ariz Rev Stat Ann § 15-872 (2002) ("A pupil [unless exempted] shall not be allowed to attend school without submitting documentary proof [of vaccination] to the school administrator . . . ."); Ark Code Ann § 6-18-702 (1999) (conditioning attendance in school on multiple vaccinations "as evidenced by a certificate of a licensed physician or a public health department acknowledging the immunization"); La Rev Stat Ann § 17: 170 (2001); NH Rev Stat Ann § 141-C:20 (1996); Conn Agencies Regs § 10-204a-2a (2000); NM Code R § 6.12.2.1-.11 (Weil 2001). See generally James G. Hodge, Jr., and Lawrence O. Gostin, *School Vaccination Requirements: Historical, Social and Legal Perspectives*, 90 Ky L J 831, 833 (2001–2002) (summarizing state laws and stating that "modern state school vaccination laws mandate that children be vaccinated prior to being allowed to attend public or private schools. Failure to vaccinate children can result in children being denied from attending school, civil fines and criminal penalties . . . .").

[86] See, e.g., Securities Act of 1933, 15 USC § 77aa(25) sched A (2000) (requiring that balance sheets and profit and loss statements included in registration statements be certified by an independent accountant); Securities Exchange Act of 1934, 15 USC § 78m(a)(2) (2000) (authorizing the SEC to require that financial statements included in annual reports be certified by an independent accountant).

[87] It might be said that some of these situations do not implicate CSSD because the First Amendment is triggered only when government compels "certain individuals to pay subsidies for speech *to which they object*." *United Foods*, 533 US at 410 (emphasis added). We do not object, so the argument might run, to a mechanic's certification that our car meets smog emission requirements, or to a physician's certification that our child meets immunization requirements. But this argument misses the point that the mechanic or the physician may at least initially give us bad news and communicate to us that our car has failed to meet emission requirements or that our child requires yet another vaccination. We may vigorously disagree with this speech, but the government will nevertheless have effectively forced us to pay for it, on pain of not driving our car or not enrolling our children in public school. The question is whether this potential disagreement should raise a First Amendment problem for these statutes. I pass over the example of required financial statements, because I assume that if a CPA is performing her job with proper professional independence her financial statements will routinely contain assertions to which her client might object.

jurisprudence generally, because First Amendment concerns are not automatically activated whenever expression is restricted.[88] I have argued the point at length elsewhere and will not repeat those arguments here.[89] Suffice it to note that because speech and expression are intrinsic to all human conduct, the regulation of conduct inevitably involves the regulation of the communication that defines the conduct. If virtually every regulation of conduct became a constitutional question, the First Amendment would rapidly become unworkable. For this reason, our First Amendment is not triggered whenever communication is regulated; we do not have a First Amendment jurisprudence of contracts, even though contracts subsist entirely within the realm of expression.[90] Constitutional review is triggered only when communication is regulated in a manner that implicates specific First Amendment values. As I have argued elsewhere, these values most conspicuously include democratic self-governance and participation in the construction of public opinion.[91]

Just as the First Amendment is not triggered by all restrictions on speech, so the First Amendment is not triggered by all government compulsions to speak. In fact we experience such compulsions all the time, and no one regards them as raising constitutional issues. Examples range from compulsory jury service,[92] to compulsory testimony before courts and legislatures,[93] to compulsory reporting of

---

[88] Schauer at 1769–86 (cited in note 82).

[89] Robert Post, *The Constitutional Status of Commercial Speech*, 48 UCLA L Rev 1, 9–10 (2000); Robert Post, *Recuperating First Amendment Doctrine*, 47 Stan L Rev 1249, 1254–55 (1995).

[90] Consistent with his dissent in *Johanns* and his acceptance of the major premise of CSSD, Justice Souter has advocated that First Amendment protections should attach to "speech as such." *Glickman v Wileman Bros. & Elliott*, 521 US 457, 478 (1997) (Souter, J, dissenting). I cannot believe, however, that Souter would want plenary constitutional review of contract law.

[91] See note 89 above.

[92] See, e.g., 28 USC § 1861 (2000) ("It is further the policy of the United States that all citizens shall . . . have an obligation to serve as jurors when summoned for that purpose."); Nancy J. King, *Juror Delinquency in Criminal Trials in America, 1796–1996*, 94 Mich L Rev 2673, 2683 ("Fining those who failed to obey [jury] summonses [was] a universal response to jury dodging throughout the colonial period, and in the early 1800s . . . .").

[93] On numerous occasions the Supreme Court has found it to be "beyond controversy that one of the duties which the citizen owes to his government is to support the administration of justice by attending its courts and giving his testimony whenever he is properly summoned." *Blackmer v United States*, 284 US 421, 438 (1932). Thus the Court has reaffirmed that "neither the First Amendment nor any other constitutional provision protects

vehicle accidents,[94] to compulsory reporting of potential public health risks like those involving child abuse,[95] to the myriad of public disclosures required by securities regulation,[96] to the labeling requirements routinely required on consumer products.[97] The very Beef Promotion and Research Act considered by *Johanns* provides

---

the average citizen from disclosing to a grand jury information that he has received in confidence." *Branzburg v Hayes*, 408 US 665, 682 (1972).

[94] Most states require drivers to report their involvement in traffic accidents that have resulted in injury or significant property damage. See, e.g., Cal Veh Code § 20002 (West 2005); NY Veh & Traf Law § 605 (McKinney 2005). While the Supreme Court has never entertained a compelled speech challenge to these statutes, in *California v Byers*, 402 US 424 (1971), the Court rejected the claim that such hit-and-run laws violate the Fifth Amendment privilege against self-incrimination, explaining that:

> An organized society imposes many burdens on its constituents. It commands the filing of tax returns for income; it requires producers and distributors of consumer goods to file informational reports on the manufacturing process and the content of products, on the wages, hours, and working conditions of employees. Those who borrow money on the public market or issue securities for sale to the public must file various information reports; industries must report periodically the volume and content of pollutants discharged into our waters and atmosphere. Comparable examples are legion.

Id at 427–28. Mandatory reporting laws of these kinds have never been thought to raise First Amendment concerns.

[95] Virtually every state has some version of a mandatory reporting law to cover cases of child abuse. See Mason P. Thomas, Jr., *Child Abuse and Neglect* (pt 1), 50 NC L Rev 293, 332 (1972). Some states have extended the duty to report abuse to other areas, as for example by making the "[f]ailure to report elder mistreatment to public authorities . . . typically a criminal offense." Seymour Moskowitz, *Saving Granny from the Wolf: Elder Abuse and Neglect—The Legal Framework*, 31 Conn L Rev 77, 117 (1998).

[96] See Troy A. Paredes, *Blinded by the Light: Information Overload and Its Consequences for Securities Regulation*, 81 Wash U L Q 417, 427 (2003) ("Disclosure is the SEC's chief regulatory tool.").

[97] Just to offer some few examples enforced by the FTC, the Fair Packaging and Labeling Act, 15 USC §§ 1451–61 (2000), directs the FTC to issue regulations requiring that all consumer commodities other than food, drugs, therapeutic devices, and cosmetics be labeled to disclose net contents, identity of commodity, and name and place of business of the product's manufacturer, packer, or distributor; the Truth in Lending Act, 15 USC §§ 1601–1667f (2000), requires all creditors who deal with consumers to make certain written disclosures concerning all finance charges and related aspects of credit transactions (including disclosing finance charges expressed as an annual percentage rate); the Wool Products Labeling Act, 15 USC §§ 68–68j (2000), requires (1) that wool product labels indicate the country in which the product was processed or manufactured, and (2) that mail order promotional materials clearly and conspicuously state whether a wool product was processed or manufactured in the United States or was imported; the Fur Products Labeling Act, 15 USC §§ 69–69j (2000), requires that articles of apparel made of fur be labeled, and that invoices and advertising for furs and fur products specify, among other things, the true English name of the animal from which the fur was taken, and whether the fur is dyed or used; the Textile Products Identification Act, 15 USC §§ 70–70k (2000), requires (1) that any textile fiber product processed or manufactured in the United States be so identified, and (2) that mail order promotional materials clearly and conspicuously indicate whether a textile fiber product was processed or manufactured in the United States or was imported.

that marketers and importers of beef and cattle shall "maintain and make available for inspection such books and records as may be required by the order and file reports at the time, in the manner, and having the content prescribed by"[98] a "beef promotion and research order" issued by the Secretary of Agriculture.[99]

There are thus innumerable circumstances in which the state forces persons to speak without raising First Amendment concerns.[100] If speech can be compelled without triggering constitutional scrutiny, *a fortiori* the subsidization of speech can be required without raising First Amendment concerns. The First Amendment interest in not being compelled to subsidize particular speech derives from the First Amendment interest in not being compelled to express that particular speech. Hence if the state can compel a person to speak without triggering First Amendment scrutiny, it can also force that person to pay for the speech. Because speaking generally consumes resources, the compulsion to speak is often simultaneously the compulsion to subsidize speech. It would in such circumstances be strange indeed to hold that requiring a person to speak does not raise First Amendment concerns, but requiring him

---

[98] 7 USC § 2904(11) (2000).

[99] 7 USC § 2903(b) (2000).

[100] This conclusion is confirmed by the Court's recent decision in *Rumsfeld v Forum for Academic and Institutional Rights*, 2006 WL 521237 (US March 6, 2006). The Court evaluated the argument of law schools that the so-called Solomon Amendment, which required law schools to provide access to military recruiters, was an unconstitutional violation of the First Amendment because it compelled law schools to speak, as for example by sending out announcements about the time and place at which students could meet military recruiters. The Court unanimously held that compelling such speech did not raise a First Amendment question:

> There is nothing in this case approaching a Government-mandated pledge or motto that the school must endorse.
> The compelled speech to which the law schools point is plainly incidental to the Solomon Amendment's regulation of conduct, and "it has never been deemed an abridgment of freedom of speech or press to make a course of conduct illegal merely because the conduct was in part initiated, evidenced, or carried out by means of language, either spoken, written, or printed." . . . Compelling a law school that sends scheduling e-mails for other recruiters to send one for a military recruiter is simply not the same as forcing a student to pledge allegiance, or forcing a Jehovah's Witness to display the motto "Live Free or Die," and it trivializes the freedom protected in *Barnette* and *Wooley* to suggest that it is.

Although the Court attempts to use the old and ultimately circular difference between speech and conduct to explain the distinction between compelled speech that raises a First Amendment question and compelled speech that does not raise a First Amendment question, for our purposes it is enough to notice that the Court does feel compelled to introduce and defend some such distinction. The Court plainly understands that a serious First Amendment question is not raised by every instance of compelled speech.

to expend the resources for that speech does. The inevitable conclusion is that the compelled subsidization of speech does not by itself trigger First Amendment scrutiny.

CSSD, however, focuses specifically on the subsidization of objectionable speech. *United Foods* asserts that "First Amendment concerns apply" whenever the state requires persons to "subsidize speech with which they disagree."[101] The basic logic seems to be that because First Amendment scrutiny should be triggered whenever a person is forced to speak in ways that she finds objectionable, First Amendment review ought also to be triggered whenever a person is forced to subsidize speech she finds objectionable. But the premise of this reasoning is false. First Amendment concerns are not automatically aroused when persons are forced to speak in ways that they find objectionable. Persons may experience as personally "galling"[102] their obligation to testify before a court or a legislature; they may wish to refuse to pronounce a verdict as a juror; they may object to their responsibility to report a traffic accident; or they may find it repulsive to report an incident of child abuse. But in all these situations we nevertheless compel persons to speak without ever raising a First Amendment eyebrow.

We also compel persons to speak in ways that they believe to be flatly incorrect. High administration officials must mouth official administration positions, whether they believe them or not, and the First Amendment will offer no solace if they are fired for voicing their actual beliefs.[103] Every day in state bureaucracies around the nation, government employees are required to draft memoranda setting forth positions with which they privately disagree.[104] We require corporations to file independent financial statements, even if they happen to disagree with the judgments made by their ac-

---

[101] *United States v United Foods, Inc.*, 533 US 405, 410–11 (2001).

[102] See *Johanns*, 125 S Ct at 2071 (Souter, J, dissenting).

[103] See, e.g., *Wilbur v Mahan*, 3 F3d 214, 215 (7th Cir 1993); *Snyder v Blagojevich*, 332 F Supp 2d 1132, 1139–40 (ND Ill 2004).

[104] See, e.g., *Hunsinger v State Pers. Bd.*, No C040744, 2003 WL 21268041 (Cal Ct App, June 3, 2003). In *Connick v Myers*, 461 US 138, 146 (1983), the Court set out the general rule that "[w]hen employee expression cannot be fairly considered as relating to any matter of political, social, or other concern to the community, government officials should enjoy wide latitude in managing their offices, without intrusive oversight by the judiciary in the name of the First Amendment." Even Justice Brennan, dissenting in *Connick*, stated his view that "[p]erhaps the simplest example of a statement by a public employee that would not be protected by the First Amendment would be answering 'No' to a request that the employee perform a lawful task within the scope of his duties." Id at 164 n 3 (Brennan, J, dissenting).

countants.[105] On pain of failure we require students in public schools to offer the right answers to questions, even if any particular student privately believes that these answers are false.[106] On pain of punishment we require soldiers in the army to salute and exclaim "Yes, Sir" when they converse with an officer, even if any particular soldier personally believes that his officer does not merit these expressions of respect.[107] On pain of tort liability we require doctors to communicate sufficient information to their patients to provide for informed consent, even if particular doctors privately believe that this information is misleading and harmful to their patients.[108] These forms of compelled speech proceed without First Amendment scrutiny. If speech of this kind can be compelled, *a fortiori* the subsidization of this speech can also be compelled. If the former does not raise First Amendment questions, neither does the latter.

These examples suggest that compelling persons to subsidize speech with which they disagree does not *automatically* arouse First Amendment concerns. No doubt constitutional scrutiny can be triggered, and easily triggered, depending upon a variety of factors, including the nature of the speech, the context of the regulation, and so forth. But the mere fact that individuals have been compelled to subsidize speech with which they disagree is not sufficient to justify constitutional scrutiny. Constitutional review is not forthcoming unless it is also demonstrated that the required subsidization of speech compromises specifically First Amendment values. As I have already noted, and as the examples we have just considered attest, these values paradigmatically involve democratic self-governance and participation in the formation of public opinion.[109]

---

[105] See note 86 above.

[106] There are numerous cases filed by students asserting that they had supplied the correct answer on an examination and were graded incorrectly. In *Susan M. v New York Law School*, 76 NY2d 241 (1990), for example, a law student objected to losing credit because she answered based on New York law a question that was intended to test her knowledge of Delaware law. Affirming the right of educators to set their own standards for what constitutes a correct examination answer, the Court stated that "the pedagogical evaluation of her test grades [is] a determination best left to educators rather than the courts . . . ." Id at 243. See also Thomas A. Schweitzer, *"Academic Challenge" Cases: Should Judicial Review Extend to Academic Evaluation of Students?* 41 Am U L Rev 267, 367 (1992) (surveying cases, and chronicling "the long-standing tradition of deference to academic evaluations [that] seems likely to remain strong for some time to come").

[107] *McCord v Page*, 124 F2d 68, 70 (5th Cir 1941) ("Military regulations requiring a soldier to salute his superior officers and . . . the enforcement of the regulations by a proper military tribunal does not violate the Constitution of the United States.").

[108] *Barcai v Betwee*, 50 P3d 946 (Haw 2002); *Brown v Dibbell*, 595 NW2d 358 (Wis 1999).

[109] See note 89 above.

Although there can be no comprehensive theoretical account of when state regulations implicate First Amendment values, we generally have well-developed constitutional intuitions about when restrictions on speech threaten to compromise First Amendment values. The problem is that these intuitions are clouded in the context of CSSD, because the very idea of compulsion seems constitutionally suspicious[110] and because laws that coerce persons to pay for the speech of others are strange and unfamiliar. The resulting confusion is plainly evident in the painful uncertainty evinced by the Court in its *Glickman–United Foods–Johanns* trilogy.

In the remainder of this essay, therefore, I shall postulate two simple heuristic principles that may prove helpful in educating our instincts in the context of CSSD. The principles function to connect the opaque and exotic circumstances of CSSD to the more familiar issues posed by cases involving compelled speech and restrictions on the subsidization of speech. I call these two principles the Non-Endorsement Principle and the Symmetry Principle.

The Non-Endorsement Principle is activated whenever subsidizing objectionable speech puts an individual in the position of appearing to endorse that speech. If the Non-Endorsement Principle applies, claims of compelled subsidization of speech merge into claims of compelled speech. Whenever the Non-Endorsement Principle applies, therefore, claims of compelled subsidization of speech will trigger constitutional review if claims of compelled speech would trigger constitutional review.

Wooley is best understood as a case involving the Non-Endorsement Principle. Although it is implausible to imagine that George Maynard was compelled actually to speak, it is clear that he was compelled to subsidize state speech by displaying the New Hampshire motto on the license plate of his car. The Court's reference to a "mobile billboard" suggests that it interpreted existing social conventions as supporting the conclusion that those who display slogans on their automobiles endorse those slogans. The particular way in which New Hampshire forced Maynard to subsidize its motto, therefore, implicated the Non-Endorsement Principle, which converted Maynard's claim of compelled subsidization of speech into a claim of compelled speech.

Because strict constitutional scrutiny would have been triggered

---

[110] See *United Foods*, 533 US at 418 n * (Stevens, J, concurring).

if New Hampshire had compelled Maynard to affirm its motto, so strict constitutional scrutiny was triggered when New Hampshire instead forced Maynard to subsidize the display of its motto in a manner that could be understood as constituting endorsement. By contrast, if New Hampshire had merely required Maynard to display a license plate with numbers, it is very doubtful that First Amendment concerns would arise, because in such circumstances a claim of compelled speech would not trigger constitutional scrutiny. From a constitutional point of view, it would be no different than the state requiring Maynard to retain and display a social security card or a draft card. The application of the Non-Endorsement Principle thus does not trigger strict constitutional scrutiny unless, in the relevant context, a claim of compelled speech would trigger such scrutiny.

Not every subsidization of objectionable speech implicates the Non-Endorsement Principle. In *PruneYard Shopping Center v Robins*,[111] for example, the Court held that state constitutional provisions authorizing "individuals to exercise free speech and petition rights on the property of a privately owned shopping center to which the public is invited"[112] did not raise First Amendment concerns, even though these provisions required owners of shopping centers to make their property available for the speech of others with whom they could be in deep disagreement.[113] The Court distinguished *Wooley* on the ground that the state constitutional provisions failed to implicate the Non-Endorsement Principle, because the views of persons "passing out pamphlets or seeking signatures for a petition . . . will not likely be identified with those of the owner."[114]

---

[111] 447 US 74 (1980).

[112] Id at 76.

[113] Recently, in *Rumsfeld v Forum for Academic and Institutional Rights*, 2006 WL 521237 (US March 6, 2006), the Court emphasized this distinction between the compelled subsidization of speech and the compelled endorsement of speech. Speaking in the context of a statute known as the Solomon Amendment that in effect required law schools to subsidize the speech of military recruiters, the Court invoked *Pruneyard* and concluded that "[n]othing about recruiting suggests that law schools agree with any speech by recruiters, . . . We have held that high school students can appreciate the difference between speech a school sponsors and speech the school permits because legally required to do so, pursuant to an equal access policy."

[114] Id at 87. The Court also noted two additional factors:

> [N]o specific message is dictated by the State to be displayed on appellants' property. There consequently is no danger of governmental discrimination for or against a particular message. Finally, as far as appears here appellants can expressly disavow any connection with the message by simply posting signs in

The distinction between compelled subsidizations of speech that implicate the Non-Endorsement Principle and those that do not is neatly captured in *Johanns'* ruling that the case should be remanded to determine if plaintiffs can establish that the advertisements of the Beef Board and its Operating Committee were actually attributable to them individually. If the advertisements are not so attributable, plaintiffs' allegations would not implicate the Non-Endorsement Principle and accordingly their claim of compelled subsidization of speech would not merge with a claim of compelled speech.

The Symmetry Principle has two prongs. The first holds that if state restrictions on the ability of persons to pay for the speech of another do not raise First Amendment questions, so also state compulsions to pay for the speech of another will not, in the absence of special circumstances like a violation of the Non-Endorsement Principle, raise First Amendment questions. Although there are of course important differences between prohibitions of action and affirmative duties to act, these differences do not typically include First Amendment interests. If restrictions on the subsidization of speech do not raise First Amendment concerns, these concerns are unlikely to be created by the mere fact of legal compulsion, which does not independently infuse First Amendment values into transactions where these values are not otherwise present.

The point is well illustrated by regulations limiting the price of professional services. We pay high fees to lawyers or doctors in order to receive the benefit of their wisdom, but no First Amendment review would be required if the government were to limit professional fees.[115] This is because we do not ordinarily regard the

---

the area where the speakers or handbillers stand.

Id.

[115] In recent years, an increasing number of legislatures and courts have placed hard limits on the amount a lawyer can receive in a contingency fee arrangement. See generally Richard M. Birnholz, Comment, *The Validity and Propriety of Contingent Fee Controls*, 37 UCLA L Rev 949, 951 n 9 (1990) ("Five states already impose a fixed or sliding scale maximum for all or most tort suits. Two states accomplish this by statute and three by court rule."). Such limits have been upheld by courts on several occasions. See, e.g., *Am. Trial Lawyers Ass'n v N.J. Sup. Ct.*, 330 A2d 350 (NJ 1974); *Gair v Peck*, 160 NE2d 43 (NY 1959). Rather that raising First Amendment issues, these laws have been subject only to the general restriction that "[p]rice control, like any other form of regulation, is unconstitutional only if arbitrary, discriminatory, or demonstrably irrelevant to the policy the legislature is free to adopt, and hence an unnecessary and unwarranted interference with individual liberty." *Nebbia v New York*, 291 US 502, 539 (1934). No one considered the First Amendment to be implicated by the Economic Stabilization Act of 1970 (ESA), which authorized the Nixon Administration to impose price controls on goods and services.

payment of fees for professional advice as transactions that are in-fused with First Amendment value. The Symmetry Principle would thus suggest that in the absence of special considerations First Amendment concerns would also not be raised by laws requiring the payment of professional fees. The fact of compulsion may arouse libertarian apprehensions, but it does not independently endow these transactions with specifically First Amendment values. That is why *Newdow* was correct to conclude that statutes providing for attorneys' fees ought not as a general matter to trigger First Amendment scrutiny.[116] Certainly no one would claim that the order requiring Newdow to pay the fees of his wife's attorney implicates the Non-Endorsement Principle.

The second prong of the Symmetry Principle holds that if state restrictions on the ability of persons to pay for the speech of another do raise First Amendment questions, state requirements that persons affirmatively provide such support will likely trigger First Amendment review. I say "likely" because sometimes First Amendment interests are understood to inhere in the right of an audience to hear, rather than in the right of a speaker to communicate,[117] and in such cases First Amendment scrutiny would be appropriate to review government efforts to restrict communication but not necessarily government efforts to compel communication.[118] In the

---

The ESA was challenged (unsuccessfully) on grounds that it constituted an unconstitutional delegation of legislative power to the president. See *Amalgamated Meat Cutters & Butcher Workmen v Connally*, 337 F Supp 737 (DDC 1971).

[116] The Symmetry Principle does suggest, however, that if restricting legal fees for public interest litigation would raise First Amendment questions, so also would the compulsory awarding of such fees. Compare *Ohralik v Ohio State Bar Ass'n*, 436 US 447 (1978), with *In re Primus*, 436 US 412 (1978). It would not follow that compulsory attorneys' fees would be unconstitutional in such circumstances, only that such fees would have to survive First Amendment review. On the distinction between First Amendment coverage and First Amendment protection, see note 82 above.

[117] From the Meiklejohnian perspective, for example, "the point of ultimate interest is not the words of the speakers, but the minds of the hearers." Alexander Meiklejohn, *Political Freedom: The Constitutional Powers of the People* 26 (1965). Meiklejohn famously remarked that "[w]hat is essential is not that everyone shall speak, but that everything worth saying shall be said." Id.

[118] This is because compelled expression would presumably increase the communication reaching an audience and so serve the underlying constitutional interest in providing an audience with information or opinion. This was the theoretical logic of *Zauderer v Office of Disciplinary Counsel*, 471 US 626 (1985), in which the Court held that compelled disclosures in the context of commercial speech would raise only de minimis First Amendment concerns. Normally commercial speech, of the kind produced by the Beef Board and its Operating Committee, is constitutionally valued because of its "informational function," *Cent. Hudson Gas & Elec. Corp. v Pub. Servs. Comm'n*, 447 US 557, 563 (1980), rather than because of a speaker's interests in disseminating it. See Post, *Commercial Speech* at 14–15

ordinary case, however, in which First Amendment rights attach to a speaker's decision to communicate or not to communicate, the Symmetry Principle holds that if a state restriction on the ability of a person to pay for speech triggers First Amendment review, so also will a state requirement that a person pay for speech, even if the Non-Endorsement Principle is not violated.

In *Buckley v Valeo*,[119] for example, the Court famously held that campaign "contribution and expenditure limitations" triggered First Amendment review because such requirements were constitutionally equivalent to direct "restrictions on political communication and association by persons, groups, candidates, and political parties."[120] The Symmetry Principle would suggest that *Buckley* gives us good ground to believe that compelling persons to contribute to specific political candidates would also raise First Amendment questions.[121]

The Court in fact drew this implication in *Abood v Detroit Board of Education*,[122] which held that serious First Amendment questions were raised by a state law creating an agency shop in which all employees were required to pay to the union that was their collective bargaining agent a fee that was equal in amount to union dues. *Abood* invoked *Buckley* to justify the conclusion that "[t]o compel employees financially to support their collective-bargaining rep-

---

(cited in note 89). *Zauderer* noticed that the "informational function" of commercial speech is not compromised when commercial speech is compelled, as distinct from restricted, because the compulsion *increases* the flow of information to an audience, and hence better serves the constitutional values at stake in commercial speech. But in *United Foods* the Court appears to have held that the First Amendment protects the rights of commercial speech speakers, rather than the rights of an audience wishing to receive the information conveyed by commercial speech. *Johanns* builds on this holding. If the Court is serious about this theoretical shift in the constitutional status of commercial speech, it will have to alter many fundamental aspects of commercial speech jurisprudence, including the application of overbreadth doctrine, the permissibility of prior restraints, the constitutionality of required disclosures of the kind approved by *Zauderer*, and so on. This is a complicated question that I discuss in Robert Post, *Compelled Commercial Speech and Coerced Commercial Association: United Foods, Zauderer, and Abood*, 40 Valparaiso U L Rev 1 (2006).

[119] 424 US 1 (1976).

[120] Id at 19. "A restriction on the amount of money a person or group can spend on political communication during a campaign necessarily reduces the quantity of expression by restricting the number of issues discussed, the depth of their exploration, and the size of the audience reached. This is because virtually every means of communicating ideas in today's mass society requires the expenditure of money." Id at 19. See also *Simon & Schuster, Inc. v Members of N.Y. State Crime Victims Bd.*, 502 US 105 (1991).

[121] This should be contrasted to the use of government tax dollars to subsidize elections in a viewpoint neutral manner. *Buckley*, 424 US at 86–93; *May v McNally*, 55 P3d 768 (Ariz 2002).

[122] 431 US 209 (1977).

resentative has an impact upon their First Amendment interests. An employee may very well have ideological objections to a wide variety of activities undertaken by the union in its role as exclusive representative."[123]

> One of the principles underlying the Court's decision in *Buckley v Valeo* was that contributing to an organization for the purpose of spreading a political message is protected by the First Amendment. Because "(m)aking a contribution . . . enables like-minded persons to pool their resources in furtherance of common political goals," the Court reasoned that limitations upon the freedom to contribute "implicate fundamental First Amendment interests."
>
> The fact that the appellants are compelled to make, rather than prohibited from making, contributions for political purposes works no less an infringement of their constitutional rights. For at the heart of the First Amendment is the notion that an individual should be free to believe as he will, and that in a free society one's beliefs should be shaped by his mind and his conscience rather than coerced by the State. . . .
>
> These principles prohibit a State from compelling any individual to affirm his belief in God, or to associate with a political party, as a condition of retaining public employment. They are no less applicable to the case at bar, and they thus prohibit the appellees from requiring any of the appellants to contribute to the support of an ideological cause he may oppose as a condition of holding a job as a public school teacher.[124]

Because *Buckley* had held that government restrictions of "support of an ideological cause" raised First Amendment issues, so *Abood* held that governmentally compelled support for such causes would raise analogous First Amendment issues, even if the speech sustained by this support could not be attributed to the contributor. The Court affirmed a symmetry between restrictions and compulsions, a symmetry that expressed the view that the same First Amendment values were implicated in each. The Court subsequently reaffirmed this symmetry in *Keller v State Bar of California*,[125] which read *Abood* to hold "that just as prohibitions on making contributions to organizations for political purposes implicate fundamental First Amendment concerns, see *Buckley v Valeo*, 'compelled . . . contri-

---

[123] Id at 222.

[124] Id at 234–35 (citations omitted).

[125] 496 US 1 (1990).

butions for political purposes work no less an infringement of . . . constitutional rights.'"[126]

United Foods cites *Abood* and *Keller* for the broad-ranging proposition that "mandated support is contrary to . . . First Amendment principles . . . ."[127] This proposition now forms the basic premise of CSSD. In his *Johanns* dissent, Souter explicitly affirms this premise and attributes it to *Abood* and *Keller*.[128] Nothing that Scalia says in his majority opinion in *Johanns* in any way limits or disavows this premise, which therefore remains the law in CSSD cases that do not involve government speech. But this premise rests on a misreading of *Abood* and *Keller*. These decisions do not hold that the compelled subsidization of speech always raises First Amendment concerns. They instead stand for the Symmetry Principle. They hold that if restrictions on subsidies for speech raise First Amendment concerns, so likely will mandated support for such speech.

The Symmetry Principle is helpful primarily because we have well-developed (if untheorized) intuitions about when restrictions on the funding of speech will trigger constitutional scrutiny. We can use these intuitions to guide us in the newer and far less familiar context of compelled subsidization of speech. *Johanns* illustrates the utility of this approach. The Symmetry Principle suggests that if government limitations on direct contributions to the state would not raise First Amendment concerns, so also, in the absence of special considerations like a violation of the Non-Endorsement Principle, compelled contributions to the state would not trigger First Amendment scrutiny. Since I very much doubt that we would regard such limitations as triggering First Amendment scrutiny,[129] the Symmetry Principle would predict that the use of compulsory taxes to support government speech ought not to trigger First Amendment review.

The heuristic value of the Symmetry Principle is that it can help us understand how the government speech exception can be inte-

---

[126] Id at 9–10 (quoting *Abood*, 431 US at 234).

[127] *United States v United Foods, Inc.*, 533 US 405, 413 (2001).

[128] Souter cites *Abood* and *Keller* as "authority for the . . . proposition that, absent substantial justification, government may not force targeted individuals to pay for others to speak." *Johanns v Livestock Mtkg. Ass'n*, 125 S Ct 2055, 2069–70 (Souter, J, dissenting).

[129] See, e.g., Tenn Code Ann § 64-7-110 (a)(16)(B) (2004) (prohibiting in certain circumstances private contributions to regional development authorities).

grated into a coherent account of First Amendment jurisprudence, which neither Scalia nor Souter is able to do. The Symmetry Principle suggests that the explanation for the government speech exception lies in the question of why government can prohibit contributions to the state without raising First Amendment concerns. The rationale of *Buckley* points toward an answer. Government restrictions on the ability to pay others to speak for us in public debate compromise our ability to participate in public discourse in ways that seek to make the state democratically responsive to our own views.[130] Such restrictions compromise First Amendment values connected to the project of democratic legitimation. These values are not at stake, however, when government restricts contributions to the state.

Because the state always speaks for the community as a whole, and never for the personal views of private citizens, the state can never become the personal spokesperson of a citizen, no matter how much money she donates to it. The state cannot properly become an instrument by which private persons attempt to make public opinion responsive to their own particular views. It follows that restrictions on donations to the state do not compromise the ability of persons to participate in public discourse. By calling our attention to this conclusion, the Symmetry Principle allows us to see that neither government restrictions on donations to the state, nor government requirements that persons contribute to the state, compromise First Amendment values connected to the project of democratic legitimation, although such restrictions or compulsions might well compromise these values in the context of contributions to a private person.

This suggests that the fundamental constitutional question posed by the government speech exception in *Johanns* is whether the Beef Board advertisements, generically considered, should be understood as "speaking for" the private and particular views of the beef industry, which represents the perspective of one group in the community, or instead as "speaking for" the official views of the state, which represents the outlook of the whole community. Cases like *Glickman, United Foods*, and *Johanns* are difficult because the industry programs created by Congress are ambiguous mixtures of public and private, so that it is hard to characterize the promotional ma-

---

[130] See Robert Post, *Reconciling Theory and Doctrine in First Amendment Jurisprudence*, 88 Cal L Rev 2355, 2366–68 (2000).

terial that they produce. It is unclear whether to classify this material for constitutional purposes as expressing the private perspectives of the cattle industry or instead as expressing the public views of the state. The formalism of Scalia's opinion may be as satisfactory a way as any to resolve this question, because, as he notes, if "the government sets the overall message to be communicated and approves every word that is disseminated,"[131] it is fair to conclude that the message speaks for the official views of the government, rather than for the particular views of private industry.[132]

Neither Scalia nor Souter can accept this explanation of the government speech exception, however, because each postulates that the fundamental First Amendment interest at issue in CSSD is autonomy, rather than participation in public debate.[133] The difficulty with regarding autonomy as a fundamental First Amendment interest is that it is omnipresent; every restriction and compulsion will to some degree compromise autonomy. It is precisely for this reason that autonomy is not usefully regarded as a foundational First Amendment interest.[134] Autonomy cannot explain why First

---

[131] *Johanns*, 125 S Ct at 2063. See note 41 above.

[132] Some lower courts have instead focused on the question of whether the speech produced by these ambiguous organizations is in fact unduly influenced by private perspectives. See note 38 above. Although this question is theoretically justified, it is not clear that it is judicially administrable. It is certainly not unreasonable for the Court to hold that it is not.

[133] See notes 36, 40, and 54 above.

[134] There is a slight indication that Souter may have in mind the constitutional value of protecting conscience, rather than protecting autonomy. Souter begins his dissent by noting:

> In 1779 Jefferson wrote that "to compel a man to furnish contributions of money for the propagation of opinions which he disbelieves, is sinful and tyrannical." 5 The Founders' Constitution, § 37, A Bill for Establishing Religious Freedom, p. 77 (1987), codified in 1786 at Va. Code Ann. § 57–1 (Lexis 2003). Although he was not thinking about compelled advertising of farm produce, we echoed Jefferson's view four years ago in *United Foods*, where we said that "First Amendment values are at serious risk if the government can compel a particular citizen, or a discrete group of citizens, to pay special subsidies for speech on the side that it favors . . . ." 533 US at 411.

Johanns, 125 S Ct at 2069 (Souter, J, dissenting). Jefferson's observation, which is frequently cited in the context of compelled speech cases, concerned the issue of the use of government tax revenue to support an established church. *R.J. Reynolds Tobacco Co. v Shewry*, 384 F3d 1126, 1140–41 (9th Cir 2004). There is a tradition in our law and our history that such taxation would compromise conscience. See *Flast v Cohen*, 392 US 83 (1968); Noah Feldman, *The Intellectual Origins of the Establishment Clause*, 77 NYU L Rev 346, 404 (2002). Souter may have meant, therefore, that compelled subsidization of government speech potentially violates the conscience of taxpayers, in the same way that the use of taxes to support an established church is understood to violate the conscience of taxpayers. There

Amendment interests are sometimes triggered and sometimes not.[135]

To understand the actual shape of First Amendment jurisprudence, we must postulate a constitutional interest that is implicated in some circumstances, but not in all circumstances. If the circumstances in which an interest is involved happen to correspond to the actual pattern of First Amendment cases, we have a good candidate for the First Amendment interest that is in fact driving judicial decision making. The interest of autonomy, which would be compromised by compulsory taxation as well as by the compelled payment of attorneys' fees at issue in *Newdow*, does not well explain the configuration of existing or desirable First Amendment jurisprudence. The interest of participation in public debate, by contrast, which is involved neither in compelled contributions to the state nor in compelled contributions to a private lawyer in a private case,[136] does have considerable explanatory power in explaining the government speech exception, as well as the contours of CSSD generally.

III. Conclusion

Johanns is a welcome development, but it leaves in place the central premise of CSSD, which is that *every* compelled subsidization of objectionable speech requires First Amendment review. This premise derives from a misreading of *Abood* and *Keller*, and it gives clear doctrinal expression to the idea, advanced by both Scalia and Souter, that autonomy is a fundamental First Amendment interest which is always at stake whenever the state forces persons to pay for the speech of others. This idea is demonstrably false unless the Court plans to constitutionalize many common legal requirements that no one presently regards as raising First Amendment issues.[137]

---

are many difficulties with this line of thought, however. It is odd to speak of violations of conscience in the context of nonideological speech like beef advertisements. And whereas the connection between conscience and religion is well explored, the relationship between conscience and speech is not. Most fundamentally, conscience, like autonomy, would seem to prove too much, because it is potentially indiscriminate. Newdow would seem to have a claim of conscience that is at least equal in force to those of the beef producers in *Johanns*.

[135] See Post, 88 Cal L Rev at 2372 (cited in note 129).

[136] See note 115 above.

[137] See text at notes 78–107.

So long as the central premise of CSSD remains unrevised, however, the holding of *Johanns* can serve as nothing more than a kind of *force majeur* necessary to foreclose potentially embarrassing applications of the compelled subsidization of speech doctrine. The lesson of *Newdow* is that in the future the Court will be required to announce other equally ad hoc decisions. The only hope of avoiding a string of precedents as self-evidently ragged as the *Glickman–United Foods–Johanns* trilogy is to repudiate the premise of CSSD and to rethink the fundamental question of when the compelled subsidization of speech does and does not raise First Amendment issues. This may in turn require reconceptualizing the nature of the fundamental interests which the First Amendment should be interpreted to protect in the context of compulsions to speak. This essay is meant to be a first small step in that direction.

TIM WU

THE COPYRIGHT PARADOX

Copyright law has become an important part of American industrial policy. Its rules are felt by every industry that touches information, and today that means quite a bit.[1] Like other types of industrial policy, copyright in operation purposely advantages some sectors and disadvantages others. Consequently, today's copyright courts face hard problems of competition management, akin to those faced by the antitrust courts and the Federal Communications Commission.[2]

How should courts manage competition using copyright? Over the last decade, writers have begun to try to understand the "other side" of copyright, variously called its innovation policy, communications policy, or regulatory side.[3] Here I want to focus attention

---

Tim Wu is Professor, Columbia Law School.

AUTHOR'S NOTE: I wish to thank Yochai Benkler, Jane Ginsburg, Scott Hemphill, Mark Lemley, Fred von Lohmann, Phil Weiser, and also Randal Picker and his team of "mob-bloggers." These views were presented in various forms on the "mob-blog," *Slate Magazine*'s end-of-term coverage, Columbia Law School's Advanced Copyright Seminar, and at UCLA Law School. I also benefited from the TPRC 2005 Grokster panel and in particular the comments of Randal Picker and Julie Cohen. Seth Graham and Stuart Sierra provided helpful assistance.

[1] Copyright today affects not only the traditional entertainment industries, but also the electronics industry, computer manufacturers, software designers, internet companies, telecommunications companies, and other sectors of the economy. Through trade agreements bilateral and multilateral, copyright also aspires to regulate those industries in the developing world as well. See, e.g., the Trade Related Intellectual Property agreements, which became law by operation of the Uruguay Round Agreements Act (URAA), Pub L No 103-465, 108 Stat 4809 (1994), a comprehensive Act dealing with matters of international trade. 18 USC § 2319A (which corresponds to § 513 of the URAA, 108 Stat at 4975).

[2] See Robert H. Bork, *The Antitrust Paradox* 3–11 (1978).

[3] See Jane C. Ginsburg, *Copyright and Control over New Technologies of Dissemination*, 101

---

on a crucial problem of decisional method that is becoming more clearly important to copyright decisions. Courts in both copyright and antitrust face a choice between what we can characterize as "bad actor" and "welfarist" models of deciding cases. The "bad actor" approach punishes alleged wrongdoers based on malicious behavior of the suspect and the prospect of harm to favored sectors of the economy, like small businesses (in antitrust) or the entertainment industries (in copyright). The "welfarist" approach, by contrast, calls for judges generally to ignore intent or "bad behavior" in exchange for a disciplined focus on questions of industry economics and consumer, or user, welfare. The welfarist approach accepts Adam Smith's premise that certain forms of malicious behavior may promote overall social well-being, on balance, though some may not.

The tension between these approaches became clear in the Supreme Court's 2005 decision in *Metro-Goldwyn Mayer Studios, Inc. v Grokster, Ltd.*[4] In *Grokster* the Court side-stepped a welfarist calculation called for by existing law, and turned instead to a "bad actor" approach. Faced with a vicious fight between disreputable firms and the incumbent industry, the Court chose to punish the bad guys. To the Court, and to many observers, the *Grokster* decision was a good political way out of a very difficult problem. As a one-shot political compromise, the decision managed to avoid outraging either the electronics or incumbent distribution industries, and was successful in that regard. However, if *Grokster* is also meant to serve as a model of how copyright should manage competition, the drawbacks of the *Grokster* model are manifest.

First, if we accept that courts should be actively choosing winners and losers among various types of market entrants, we need to ask whether *Grokster*'s focus on intentionally bad behavior is a good way to create market-entry rules. As discussed below, the approach can be defended, particularly under the facts of *Grokster* itself. But at its worst, the Court's approach in *Grokster* risks putting copyright where antitrust was in the 1960s, punishing businesses without ask-

---

Colum L Rev 1618 (2001); Kathryn Judge, *Rethinking Copyright Misuse*, 57 Stan L Rev 901 (2004); Joseph Liu, *Regulatory Copyright*, 83 NC L Rev 87 (2004); Randal C. Picker, *From Edison to the Broadcast Flag: Mechanisms of Consent and Refusal and the Propertization of Copyright*, 70 U Chi L Rev 281 (2003); Timothy Wu, *Copyright's Communications Policy*, 103 Mich L Rev 278 (2004); see also Yochai Benkler, *Intellectual Property and the Organization of Information Production*, 22 Intl Rev L & Econ 81 (2002).

[4] 125 S Ct 2764 (2005).

ing whether consumer welfare is served or harmed by the business model in question. That is not to say *Grokster* is an easy case either way. But it can be a dangerous business to create industrial policy focused on the perceived malice of the defendant as opposed to measures of economic consequence. That, at least, is what antitrust writers long ago concluded. As the late Phillip Areeda put it, "'purpose' or 'intent' have been particularly slippery, ambiguous, and unsatisfactory in the antitrust world."[5] The problem that antitrust scholars point out is that "bad behavior" is sometimes just another name for competitive behavior, of the kind the legal system might want to encourage.

Second, even within the welfarist approach to copyright, an old but still uncomfortable question remains. How comfortable are we with the federal courts, as in *Grokster* or *Sony*, using the copyright code to set market-entry policy for new technologies at all? The answer is not entirely obvious. Some might argue that since copyright infringement is a tort, the Court has the duty to work out a full theory of secondary liability. Others might prefer the federal courts' relative insulation from interest-group politics. But arguably what the Court is doing with copyright's competition policy is as technical and economic as the problems the Supreme Court routinely defers to the Federal Communications Commission. The case *National Cable & Telecommunications Assn v Brand X Internet Services*,[6] released the same day as *Grokster*, makes this institutional contrast clear. In both cases the Court faced hard problems of technology and economics. In *Grokster*, the Court has little hesitation in making policy for an extremely complex and evolving technological problem, but in *Brand X* the Court bent over backward to defer to an expert agency.

What the courts in cases like *Grokster* are doing is akin to trying to decide on the right level of an industrial subsidy in the face of technological change. That is a hard challenge for any branch of government, including Congress, and indeed Congress's interest-group-dominated method has a mixed record.[7] But as the federal

---

[5] Phillip Areeda and Herbert Hovenkamp, 3 *Antitrust Law* ¶ 601 (2d ed 2002).

[6] 125 S Ct 2688 (2005).

[7] Perhaps the best-known failure is the Audio-Digital Home Recording Act of 1992, which was an effort to handle the invention of digital recording technology. The Act focused on the digital audio tape, which it simply managed to render uncompetitive, and as a whole the Act was almost irrelevant to the struggle over digital copyright discussed in this article.

courts continue to encounter the question of just how much protection is warranted in the face of disruptive technologies, the questions of institutional competence may become even more intense.
Stated otherwise, beyond the question of decisional method lie unanswered questions of legal process.[8] Where does the courts' relative
institutional competence to handle adjustments to copyright in the
face of technological change begin and end? That is not an easy
question to answer. Yet it is beyond question that at some point the
Court may need to relearn how to hand problems over to a congressional process.

I. How Copyright and Antitrust Manage Competition

While traditionally associated with the promotion of individual authorship, copyright in operation also creates industrial policy. It provides some level of support and protection to a group of
favored industries—the film industry, recording industry, software,
and publishing—at some expense to other industries and consumers.
The theory is that, absent such protection, the favored industries
would not be viable, hence the need for government protection.[9]
For various reasons, expressive works are unusual and less likely to
be produced at optimal levels absent government intervention. Yet
this leaves open a very hard question: What is the right degree to
which other industries should sustain such costs to support the
creation of expressive works that is necessary to copyright-depen-
dent industries?

These problems are faced in their most difficult form when copyright considers the market entry of new technologies of copying
and distribution, like the electronics and telecommunications industries.[10] New communications industries, like radio, cable, or internet distribution, inevitably threaten existing companies. And
copyright, for better or worse, has emerged as a central tool for
managing the market entry of certain types of disruptive technology.
The challenge is, in some rough way, to allow new technologies to

---

[8] Cf. Henry M. Hart, Jr., and Albert M. Sacks, *The Legal Process: Basic Problems in the
Making and Application of Law* 158 (William N. Eskridge, Jr., and Philip P. Frickey, eds,
1994) ("What is each of these institutions good for? How can it be made to do its job
best? How does, and how should, its working dovetail with the working of the others?").

[9] There are some analogues in copyright policy to strategic trade policy. Cf. Elhanan
Helpman and Paul Krugman, *Trade Policy and Market Structure* (1989).

[10] See generally Picker, 70 U Chi L Rev (cited in note 3).

emerge while still fairly protecting the incentives to create expressive works. Those are not goals easily reconciled, and the result has always been some kind of messy trade-off.

The copyright system in the twentieth century often dealt with these problems through a mixed congressional and court-driven process that led to legally managed settlements called compulsory licensing schemes.[11] Stated briefly, the new industry and the incumbent distributors, sometimes over a period of decades, would fight both in the courts and in Congress until finally arriving at a settlement. These deals, placed directly in the copyright statute as compulsory licensing schemes, typically struck a balance. The new industry got a right to access copyright works crucial to its commercial success. In exchange, the new industry would make some kind of ongoing transfer payment, set by statute, to the incumbent copyright owners and incumbent distributors.[12]

Since the 1980s, copyright has mainly taken a different approach and used a different policy tool for managing market-entry problems. Perhaps in reaction to the decades-long battles that led to compulsory licenses, the new system is more clearly court managed. It is usually called the *Sony* system, after the decision on the legality of the Sony Betamax VCR in *Sony Corp. of America v Universal City Studios, Inc.*[13] As the Court said at the time, it was "strik[ing] a balance between a copyright holder's legitimate demand for effective [protection] . . . and the rights of others freely to engage in substantially unrelated areas of commerce."[14]

What is the *Sony* rule, and how does it manage competition? The *Sony* Court ruled the VCR a legal technology, despite the fact that it could be and was used for infringing purposes. Interestingly, the *Sony* Court claimed to be deferring to a congressional resolution of the battle between Hollywood and Sony—yet it still went ahead and created a judge-centric rule meant to distinguish desirable from undesirable market entrants. The Court said (using language that most copyright lawyers know by heart) that a manufacturer of copying technology is not liable for the infringements of its users "if the product is widely used for legitimate, unobjectionable pur-

[11] See Wu, 103 Mich L Rev at 288–97, 309–25 (cited in note 3).
[12] Id.
[13] 464 US 417 (1984).
[14] *Sony Corp. v Universal City Studios, Inc.*, 464 US 417, 442 (1984).

poses." "Indeed," said the Court, "it need merely be capable of substantial non-infringing uses."[15]

While there is great disagreement over the meaning of the *Sony* rule, its *method* is fairly clear. At bottom, the *Sony* test asks courts to conduct some weighing of the social costs and benefits of any new technology. The disagreement over meaning arises over what can legitimately constitute a cost or benefit of a new technology, and in which direction the presumptions should run.

There are obvious ambiguities on both sides of the *Sony* ledger. The benefits are a technology's "legitimate purposes"—the benefit to consumers of a new technology (in *Sony* itself, the luxury of taping TV programs and watching them later). Later courts, including the *Grokster* Court, describe this as the interest in "innovation," and it can also be described as the consumer surplus generated by a rightward shift in the supply curve.[16] But here is the problem: should the Court focus on consumer uses clearly manifest at the time of decision, or try to take into account future uses of the technology? In other words, if a new technology has a social value of 10 today, but a future value of 1,000, is it worth a present harm of 100?[17] The Court, in *Sony*, unsurprisingly, did not answer that question.

One reading of *Sony* takes the language "merely capable" to create a presumption—that judges should not block any technology unless it is absolutely clear that the product is not even theoretically capable of uses that are not illegal. While not quite so saying, the Ninth Circuit came close to endorsing this position in the *Grokster* litigation.[18] But others firmly reject the idea that *Sony* has any such presumption. Judge Posner has interpreted *Sony* as limited to extant uses on the record. "It is not enough" he said, "that a product or service be physically capable, as it were, of a noninfringing use."[19]

Aside from the meaning of "merely capable," it is also not so easy to say what should count as a cost. Courts say the costs are those of "infringement," but what does that mean? The difficult fact is that if we ignore dynamic effects, infringement benefits consumers.

---

[15] Id.

[16] See Wu, 103 Mich L Rev at 292–95 (cited in note 3).

[17] Cf. Randal C. Picker, *Copyright as Entry Policy: The Case of Digital Distribution*, 47 Antitrust Bull 423 (2002).

[18] *Metro-Goldwyn-Mayer Studios, Inc. v Grokster Ltd.*, 380 F3d 1154 (9th Cir 2004).

[19] *In re: Aimster Copyright Litigation*, 334 F3d 643, 653 (7th Cir 2003) (Posner, J) ("It is not enough, as we have said, that a product or service be physically capable, as it were, of a noninfringing use [to escape liability under contributory infringement].").

Any single instance of infringement is not a cost at all, but just a transfer of wealth to the individual infringer. Rather in the sense that Jesus was able to feed 5,000 people with "five loaves, and two fishes,"[20] millions of infringing consumers get something that costs $15 for free, and no honest economist can ignore billions in consumer surplus.

The costs, of course, are dynamic—the diminution of incentives to produce things that society wants produced. Without reasonable financial incentives to create new works, unpaid creativity may continue,[21] but investments in commercial entertainment will diminish or disappear. But here the tricky question is distinguishing the costs to *authors* as opposed to *distributors*. Given the advent of a new technology, some of the "costs" may represent the fact that outdated technologies are being put out of business, in the sense that computers imposed costs on the typewriter industry. Should a court try to figure out whether the costs of infringement are really costs that will be felt by authors, as opposed to incumbent distributors?

One more thing needs to be said. The *Sony* Court tried to fit its rule somewhere within the traditional common-law doctrine of contributory liability. So while everyone knows that *Sony* asks courts to judge the costs and benefits of a new technology, its doctrinal cast is different. *Sony* purports to be about *mens rea*—deciding whether constructive knowledge of infringement is sufficient to constitute knowledge for purposes of contributory liability. (Non-copyright lawyers are often surprised to find out that major questions of competition policy are settled this way.) As we shall see, this link to "knowledge" is the "bad actor" side of the test for contributory liability. The idea is that, regardless of the costs and benefits discussed in *Sony*, a company that knowingly helps infringe copyright ought be liable no matter how beneficial its technology is.

The *Sony* court did something unusual: it put an economic test in the middle of a *mens rea*-driven standard. That, as we shall see, had important consequences for the *Grokster* litigation. But first we turn to antitrust, where Courts have been asking *Sony*-like questions for more than a century.

---

[20] Matthew 14:15–21 (King James).

[21] For a description of some of the mechanisms underlying noncommercial creativity, see Yochai Benkler, *Coase's Penguin, or Linux and the Nature of the Firm*, 112 Yale L J 369 (2002).

II. Two Antitrust Approaches

In antitrust, courts regularly face the same "industry injury" problem just described in the copyright context. In copyright, the problem is that one company's business model (in *Sony*, the VCR) is seen as injurious to the business model of others (in *Sony*, the film industry). Antitrust is similarly faced with problems of allegedly injurious behavior between firms. Predatory pricing, plaintiffs have long argued, is a dastardly practice that big business uses to kill the little guy. Mergers will create dangerous giants that will drive smaller competitors out of business. A variety of business practices, many of which are quite ungentlemanly, are alleged to be dangerous. The challenge for courts is to figure out which of the many forms of "bad behavior" should amount to illegal behavior.

Over the course of antitrust history there have been many schools of antitrust thought, and this article is no survey.[22] But on this issue of intent and motive, to simplify enormously, over the last several decades we have seen reflections of two main and competing decisional approaches, the "bad actor" and "welfarist" approaches.

The "bad actor" approach to antitrust aims to punish or block various ill-intended business practices that are regarded as wrongful, and likely damaging to favored sectors of the economy. In the case law, it is distinguished by an emphasis on motive or "economic purpose," rather than net economic effect or consumer welfare. During the 1950s, 1960s, and 1970s, when the approach was at the peak of its popularity, the courts did not allow what they considered "bad" practices to be justified by the prospect of gains in business efficiency.[23] They were willing to punish what they called bad behavior regardless of proof of injury to consumers or to the economy as a whole. Conduct was punished on the basis of its effects on favored sectors, such as "small dealers and worthy men," against the abuses of the market.[24]

A well-known symbol of the "bad actor" method is the famous case of *Brown Shoe Co. v United States*,[25] decided in 1962. *Brown*

---

[22] This is an enormous simplification. The history of battling "schools" of antitrust thought is described in Herbert Hovenkamp, *Antitrust Policy After Chicago*, 84 Mich L Rev 213 (1985); Herbert Hovenkamp, *The Reckoning of Post-Chicago Antitrust*, in Antonio Cucinotta et al, eds, *Post-Chicago Developments in Antitrust Law* 1 (2002).

[23] See Bork, *The Antitrust Paradox* (cited in note 2).

[24] *United States v Trans-Missouri Freight Ass'n*, 166 US 290, 343 (1897).

[25] 370 US 294 (1962).

Shoe concerned a proposed merger between two shoe manufacturers and retailers who, collectively, would control about 5 percent of the manufacturing market and 2.1 percent of the retail market (this number was higher in some cities). Despite the relatively small numbers, the Court blocked the merger, in large part based on the purpose of the merger. The Court ruled that it was essential to examine the "very nature and purpose of the arrangement"—the "economic purpose" of the merging companies. The merger, it turned out, was motivated not by an interest in rescuing a failing company, or even by an interest in allowing two small companies to defeat larger opponents. Instead, it featured two successful companies who hoped to use their new size to aggressively expand their market share. That, said the Court, was a trend that should be halted.[26] The Court justified the decision by declaring that antitrust had a particular concern for a certain "economic way of life."[27] That meant using the law for the protection of certain sectors of the economy—to protect against adverse effects "upon local control of industry and upon small business."[28]

As everyone familiar with antitrust knows, the "bad actor" approach represented by *Brown Shoe* has been not only criticized, but also renounced, and ultimately upended. Most of the attack came from the "Chicago School," historically composed of people who at some point or another worked with Aaron Director at the University of Chicago. Writing in 1976, for example, Richard Posner said of *Brown Shoe*, "one has no sense that the Court had any notion of how a non-monopolistic merger might affect competition."[29] Robert Bork, in his book *The Antitrust Paradox*, wrote that "[i]t would not be overhasty to say that the *Brown Shoe* opinion is the worst antitrust essay ever written." Bork, paraphrasing Justice Stevens, also left us with this memorable description of the "bad actor" approach to antitrust:

> Antitrust . . . is in the good old American tradition of the sheriff of a frontier town: he did not sift evidence, distinguish between suspects, and solve crimes, but merely walked the main street and every so often pistol-whipped a few people.[30]

---

[26] Id at 333.

[27] Id.

[28] Id.

[29] Richard A. Posner, *Antitrust Law* 102 (1976).

[30] See Bork, *The Antitrust Paradox* at 6 (cited in note 2).

Even Phillip Areeda, writing at greater distance from the Chicago School, wrote that "in the great majority of antitrust cases, talk of 'purpose or intent' is largely diversionary or redundant . . . one must concentrate on conduct and define its characteristics that are undesirable."[31]

The principal criticism advanced by the Chicago School was simple: the courts had relied too much on considerations like "bad motives" and failed to justify their intervention by any reference to the effects on the economy as a whole. The Chicago School proposed the alternative and now dominant approach, a welfarist approach. Its central argument is that the maximization of consumer welfare should in all cases be the primary goal of competition policy. In judicial practice, that meant that every condemnation of a given business practice should be accompanied by some proof that the practice in general is actually bad for the consumer.

In contemporary antitrust theory and judicial practice, the welfarist approach now dominates. Yet that does not mean that we have Robert Bork's antitrust law. There remains much disagreement within the welfarist decisional method over whether writers like Bork were correct about what counts as harmless or efficiency-promoting business practice. For example, many scholars in the "new institutional economics" school take a very different view of vertical integration than Bork did.[32] But the Chicago School's larger point—that damage to consumer welfare should be the sine qua non of antitrust illegality—is today essentially uncontested.[33]

A. GROKSTER

It was perhaps inevitable that the Court in copyright would one day face a *Brown Shoe*-like case, and it turned out to be *Grokster*. The *Grokster* case was the culmination of nearly five years of constant litigation centered on the invention of mass "file-sharing" technology in the late 1990s.[34] The questions in *Grokster* were

---

[31] Areeda and Hovenkamp, 3 *Antitrust Law* ¶ 651 (cited in note 5).

[32] See Hovenkamp, *The Reckoning of Post-Chicago Antitrust* (cited in note 22).

[33] Essentially, but not entirely. See, e.g., David W. Barnes, *Revolutionary Antitrust: Efficiency, Ideology, and Democracy*, 58 U Cin L Rev 59 (1989) (defending *Brown Shoe* approach as more consistent with American democracy); Kenworthey Bilz, *Populist Wealth in Legal Economic Analysis* (Oct 12, 1998) (unpublished manuscript).

[34] For an account of the evolution of file-sharing technologies, see Timothy Wu, *When Code Isn't Law*, 89 Va L Rev 679, 726–43 (2003).

created, at the broadest level, by the popularization of the internet, which makes possible mass dissemination of expressive works without the industries that have long specialized in such dissemination. To be blunt, the internet threatened to make large parts of the incumbent distribution industries obsolete. Online distribution is a particular threat to the recording industry and its favored model of the retail compact disc.

File-sharing, or "peer-to-peer" (P2P) software, in its various forms, is a type of program that lets people share information without help from any centralized distributor. These programs make it easy for millions to copy and distribute information without permission, while the copyright law has long been premised on the fact that doing so is hard.[35]

The file-sharing attack on industry structure came in waves. As everyone knows, the first came from a college dorm and a student nicknamed "Napster." His Napster program was the first to make file-sharing a mass phenomenon. But Napster's design also gave its owners both knowledge and control of the sharing it facilitated, and Napster was quickly buried by the Ninth Circuit.[36]

The *Grokster* litigation, the second wave, was a truer test of file-sharing technology. Napster's greatest successor was a program named Kazaa, produced by an Amsterdam-residing Swede named Niklas Zenstrom, aided by a mysterious team of Estonian programmers. Kazaa's basic design concept was adopted or licensed by other companies, including "Grokster," the first defendant by alphabetical order in the *Grokster* litigation. The difference between Napster and Kazaa is slightly technical, but suffice it to say that Kazaa was by design much closer to a purely neutral file-sharing technology.[37] The programs could be used to swap just about any kind of file, and the producers of Kazaa or Grokster had no immediate control over their users and no specific knowledge of what any one user was up to.

I have described file-sharing technology as just a technology for sharing information. But despite the great labors of the defendants

---

[35] Jane C. Ginsburg, *Putting Cars on the "Information Superhighway": Authors, Exploiters, and Copyright in Cyberspace*, 95 Colum L Rev 1466, 1488 (1995) (discussing the role of intermediaries); Wu, 89 Va L Rev (cited in note 34) (same).

[36] See *A&M Records, Inc. v Napster, Inc.*, 239 F3d 1004 (9th Cir 2001).

[37] See Wu, 89 Va L Rev (cited in note 34), for a description of the technical differences between Napster and Kazaa.

and other groups, the social meaning of file-sharing was and is quite different. Programs like Kazaa and Grokster have always been understood not just as a new means of disseminating information, but as a way to get music and sometimes movies for free. They had a reputation, in other words, as pirates.

For many, P2P's rebellious nature was the whole point—it was a new technology that might liberate music from the chokehold of what some saw as a corrupt and abusive recording industry. Professor Siva Vaidhyanathan has called the use of file-sharing networks "civil disobedience." As Justin Frankel, "the world's most dangerous geek," put it, the point of file-sharing programs was "giving power to people, and what can be wrong with that?"[38]

But P2P's reputation did not help in the quintessentially uptight city of Washington, D.C. The file-sharing movement was seen less as a legitimate market entrant and instead as a bunch of radicals hailing from the West Coast and Amsterdam. The contrast with Sony from the 1970s is important. Then, the film industry tried to portray Sony as a foreign "invading" force—Jack Valenti, lobbyist for the film industry, called the VCR "a great tidal wave just off the shore."[39] But it did not work.[40] Sony was the inventor of the Walkman and other gadgets, and widely beloved. It came to Court as a respectable, even earnest company whose products were used by decent citizens. That cultural difference between Kazaa on the one hand and Sony on the other arguably made a difference in the *Grokster* litigation.

The Court, in deciding *Grokster*, faced the problem of method we described in the antitrust context. Would it try to decide the case under *Sony* by assessing whether, on balance, the benefits of Grokster's technologies were worth the costs measured in terms of authorial incentives? Or might it be easier to decide the case by looking at the motives of the actors involved? In Bork's terms, might it just be easier to pistol-whip a few bad guys?

The Court took the easy way out, and the reasons are easy to understand. The Justices could not agree on the hard question—

---

[38] David Kushner, *The World's Most Dangerous Geek*, Rolling Stone (Jan 13, 2004).

[39] Home Recording of Copyrighted Works: Hearings on HR 4783, HR 4794, HR 4808, HR 5250, HR 5488, and HR 5705 before the Subcommittee on Courts, Civil Liberties, and the Administration of Justice of the House Committee on the Judiciary, 97th Cong, 2d Sess 5 (1982) (statement of Jack Valenti, President, Motion Picture Assoc. of America).

[40] James Lardner, *Fast Forward: Hollywood, the Japanese, and the Onslaught of the VCR* 21 (1987).

whether the *Sony* rule, which calls for some balance of costs and benefit, allowed Grokster to survive (in concurrences, they split 3–3 on the question). The Seventh and Ninth Circuits had announced very different views of what *Sony* should mean. And the briefing also gave the Court plenty of reasons for staying away from *Sony*. Both sides warned of the terrible consequences of adjusting the *Sony* rule. The recording industry and some academics warned of chaos that might attend adopting an expanded *Sony* that declared Grokster legal.[41] On the other side, the computer hardware, software, and electronics industries and others warned of the toil and trouble that would attend the destruction of their beloved *Sony* safe harbor.[42] Whatever the Court did with *Sony*, it was sure, or so the amici seemed to suggest, to make life in America unlivable.

Meanwhile, there was a much easier way out. All of the Justices could plainly see that Grokster, Kazaa, and the like were running a crooked business. Everyone knew these companies were not "legitimate" market entrants like Sony, but rather companies trying to make a quick buck on copyright infringement. So the Court pistol-whipped Grokster out of business. In doing so, it purported to leave *Sony* alone, hoping to mollify everyone by grabbing a rule from the patent statute that fit what it did not like about Grokster's business model. The Court created a test designed to catch companies with a bad attitude.

The result is the "active-inducement" test, the first test in copyright history that asks a court to look at a defendant's business model and decide whether its motives are crooked. It is a test that bears strong similarities to similar intent-based approaches in an-

---

[41] See, e.g., *Brief for Motion Picture Studio and Recording Company Petitioners*, at 19, *Metro-Goldwyn-Mayer Studios Inc. v Grokster Ltd.*, 125 S Ct 2467 (arguing that the Ninth Circuit's *Sony* theory "perversely encourages such efforts to defeat copyright enforcement, and disadvantages businesses that seek in good faith to prevent violations of copyright holders' rights."); *Brief of Amici Curiae Law Professors, Economics Professors, and Treatise Authors, Metro-Goldwyn-Mayer Studios Inc. v Grokster Ltd.*, 125 S Ct 2467 (upholding Ninth Circuit "could negatively affect myriad existing technologies, undermine the copyright system, destroy the economic viability of legitimate file-sharing services, and retard future innovation in both the technological and authorial communities.").

[42] See, e.g., *Brief of Intel Corporation as Amicus Curiae Supporting Affirmance*, at 5, *Metro-Goldwyn-Mayer Studios Inc. v Grokster Ltd.*, 125 S Ct 2467 (if Sony were uprooted, "innovators, such as Intel, would have no choice but to withhold from the market socially and economically useful products. The national economy, which has grown through technological innovation over the 20 years since this Court decided *Sony*, would suffer.") .

titrust law. But before getting to an analysis of that test, a few notes on the opinion.

The *Grokster* opinion is notable, compared to the Court's earlier decisions, for how little awe the Court seemed to have for the internet. Back in 1997, the Court called the internet "a unique medium—known to its users as 'cyberspace'—located in no particular geographical location but available to anyone, anywhere in the world . . . ."[43] But by 2005, the honeymoon was over. The fact that the internet was part of the litigation was important, but there was little of the technolibertarianism that characterized many of the internet decisions of the 1990s. Stated otherwise, with *Grokster*, internet analysis has come to splinter largely based on usage, or application.[44]

Second, the Court described a central question in copyright as follows:

> The more artistic protection is favored, the more technological innovation may be discouraged; the administration of copyright law is an exercise in managing the trade-off.[45]

That is not the traditional way that the Court discusses copyright's balance. The traditional way of describing the balance is that copyright is either "a tax on readers for the benefit of writers," or "a balance of competing claims upon the public interest: Creative work is to be encouraged and rewarded, but private motivation must ultimately serve the cause of promoting broad public availability of literature, music, and the other arts."[46] The Supreme Court's words in *Grokster* may reflect some awareness that the Court was dealing with the "communications policy" side of copyright, or regulation of new and old technologies of dissemination, where the interests at stake are indeed different than in the purely authorial context.

On to the test itself. The active-inducement test itself says that a company is to be punished if it "distributes a device with the object of promoting its use to infringe copyright."[47] That, the

---

[43] See *Reno v ACLU*, 521 US 844, 851 (1997).

[44] See Timothy Wu, *Application-Centered Internet Analysis*, 85 Va L Rev 1163 (1999) (describing future where internet cases split by application type).

[45] 125 S Ct at 2775.

[46] *Twentieth Century Music Corp. v Aiken*, 422 US 151, 156 (1975).

[47] 125 S Ct at 2780.

Court explained, is "shown by clear expression or other affirmative steps taken to foster infringement."[48] What such "affirmative steps" might be, the Court did not explain completely, but it did find enough of them evident in the *Grokster* litigation. Most important, said the Court, were three things: solicitation of infringement, design, and commercial interest.

The programs in question had a suspect lineage: all were designed to appeal to the users of the "notorious . . . Napster."[49] The Court made much of the fact that one of the defendants, Streamcast, developed advertising materials that called the product the "#1 Alternative to Napster." (Notably, the advertisements were not actually released, on the advice of Streamcast's lawyers.) Second, none of the companies designed their products to prevent infringement (though the Court quickly added that merely not designing a product to prevent infringement was not enough—more on this in an instant). And, finally, the Court pointed out, ad-driven business models need volume to succeed, and since the demand is for infringement, their commercial interest was served by infringement.[50] The Court found what it wanted to confirm what it already thought: these guys were up to no good.

Readers who are not copyright lawyers may be curious to know how, exactly, a major economic decision about the future of industry competition could come to be influenced by the contents of a proposed advertising campaign. The doctrinal answer is, as we discussed above, that the common law of contributory copyright liability left an opening, for it makes everything depend on the *mens rea* of the alleged contributory infringer. *Sony*, while really a decision about market entry, is doctrinally a decision about when constructive knowledge suffices to create contributory copyright liability. In other words, for better or worse, you can find a "bad actor" approach already built into copyright's common-law contributory infringement doctrine.

Another reason, which may seem absurd to non-lawyers, is that there was a pleasing doctrinal symmetry in adding an active-inducement test to copyright. In *Sony* itself, the Court had declared that the "substantial non-infringing" test was based on a doctrine

---

[48] Id.
[49] Id at 2772.
[50] Id at 2781–82.

in § 271(c) of the patent statute. The active-inducement test is just one statutory section away, in § 271(b). (As Randal Picker put it, "you might say it took the Court 20 years to move us one section into the patent law."[51]) Since the patent law has these two bases for infringement, why not copyright?

B. WHAT DOES GROKSTER MEAN?

Within hours of the decision's release, copyright watchers were asking, "but what does it mean?" The "induce" formulation, as many have complained, is open-ended. What is a "clear expression or other affirmative steps taken to foster infringement?" As Rebecca Tushnet asked, are Apple's famous "rip, mix, burn" advertisements enough?[52] We may organize the discussion by saying that *Grokster* leaves behind three sets of questions. First, what is left of *Sony*? Second, what, exactly, does *Grokster* say about product design? And, third, what will *Grokster* mean for actual copyright litigation?

The main doctrinal question after *Grokster* is what, if anything, remains of the *Sony* safe harbor. It is true that the Court on several occasions expressly said it was leaving the *Sony* rule alone, that it would "leave further consideration of the *Sony* rule for a day when that may be required."[53] But if the *Grokster* rule makes *Sony* irrelevant for most cases, then *Sony* may merely be preserved, as Fred Von Lohmann puts it, "in amber."

The question can be framed by asking what happens to the next program that has only a few, or even none, of the elements *Grokster* described as probative to an intent to induce infringement, yet still is widely used for infringement. Recall that *Grokster* named three things that courts might look at as acts probative of inducement:

(1)   Promotion or solicitation of infringement (i.e., advertising);
(2)   Failure to filter; and
(3)   A business model dependent on massive infringement.

---

[51] See Randal Picker, Remarks at the Telecommunications Policy and Research Conference (Sept 23, 2005).

[52] Posting of Rebecca Tushnet to http://www.scotusblog.com/discussion/archives/grokster/ (June 28, 2005).

[53] 125 S Ct at 2779; see also id at 2781 n 12.

(The Court also added that neither evidence of (2) nor (3) standing alone would be sufficient evidence of intent.[54])

Consider three problems. First, a "copyright liberation" website might promote infringement and fail to filter, but have no business model.[55] Second, a company (Apple is arguably in this category) might benefit and arguably depend on mass infringement, yet not take any steps to encourage it, and even use encryption technology to discourage infringement. And, finally, consider the "passive enabler" site that facilitates infringement, yet otherwise does nothing: it takes no proactive steps, other than existing to encourage infringement. For these kinds of problems, does copyright liability attach, and is *Grokster* the relevant rule, or *Sony*?

A key question for each of these examples is whether the bare fact of massive infringement means that the software manufacturer has the "object of promoting [the program's] use to infringe copyright." It is not a question answered in the opinion, and it seems the only way to get at it is to ask whether willful blindness suffices to create liability under *Grokster*. To restate, if you know, for contextual reasons, that your program will be used for massive infringement, and you release the product anyway, is the act of releasing the product the inducement of copyright infringement?

We can discuss three ways to answer the question. Jane Ginsburg provides the first. She believes that these kinds of hard *Grokster* problems will be effectively converted into *Sony* problems. "Speculation is hazardous," she writes, "but one might predict that where a device facilitates infringement on a massive scale, its distributor will likely be found to have intended that result. Where the infringement is relatively modest in scale, inducement will not be found, but neither will the *Sony* threshold for liability be crossed."[56] In other words, whatever the labels, everything will ultimately turn on the old *Sony* question of whether the technology facilitates too much infringement. We can call this theory the *Grokster*-via-*Sony* theory—the idea being that a device that fails *Sony* can easily and automatically be called a copyright inducer under *Grokster*.

A second and perhaps less rigorous prediction is that the answer

---

[54] Id at 2780–82.

[55] This example is taken from Jane Ginsburg and Sam Ricketson, *Inducers and Authorizers: A Comparison of the U.S. Supreme Court's Grokster Decision and the Australian Federal Court's KaZaa ruling* 7 (January 6, 2006, draft on file with author).

[56] Id at 6–7.

may end up having much to do with what I have called a program's "lineage." The Court in *Grokster*, in effect, was trying to kill a family line—Napster and its progeny. And one prediction is that programs inspired by and designed to do what Napster did—make file-sharing easy for millions of people—will result in liability under *Grokster*. The idea is that if you design a follow-on program, you must know that you are trying to facilitate massive infringement, whether under a willful blindness theory or otherwise. Meanwhile, passive enablers that do not share *Napster*'s lineage are safe.

The lineage theory suggests that *Sony* remains the rule for technologies that never knew Napster—technologies clearly and obviously designed for purposes other than infringement and used predominantly for that purpose. For example, email and Microsoft's Explorer browser are in practice used to facilitate massive copyright infringement. But they do not have any historical connection to Napster/Grokster, are widely used for legitimate purposes, and were never designed for copyright infringement. Also, perhaps critically, their business model does not depend on infringement in an obvious way.

The third theory is the "active-step" theory. The Supreme Court said in *Grokster* that

> mere knowledge of infringing potential or of actual infringing uses would not be enough here to subject a distributor to liability. Nor would ordinary acts incident to product distribution, such as offering customers technical support or product updates, support liability in themselves. The inducement rule, instead, premises liability on purposeful, culpable expression and conduct, and thus does nothing to compromise legitimate commerce or discourage innovation having a lawful promise.[57]

This suggests that so long as companies either do not actively take a single step to encourage infringement, they simply cannot be liable under an inducement theory. Instead, in the absence of any active steps, the relevant test is, again, *Sony*. If this reading is right, willful blindness is irrelevant—there has to be some affirmative act in question for inducement liability to exist.

The passive-enabler question is sharpened by considering BitTorrent. BitTorrent has been widely seen as the "next wave" in file-sharing software—one even more powerful than Kazaa, and

---

[57] 125 S Ct at 2780.

more often used for legal reasons.[58] As it stands, both the *Grokster-via-Sony* and the lineage theory predict bad news for BitTorrent sites. Even passive sites will be held liable for inducing a copyright violation if they make the technology available with what they know, unless they take advantage of a *Grokster* safe harbor, as I describe in a moment. Conversely, if the active-step theory is right, a site that is purely passive cannot find itself liable under *Grokster* (though it may still face *Sony* liability).

But to fully answer the question, we need to turn to the topic of safe harbors. What did *Grokster* really say about product design? Does it require all copying devices to have filters or centralized control? Discussing product design and, in particular, filtering, *Grokster* said the following in footnote 12:

> Of course, in the absence of other evidence of intent [other than a failure to screen], a court would be unable to find contributory infringement liability merely based on a failure to take affirmative steps to prevent infringement, if the device otherwise was capable of substantial noninfringing uses. Such a holding would tread too close to the *Sony* safe harbor.[59]

This language says that failure to filter is not, by itself, enough to prove infringement given a product that is otherwise legal under *Sony*. This language supports the conclusion that companies like email providers cannot be secondarily liable merely because they do not block all emails carrying infringing works. Yet one might also infer from this language that *Grokster* creates a kind of safe harbor that may prove important. It may be read to suggest that a product that *does* filter is presumptively not a product that is intended to promote infringement, even if it does, in practice, facilitate infringement.[60] In other words, *Grokster* is good news for Apple's iPod and iTunes download store, which, as in the example below, do lead to infringement, but also make some effort to prevent

[58] See Wikipedia, BitTorrent, http://en.wikipedia.org/wiki/BitTorrent.

[59] 125 S Ct at 2781 n 12.

[60] The question is then this: What happens if a company puts in place a filter, or an encryption system, designed to prevent infringement, that fails? For example, while the iPod is meant to prevent people from sharing files, many have learned how to disable the protections. Is the manufacturer liable if its systems fail? Does the analysis then turn to a *Sony* question—namely, how often is the system used legally, versus illegally? My guess is that a good-faith effort to filter will be enough, but only time will tell.

illegal copying. The opinion may even have been written with the iPod in mind.

The final set of important *Sony/Grokster* questions is procedural. What difference will *Grokster*, as opposed to *Sony*, make in actual copyright litigation? Will *Grokster* make it much easier to threaten innovators with lawsuits? We can probably assume that every copyright plaintiff will, as a matter of course, bring an inducement count in any future litigation. For summary judgment purposes, might we expect that *Grokster*, and not *Sony*, will drive the litigation? Perhaps the evidentiary issue of "intent" will be harder to escape on summary judgment, and in any cases more expensive to litigate than design alone. And that, obviously, favors copyright plaintiffs with lots of resources.[61]

In short, the procedural consequences of *Grokster* may be the most important for the future of innovation. One rather pessimistic view suggests that the *Grokster* rule will help big innovators at the expense of smaller innovators. As an innovation test, it creates some degree of uncertainty, which will lead to more deal-making, more settlement, and payoffs to industry, as in the example of Apple's iTunes. A competitor to Kazaa at the time of litigation, iTunes keeps prices relatively high relative to its costs, and hands over much of its proceeds to the old recording industry, the existing copyright distributors. That, the argument goes, hurts smaller, newer innovators, who will never have the resources to pay off the incumbent industries. Indeed, it is hard to imagine wanting to start or fund a company that has to worry a lot about *Grokster* issues, and lacks either the size or wherewithal to find partners.

Is there a contrary view of *Grokster*? It must be correct that, on balance, a new theory of liability does not help the new firms whose business models touch and concern copyrighted materials. But we also know that the decision was, as we have said, an effort to be minimalist—to kill Grokster without guaranteeing permanent life support for the recording industry.[62] And so a contrasting view is that *Grokster* may not mean much ("what decision?").

If the active-step theory of *Grokster* is right, then the consequences of *Grokster* may be fairly minimal. It all comes back to what is likely to be the hardest question at summary judgment: to what

---

[61] Fed R Civ P 56(f).

[62] Cf. Cass R. Sunstein, *Minimalism at War*, 2004 Supreme Court Review 47.

extent can "intent" be inferred from "design." This is the same as the question discussed above—whether passive knowledge of widespread illegal use, plus a failure to design software or hardware to do anything about it, is enough to count as inducement.

III. GROKSTER'S COMPETITION POLICY

Grokster was a political compromise. But the deeper questions raised by *Grokster* are not what "induce" means, or even whether *Grokster* was a successful political settlement.[63] The question is how far the Court should go in deciding these kinds of cases with inducement rules that study the behavior of the particular companies in question. Why should the law care what some Swedish businessman was thinking when he wrote advertisements for Kazaa? Should the contents of proposed advertising campaigns really tip American industrial policy one way or another?

Remember what the Court is doing: it is blessing or cursing the market entry of a given technological device. Whether the object was to "promote its use to infringe copyright" is arguably irrelevant. The right question is this: either a given technology is worth its costs, or it is not. Either Grokster's or BitTorrent's efficiencies and gains in user welfare are worth the damage to authorial incentives, or they are not. That is not an easy question, necessarily. But why should we care what Streamcast's advertising manager was thinking?

While I do not want to say that an intent test will never be a useful tool in copyright, the argument is that it is not the right tool for handling market-entry problems. Let us look at the argument in favor of relying on a test of bad behavior. One defense might be that the *mens rea* of a defendant is, in fact, a good or useful way of deciding whether a given technology is worth its costs. A defense of this approach runs something as follows. *Mens rea* tests are good for identifying particularly dangerous actors. The criminal law does, for example, offer different punishments for people who kill people, depending on what they were thinking at the time. In that context, the premeditated killer is more dangerous to leave at large than, say, someone who was provoked. Translated to copyright, the idea might be that between company A and company B, even if both

---

[63] See Congressman Rich Boucher, Remarks at Stanford Law School (Sept 19, 2005) (praising *Grokster* decision as "wise" because no one came to Congress afterward seeking legislation).

use the exact same technology, if company A encourages others to infringe copyright, it is the more dangerous actor and should be stopped.

A second answer is that the whole intent analysis in *Grokster* is really just a proxy for weeding out companies engaged in something the copyright law knows to be bad. In support of this position we have Justice Kennedy's question at oral argument:

> JUSTICE KENNEDY: What you want to do is say that un-lawfully expropriated property can be used by the owner of the instrumentality as part of the startup capital for his product.
> MR. TARANTO: I—wel—
> JUSTICE KENNEDY: And I—just from an economic stand-point and a legal standpoint, that sounds wrong to me.[64]

Justice Kennedy's arguments suggest that while we might not know much about copyright, we at least know that infringement upsets whatever balance the statute intended. So looking to matters like intent, advertising campaigns, and so on functions as a kind of radar that detects mass infringement and lets a court put a stop to it.

But if the point of focusing on inducement is that it suggests mass infringement, why not just do so directly? Why not just ask whether the device creates too much infringement, and therefore too much damage to authorial incentives? If infringement is in the end what we care about, the whole examination of the conduct of defendant companies may just be a distraction. And the problem, as antitrust law shows, is that the distraction can quickly take on a life of its own.

In the 1960s, the courts in cases like *Brown Shoe* were confident that a focus on motives, as opposed to effects, was a good way to regulate competition. But the problem is that even when people have what may seem like bad intentions, what they are doing may nonetheless be good for the economy. The point—that bad behavior may serve the common good—is really not new it all. It is Adam Smith's idea that much public good can result from self-interested, and even ungentlemanly, behavior. "It is not from the benevolence

---

[64] See Oral Argument Transcript at 36, *MGM Studios, Inc. v Grokster Ltd*, 125 S Ct 2764 (No 04-480), available at http://www.supremecourtus.gov/oral_arguments/argument _transcripts/04-480.pdf.

of the butcher, the brewer, or the baker, that we expect our dinner, but from their regard to their own interest."[65]

My argument that the court should care about infringement and its effects, period, is susceptible to one further, and powerful, objection. In antitrust, there seems to be a better sense of what constitutes a well-functioning, competitive market. Meanwhile, as George Priest said of intellectual property generally, it is much harder to say what constitutes optimal copyright scope.[66] Copyright policy is aiming for something hard—the optimal subsidization of desirable behavior. The good thing about *Grokster* is that it did not actually focus on the *Sony* question, because the *Sony* question is just too hard for a court to answer. Instead, *Grokster* killed a few bad apples, and left the rest to the market.

While I appreciate the force of this argument, I think it leads in a completely different direction. It suggests not only that the Court should not try to differentiate the good guys from the bad guys, but that it should not be asking *Sony* questions either. Instead, it suggests that the Court should get out of the entire business of trying to bless or curse technologies, and implicitly adjusting the optimal subsidy to existing copyright industries. Instead, the Court should do everything it can to delegate these problems back to Congress. We will consider these arguments in the last section.

Whether it uses *Grokster* or *Sony*, the Court has put itself, and lower courts, in the position of picking winners and losers out of the market entrants that the next decade will bring. In this respect the Court is, as we have already said, conducting industrial policy, along lines very similar to what the FCC does. Yet for a variety of reasons courts have long deferred to either Congress or the FCC when faced with such problems—because the questions are economic, and highly technical.

National Cable & Telecommunications Assn v Brand X Internet Services[67] was released on the same day as *Grokster*, but the contrast in decisional method could not be stronger. The underlying policy question in *Brand X* was challenging: How should broadband competition be managed? Should the government try to prevent vertical

---

[65] Adam Smith, *An Inquiry into the Nature and Causes of the Wealth of Nations* 119 (first printed 1776, Penguin Classics ed, 1999).

[66] See George Priest, *What Economists Can Tell Lawyers About Intellectual Property*, 8 Res Law & Econ 19 (1986).

[67] 125 S Ct 2688 (2005).

integration by DSL and cable operators? And should it try to create a similar regulatory structure for the two main competitors? As we will see, the Court was so allergic to trying to answer these questions and pick winners and losers that it bent backward to get itself out of broadband policy. That makes it more surprising that the Court has not tried to do the same in copyright.

The legal issue in *Brand X* was a *Chevron* question: whether the FCC had violated the plain language of the Telecommunications Act when it classified internet cable-modem services as an "information service." In telecommunications law jargon, an "information service" is a highly discretionary category where the FCC has the power to impose as few or potentially (though it has not yet tried) as many regulatory requirements as it wants. "Information service," to exaggerate slightly, means carte blanche for the FCC and whatever it thinks might be best. In *Brand X*, the Court, relying on *Chevron*, deferred to the commission's decision that cable-modem services could be classified as an "information service."

Deference sounds like a good idea—the only problem is something called *Chevron* and the plain language of the Telecommunications Act. Unfortunately, cable-modem service does not come close to fitting the statutory definition of "information service."[68] What cable operators offer is usually a package of internet service plus the basic transport service, although sometimes the internet services are provided or offered by a third party. The raw transport of bits is a much closer fit with another legal category, "telecommunications."[69] But being a "telecommunications" service imposes all kinds of regulatory requirements. And since the Court, we can surmise, wanted to give the FCC room to decide how much regulation was appropriate, it had to somehow squeeze cable-modem services into the "information service" definition.

Consequently, the opinion in *Brand X* is a little off, and what it says about administrative law and the internet will, one hopes, be forgotten soon. Briefly, the FCC relied on the idea that internet and transport services are offered as a single integrated package.

---

[68] "The term 'information service' means the offering of a capability for generating, acquiring, storing, transforming, processing, retrieving, utilizing, or making available information via telecommunications, and includes electronic publishing . . . ." 47 USC § 153(20) (1997).

[69] "The term 'telecommunications' means the transmission, between or among points specified by the user, of information of the user's choosing, without change in the form or content of the information as sent and received." 47 USC § 153(43) (1997).

The Court concluded that the FCC was justified in calling that package an "information service." But the premise is wrong as both a technological and a business matter.

AOL and Earthlink, among others, are called internet service providers, or ISPs for short. They offer internet services, and even offer such services, on some networks, to cable-modem customers. That stubborn fact impeaches the "single-service" theory, because if companies other than cable operators actually offer the internet side of the service, the transport service is *all* that the cable operator offers. Justice Scalia said, in dissent, that it would be odd to say that a pizzeria that delivers pizza does not offer a "delivery service."[70] But the truth is even starker than Justice Scalia described. Imagine a company that did nothing but deliver other companies' pizzas. If that company does not offer delivery services, then what, exactly, do they offer?

Fortunately, the Court has shown no need to be consistent in how it characterizes the internet across different kinds of cases. What is more interesting is that all of the bending and squeezing out of *Chevron* and the plain language of the Act was for the purpose of getting the Court out of telecommunications policy. The Court did not want to decide the truly difficult economic questions facing the broadband industry. It did not want to decide whether open-access rules for cable might speed or restrict deployment, and whether horizontal parity might be a good idea. The result of the *Brand X* decision was to give the FCC more room to decide on the future of broadband.

That "bend-over-backward" deference is what makes the contrast with *Grokster* so sharp. In both cases, the Court faced difficult economic questions centered on new technologies and dynamic industries. Yet in *Grokster* the Court decided that it was fully competent to decide that a given business model based on a new technology was not a good idea for the national economy. In *Brand X*, the same Court is positively terrified of trying to answer what amount to similar types of questions. There were no obvious good guys and bad guys in *Brand X*, but is that really what should make the difference?

All this suggests that perhaps the most principled outcome in *Grokster* would have been for the Court to take a different course

---

[70] 125 S Ct at 2714 (Scalia, J, dissenting).

even than that suggested by the *Sony* decision. As we said earlier, *Sony* professed to defer to Congress, yet at the same time created a substantive rule for the market entry of new technologies. The Court might have gone back further, before *Sony*, and taken the approach of earlier cases like *Fortnightly Corp. v United Artists,*[71] *Teleprompter Corp. v Columbia Broadcasting Systems,*[72] and *White-Smith Music Publishing Co. v Apollo Co.*[73] In each of those cases the court confronted the same problem it had in *Grokster* and *Sony*— a new technological industry (the record and piano player, and various kinds of cable television) facing off against an incumbent industry. The Court in those cases said, in essence, we don't have a clue, found no copyright liability, and left things for Congress to fix. The Court in those cases made it clear that the Copyright Act, as written, had no answers to the problem presented, and that the Court did not trust itself to fashion one.

It is a little too easy to say the Court should have just deferred; some of the disadvantages of institutional deference are worth discussing. Had the Court let *Grokster* off with a note to Congress, the result would have been some kind of congressional settlement of the dispute. However, that is another name for an interest-group free-for-all that would have been time consuming, expensive, and may have damaged whatever integrity the copyright code still has.[74] The congressional or, more accurately, interest-group mode of copyright policy-making has well-documented weaknesses. Its record is a mix of arguable successes along with many outright failures.[75]

It may be that the Court in *Grokster* managed to replicate what Congress would have done, in less time. But as the comparison with telecommunications law makes clear, in the long run, the Court will need to ask itself when it is and is not competent to set industrial policy for the information sectors through ever more elaborate in-

---

[71] 392 US 390, 399 (1968).

[72] 415 US 394 (1974).

[73] 209 US 1 (1908).

[74] As David Nimmer points out, interest-group-driven amendments have made a mess of the copyright statute. See David Nimmer, *Codifying Copyright Comprehensibly*, 51 UCLA L Rev 1233, 1238 (2004).

[75] For a general history of the interest-group process in copyright and its results, see Wu, 103 Mich L Rev (cited in note 3); Jessica Litman, *Copyright Legislation and Technological Change*, 68 Ore L Rev 275 (1989); Jane Ginsburg, *Copyright and Control Over New Technologies of Dissemination*, 101 Colum L Rev 1613, 1622 (2001).

terpretations of the copyright statute. Copyright, in this respect, faces a question of legal process that is difficult to answer. When do courts remain competent to answer the economic questions presented by disruptive technologies, and when does deference back to Congress become a better course of action? At a minimum the Court needs to give itself the option, when it faces copyright questions that are just too hard, to direct the problem to Congress with a "fix-me" attached.

IV. CONCLUSION

When compared with either antitrust or communications laws' management of competition, copyright's approach is unusual. No one doubts that the underlying questions are hard no matter who asks them. Yet courts have taken to regulating the information industries by asking questions that have very little to do with the economic effects on the industries regulated. Discussing matters like "knowledge" or "inducement" is an unusual way to take into account matters like industry structure, innovation, and other macro-economic questions.

The results may be defensible in individual cases. But as rules for industry, they will be something of a random walk: sometimes defensible, but often not. The fact is that courts in antitrust, copyright, and telecommunications cases are now facing very similar problems. In coming years, the Court and other federal courts should self-consciously accept the role they are playing in setting the terms of competition in information industries, and strive to make industrial policy the best it might be.

JOHN O. MCGINNIS AND
MICHAEL B. RAPPAPORT

THE JUDICIAL FILIBUSTER, THE

MEDIAN SENATOR, AND THE

COUNTERMAJORITARIAN DIFFICULTY

I. Introduction

In recent years, the filibustering of judicial appointments has generated enormous controversy. While the controversy has focused on a range of issues,[1] the most important issue—the filibuster's effect on the nature of Justices who can be confirmed—has largely been neglected. In this article, we show that the application of the filibuster to judicial confirmations has fundamental implications for both the composition of the courts and the nature of constitutional

John O. McGinnis is Class of 1940 Research Professor, Northwestern University Law School. Michael B. Rappaport is Professor, University of San Diego School of Law.

Authors' note: The authors would like to thank Lee Epstein, Barry Friedman, Tonja Jacobi, David Law, Shaun Martin, David McGowan, Thomas Merrill, Mark Movsesian, Jide Nzelibe, Richard Posner, Max Schanzenbach, and participants at a Case Western Law School workshop for their helpful comments.

[1] The issues focused upon in the debate include whether the filibuster can be eliminated by a majority vote through the nuclear or constitutional option, see Martin B. Gold and Dimple Gupta, *The Constitutional Option to Change Senate Rules and Procedures: A Majoritarian Means to Overcome the Filibuster*, 28 Harv J L & Pub Pol 205 (2004); Michael B. Rappaport and John O. McGinnis, *Confirming Judges: The Constitutional Option*, San Diego Union Tribune (Mar 11, 2005), whether its use in this context is unprecedented, and whether the President can respond to a filibuster through the use of a recess appointment. See Michael B. Rappaport, *The Original Meaning of the Recess Appointments Clause*, 52 UCLA L Rev 1487 (2005); Edward Hartnett, *Recess Appointments of Article III Judges: Three Constitutional Questions*, 26 Cardozo L Rev 377 (2005).

law. If employed, the filibuster will change the kind of Justices who are confirmed and so over time reshape the Supreme Court itself. It also holds the promise of tempering the countermajoritarian difficulty, "the central preoccupation of modern constitutional law."[2]

We demonstrate these dramatic effects by turning to positive political theory, a branch of political science that is in the process of making legal theory more analytic and precise.[3] With the help of spatial models, we show that supermajority confirmation rules, of which the filibuster rule is an example, will tend to make Justices more moderate, where moderate means having a jurisprudential view closer to the view held by the median Senator. We thus identify an apparent paradox that a supermajority rule for judicial confirmation actually furthers the views of the legislative majority.

Our analysis of the filibuster rule reveals the political forces that may help this new practice endure, laying bare the motivations that led to the recent Filibuster Deal entered into by the "Gang of 14." While many have praised this group of moderate Senators for their statesmanship in agreeing not to employ the "nuclear option" to end the filibuster,[4] we show that their deal actually reflected their political self-interest. Because the filibuster rule generates the appointment of more moderate Justices, these moderate Senators, Democrat and Republican alike, are better off when the filibuster is permitted. Our analysis also allows us to predict that a key provision of the Filibuster Deal, which prohibits filibusters of judicial nominees except in extraordinary circumstances, is likely to be interpreted to permit ideological objections to a nominee. Such objections help moderate Senators avoid extreme nominees whom they dislike.

Second, our argument that the filibuster rule generates more moderate judicial appointments also suggests that the rule will temper the countermajoritarian difficulty—the problem created by an unelected judiciary invalidating the decisions of the popularly

---

[2] Akhil Reed Amar, *The Consent of the Governed: Constitutional Amendment Outside Article V*, 94 Colum L Rev 457, 474 (1994) (noting that scholarship has lately been "preoccupied with the 'countermajoritarian difficulty'").

[3] Positive political theory is a growing movement that analyzes law through a combination of rational choice and institutional analysis. See Frank B. Cross and Emerson H. Tiller, *Judicial Partisanship and Legal Doctrine: Whistleblowing in Courts of Appeal*, 107 Yale L J 2155, 2176 (1997); Tonja Jacobi, *The Impact of Positive Political Theory on Old Questions of Constitutional Law and Separations of Powers*, 100 Nw U L Rev 259 (2006).

[4] See Howard Kurtz, *The Gang of 14, Blogged Down the Middle*, Wash Post (May 29, 2005) at D-1.

elected branches. We suggest that the median Senator is a reasonable proxy for the median voter in the electorate. Therefore, a supermajority confirmation rule that generates appointments that accord with the median Senator's view is also more likely to produce Justices who act based on a majority of the public's view of judicial review. In this way, judicial review would be more likely to impose the limitations on popular government that a majority of the people desire. While this form of judicial review would be more democratic, it would still operate to impose longer-term constitutional principles on the popularly elected branches.

In developing this argument, we offer a fundamental reconceptualization of the countermajoritarian difficulty by unpacking it into three components—jurisprudential, temporal, and confirmational. We show that the first two components are deeply embedded in the institutional requirements of judicial review. But the third component—the selection of Justices who at the time of their appointment are likely to exercise judicial review differently from what the public would prefer—stems only from majoritarian appointment rules. Since this component serves no useful function, it should be eliminated.

We then relax the assumption in our model that the President and the Senate have perfect information about the ideology of the nominee for the Supreme Court. This allows us to explore stealth nominees (about whom the President has information that the Senate lacks) and uncertain nominees (about whom both the President and the Senate lack information). We show that the presence of a filibuster rule will lead the President to attempt to nominate more stealth nominees, although that strategy turns out to have some costs for him as well as the Senate. We also demonstrate that the greater use of stealth nominees will temper but not eliminate the two greatest virtues of the filibuster—generating more moderate nominees and eliminating an unnecessary component of the countermajoritarian difficulty.

Our model also clarifies other important aspects of the confirmation process that might otherwise seem confusing or irrational. For instance, the filibuster is likely to have a greater effect on lower court nominees than Supreme Court nominees, because charges of obstructionism limit the ability to filibuster and are more effective at the Supreme Court level. A filibuster rule also will lead to less moderate Justices than would an express sixty-vote confirmation rule on the merits, because mounting a filibuster rather than voting according to an express rule will generate more charges of obstructionism. Supermajority confirmation rules, including the filibuster, also make the timing of vacancies more salient. As the President's term nears its end, he will not be able to fill vacancies with Justices as close to his preferences as he would earlier in the term. Filibustering under those circumstances has more benefits to the opposition party, because the President is less likely to be able to make a second or third nomination.

Finally, decisions whether to filibuster will sometimes be strategic in that Senators rationally consider the effect of a filibuster on subsequent vacancies. For instance, a minority party opposed to the President may filibuster a nominee that it otherwise deems ideologically acceptable when the party wants to gain a reputation for toughness to facilitate its subsequent bargaining with the President over judicial nominees. Conversely, that party may decline to filibuster an ideologically unacceptable nominee to gain a reputation for reasonableness with the public so it can more easily filibuster future nominees whom it believes will be even farther from its ideologically ideal point.

Part II sets forth our spatial model and applies it to compare the behavior of Senators and the President under majority rule and supermajority rule. We modify the model to consider three situations: Senators acting independently of political parties, Senators acting as members of superstrong parties, and Senators acting as members of parties with substantial, albeit not controlling, influence on their vote. Part III applies the model to explain key features of the Filibuster Deal, including the advantages it provides to moderates. Part IV offers a new conceptualization of the countermajoritarian difficulty and shows how a supermajoritarian confirmation rule tempers that difficulty by reducing its most indefensible component. Part V relaxes the assumption that the President and Senate will have perfect information about the candidates. It shows that a filibuster rule will generate more stealth candidates, but that this effect will not greatly reduce its advantages in creating more moderate Justices and tempering the countermajoritarian difficulty. Finally, Part VI uses our model to explain several features of the current confirmation process.

II. The Model

To understand how majority and supermajority rules operate as to judicial appointments, we employ a simple spatial model.[5] Spatial models have been widely used in the political science literature[6] and are readily applicable to the appointment of Justices. As with all models, our model makes certain simplifying assumptions in order to help us understand the essential features of a more complicated reality.

This section develops a spatial model for the judicial confirmation process. Our principal model is one dimensional in which the single dimension consists of the ideological preferences by which Senators and the President assess a judicial nominee.[7] We then make this model more realistic by adding other values besides ideology that political actors systematically consider. We also vary the model to reflect Senators' consideration of the preferences of their political parties.

All variations of the model underscore our most important conclusion: both an express supermajority rule and a filibuster rule tend to produce Justices that are more centrist ideologically than does majority rule.

A. ASSUMPTIONS: THE SPAN OF SENATORS AND THE PLACEMENT OF THE PRESIDENT

Our principal model assumes that Senators and the President evaluate judicial candidates based on a single dimension—their assessment of the candidate's ideology.[8] Under this assumption,

---

[5] For an introduction to spatial models, see Peter C. Ordeshook, *Game Theory and Political Theory: An Introduction* 23–26 (Cambridge, 1986). A good example in the law review literature is a famous article explicating Chadha. See William Eskridge and John Ferejohn, *The Article I, Section 7 Game*, 80 Georgetown L J 823 (1992).

[6] See, e.g., Keith Krehbiel, *Spatial Models of Legislative Choice*, 13 Legis Stud Q 259, 273–94 (1998).

[7] The term "dimension" in the literature of spatial models is used to describe a particular axis of policy choice. See Thad Kousser and Mathew D. McCubbins, *Social Choice, Crypto-Initiatives and Policymaking by Direct Democracy*, 78 S Cal L Rev 949, 951 (2005). If a political actor considers only one kind of policy choice in making a decision, then the model will be one-dimensional. If he considers two or more policy variables, the model will be multidimensional.

[8] The view that Justices vote based at least in part on ideology is widely accepted in the political science literature, even if it is controversial in the legal literature. See, e.g., Jeffrey A. Segal and Harold J. Spaeth, *The Supreme Court and the Attitudinal Model* 256–60 (1993) (providing ideological scores for all Justices).

the political actors' evaluations of candidates run on a straight line ranging from the left end of the political spectrum to the right end. While there are actually 100 Senators, the model is simpler if there is an odd number. Because the Vice President can break ties,[9] we will assume that there are 101 Senators. Thus, in Figure 1, we place the 101 Senators along a line, with the most liberal Senator (S1) on the extreme left and the most conservative one (S101) on the extreme right.

Each Senator is placed at his ideal point—the position in the ideological spectrum that he would prefer the nominee to hold. We assume that the political actors' preferences are single-peaked, that is, that they prefer points closer to their ideal than farther away.[10] Under majority rule, an important Senator is S51, the median Senator. Given certain assumptions, a nominee cannot be confirmed under majority rule unless the median Senator supports his confirmation. Similarly, under supermajority rule, the important Senator is the "pivotal Senator." The pivotal Senator is the Senator ideologically closest to the President whose support he needs to obtain the supermajority consensus necessary for confirmation. For instance, as we describe below, a conservative President needs to get the support of S42 under a supermajority rule requiring sixty votes for confirmation.

For heuristic purposes, we also assume that the Senators' ideal points are equally spaced on the line, so that the ideological distances between any two consecutive points are equal.[11] It is im-

$$
\begin{array}{ccccc}
 & & & \text{P} & \\
\hline
1 & 42 & 51 & 75 & 101 \\
\end{array}
$$

Fig. 1

[9] See US Const, Art I, sec 3, cl 4 ("The Vice President of the United States shall be President of the Senate, but shall have no vote, unless they be equally divided."). Of course, the Vice President does not cast a vote under supermajority rules, including cloture, as there are no ties, but we ignore that complication here.

[10] See Krehbiel, 13 Legis Stud Q at 263 (cited in note 6). We also assume that the political actors' preferences are symmetrical, so that a Senator is indifferent between nominees at an equal distance from his ideal point in either direction. For example, S51 will be indifferent between a nominee at 55 and a nominee at 47.

[11] The assumption that the Senators' ideal points are equally spaced means that the ideological distance between any two Senators who are an equal distance apart from one another is equal. For example, the distance between S30 and S40 is equal to the distance between S60 and S70. Under this assumption, the median Senator is not merely central

portant to note, however, that our basic conclusion that a super-majority rule leads to the confirmation of more moderate Justices does not depend on this last assumption. As we discuss below, however Senators are bunched ideologically, our basic conclusions continue to hold on more modest assumptions about the ideological distances between the President, the median Senator, and the pivotal Senator.[12]

The President can also be placed on this line, depending on his preference for a judicial candidate. In Figure 1, we have located the President at 75 (P75) to suggest a reasonably strong conservative, such as George W. Bush. It is not an accident that we have placed the President close to the median Senator of his party rather than to the median Senator of the entire Senate. There are strong reasons to believe that the President will hold more extreme ideological views than the median Senator. Presidents must obtain nominations from a primary electorate that is composed largely of members of his own party. Moreover, primary voters tend be more ideologically extreme than voters in the general electorate. Consequently, rather than reflecting the views of the median voter of the electorate, Presidents are more likely to reflect the views of the median voter of their party, or even to be more extreme.[13] While presidential candidates do attempt to reach out to the median voter during the general election, they remain concerned to turn out their base and thus make commitments that do not reflect purely majoritarian sentiment.[14] As a result of these forces, the last seven elected Presidents appear to have reflected the median views of their party more than the median views of the electorate.[15]

---

in the sense that there are an equal number of Senators to the right of him as to the left of him. He is also central in that the ideological distance from S51 to S101 will be equal to that from S51 to S1.

[12] As discussed in note 35 and accompanying text.

[13] Political scientist David King of Harvard University has well described the factors that have led to this situation. See David C. King, *Who's Partying*, USA Today (Aug 4, 2000).

[14] The so-called "securing the base strategy" has received a lot of attention both in the press, see, e.g., David Brownstein, *Bush Aims to Solidify His Base*, Los Angeles Times (Aug 24, 2004), and in academic commentary, see, e.g., Morris Fiorina, *What Ever Happened to the Median Voter* (paper on file with authors). Moreover, one of the popular ways of securing the base is to pledge to appoint a Justice acceptable to it.

[15] We have evidence from the modeling of social scientists that Presidents George W. Bush and Bill Clinton are closer to the median representatives of their party than to the median representatives. See Keith Poole, *Estimating a Basic Issue Space from a Set of Issue Scales*, http://voteview.com/basic.htm. We do not have similar proof of this proposition for previous Presidents in the modern era, but we believe that Lyndon Johnson, Richard

By contrast, electoral forces tend to produce a body of Senators who are more likely to reflect both the center and the extremes of the larger electorate. Senators are arrayed over a wider ideological space because of variations in the composition of voters in the states. New England Republicans are more liberal than most Republicans and thus Republican Senators elected from those states will be more centrist.[16] Similarly, Southern Democrats are more conservative than most Democrats, which generates more moderate Democrats.[17] Consequently, there are likely to be a range of Senators from the President's party with more moderate views than the President.

While this single-dimensional model has the virtue of simplicity, we can add factors to capture more of the story and make our analysis more useful. In our view, the political ideologies of the Senators and the President are the most important parts of the confirmation process, but they do not sufficiently dominate the process so that other matters can be ignored. In particular, we believe that a useful model of the judicial appointment process must recognize that Senators care about two other values besides the ideology of the candidate—minimizing the time judicial offices are vacant and not being viewed as obstructionists. One could understand these values more formally as part of each Senator's utility function. We also consider in some versions of our model the desire of Senators to vote with their political party.

Like the Senators, the President is also concerned about leaving offices vacant. The President, however, is not concerned about obstruction but about something similar—divisiveness. Just as Senators do not want to be thought by the public to be obstructing the normal business of government, the President does not want to be thought to be nominating such divisive candidates that the

---

Nixon, Jimmy Carter, Ronald Reagan, and George Bush the elder similarly reflected more the median views of the members of their party in each house of Congress rather than the median voter generally. The explanation for the movement of Presidents toward the extremes of the political spectrum in this period is attributable at least in part to the emergence of primaries as the principal means of selecting presidential candidates. See Fareed Zakaria, *The Future of Freedom* 180–84 (2003).

[16] See Roberta Romano, *The Political Dynamics of Security Regulation*, 14 Yale J Reg 27, 383 n 222 (1997) (showing political divergence of New England Republicans from Republicans in general).

[17] See id (showing political divergence of Southern Democrats from Democrats in general).

confirmation process impedes the smooth operation of government.

If we were to incorporate additional dimensions into our graphs, that approach would significantly complicate them and their ability to convey our analysis. In our view, the benefits of complicating the graphs from greater accuracy are greatly outweighed by the disadvantages from reduced comprehensibility.[18] Therefore, our model will graph the single dimension of political ideology, while verbally adding the other considerations where they are needed in the analysis.

B. THE DECISIONS TO NOMINATE AND TO CONFIRM

Under a one-dimensional analysis, each Senator would prefer nominees at their ideal point. When the President nominates someone at a point different from a Senator's ideal point, the Senator must decide whether or not to support the nominee. For example, Senator Jesse Helms had to decide whether to vote for Sandra Day O'Connor although she was presumably less conservative than his ideal point.[19] Here we outline the considerations affecting a Senator's decision whether to support a nominee departing from his ideal point under both a one-dimensional analysis and an analysis that takes other values into account. We also briefly discuss the considerations that lead the President to nominate someone who departs from his ideal point.

There are several ways to look at a Senator's decision whether to vote to confirm a nominee who departed from his ideal point. Under the simplest approach, a Senator would decide whether to vote to confirm a nominee by deciding whether he preferred the ideological composition of the Court with the nominee or without

---

[18] The benefits of modifying our graphs are not sufficient, because in general the additional dimensions are unlikely to alter systematically the causal effects of the ideological differences. First, these other dimensions are, in the main, of less importance to the Senators and the President. Second, these other dimensions are also unlikely to diverge significantly across Senators. For example, if all Senators prefer higher-quality Justices or shorter vacancies to the same extent, then the differences in the positions of the Senators will all be the result of their ideological preferences. Finally, cycling, which can cause problems with the addition of other dimensions, is also not likely to be a problem in the judicial area, because there are generally only two choices about a nominee—confirm or reject. See, e.g., Maxwell L. Stearns, *Standing Back from the Forest: Justiciability and Social Choice*, 83 Cal L Rev 1309, 141 (1995) (limiting voting options can prevent cycling).

[19] 127 Cong Rec 21375 (1981) (noting that Senator Jesse Helms voted to confirm Sandra Day O'Connor).

him. Even if the nominee diverged from the Senator's ideal point, the Senator might still decide that he preferred the nominee to leaving the office vacant if the nominee would be close enough to the Senator's ideal point.[20]

This approach to modeling a Senator's decision whether to confirm, however, is too simple. Senators consider additional factors other than whether they prefer the ideological composition of the Court with the nominee than without him.[21] First, Senators also care about the extent to which there is a vacancy in the judicial office. The rejection of a nominee will usually lead to a longer period in which the office is vacant. Senators will generally prefer, holding the ideological views of the nominee constant, that there be shorter vacancies. They will prefer that nominees they support on ideological grounds be appointed more quickly. They will also prefer, even apart from the ideology of the nominee, that someone serve in the job so that the work of the judiciary can be performed.[22] Consequently, a Senator who was otherwise unwilling to support a nominee on ideological grounds nonetheless might vote for him in order to avoid an extended vacancy.

The desire of Senators to avoid a vacancy is likely to be much

---

[20] One way to think about a Senator's choice as to whether he prefers the ideological composition of the Court with the nominee or without him is as follows: the Senator will vote for the nominee if the Court would be closer to his ideal point with the nominee than with the eight existing members of the Court. See Byron J. Moraski and Charles R. Shipan, *The Politics of Supreme Court Nominations: A Theory of Institutional Constraints and Choices*, 43 Amer J Pol Sci 1069 (1999). This approach, however, ignores the other considerations that we believe influence a Senator's decision how to vote, including whether the President's next nominee would be closer to the Senator's ideal point. See note 25 and accompanying notes.

[21] Presidents will also take factors like the continuation of the vacancy into account in deciding whom to nominate. See note 26 and accompanying text.

[22] Of course, not all appointments will formally involve an existing vacancy. Justice Sandra Day O'Connor's resignation took effect when her replacement was confirmed by the Senate. See Letter from Justice Sandra Day O'Connor to President George W. Bush (July 1, 2005), http://www.cnn.com/2005/LAW/07/01/oconnor.letter.nobanner/. If Justice O'Connor could have fully performed the duties of her office until a replacement were confirmed, then there would have been less incentive to confirm a new nominee because no real vacancy would have occurred after her announcement that she intended to retire. But Justice O'Connor's availability to serve after her announcement is less important than might be thought, because a Justice who has resigned pending confirmation is not, practically speaking, a fully effective Justice. A lame duck Justice raises questions of logistics. For instance, during the incumbency of a lame duck Justice, there is the question of who will decide cases which she heard argued, but which would normally be issued after she left the Court. It also raises questions of legitimacy: should she take momentous decisions for the nation as a lame duck? It may still appear to the public that the Court needs a new Justice. Thus, even when Justices resign pending confirmation, Senators would want to fill the vacancy, other things being equal.

stronger for Supreme Court nominees (who are our main focus here) than for lower court nominees. As we discuss below, both politicians and the public consider a Supreme Court vacancy to require immediate attention and quick action. By contrast, lower court vacancies are not normally deemed to be pressing matters and court of appeals vacancies can last for several years without receiving much notice.

Second, a Senator may also care about the reaction of his state's electorate to his vote to confirm or reject a nominee. Of course, a Senator will prefer that the voters agree with his assessment of a nominee. A similar but distinct issue that we emphasize here is that a Senator may be concerned that his vote against a nominee not be regarded as obstructionist. It seems that the public often does not like actions, taken on a partisan basis, that impede the smooth operation of the government.[23] This public reaction would be most forceful when a large majority of the relevant political actors favor a nominee, but the actions of a small number are able to block him. Such is the case when the President nominates and a majority of the Senate supports a candidate, but a minority is able to filibuster him.[24]

Finally, and perhaps most importantly, Senators will consider who the next nominee might be if the existing nominee is rejected. To a significant extent, Senators are not deciding between the existing nominee and no nominee, but instead between the existing nominee and the next nominee. Because an extended Supreme Court vacancy is not deemed acceptable and Justices serve much longer than the length of any vacancy, the dominant ideological consideration for Senators will not be whether the current nom-

---

[23] The public has often regarded the filibuster as a source of obstructionism. Catherine Fisk and Erwin Chemerinsky, *The Filibuster*, 49 Stan L Rev 181, 195 (1997). The public also punished the Republican party, whom it held responsible for shutting down the government in 1995. See Bruce Ackerman, *Revolution on a Human Scale*, 108 Yale L J 2279, 2342 (1998) (describing public reaction to Republican tactics).

[24] There are, of course, many other considerations that potentially may affect the decision whether to vote to confirm or reject a nominee. These considerations include the perceived quality of the nominee, see Lee Epstein, Jeffrey A. Segal, Nancy Staudt, and René Lindstädt, *The Role of Qualifications in the Confirmation of Nominees to the U.S. Supreme Court*, 32 Fla St L Rev 1145 (2005), different Senators' views as to the legitimacy of the President being allowed to select a nominee that reflects his ideology, and other benefits that the President might provide in exchange for a Senator supporting his nominee. In our view, these considerations are not needed to draw the conclusions we reach, nor would they change those conclusions. Thus, we mainly choose to omit these and other considerations from our analysis.

inee will move the existing eight-member Court closer to the Senator's ideal point but whether a Senator prefers the current nominee to the next nominee he believes the President would select. For example, if a centrist Senator like S51 believed that P75's next nominee would be more centrist than his present nominee, S51 might vote against the present nominee even though the present nominee would move the existing eight-member Court closer to S51's ideal point. Thus, expectations about the next nominee can be extremely important.[25]

These considerations governing a Senator's decision whether to vote to confirm are mirrored by similar considerations that govern the President's decision about whom to nominate. Like the Senators, the President cares about ideology and about avoiding vacancies. Thus, he is likely to nominate someone as close to his ideal point as he believes has a reasonable chance of being confirmed. The President, however, would not be concerned with avoiding charges of obstructionism, but with avoiding charges of the analogous sin of divisiveness—of nominating someone so ideologically extreme that it causes the Senate to have to reject him. If the President is seen as divisive and his nominee is rejected, the President is likely to see his popularity fall and to be forced to

---

[25] Many spatial models of the judicial appointment process employ a point on the line that is marked as the status quo. The status quo represents the state of the world that exists prior to the nomination and what would continue to hold if the nomination is defeated. The use of a status quo helps to capture the decision that a Senator faces of whether to accept the nominee or to reject him (and revert to the status quo). Typically, the models view the status quo as the existing eight-member Court. See, e.g., Moraski and Shipan, 43 Amer J Pol Sci (cited in note 20). Our figures, however, do not identify any point as the status quo, because in our model the status quo is not a stable point. In our model, a Senator deciding whether to reject a nominee must consider not only the eight-member Court that would continue if the nominee is rejected, but also the next nominee that the President is likely to make. Without considering these expectations concerning the next nominee, the status quo concept is misleading. For example, if the existing nominee would make the eight-member Court less conservative, models that employ the eight-member Court as the status quo would predict that a left-wing Senator would vote to confirm that nominee. But if that Senator believes that the President's next nominee would be even less conservative, he would vote against the existing nominee. While expectations about the next nominee must be included in the definition of the status quo, such expectations are not stable. They will depend on the circumstances under which the first nominee was rejected. Moreover, because the confirmation process is iterative, those expectations are updated as the actors receive more information and political circumstances change. Accordingly, because the status quo is unstable and a construct of expectations and preferences, we do not identify a fixed status quo. Instead, we use the ideological values of the Senators, the President, and the nominees in the figures to represent the basic aspects of the choice situation. We then proceed to analyze the political actors' decisions with these considerations in mind.

nominate someone farther from his ideal point.[26] The President's desire to avoid divisiveness suggests once again that he will nominate someone who he believes has a reasonable chance of being confirmed.

Finally, it is worth emphasizing that the President's decision who to nominate and the Senators' decisions whether to confirm are significantly affected by the expectations of these political actors. For example, the President may desire a nominee at 75, but he may choose to nominate someone at 65 because that person is more likely to be confirmed. His decision to depart from his ideal point, then, will be based on his expectations about how the Senate will respond to a nomination. Many of the Senators, however, will base their decisions whether to accept a nominee on expectations about the President. If they turn down the present nominee, will that lead the President to nominate one who is less conservative?

The importance of expectations in the decisions to nominate and confirm suggests that the President and the Senators will have incentives to influence the expectations about their actions.[27] For example, the President might seek to posture in such a way as to suggest that he is strongly committed to nominating a conservative nominee, so that the Senators do not believe he would moderate his selection of a second nominee in the event his first nominee is rejected.

While these considerations suggest that the appointment decision can be quite complicated, our analysis will focus mainly on ideological preferences, bringing in the other factors individually when needed. Moreover, our focus is not to explain all aspects of the appointment process, but instead to explore the differences that are likely under majority rule and supermajority rules, including the filibuster rule. Using this strategy, we now show that an express supermajority rule would tend to produce more moderate nominees than would majority rule, and that Senate moderates therefore would prefer the supermajority rule. We then

---

[26] This analysis suggests that not all nominees who are rejected will harm the President's popularity and influence. If the Senate's rejection of a nominee is seen as unfair and is itself unpopular (admittedly, an event that may be unlikely), then the President will not be viewed as divisive and bear the resulting consequences. Instead, the Senate will be viewed as obstructionist.

[27] Cf. Gary Goodpaster, *A Primer on Competitive Bargaining*, 1996 J Disp Res 325, 328 (1996) (discussing situations where the strategy of one party depends on the expectations of the other).

show that largely the same result is produced by the implicit supermajority rule of the filibuster.

C. APPOINTMENTS WITHOUT PARTY VOTING

Our analysis of the judicial appointments process under majority and supermajority rules proceeds in three steps. First, we look at the appointments process without the influence of political parties. Then, we move to the opposite extreme and examine how the process would work if parties are superstrong and Senators always follow the positions adopted by their parties. Finally, we consider the more realistic situation where Senators prefer to follow the positions of their parties but are willing to depart from their positions under certain circumstances. The result there not surprisingly turns out to be a mixture of the appointments process without parties and with superstrong parties.

The analysis without parties assumes that each individual Senator votes whether or not to confirm without considering the preferences of his political party. To analyze this situation, assume the simple spatial model discussed above with a conservative President with an ideal point of 75. This situation is illustrated in Figure 2. If the President nominates someone at his ideal point of 75, will that person be confirmed under majority or supermajority rule?

Under majority rule, confirmation would require majority support. The most obvious majority coalition would involve the fifty-one Senators ranging from S51 to S101. While Senators who are close to 75 are very likely to support the nominee, the question is whether a Senator whose ideal points are farther away will support him. The President's nominee will need the support of moderate Senators, such as the median Senator, S51, and the most conservative Senators, such as S101.

To begin with S101, why would he support the President's nominee, even though he would prefer someone much more conservative? While he, of course, would have the same general reasons

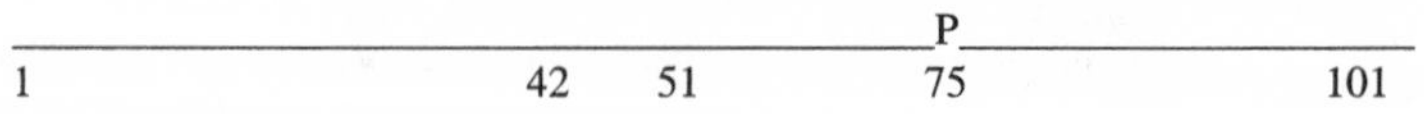

			P	
1	42	51	75	101

FIG. 2

to support the nominee that all Senators do—a desire to end the vacancy and not to be viewed as obstructionist—what seems most important for S101 is the notion that this is a conservative President and S101 is unlikely to do better with the next nominee. There are three reasons for this. First, voting against the President's nominee raises the possibility of the confirmation of a nominee significantly farther from his ideal ideological point. If there is any significant chance that the next President might be a Democrat (with an ideal point, let us say, of P25), then S101 would be better off supporting the current President's nominee.

Second, even if the vacancy were to last a shorter time and the appointment were to be made by the existing President, the period of the vacancy is likely to prove a significant cost to S101. The period when the office is vacant is a loss to S101 of a nominee who he is likely to prefer to the existing set of Justices who now serve (or to the Justices who are likely to be appointed by future Presidents). More precisely, if S101 would prefer the courts with a new 75 Justice to the courts without this Justice, then the period of the vacancy must be regarded as a cost.

Finally, a decision by S101 to reject a nominee at 75 is not likely to result in the appointment of a more conservative Justice.[28] S101 simply has no reason to expect that any nominee that the President would nominate after the defeat of the first will be more conservative. While a nominee farther to the right might secure S101's vote, it is also possible to cause S51 to abandon the nominee. Thus, S101 appears to have an incentive to confirm the President's nominee, even if the Senator would prefer more conservative nominees.

By contrast, S51 has less incentive to go along with P75's nominees. Most importantly, S51 is not likely to regard P75 as closer to his views than future Presidents. Indeed, S51 will be largely indifferent between P75's nominees and a future P25's. For much the same reason, S51 is also likely to regard the vacancy of a Justice at 75 to be far less costly than does S101. Finally, it is also more likely that S51 will believe that voting against a nominee at 75 will result in a more moderate nominee. If S51 votes against the

---

[28] If the nominee is much more moderate than 75, conservatives might oppose the nominee on the theory that the President will move toward his ideological optimal point with the next nomination. Such a view may explain conservative Senators' (and conservative interests groups') opposition to President George W. Bush's nomination of Harriet Miers.

nominee, then the President will need to nominate someone else. Unlike S101, S51 can credibly threaten to vote against another nominee unless the nominee were more to his ideological liking, because the cost to S51 of the President not making the appointment is far less than to S101.[29]

As a result, we would predict that moderate Senators would have more leverage over the nomination in these circumstances than would more conservative Senators. Consequently, one can predict that the nominee will lie somewhere between P75 and S51's preferences.[30]

Now consider how the nomination would operate under a supermajority rule that requires sixty Senators to confirm a nominee. The pivotal Senator is no longer S51, but S42.[31] Thus, the President must secure his consent to the nomination, and therefore the result in this situation is likely to lie between S42 and S75. Since S42 is more liberal than S51, it is likely that the President will have to nominate someone more liberal to secure confirmation. While S51 under majority rule was largely indifferent between a nomination by the existing President and a future Democratic President, S42 would actually prefer a nomination by a Democratic President. Thus, S42 has even less incentive to compromise with the President than S51 had under majority rule. This suggests that S42 would have more leverage to insist on a more liberal nominee than S51 would, since S42 has a much more credible threat not to support the nominee.[32]

The most significant limitation on the power of S42 would be S42's desire not to be viewed as obstructionist. If the people in S42's state believe that a single Senator should not oppose an

---

[29] One countervailing consideration is that moderates may be somewhat more likely than those on the extreme end of the spectrum to fear charges of obstructionism. If moderates come from states where there are more competitive general elections, one might think they will want to appeal to swing voters with whom charges of obstructionism would carry the most weight.

[30] We discuss below the degree to which this situation resembles a bilateral monopoly. See notes 45–46 and accompanying text.

[31] S42 is the pivotal Senator under a sixty-vote supermajority rule because our model has 101 Senators, see note 9 and accompanying text, and thus there are fifty-nine Senators to his ideological right.

[32] It is true that S101's threat to refuse to support a centrist nominee might operate as some check on the extent of S42's demands, but S101 would be less able to check S42 than he would S51 under majority rule. S101 will recognize that it is more difficult to secure a supermajority coalition and therefore will be likely to moderate how much of a conservative he will insist on, or else risk causing a large number of rejections of nominees.

appointment on ideological grounds when there are a large number of people who favor it, then the Senator may be constrained to support nominees he would otherwise reject. Under a three-fifths supermajority rule, the President and fifty-nine Senators would be willing to support a nominee. The difficulty of securing a supermajority suggests that the public would feel more strongly that a Senator should not oppose the nominee when his vote would allow confirmation than under majority rule. This is all the more true if, as seems likely, the nominee were someone who was relatively moderate as compared to the political preferences of the President.

In the end, then, we can make two predictions as to how the supermajority confirmation rule will compare to the majority confirmation rule. First, one would expect that the nominees who secure confirmation under the supermajority rule will tend to be more moderate than those under majority rule.[33] Despite the complications discussed above, the fact that S42 is more liberal than S51 suggests that the President's nominee will be closer to the median Senator under a supermajority rule than under majority rule. While the appointee will lie somewhere between the ideal points of S51 and P75 under majority rule, he will lie somewhere between the ideal points of S42 and P75 under supermajority rule.[34]

---

[33] The only circumstance in which the candidate confirmed would be less moderate under majority rule is where the pivotal Senator had such leverage in bargaining with the President that under majority rule the Justice confirmed was very close to S51 and under supermajority rule close to S42. But the received wisdom is that the President has the greater leverage in the confirmation process. See Michael J. Gerhardt, *Toward a Confirmation Understanding of the Appointments Process*, 21 Harv J L & Pub Pol 467, 479–81 (1998). In part, this leverage depends on the public perception that the President has discretion to nominate Justices so long as they are qualified. Even in the absence of such a perception, we believe that the President has at least as much leverage as does the Senate, if not more. Senators who are deciding whether to vote against a nominee must consider the possibility that they will be seen as obstructionist. They must also consider that they will be even more vulnerable to charges of obstructionism should they choose to oppose the next nominee. For his part, the President must consider the possibility that he will be seen as divisive. This will affect his initial decision who to nominate as well as his decision who to nominate if his first nominee is rejected. Thus, both the President and the Senate bear costs for failed nominations. The President, however, has an advantage. If the Senate rejects one of the President's nominees, he may be able to nominate someone at largely the same ideological point and still avoid charges of divisiveness by differentiating his second nominee in other ways—by gender, ethnicity, or professional experience. The prospective costs of obstructionism of the Senate, then, may rise more quickly than those of divisiveness for the President, which would give the President greater leverage in the confirmation process.

[34] While we locate the President at 75, he does not have to be nearly at such an extreme

This conclusion does not change substantially if we relax the assumption of equally spaced Senators. Without the assumption of equally spaced Senators, groups of Senators might be bunched together toward the left or the right. This array might change the results if it meant that the median Senator, S51, or the pivotal Senator, S42, were to prefer judicial candidates who were significantly more to the left or to the right than they would be if the Senators were equally spaced. It turns out, however, that given the location of the President, the distribution of Senators would have to radically diverge from the equally spaced assumption for the supermajority rule not to produce more moderate results.

To take just one example, it is possible that the pivotal Senator, S42, might have views so far to the left that only left-wing nominees could be confirmed. If S42 were sufficiently left wing, then the nominees confirmed under the supermajority rule might be farther to the left from the ideological midpoint than the nominee who would be confirmed under majority rule would be to the right. In our model, however, that is likely to happen only if the pivotal Senator had the equivalent of the views of S3 under the equally spaced assumption. Thus, our general results continue to hold in the most plausible circumstances even if Senators are not equally spaced.[35]

---

point for a supermajority rule to generate more moderate Justices than would majority rule. To illustrate this point, assume that the President is at 57 and the Senate is willing to confirm a Justice who is at the midpoint between the President's ideal point and the median Senator under majority rule (or the President and the pivotal Senator under supermajority rule). Majority rule will lead to a compromise between the President and S51 that results in a Justice at 54. In contrast, a sixty-vote supermajority rule will lead to a compromise on a Justice between the President and S42 that results in a Justice at 49.5. Thus, even if the Republican President is modestly conservative, a sixty-person supermajority rule will produce a Justice who is closer to 51 and thus has a moderate ideology.

[35] The result of varying the ideological position of the pivotal Senator can be intuitively grasped with simple calculations. We here make the modest assumption that the President and Senator have equal bargaining power. (For that assumption, see note 33.) Under majority rule, the ideology of the confirmed Justice will be the average of 75 and 51, or 63, which is 12 from the median of 51. Under supermajority rule the average of 75 and 3 will be 39, which is 12 from the median. Thus, the supermajority rule will lead to more moderate Justices so long as the pivotal Senator has views less left wing than S3 would have under an equally spaced model. We ultimately derive this result from an inequality relating the ideological values (as opposed to the positional values) of v, the pivotal Senator, m, the median Senator, and p, the President. The right-hand side of the inequality represents the expected distance from 51 (perfect moderation) of the ideological value of a Justice confirmed under supermajority rule. The left-hand side represents the expected distance from 51 of the ideological value of a Justice confirmed under majority rule. If the left-hand side is larger than the right, the supermajority rule will lead to more moderate Justices. The general inequality is then: $51 - (p + v)/2 < (p + m)/2 - 51$. In our example above, we assumed that the median Senator is at 51, the ideological value of the most

Second, one would also predict that, even holding the ideology of the nominee constant, it will be more difficult to secure agreement on a nominee under a supermajority rule. Under a supermajority rule, the differences of opinion between the members of the coalition will be greater. Thus, the stakes will be larger—possible nominees ranging from 42 to 101 rather than 51 to 101—and therefore provide the Senators with more incentive to engage in strategic behavior to secure a nominee closer to their ideal point.[36] In addition, under a supermajority rule, there would need to be a larger coalition of Senators ready to confirm than under majority rule.[37] Even if one assumes that the larger coalition is no more ideologically diverse than a smaller one,[38] holding a larger coalition together is likely to be more difficult, since it is harder to find a common agreement among more parties.

D. APPOINTMENTS WITH SUPERSTRONG POLITICAL PARTIES

Now consider appointments when the Senators have a preference to vote with their party. In analyzing this situation, we first assume that Senators place overriding importance on voting as a party.[39] Thus, all members vote as their party desires. In the next section, we relax the assumption and address the more realistic situation where Senators have a preference, but not an overriding one, to vote as their party desires.[40]

---

moderate Justice possible. We believe this is a reasonable assumption because the most moderate Senators seem to approximate the ideological center. One could, of course, vary that assumption as well and analyze the result under the general inequality above.

[36] See Mark Lemley, *The Economics of Improvement in Intellectual Property Law*, 75 Tex L Rev 989, 1084 (1997) (strategic behavior increases the more is at stake).

[37] See Gregory Sidak, *To Declare War*, 41 Duke L J 27, 57 (1991) (assembling larger coalition raises transactions costs to politicians).

[38] Cf. Michael Greve, *Business, the States, and Federalism's Political Economy*, 25 Harv J L & Pub Pol 895, 904 (2002).

[39] There has been a high degree of party voting in Supreme Court nominations. See John D. Felice and Herbert F. Weisber, *Senate Confirmation of Supreme Court Justices: The Changing Importance of Ideology, Party, and Region in Supreme Court Nominees, 1953–88*, 77 Ky L J 509, 511–12 (1989) (exploring correlation between party membership and Supreme Court confirmation votes). Moreover, party-line voting seems to be on the rise generally during the George W. Bush administration. See John Maltese, *Confirmation Gridlock: The Federal Judicial Appointments Process Under Bill Clinton and George W. Bush*, 5 App Prac & Process 1, 12 (2003)

[40] We assume here that, as is usually the case, the minority party has at least 41 Senators in its caucus. For 42 out of 56 years since 1950, the minority party has had more than 49 percent of the seats, permitting it to conduct a partisan filibuster. See http://www.senate.gov/pagelayout/history/one_item_and_teasers/partydiv.htm. All of the years in which the majority party had more than 60 percent of the years were ones in which there

In this section, we continue the assumption of a Republican President at P75. Introducing parties, we now assume that the Republicans have fifty-five Senators (S47 through S101) and the Democrats have forty-six (S1 through S46). While the Senators in each party have differing ideal points, they choose to vote as a group and therefore need to establish a party position. We assume that the party chooses the ideal position of the party's median Senator for at least two reasons. First, it operates to minimize the maximum disparity of party members from the party position. Any other point would involve a larger overall disparity of members from the party's position. Second, the median is also the position that a majority of the party would choose against any other possible position.[41]

In Figure 3, the Republican Party will act to further the preferences of its median Senator, S74, and the Democratic Party chooses to further the preferences of its median Senator, which we will deem S24.[42] In this situation, there are only three players: S24, S74, and P75. Under majority rule, the Republicans and the President will join together to confirm nominees at 74 or 75.

Under supermajority rule, however, confirmation of a nominee will also require the approval of the Democrats. As there is only one Democratic vote, confirmation will require the unanimous support of both parties for the President's nominee. While there is no obvious way to predict the precise result of this arrangement, any agreement will involve a compromise between these three

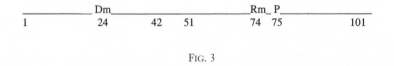

	Dm			Rm_ P		
1	24	42	51	74	75	101

FIG. 3

were large numbers of conservative Southern Democrats who had to some extent a separate political identity. See Robert Caro, *Master of the Senate* 89–97 (2003) (discussing the identity and power of the Southern caucus in the fifties and sixties). Thus, it is far from clear that there was an ideologically filibuster-proof majority even in those years.

[41] The argument in this paragraph of the text assumes single-dimensional voting. See Maxwell L. Stearns, *From Lujan to Laidlaw: A Preliminary Model of Environmental Standing*, 11 Duke Envtl L & Pol 312, 346 (2001) (explaining how majority rule leads to the adoption of the position of the median voter when the issue runs along a single dimension). It also assumes equal ideological space between Senators, although our conclusions hold under much weaker assumptions. Cf. notes 34–35 and accompanying text.

[42] Actually, the median Senator of the Democrats is either S23 or S24, but we assume for simplicity that it is S24.

players. Considering the various factors that are part of the utility function of the Senators, one would predict a result along the following lines.

Although the President and Senate Republicans would desire a nominee close to their ideal points, the Democrats would be unwilling to agree. The Democrats would want to hold out for a nominee closer to their ideal point since they would be happier to have the next President make the appointment. There would, however, be limits on the Democrats' behavior. They would regard vacancies as being undesirable. More importantly, if they insisted on a nominee closer to their ideal point than that of the President and the Senate Republicans, the Democrats would appear to be open to a charge of obstructionism. Taking these considerations into account, one would expect that an agreement could be reached only for a compromise nominee between 24 and 75. Thus, the nominee would be considerably closer to the center of the political spectrum than the nominee at 74 or 75 that would be produced by majority rule.

Although the result will represent a compromise between the President, the Senate Republicans, and the Senate Democrats, it is unlikely to be an amicable agreement. Instead, one might view the situation as resembling a bilateral monopoly,[43] where both the President and the Democratic Party will jockey strategically in order to strike the best deal.[44] While both the President and the Democratic Party would have a common interest in confirming someone, they disagree over how close the Justice should be to each of their ideal points.[45] As with any bilateral monopoly, one

---

[43] One can define a bilateral monopoly even in situations that are not strictly economic as "'a situation where two parties are forced to deal exclusively with one another and to reach agreement in order to derive any profit from the interaction.'" Richard D. Friedman, *Antitrust Analysis and Bilateral Monopoly*, 1986 Wis L Rev 873, 873 (quoting Druckman and Bonoma, *Determinants of Bargaining Behavior in a Bilateral Monopoly Situation II: Opponent's Concession Rate and Similarity*, 21 Behavioral Sci 252 (1976)).

[44] The Senate Republicans' preferences are so close to the President that we leave them out of our analysis of bilateral monopoly.

[45] Formally, there are aspects of a bilateral monopoly even under our model without parties in which a deal is struck under majority rule between S51 and P75 (or under supermajority rule between S42 and P75). For example, a deal with S51 under majority rule (or with S42 under supermajority rule) offers the clearest route to confirmation, to the extent that these Senators are decisive and exercise bargaining leverage. Yet the compromise that occurs in a world without parties differs from a true bilateral monopoly in certain respects. First, there are other Senators party to the negotiations, who would also have an incentive to induce a better deal. Thus, if under majority rule S51 sought to get a better deal, S101 might refuse to support a nominee and threaten to hold out for a more

would expect significant transaction costs, as each party negotiates and engages in threats in order to extract a better deal. For example, the Democratic party might withhold support from a nominee it would otherwise support in an effort to extract a less conservative nominee.

Significantly, the results for a Senate without political party influence and for a Senate with superstrong parties are consistent in two important respects. First, in both situations, one would expect that the nominees confirmed under the supermajority rule to be more moderate than under majority rule. Second, in both situations, it should be harder to reach an agreement under supermajority rule than under majority rule. Under the supermajority rule, there is a greater divergence between the preferences of the Senators and there are more parties to any coalition that is to be negotiated. These circumstances make an agreement more difficult, especially given the possibility of strategic behavior.

E. APPOINTMENTS WITH WEAKER POLITICAL PARTIES

Finally, we address the more realistic situation of appointments with weaker political parties.[46] Here we assume that Senators have some preference to act in conformity with their parties, but that this preference can be overridden if the Senator's other preferences cut strongly against what his party wants. This section continues the assumptions from the previous section about the ideal points of the President (75), the Senate Republicans (74), and the Senate Democrats (24).

Our analysis suggests, as one might expect, that the result for weaker parties falls between the results for no political parties and those for superstrong parties. Consider first the situation under majority rule. Under superstrong parties, we predicted a nominee

---

conservative nominee. Second, while P75 does have a veto, it is not clear that S51 has one. Once one departs from ideology and looks to other values (such as valuations of vacancy or desire to please the public) or perceptions (such as differing views as to how the President would respond to a rejection), it is possible that S50 might support the nominee, even though S51 would not. While S50 has ideological views that are farther from the nominee's ideology, other factors at work in this situation make him a viable candidate to be the decisive Senator approving the nominee. Thus, practically, S51 would have limited monopoly power.

[46] Whether or not political parties are undergoing a revival in power today, they are weaker in the United States than in many other democracies. See Terri Perreti, *The Virtues of "Value Clarity" in Constitutional Decisionmaking*, 55 Ohio St L J 1079, 1089 (1992). Politicians thus often vote independently of party.

between the President's view (P75) and the median Senate Republican's view (S74). With no parties, we predicted a nominee between the President's view (P75) and the median Senator's view (S51). Under weak parties, we predict a compromise between these two results.

To see this point, start with the assumption that the Senators follow their party positions. While this might suggest a nominee of 74 or 75, the most liberal Republicans, such as S47, would not necessarily be happy under this arrangement and might have an incentive to vote against the nominee. Of course, since the Republicans have a fifty-five-vote majority, they can lose four Senators and still prevail. Thus, the key Senator for them is S51—the same Senator the President needed to secure under majority rule without parties. While one would therefore expect that the result will be a compromise between P75 and S51, as under majority rule without parties, there is a difference here. S51 has some preference to follow the position of his party. Thus, he is less likely to depart from the President's nominee than he would be under majority rule without parties, and therefore the compromise between P75 and S51 will be closer to the P75 end than it would if there were no party influence.

A similar analysis applies to appointments under the supermajority rule. Under the supermajority rule without political parties, the compromise was between P75 and S42. Under the supermajority rule with superstrong parties, the compromise was between P75 and S24. Assume initially that the Democrats vote as a party. With weak parties, the question is on what terms the most conservative Democrats, S42–S46, would be willing to make a deal with the President and the members of his party. Those Democrats would, if they were not influenced by their party's position, choose to make a compromise between S42 and P75.[47] While their party loyalty would cause them to be willing to adopt a harder line with the Republicans than they otherwise would,

---

[47] As discussed in the section addressing appointments without political parties, the main incentive that conservative Democrats, such as S42, have to compromise with the President and the Republicans is the desire to avoid being accused of being obstructionists. S42 does not have a strong ideological incentive to compromise with the Republicans, since he would happier ideologically if the next President made the appointment. Another reason to compromise is if the conservative Democratic Senator comes from a centrist state, where the public expects him not to use ideology to obstruct government. Assuming that centrist Senators come from more competitive districts, this situation would lead them to take fuller account of voters' preferences.

they would only be willing to sacrifice their own preferences to those of their party to a limited extent. Consequently, one would expect the compromise under a supermajority rule with weak parties to be somewhere between S42 and P75, but to be considerably closer to S42's ideal point than under a supermajority rule with no party influence.[48]

While the results for majority and supermajority rules with weak parties fall between those for the other two models, all of the models share the same two predictions: that the nominees who are confirmed under supermajority rule are likely to be more centrist under majority rule, and that it is likely to be more difficult to reach an agreement under supermajority rule than under majority rule.[49]

F. THE FILIBUSTER AND THE EXPRESS SUPERMAJORITY RULE

While we have compared the effects of a supermajority rule with those of majority rule, it is also important to examine the effects of allowing filibusters. Under existing Senate rules, a majority of the Senate has the power to confirm a nominee, but Senators can attempt to prevent a vote on the nominee through a filibuster.[50] The filibuster will continue unless sixty Senators vote

---

[48] While we describe the result under weak parties as lying somewhere between 42 and 75, one might wonder whether it could turn out to be lower—between 24 and 42. In order to reach as far as that interval, S42's commitment to the Democratic Party's preference would have to be so strong that it would outweigh not merely his own preference but also the preferences of the President and of the Republicans (who collectively desire a nominee at 74). This result seems inconsistent with the assumption of our model that S42 only has a limited preference to vote with his party.

[49] While we focus on the situation when the President and the Senate majority are from the same party, supermajority rules will also result in judicial appointments that are more centrist when the President and the Senate majority are from different parties. For example, suppose that P75 faces a Senate that has fifty-five Democratic Senators (S1–55). Under majority rule without party voting, the result would be between 51 and 75. Under majority rule with weak party voting, the forces of party loyalty would move the result more toward 51. Assuming that the forces of party cohesion move the result two-thirds of the way toward 51, the result would be 59. Under supermajority rule, the result would be between 42 and 75, and the two-thirds assumption yields a result of 49. It is only when the President is more centrist and he faces a Senate from the other party that supermajority rules can result in less moderate nominees. If the President were more moderate than 60, then a supermajority rule might result in a less moderate result than majority rule. And even this result would not stand if the party effects are weaker than our two-thirds assumption. Finally, Presidents will rarely be so centrist. See notes 13–15 and accompanying text.

[50] See *Congressional Quarterly's Guide to Congress*, Standing Rules of the United States Senate, Rule XXII 68-A (4th ed 1991).

to end it by invoking cloture.[51] Thus, the filibuster rule resembles a supermajority rule because 60 percent of the Senate is needed to overcome it and secure a vote on the nominee.

Despite its similarity with an express supermajority rule, the filibuster rule will depart less from simple majority rule than will an express supermajority rule because Senators who choose to filibuster are more vulnerable to the charge of being obstructionists than those who vote against a nominee under the express supermajority rule. The filibuster is a discretionary device. Senators who have chosen to use it seem to have intentionally made the appointment more difficult, and therefore such Senators might seem obstructionist. Under an express supermajority rule, by contrast, Senators opposing a nomination appear to be simply voting their judgment rather than deciding to make it more difficult to fill a vacancy.[52] This disincentive to employ the filibuster is reinforced by the filibuster's historic use against civil rights legislation, which gives it a bad odor and further raises the costs of using it.[53] Moreover, the filibuster may be weak if the threat of its use can be countered by the threat of the nuclear option.[54] As we describe below, key Senators have agreed for now to sheathe this threat, but there remains the ever-present possibility that some will decide to unsheathe it. Thus, the application of an express supermajority rule to judicial confirmations, particularly one written in the Constitution itself, is likely to move judicial appointments more toward the preferences of the median Senator than the filibuster rule.

---

[51] Id.

[52] For instance, Senators are subject to less criticism for obstructionism when they block a treaty with majority support from being ratified, because the Constitution includes an express supermajority rule for ratification. See US Const, Art II, § 2, cl 2 (stating that the President shall have the power, by and with the consent of the Senate, to make treaties, provided that two-thirds of the Senate concur). Of course, other differences between treaties and appointments are relevant to the public reaction. While appointments to the Supreme Court are thought to be required for that Court to function properly, most treaties are not needed for the nation to operate, and therefore a decision to vote against them might not be seen as obstructionism. But there are exceptions. See Steven Charnovitz, *Using Framework Statutes to Facilitate U.S. Treatymaking*, 98 Am J Intl L 696, 704 (2004) (noting that Senators who opposed the Versailles treaty, which had majority support, are often accused of obstructionism).

[53] See Sarah A. Binder and Steven S. Smith, *Politics or Principle? Filibuster in the United States Senate* 11 (1997) (showing that the filibuster in the forty years before 1940 was used principally to bottle up civil rights legislation).

[54] See David S. Law and Lawrence B. Solum, *Judicial Selection, Appointments Gridlock and the Nuclear Option*, 15 J Contemp L Issues (forthcoming 2006).

III. The Filibuster Deal

This model of the appointment process can be used to shed light on several different important issues. In this section, we show that the model has important implications for the recent Filibuster Deal entered into by the "Gang of 14"—seven moderate Republican Senators and seven moderate Democratic Senators.[55] The deal was an effort to avoid the use of the nuclear or constitutional option by Republicans that would have modified the filibuster rule as applied to judicial nominations.[56] Under the deal, which extends until the end of the current Congress, the Senators agreed not to filibuster judicial nominees except under "extraordinary circumstances."[57]

The Filibuster Deal raises at least three significant questions. First, why did these Senators, especially the Republican ones, choose to enter into the deal? Based on the language of the agreement and statements in the press, the Senators claim that they acted out of a public spirited desire to place Senate traditions above partisan benefits. While we do not presume to know their motivations, we can state that the deal did not represent a sacrifice on the part of these Senators for some larger goal. Instead, these moderate Senators, including the Republicans, furthered their own ideological interests in making the deal.[58]

Our model has shown that centrist Senators do better under both an express supermajority rule and under a filibuster rule than under simple majority rule. Under the model with weak parties, majority rule would produce a nominee between 75 and 51, but

---

[55] See James Kuhnhenn, *Senate Back from Brink: Pact Allows Votes on 3 Judicial Picks, Preserves Filibuster*, The Record (May 24, 2005) at A-1 (listing the seven Republican and seven Democratic Senators party to the filibuster deal).

[56] See Sheryl Gay Stolberg, *The Elusive Middle Ground*, New York Times (May 29, 2005) at sec 4, p 1 (recounting how the filibuster deal averted the nuclear option).

[57] See Memorandum of Understanding on Judicial Nominations (May 23, 2004), found at http://www.freerepublic.com /focus/f-news/1409009/posts.

[58] Most of the Senators party to the Filibuster Deal are ideologically closer to the center of the Senate than the typical member of their party. For instance, all of the Republican members of the Gang of 14 have better 2004 ratings by the Americans for Democratic Action, a liberal group, than the average Republican Senator, and four of the Democratic Senators have worse ratings than the average Democratic Senator. See ADA Voting Records at http://www.adaction.org/votingrecords.htm. Another of the Democratic Senators, Ken Salazar of Colorado, has no ratings yet because he was just elected to Congress. But he ran as a moderate Democrat. See T. R. Reid, *Democrats May Use Colorado Results as Political Primer*, Wash Post (Nov 21, 2005) at A18 (discussing Salazar's victory as a moderate).

probably closer to 75, because of the party effect. Collectively, the Senate Republicans' ideal point is at 74, and they would exert substantial leverage on their moderates to vote for nominees closer to the party's ideal point. Let us assume that these forces produce a nominee at 67, which is two-thirds of the way toward 75 from 51. Under a supermajority rule with weak parties, the nominee would be someone between 75 and 42, but closer to 42, due again to the party effect. Collectively, the Senate Democrats' ideal point is at 24, and they would exert leverage on their moderates to vote against nominees who are farther from their ideal point. Let us assume that these forces produce a nominee at 53, which again is two-thirds of the way toward 42 from 75. Under these assumptions, then, the result under supermajority rule is 53 as compared to 67 under majority rule.

Centrist Senators of both parties would prefer this result. While it is no surprise that the Democrats do better under a supermajority rule, it might surprise some that the moderate Republicans also prefer it. The moderate Republicans' preference for the result under the filibuster rule occurs for several reasons. In part, it occurs because the political parties move the results under majority rule farther to the extremes. But it even occurs under the model without political party influence. There it is caused by the need to compromise with a President who is not in the center of the political spectrum.[59] Significantly, the benefits to both moderate Republican and Democratic Senators would continue if the President and Senate switched to Democratic control.

A second question that might be asked about the Filibuster Deal is how the Gang of 14 Senators are likely to interpret the term "extraordinary circumstances."[60] Commentators have noted that the force of the deal largely turns on whether, and to what extent, "extraordinary circumstances" includes the ideology that the nominee holds.[61] While the language of the agreement itself does not specifically answer the question, our model suggests that the parties to the deal would want to include consideration of judicial

---

[59] We discuss the reasons that Presidents tend not to occupy the political center, see notes 13–15 and accompanying text.

[60] See William Schneider, *How "Extraordinary,"* National Journal (June 4, 2005) (seeing the meaning given to extraordinary circumstances as key to understanding the import of the deal).

[61] Id.

ideology as part of the "extraordinary circumstances" that warrant filibuster, because they will want to narrow the range of ideological appointments.[62] The one countervailing consideration is that Senators from the President's party receive patronage and fund-raising help from the President that might be endangered by breaking with his nominee. It will be the tension between those interests and the Senators' judicial preferences that will determine whether they defect from the Filibuster Deal to embrace the nuclear option.[63]

A third question about the Filibuster Deal is whether it is likely to continue past the existing Congressional term. While specifically limited to this term, the deal might be extended explicitly or implicitly into the future. Indeed, the extension of the agreement would appear to be crucial. If not extended, it would be possible for the Democrats to secure control of the presidency and the Senate in 2008, and then, when the Republicans filibustered Democratic nominees, for the Democrats to invoke the nuclear option to end the Republican filibusters. In this scenario, the moderate Republicans who joined the Filibuster Deal would have made a bad deal for the Republicans that gave up much more than they received in return.

Our model suggests, however, that the Filibuster Deal is likely to continue through the next term. If the centrist Republicans and Democrats benefit from the Filibuster Deal now, then it is likely that they will continue to benefit from it in the future, because the same institutional concerns are likely to continue to hold. Thus, if the filibuster rule came into jeopardy, one could expect the centrists to enter into a new Filibuster Deal to preserve it.[64]

---

[62] In his public comments, one Senator has shown how to navigate the shoals of this problem. Lindsey Graham has said that "extraordinary circumstances" should not include consideration of judicial "ideology," but may include consideration of judicial "activism." See ABC's *This Week* (July 10, 2005). Of course, the difference between ideology and activism is not very clear, either under the realist assumptions of our model or the similar assumptions embraced by many Senators.

[63] If Presidents are less important to the reelection of members of their party than they once were, see Michael Fitts, *The Vices of Virtue: A Political Party Perspective on Civic Virtues Reform of the Legislative Process*, 136 U Pa L Rev 1527, 1629 (1988), Senators may be more immune to such pressures.

[64] One might wonder why the Republican Senators in the Gang of 14 were willing to depart from the preferences of their party to join the agreement, but were unwilling to ignore their own party's views when voting on nominations. After all, under the weak parties voting model, the centrist Senators do not fully consider their own ideological preferences, but modify their votes to take their party's preferences into account. There

IV. Supermajority Appointments, the Countermajoritarian Difficulty, and Democratic Judicial Review

While a supermajority confirmation rule, whether an express rule or the filibuster rule, furthers the interests of centrist Senators, it also has a more public interested function: A supermajority confirmation rule helps to remove a portion of the countermajoritarian difficulty that performs no useful function in our constitutional system. Thus, supermajority appointment rules promote a more democratic form of judicial review without sacrificing constitutional principle. As compared to a majority rule for the confirmation process, supermajority rule moves the Justices more toward the views of judicial review of the median Senator.[65] And the views of the median Senator are generally more representative of the views of the median voter in the electorate than those of the President. Consequently, a supermajority rule helps to promote the appointment of Justices who hold views on constitutional matters that accord with the median voter of the electorate and therefore with those of a majority of the public.[66]

---

are three reasons that explain their actions. First, the Filibuster Deal could be made more attractive to the Republican Party than could moderate Republican votes against a Republican President's nominee. The moderate Republicans were able to secure the confirmation of three circuit court judges who had been filibustered—Janice Rogers Brown, Patricia Owen, and William Pryor. See Ronald Brownstein and Janet Hook, *High Court Nomination May Prove a Deal-Breaker*, Wash Post (July 7, 2005) at A-20 (understanding confirmation of these judges as a consequence of the deal). Moreover, they also received a promise from the conservative Democrats not to filibuster except in extraordinary circumstances, although that promise was admittedly vague. Second, the Filibuster Deal as a whole also provided the signatories with a great deal of additional benefits. They could portray themselves, and were portrayed in the media, as public spirited Senators who had placed Senate traditions over their own narrow interest. See, e.g., *The Center Holds*, Wash Post (May 24, 2005) at A16. This would enhance their prominence and presumably their electability and influence. Finally, the Filibuster Deal also provided the Republican Senators with greater benefits. If the Republican Senators simply ignored their party's interests, then presumably the result would be a compromise between their ideal point and the President's. Under a filibuster rule, though, the results are closer to those they desire. The compromise is between the President and S42—a Democratic Senator—and the result is likely to be closer to the moderate Republican Senator's ideal point. Another option for the Republican Senators was to vote against the Nuclear Option and thereby to preserve the filibuster in that manner. But obviously the Republican Senators did better under the Filibuster Deal, since they secured far more for their party and did not have to vote against their party on an issue that would no doubt have provoked strong payback.

[65] See note 49 and accompanying text.

[66] Our argument that promoting the views of the median voter also promotes the views of the majority of voters assumes that voters evaluate judicial nominees based on a single dimension. Under the famous median-voter theorem, the preferences of the median voter will always be the preferences of the majority. While we recognize that voters may consider other matters, we believe that the ideology of the nominees is the principal matter on which voters focus. Moreover, we also believe that in many cases voters have largely

The countermajoritarian difficulty is the problem created by unelected Justices striking down the decisions of the democratic branches.[67] To understand how a supermajority rule reduces the least defensible component of the countermajoritarian difficulty, we first must describe more precisely the benefits of judicial review and the nature of the countermajoritarian difficulty. These matters are more often casually referenced than carefully analyzed.

We assume here a relatively realist view of judging under which Justices vote their preferences on constitutional questions rather than being constrained by a constitutional methodology.[68] On that assumption, judicial review nevertheless may have social benefits: While Justices vote on the basis of preferences, their institutional background and incentives provide them with different preferences than politicians. First, institutional constraint requires the Justices to write opinions and follow prior precedent, unless they justify departure.[69] The requirement of writing opinions provides Justices with a greater incentive than elected politicians both to be consistent and to follow the decisions of their predecessors. Second, Justices have internalized a norm in playing by the rules laid down: this craft norm serves as a constraint, however soft, on the kind of decisions they reach.[70] Finally, Justices do not have to stand for election and therefore need not conform their decisions to the views of what may be a temporary majority. For all these reasons, Justices' preferences are often, albeit not always, based on more principled, long-term considerations than elected politicians—considerations that may over the long run lead to greater stability and prosperity for the republic. For instance, whereas legislators might pass statutes that seek to suppress either overtly

---

identical preferences as to other values. For example, it is plausible to believe that they all prefer more qualified nominees to an equal extent. In that event, the median-voter theorem would continue to hold.

[67] See Barry Friedman, *The History of the Countermajoritarian Difficulty, Part One: The Road to Judicial Supremacy*, 73 NYU L Rev 333, 334 (1998) (describing the problem as "how to explain a branch of government whose members are unaccountable to the people, yet have the power to overturn popular decisions").

[68] We focus on Justices, not all judges, because lower court federal judges have a limited ability by themselves permanently to block the will of democratic branches. See notes 91–92 and accompanying text.

[69] See Ronald A. Cass, *Judging Norms and Incentives of Retrospective Decisionmaking*, 75 BU L Rev 941, 971 (1995).

[70] See Richard Posner, *What Judges Maximize (the Same Thing Everyone Else Does)*, 3 S Ct Econ Rev 1 (1995) (discussing importance of judges' interest in playing by rules as a guide to their behavior).

or subtly the speech rights of their partisan opponents, the Court is less likely to uphold such statutes.

Based on this view of judging, we can unpack three separate components of the countermajoritarian difficulty. The first component is created by the difference in the public's views as to how legislators and Justices should decide matters. Because people generally accept that Justices should decide based on longer-run and more principled considerations, whereas legislators should be more focused on policy trade-offs and shorter-run public sentiments, there is a space for a Court with a majority of the electorate's views of jurisprudence to strike down legislation with majoritarian support.[71]

The median Senator represents somewhat imperfectly the median voter of the electorate and thus the majority of the polity.[72] Accordingly, a Court with the views of constitutional law embraced by the median Senator might strike down legislation supported by that Senator.[73] That gap ultimately reflects the reality that the

---

[71] A similar assessment of the public's view of judicial review is suggested in Barry Friedman, *Mediated Popular Constitutionalism*, 101 Mich L Rev 2596, 2606 (2003). One may find evidence for this view in some of the conceptions of political scientists of "diffuse support" and "specific support." Id at 2626. Our interpretation of these data is that individual members of the public understand that the Justices will sometimes invalidate popular statutes, but their diffuse support will continue, unless the Justices make too many decisions with which they disagree. See also William Ford, *The Threshold Question: Public Thinking about the Constitution* (working paper on file with authors) (providing experimental evidence that the public has preferences about constitutional jurisprudence that are distinct from their policy preferences).

[72] The imperfections are of two kinds. First, by giving the same representation to small and large states alike, the Senate is malapportioned and may therefore not represent majority sentiment. That malapportionment effect is often exaggerated, however, because the Senate reflects majority will relatively well on issues where the preferences of voters in small states do not differ systematically from preferences of voters in large states. See John O. McGinnis and Michael B. Rappaport, *Our Supermajoritarian Constitution*, 80 Tex L Rev 703, 746–48 (2005). Moreover, political scientists have recently mapped the ideological composition of the Senate and the House and found their contours very similar. See Keith Poole, *Estimating a Basic Issue Space from a Set of Issue Scales*, http://voteview.com/basic.htm. Second, sometimes because of agency costs, the legislators do not represent their constituents' sentiments. For instance, it may be the case that federal legislators will consistently object to Justices who want to constrain federal powers, although that position would be far more popular with the majority of their constituents.

[73] The public view of the judicial function will take into account both substantive views—such as how strong should be the content of civil rights—and methodological views—such as how strong should be the respect for precedent. Thus, the median voter (and Senator for that matter) may face trade-offs in reaching the ideal Justice. In evaluating a prospective Justice, the median actor may be willing to give up some proximity to his view of the ideal content of constitutional provisions for proximity to his view of the appropriate methodology, including adherence to precedent.

public wants their Justices to behave differently from their legislators.[74]

This component of the countermajoritarian difficulty is inherent in any concept of judicial review. Constitutions represent popularly imposed restraints on democracy. The polity wants Peter Sober to check Peter Drunk.[75] Thus, Senators will want to confirm a Supreme Court that would on occasion invalidate laws that the Senators themselves would pass.

The second component of the countermajoritarian difficulty is the temporal component created by the necessarily shifting nature of viewpoints over time. Justices currently on the Court may not reflect the jurisprudential views of the current Senate (which is the proxy for the current majority of the electorate) for three different reasons. First, the views of the median Senator when a Justice was confirmed may differ from the views of the current median Senator. Second, Justices during their tenure may fundamentally change their views and may not even reflect those of the previous Senate, let alone the current Senate.[76] Third, the issues coming before the Court may have changed since the Justice was confirmed.[77] Thus, the Justice's views on the new issue mix before the Court may never have received any serious democratic vetting even by a previous Senate.

This aspect of the countermajoritarian difficulty is inherent in giving Justices on the Court tenure of any substantial length, let alone the life tenure contemplated by the Constitution. Conferring terms of significant length appears to be necessary to the longer-

---

[74] By confirming such Justices the public is engaging in a precommitment strategy familiar to students of constitutional law. See Jon Elster, *Ulysses Unbound: Studies in Rationality, Precommitment and Constraints* 1–87 (1989). For instance, the public may generally adhere to a set of principles about the protection of civil rights, but recognize that at times of passion its legislative agents may reflect its current passions rather than its enduring commitments. Therefore, the public would like the judiciary to be the agent of its longer-term principles and police the agents of its more turbulent and short-term desires.

[75] The source of this colorful phrase is Justice David Brewer. David J. Brewer, *An Independent Judiciary as the Salvation of the Nation*, in Proceedings of the New York Bar Association (1893), reprinted in 11 Annals of America 423, 428 (1968).

[76] The most famous recent example is Harry Blackmun. See Linda Greenhouse, *Becoming Harry Blackmun* (2005). But other Justices have moved left as well. See Andrew Martin, Kevin Quinn, and Lee Epstein, *The Median Justice of the Supreme Court*, 83 NC L Rev 1275 (2005) (arguing that the Court has moved left as Justice O'Connor has moved left).

[77] For instance, Justices were appointed and confirmed in the New Deal largely on the basis of their views about federal regulatory power. They then divided on issues of civil liberties that were not central concerns in their appointment.

run decision making we associate with judicial decision making. However, that judicial terms need to be long does not necessarily imply that they should be for life. Recently, a debate has broken out over whether life tenure for Supreme Court Justices is wise.[78] The most important aspect of this debate, in our view, should be whether life tenure unduly exacerbates this component of the countermajoritarian difficulty. In any event, the only way to address this particular component is to shorten Justices' terms.

This component of the countermajoritarian difficulty may also be exacerbated by the uneven intervals at which Supreme Court Justices are appointed. Because one President may have the opportunity to appoint a disproportionate number of Justices, these Justices may give undue weight to the views of the President and the Senate at a particular moment in history. Staggered terms where Presidents have the opportunity to appoint a fixed number of Justices during their presidencies would thus help address the temporal component of the countermajoritarian difficulty.[79]

But there is a third aspect of the countermajoritarian difficulty that is not inherent in the concept of judicial review or substantial judicial tenure. When Supreme Court Justices can be confirmed by majority vote, a Justice may not even reflect the median Senator's view of judicial review at the time of his confirmation, but instead may have more extreme views. This gap can occur because, as discussed above, Presidents are likely to nominate and secure the confirmation of Justices with more extreme views than the median Senator.

Unlike the other two components of the countermajoritarian difficulty, which are necessary to our practice of judicial review, this component is unambiguously undesirable. It does no useful work. Significantly, a confirmation supermajority rule, including the filibuster rule, helps to address one component of countermajoritarian difficulty by moving Justices toward the views of the median Senator (and of the median voter of the electorate). In this way, the supermajority confirmation rule can preserve the benefits of judicial review, while reducing some of its costs.

It might be objected that we mischaracterize the counterma-

---

[78] See Steven Calabresi and James Lindgren, *The Problem of Prolonged Tenure in Supreme Court Justices*, in Roger C. Crampton and Paul D. Carrington, eds, *Term Limits for Supreme Court Justices* (2006).

[79] See id.

joritarian difficulty by focusing on the median voter of the electorate, because federal legislation itself does not precisely reflect the median voter but is a product of a tricameral process encompassing the House, Senate, and President.[80] The legislative process no less than the confirmation process moves the ideological "center of gravity" of legislation toward the President and away from the median Senator.[81] Under this view, judicial review is only countermajoritarian to the extent that it departs from the results of the legislative process, even if that process does not reflect the views of the median voter. But even if we accept this view and understand the countermajoritarian difficulty as the gap between the ideological centers of gravity of the tricameral process and the confirmation process,[82] a supermajoritarian confirmation rule reduces that gap.

First, the federal legislative process includes the filibuster rule for most legislation, particularly the kind of legislation that is subject to judicial review.[83] The filibuster rule in this context permits the minority party to exercise the same kind of moderating influence on legislation that it does on the appointment process. Thus, a filibuster rule in the appointments process would help close any gap between the likely ideological centers of gravity of legislation and of the confirmation process.

Second, even apart from the filibuster rule's effect, the legislative process is likely to reach more moderate results than the confir-

---

[80] See McGinnis and Rappaport, 80 Tex L Rev at 769–74 (cited in note 72) (discussing the tricameral structure).

[81] See Keith Krehbiel, *Pivotal Politics* 118 (1998) (everyone agrees that the President's veto power enhances his power in legislation).

[82] It is by no means clear that one should, in discussing the countermajoritarian difficulty, compare the results of judicial review with the results of the actual legislative process rather than with the results that the median voter would enact. The correct comparison depends on the reasons why the legislature departs from the median voter's views. If the legislature departs for undesirable reasons (such as agency costs), then exercising judicial review based on the actual views of the public may still be desirable, because one would not want agency costs to infect the appointment process as well as the legislative process. Even if the legislature departs for desirable reasons (such as allowing for the expertise that committees provide), it is not clear that this departure should be followed in the appointment process, unless those same reasons apply equally in that process.

[83] The filibuster rule does not apply to budgetary legislation or trade fast track legislation, see Donald Tobin, *Less Is More: A Move Toward Sanity in the Budget Process*, 16 SLU Pub L Rev 115, 120 (1996) (filibuster rule removed from budget reconciliation process); Philip H. Potter, *Comments on the Fast Track Process for Review of NAFTA*, 1 US-Mex L J 343 (1993) (filibuster rule removed from trade agreement process), but trade and spending bills do not bulk large in the kind of legislation that raises constitutional issues.

mation process under majority rule. In the appointment process, the President has essentially an absolute agenda-setting power,[84] which he will use, because of his likely ideal point, to nominate more extreme candidates than the median Senator would prefer. By contrast, in the legislative process, both Congress and the President have influence over the agenda, and therefore the legislative agenda is likely to be less extreme. A supermajoritarian confirmation rule would tend to counteract this difference between the appointments and the legislative process.[85]

A related advantage of a supermajority confirmation rule is that Justices confirmed in the shadow of the rule will enjoy greater legitimacy, because they will necessarily have bipartisan support. Because of this bipartisan support, partisans on both sides will be less invested in sniping at their decisions. Moreover, more moderate constitutional decision making in line with the views of the median Senator and the median voter—and therefore supported by a majority of the people—will also enable the Court to maintain greater public support. Now, it may be argued that greater public support for the Court is not an unmitigated good, because the Court may take advantage of it to engage in "activist" decisions. But if one has a realist view of "activism" as a decision not supported by the majoritarian view of judicial review, such activism is less likely under a supermajoritarian confirmation rule.

While a supermajoritarian confirmation rule for Justices helps reduce the extent of the countermajoritarian difficulty, it also has some costs. A supermajoritarian confirmation rule will raise transaction costs, because more time will be necessary to put together the coalition necessary for the Justice to be confirmed.[86] The

---

[84] See James Salzman, *Labor, Rights Globalization and Institution: The Role of Influence of the Organization for Economic Cooperation and Development*, 21 Mich J Intl L 769, 783 (2000) (President is absolute agenda setter with respect to Supreme Court nominees).

[85] It does not follow from our analysis that the legislative process and the confirmation process should necessarily have the parallel structures to assure the same ideological center of gravity. Providing the President with the authority to nominate provides a kind of accountability that has particular value in the appointment of lifetime members of the judiciary. This was the argument that the Framers made for lodging the nomination power solely in the President. See, e.g., Federalist (Alexander Hamilton) in Clinton Rossiter, ed, *The Federalist Papers* 461 ("The blame of a bad nomination would fall upon the President singly and absolutely."). That accountability can be preserved, however, even if the voting rule for confirmation is supermajoritarian.

[86] For discussion of how supermajority rules lead to more transaction costs, see James M. Buchanan and Gordon Tullock, *The Calculus of Consent* 68–70 (1962) (discussing how more inclusive voting rules raise decision-making costs); McGinnis and Rappaport, 80 Tex L Rev at 703, 745 n 175 (cited in note 72).

higher transaction costs are the result primarily of two effects. First, under a supermajority rule, including the filibuster, the coalition will need to encompass sixty Senators rather than fifty-one. Second, the larger coalition will encompass greater ideological diversity, leading to more wrangling.[87]

The transaction costs of a supermajoritarian confirmation rule are not limited to additional negotiations among politicians, but may also lead to longer vacancies, which may impair the Supreme Court's efficiency. Moreover, in rare cases, the higher transaction costs may even cause vacancies to carry over into an election season.[88] That kind of prolonged vacancy may inject the confirmation of a particular nominee into a political campaign, creating the danger of undue politicization of the judiciary.

One caveat about the advantages of the judicial filibuster rule involves transition costs. The filibuster rule would work much better and the transaction costs would be lower if both parties have agreed to its use. The Democrats, however, appear to have deployed the judicial filibuster in a relatively unprecedented manner.[89] As a result, President Bush and his supporters do not appear to recognize its legitimacy, causing them to resist the device. This resistance can lead to bitter fights and longer vacancies rather than to agreement on more moderate nominees. These fights could be minimized, however, if both parties accepted the legitimacy of the judicial filibuster and agreed to applying it to confirm Supreme Court Justices.[90] One way to reach such an agreement would be

---

[87] For a discussion of how ideological diversity will lead to greater transaction costs, see notes 37–38 and accompanying text.

[88] We think these will be relatively rare cases, because the President will have incentives to make sure that his Supreme Court nominees are confirmed before the end of his current term.

[89] It is true that Republicans and Southern Democrats together successfully filibustered the nomination of Abe Fortas in 1968. See Laura Kelman, *Law and Character: Does Character Affect Judicial Performance?* 71 U Colo L Rev 1385, 1395 (2000). But this was not a partisan filibuster and concerned ethical issues of the kind that eventually forced Fortas to resign from the bench. Id. The routine use of partisan filibusters to deny votes on judicial nominees is a new phenomenon, although one fully within the rules of the Senate, which make no distinction between nominations and legislation. See Standing Rules of the United States Senate, Rule XXII 68-A, *Congressional Quarterly's Guide to Congress* (cited in note 50). We have previously written that the filibuster rule is constitutional, although the majority must be able to change it. See John O. McGinnis and Michael B. Rappaport, *The Constitutionality of Legislative Supermajority Rules: A Defense*, 105 Yale L J 483, 498 (2005).

[90] The Filibuster Deal provides some legitimacy, but much less than would the agreement of the full Senate, particularly because the deal tracks the peculiar political interests of so many of its signatories.

for the Senate to adopt the judicial filibuster rule prospectively, applying it only to the Supreme Court nominations of future Presidents, who might turn out to be either Republicans or Democrats.

A final caveat is that the normative case for a filibuster rule at the lower court level is much weaker than at the Supreme Court level. Inferior federal courts by themselves cannot entrench new constitutional norms against the democratic process, and thus the countermajoritarian difficulty in this context is far less acute. Furthermore, by tradition, home-state Senators substantially influence appointments to the district courts and, even to some extent, to the appellate courts, weakening the influence of an ideologically extreme President.[91] Finally, the diversity afforded by some outlier appointments to the lower courts, particularly brilliant outliers, may benefit the nation's jurisprudence by providing innovative thinking and bracing critiques that a more moderate Supreme Court could then either accept or reject.[92]

V. Imperfect Information: Stealth and Uncertain Nominees

A. THE BENEFITS AND DRAWBACKS FOR THE PRESIDENT OF STEALTH AND UNCERTAIN NOMINEES

In our previous discussion, we have assumed that the President and the Senate have perfect information about the ideological position of the nominee. While this assumption is simplifying and useful, relaxing it allows us to explain additional aspects of the confirmation process. In particular, Presidents may nominate individuals for whom there is less information about their judicial views as a means of securing their confirmation. In this section,

---

[91] See Tracey E. George, *Judicial Independence and Ambiguity of Article III Protections*, 64 Ohio L J 221, 234 (2004) (discussing Senators' influence on lower court appointments).

[92] While this article addresses some of the effects of the filibuster rule, we make no attempt to address all the effects. The supermajority rule, for instance, will also have the beneficial effect of raising the quality of nominees in terms of credentials, ability, and other factors which are generally thought to be characteristic of an excellent Justice. Because Senators of both parties find it harder to oppose high-quality nominees, the President may often be able to increase the chances of confirming a Justice by selecting a high-quality nominee. As a supermajority rule forces the President to compromise with Senators of more distant ideal points, the value of high-quality nominees in gaining a favorable compromise becomes more substantial. As the nomination of Harriet Miers illustrated, selecting a nominee without excellent credentials has a significant chance of failure when a filibuster is possible. Under majority rule, by contrast, the President will more often be able to select nominees who have less than excellent credentials and still have them confirmed, because he will not need a nominee of high quality to gain the support of Senators who are closer to his ideal point.

we show that the President may nominate such individuals, but that this strategy is unlikely to change the overall effect of a supermajority confirmation rule.

We can distinguish between two different ways in which the President might nominate someone about whom there is imperfect information: stealth nominations and uncertain nominations. Under a stealth nomination, the President selects someone about whom he has good information, but about whom the Senate lacks information. This asymmetry of information is a significant advantage to the President. The ideal nominee for a President at P75 would be a nominee who actually has views at 75, but who appears to the Senate to be more moderate.[93] In this way, the President could choose a nominee that he desires while getting Senate moderates to confirm him. A less ideal and more realistic stealth nomination would involve a nominee who the President believes is at 75, but about whom the Senate does not know where between 50 and 80 he stands.

While a stealth nomination would be advantageous to the President, there are reasons to doubt that the Senate could be fooled in this way. First, the Senate can access publicly available information as easily as can the President. Second, if the President does have private information, much of it is likely to be revealed to the Senate as a whole. The President will need to release some of this information to persuade his own coalition, especially the conservatives, that the nominee is sufficiently conservative. Moreover, the Senate can and does ask nominees what questions they were asked by the executive branch in the period leading up to the nomination.[94] It seems quite unlikely that there would be revealing information about the nominee that the executive branch could keep secret.[95]

---

[93] How moderate is ideal depends on such matters as the confirmation voting rule and the strength of party voting. Under a filibuster rule, if the parties are superstrong with Democrats possessing an ideal point of 25, it may be ideal to give the nominee a moderate appearance of 51. But if there is not strong party voting, the President needs only to nominate a candidate within the moderates' ideological range, say a 61. Nominating a candidate who appears to be a moderate conservative rather than simply a moderate helps him keep members of his own party happy.

[94] See Senate Judiciary Questionnaire for John G. Roberts, found at http://www.nytimes.com/packages/pdf/politics/20050802Roberts.pdf (asking Judge Roberts about contacts with White House). This kind of question attempts to eliminate any asymmetrical information advantage for the President.

[95] Senators will be suspicious that the President has inside information. The President will thus have an incentive to find a candidate about whom he has inside information, because Senators will assume that the President selected a candidate on the basis of such

While a stealth nomination is unlikely to deceive the Senate, it may still increase the chance of Senate confirmation by its effect on the public. The differential effect on the Senate and the public turns on the difference between hard and soft information. By soft information we mean information that relates to the candidate's predispositions, such as information about his friendships and connections gleaned from government service. In contrast, hard information is specific information about positions on particular issues. The President may have much "soft" information that the nominee is near his ideological point.

It will be difficult to hide soft information from the Senators for the reasons we have discussed above. But the soft information is more useful to the President than to Senators, because he can sift through all the soft information in making his nomination. By contrast, it is difficult for Senators to use soft information to justify opposing a nominee and particularly difficult to use it to justify a filibuster. A public less schooled in confirmation matters will regard soft information as far less probative and tend to dismiss as unfair attempts to claim that such information can disqualify a nominee. This discrepancy between what the President knows and the Senators can effectively use allows the President to nominate someone who is closer to his ideal point. But in terms of usable information available to the Senate, the candidate appears more moderate.

Another reason stealth nominations may secure confirmation is that they make it less likely that moderate Senators will be held responsible for mistakes. If the appointment deviates from a Senator's expectations, with S55 supporting the appointment of a nominee at 90, a stealth nominee provides the Senator with some cover.[96] S55 could explain to his constituents that he had not expected the nominee to be so conservative.[97]

---

information, even if he did not do so. This problem is analogous to the market for lemons. Because the seller has an asymmetric information advantage over the buyer, the buyer will assume that he is making use of this advantage, unless he can find a way to precommit not to make use of it. See generally George Alerkof, *"The Market for Lemons": Quality Uncertainty and the Market Mechanism*, 84 Q J Econ 48 (1970).

[96] One might say that stealth nominees blunt presidential accountability as well, if the nominee turns out to be far from the President's (and his party's) preferred ideological point. But the President is more identified with the nominee because of his act of nomination than Senators are by virtue of their confirmation vote. And more than any other politician, the President has a historical legacy to protect. See Elena Kagan, *Presidential Administration*, 114 Harv L Rev 2245, 2335 (2001).

[97] A nominee about whom there is only soft information is also likely to reveal his views only over time, further reducing potential recriminations from a wrongly cast vote. Having

While a stealth nomination involves a nominee about whom the President, initially at least, has more information, an uncertain nomination involves a nominee about whom both the President and the Senate lack good information. Uncertain nominations are less desirable for the President. The President, of course, would prefer to know the exact content of his nominee's ideology. Uncertainty might lead him to nominate an individual far away from his ideal point. If instead of nominating someone at 75, the President nominates someone who is equally likely to be anywhere between 55 and 95, this creates a significant risk that the nominee will not share the President's views.[98]

The disadvantages to the President of an uncertain nominee may even be greater than this example suggests. There are reasons to wonder whether an uncertain nominee, whose views seem to lie anywhere between 55 and 95, is actually more likely to have views toward the moderate range. To be an uncertain nominee, an individual must have generated little hard information in the course of a long and relatively distinguished career. There are good reasons to believe that such persons would, on average, skew toward the moderate side. Persons who hold more extreme views are likely to seek to express them or to associate with others who share them. If an individual does not express any views or establish associations regarding them, they are more likely either not to hold specific views or to share the views of the overall society. Further, it seems likely that the distribution of views in the populace and among lawyers skews toward the moderates.[99] Thus, even restricting oneself to Republicans from whom P75 would choose a nominee, there are

---

kept his views secret and refusing to reveal them, he has an incentive to continue his unknown positions for a time. Thus, he is likely to write narrow opinions at least at first. A more radical, broader opinion would suggest that the Justice had hoodwinked the Senate through the judicial appointment process. For instance, some criticized Justice Clarence Thomas, because opinions they deemed very radical seemed out of keeping with his moderate and anodyne comments at his confirmation hearing. See, e.g., *Youngest, Cruelest Justice*, New York Times (Feb 24, 1992) at A24 (criticizing his dissent in *Hudson v MacMillan*, 501 US 1, 28 (1992) in part because of its alleged departure from the tenor of his confirmation hearing testimony).

[98] One would assume that the President, like most individuals, is risk averse. That means he prefers the certainty of a single outcome to the uncertainty of a range of outcomes, even if the expected value of the average of the range is as high as the single outcome. Robert A. Josephs et al, *Protecting the Self from the Negative Consequences of Risky Decisions*, 62 J Personality & Soc Psychol 26, 26 (1992) (defining risk aversion).

[99] Technically, the claim is that political views have a normal or bell-shaped distribution, with more people bunching at moderate views and fewer at either extremes.

likely to be more moderate candidates in the pool than extreme candidates.

Despite these disadvantages of uncertain nominees, the President might be willing in some cases to choose such a nominee if it would increase confirmability. Would the Senate be more likely to confirm an uncertain nominee than a certain one? Uncertainty about a nominee by itself does not appear to be an advantage. It is not obvious that the Senators, considering their own preferences, would prefer a nominee somewhere between 55 and 95 to one at 75. Like the President, they too prefer certain information. But other reasons might support confirmation. The same two reasons that made it more likely that a stealth nominee would be confirmed—that the Senate will not have hard information supporting a filibuster and that the absence of hard information will lessen the Senator's accountability—also support confirmability of an uncertain nominee. Moreover, moderate Senators may be more likely to support an uncertain nominee if they believe, as discussed above, that such nominees are more likely to have moderate than extreme views.[100]

Overall, then, the appointment of an uncertain nominee is less attractive to the President than a stealth nominee. With a stealth nominee, the President will have good information about the nominee, whereas the President will have poorer information about an uncertain nominee. Thus, the risks are greater to him from an uncertain nominee. It is possible, however, that an uncertain nominee will be more likely to be confirmed. An uncertain nomination not only denies information to the Senate that can be used to justify a filibuster, but also gives them some reason to believe that the nominee will be more moderate than might otherwise be expected. Of course, though, this increased confirmability comes at the expense of the President's expectation that the nominee will be conservative.

While the President might like to employ stealth nominees about whose ideological point he is certain, he will probably not be able

---

[100] Senator Schumer seemed to have this effect in mind in planning his strategic response to President Bush's selection of a replacement for Justice O'Connor. In a cell-phone conversation that was overhead, Schumer noted "how hard it was to predict how a Supreme Court justice would turn out: Even William Rehnquist is more moderate than they expected. The only ones that resulted how they predicted were Scalia and Ginsburg. So most of the time they've gotten their picks wrong, and that's what we want to do to them again." See http://www.confirmthem.com/?p=804 (July 6, 2005) (reporting the overhead conversation).

to accomplish this goal because hard information about the nominee is likely to be known to the Senate. Although the President may be able to rely on soft information in making his selection, soft information is less reliable than hard information. Thus, in the real world, it is likely that any plausible stealth nominee will also have an element of uncertainty about him, creating an additional cost for the President.[101]

B. FILIBUSTERS AND STEALTH NOMINEES

We thus conclude that in a world of imperfect information, the President will sometimes attempt to use stealth nominees, but that strategy will often require him to appoint more uncertain nominees than he would like. Under a supermajority confirmation rule, the President will have greater incentives to undertake a stealth strategy than under majority rule. Because a supermajority rule will make it more difficult for the President to secure confirmation of nominees at his ideal point, one would expect that the President will be more inclined to use stealth and uncertain nominees under supermajority rules as a means of increasing the chances of securing confirmation. Indeed, stealth and uncertain nominations would be especially useful in limiting the use of Senate filibusters, since they deprive opponents of the nomination of hard information suggesting that the nominee has extreme views.

One might fear that the "stealth and uncertainty" strategy would temper one of the main benefits of the filibuster rule—moving nominees toward the center—because that strategy would allow

---

[101] The strategy of nominating a stealth candidate about whom the President has substantial soft information that he is near his ideological point is not merely hypothetical. It may well be the strategy George W. Bush employed when he nominated Judge John Roberts to fill the position of Chief Justice. Judge Roberts had worked for conservative Republican administrations and had been associated as clerk and subordinate to leading conservative legal figures, like William Rehnquist and Kenneth Starr. (For details of Roberts's biography, see http://www.usdoj.gov/olp/robertsbio.htm.) But, unlike previous nominee Robert Bork, he had not written controversial academic articles. Moreover, his limited time on the bench meant that he had a judicial record too insubstantial to attack.

Yet, precisely because of the lack of hard information, the appointment carries more risk to the President that Roberts will diverge from his ideal ideological point. David Souter is sometimes understood as a stealth candidate of the first President Bush. See John Copeland Nagle, *Choosing the Judges who Choose the President*, 30 Cap U L Rev 499, 514 (2002). But he did not work out well for the President. One difference between Roberts and Souter is that Roberts worked at the highest level in Washington legal circles, generating better soft information about how he would behave in the Washington limelight than could be gleaned about a candidate who spent his entire career in a small state like New Hampshire.

the President to confirm Justices closer to his ideal point. But even if this strategy would reduce the moderating effect of the filibuster rule, it would certainly not eliminate that effect. Moreover, as discussed above, it seems likely that nominees about whom there is uncertainty would be less extreme in the first place.

One might also wonder whether this kind of strategy would temper the reduction of the countermajoritarian difficulty—another normative virtue we claim for the filibuster rule. One consequence of the President's adoption of a strategy of stealth and uncertainty is that it reduces the kind of hard information of which citizens can most easily make use. It thus creates more difficulties for the public in assuring that the Justice being confirmed reflects its ideology.

We believe that this strategy may weaken the normative attractions of the filibuster, but only to a small degree. First, the filibuster will still, as discussed above, move the nominee toward the center and thus closer to the median Senator's, and presumably the median voter's, view of judicial review. While the filibuster reduces the extent of the countermajoritarian difficulty, it largely does so indirectly by moving the nominee toward the median Senator rather than directly by engaging the views of the voters.

Second, the provision of abundant hard information may, paradoxically, result in less desirable Justices. As described above, judicial review under our realist conception involves Justices making longer-term decisions that are more consistent across issues and more continuous with the past. Justices should therefore be selected based on how well they will perform this function. Too much hard information, however, may actually result in the selection of worse Justices. In a world where there is limited public attention, and certain political issues have extreme salience, hard information about how a Justice will decide an issue may cause that Justice to be selected based on that issue rather than on their overall ability to perform the judicial function.[102]

Finally, it should be noted that the greater uncertainty about

---

[102] Our claim in the text is a limited one. We are not arguing that the public will have the best kind of information for judging a nominee under a supermajority rule that leads to stealth and uncertain nominations. What is the best amount and mix of information about a nominee is a difficult question. Our point is that it should not be assumed that more hard information is always better than less. In a politicized environment, with limited public attention, less hard information may result in better Justices, and therefore what might seem a disadvantage of supermajority rules may not be one.

the precise ideological points of the Supreme Court Justices may maintain the mystery and to some people the legitimacy of the Court. If one had perfect information about the Justices' positions before they took the bench and could anticipate their rulings, the excitement of argument and decision would dissipate and the sense of the Court as a living institution would drain away. No one would have invested the Delphic oracle with majesty if everyone could predict its predictions. The mystique of an institution that lives by rulings depends to some degree on the uncertainty of what those rulings will be. As Walter Bagehot, the famous chronicler of the British Constitution, said about another nontransparent institution, "we must not let daylight in upon the magic."[103] To be clear, we are not here endorsing the virtues of magic over transparency, but we do believe that this characteristic of the Court is preserved by some uncertainty about Justices' particular views during the confirmation process.

VI. Implications of the Model for Confirmation Politics

In this section, we look at some of the implications of our model for the confirmation process. There are some misconceptions and perplexities that our model helps dispel. First, it might be thought that a minority party opposing the President will make its decisions about whether to filibuster on the basis only of the ideology of the nominee. But in reality the party will consider the effects of its filibuster on future vacancies as well. Thus, the minority party will sometimes make strategic decisions to filibuster or not to filibuster.[104] Second, it might be thought that the filibuster rule will have similar effects on the confirmation of both Supreme Court Justices and lower court judges. In fact, the rule will tend to be more effective in moderating the views of lower court judges, because obstructionism is a more potent and visible charge in a Supreme Court appointment fight. Finally, the filibuster rule makes the timing of vacancies even more important, limiting the President's ability to confirm nominees close to his ideological preferences late in his term.

---

[103] See Walter Baghot, *The English Constitution* 53 (speaking of the British monarchy) (1867).

[104] Even without strategic filibustering, our model suggests that Senators will take account of the ideology of nominees that the President will nominate in the event that the Senate blocks his earlier nominee to that vacancy. See note 25 and accompanying text.

A. STRATEGIC FILIBUSTERING

It might seem from our previous discussion that the Senators and their parties will make decisions about whether to vote for or against a nominee only on the basis of factors that bear on the desirability of a nominee filling a particular vacancy, such as his ideology and the concern about the continuing vacancy his appointment fills. But politics always has a future as well as a present. Depending on circumstances which we can categorize, Senators will make strategic decisions on a nominee in light of that future, leading them on occasion to filibuster a nominee who is ideologically acceptable considered on his own terms and not to filibuster a nominee who might be ideologically unacceptable considered alone.

A strategic decision to filibuster an ideologically acceptable nominee can occur for two reasons. First, as described above, the President and the minority party in the Senate are locked in a bilateral monopoly. Neither can get a nominee confirmed without the other's acquiescence. While a compromise can be struck between their ideal ideological points, no equilibrium dictates what that compromise will be. Thus, it is in the interest of each to gain a reputation as a tough bargainer.[105] The Senate minority can bolster that reputation through filibustering a nominee who would otherwise be acceptable. The more vacancies that are in prospect, the greater the value of a reputation for toughness. Thus, one explanation of the Senate Democrats' decision to filibuster lower court nominees early in President Bush's term was their recognition of the high probability that one or more of the aging Justices would soon resign.[106]

Second, the President has incomplete information about the minority party's preferences.[107] He may be uncertain of how ideo-

---

[105] See Edward B. Rock and Michael L. Wachtler, *Labor Law Successorship: A Corporate Law Approach*, 92 Mich L Rev 103, 243 (1992) (discussing need for tough reputation in context of bilateral monopolies).

[106] The Senate Democratic caucus may have also wanted to filibuster nominees who they thought might prove particularly attractive Supreme Court nominees, such as Miguel Estrada. Another advantage was that Senate Democrats practiced the political mechanics of the judicial filibuster. Still, a third and perhaps most important advantage was that filibusters of lower court judges began to acclimatize the public to filibusters, making them appear less shocking to the nation and thus easier to conduct against Supreme Court nominations.

[107] Thus, there are two kinds of problems of imperfect information in the confirmation process. One is imperfect information about the nominee's ideological point, see notes

logically extreme a nominee the minority party would confirm. In economic terms, he is uncertain about the minority party's "reservation price."[108] It may be in the minority party's interest to filibuster an acceptable nominee to mislead the President about its reservation price in the hopes of getting a nominee even closer to its preferences.[109]

The uncertainty about the reservation price also helps explain the practice of consultation and in particular the lengths to which President Bush has gone to seek consultation in the shadow of the filibuster.[110] While the President has no constitutional obligation to seek advice from the Senate prior to the nomination,[111] it is in his interest to try to determine the reservation price of key Senators and, particularly under the filibuster rule, of its minority party. A consultation process is one way to do that. Of course, Senators have an interest in disguising their reservation price by suggesting nominees that may be close to their ideal point and thus be nonstarters for the President. Accordingly, the consultation process is itself strategic with a high ratio of blustering and posturing to genuine advice.

We do not believe that strategic filibustering is likely to play a substantial role, because the minority party will be restrained in strategic filibustering by its most moderate members. For moderates, filibustering a nominee who is acceptable even to the median member of their party, let alone their own more moderate preferences, will not be very palatable. Nevertheless, the prospect of strategic filibustering imposes a cost on moderates, because they must pay a price to buck their party. We believe, however, that this cost would be quite modest in comparison to the gains in

---

93–101 and accompanying text. The other, which we discuss in this section, is imperfect information about the preferences of other political actors.

[108] Cf. Martin Shapiro, *Administrative Discretion: The Next Stage*, 92 Yale L J 1487, 1514 (1983) (talking about the manner in which administrative agencies may demand more than their reserve price in negotiations).

[109] There is similar testing that takes place in legislation. When Congress does not know the exact preferences of the President in legislation, the President may veto legislation for strategic reasons. See Charles M. Cameron, *Veto Bargaining, Presidents and the Politics of Negative Power* 110–14 (2000) (discussing strategic vetoes).

[110] See John M. Broder, *Have a Seat, Your Honor (Presidents Wish It Were That Easy)*, New York Times (July 10, 2005) at sec 4, p 3 (discussing extensive consultations of President Bush).

[111] See John O. McGinnis, *The President, the Senate and the Confirmation Process: A Reply to Professors Sunstein and Strauss*, 71 Tex L Rev 633 (1993).

moving nominees toward their preferences and thus, on balance, moderates will still prefer a filibuster rule.

Conversely, there may also be strategic decisions not to filibuster a nominee who is outside the range of the minority party's ideological acceptability. For instance, the minority party may foresee that the nominee for the next vacancy will be worse than the nominee to this vacancy. Filibustering the current nominee may give the minority party a reputation for obstructionism that would provide the President with greater ability to win that subsequent fight. We believe this strategy of withholding a filibuster would be used more often with Supreme Court nominees than with lower court nominees, because the public is far more aware of the confirmation of the former than the latter. Senators can create substantial political capital with the public only with visible political actions.

B. LOWER COURT JUDGES VERSUS SUPREME COURT JUSTICES

The second implication of our model is that the filibuster will have less influence on the ideology of Supreme Court Justices than lower court judges. The reason is that the public will almost certainly give more credence to charges of obstructionism at the Supreme Court level. The Supreme Court nomination is more visible, thus making the public more aware that the nomination is being blocked from an up or down vote by a parliamentary tactic. The public may also be concerned about the legitimacy of the Court's operating without its full complement of Justices. A vacancy is far more harmful to the Supreme Court than to the court of appeals, because an essential part of the Supreme Court's perceived function is to resolve close cases for the nation, which an eight-member Court may be unable to do. Filibustering a Chief Justice may be particularly difficult, because a vacancy at the apex of the judiciary might seem intolerable.[112]

---

[112] We have discussed above, see note 22 and accompanying text, the reasons that a Justice's resignation pending a confirmation may inhibit the Justice from fully functioning. Nevertheless, insofar as this distinction between resignation pending confirmation and outright resignation has a practical effect on the confirmation process, we would predict that the rise of the filibuster may encourage some Justices to resign outright rather than pending the confirmation of their successor when the President is likely to name a successor to their liking. Such outright resignations ensure that the Court will be short staffed until their successor is confirmed and strengthen the President's hand in gaining confirmation.

C. TIMING

The third implication of the model is that the filibuster will be more effective in producing moderate nominees the later in the President's term the nomination occurs. As the end of the term approaches, the benefits for the minority party of opposing the President's nominee increase. Blocking the nominee may lead the seat to remain vacant through the next election with the consequence that a President of the opposing party may get to make the nomination. With party voting, minority-party Senators can effectively shut down the confirmation process late in the term as the time remaining becomes too short to permit effective charges of obstructionism. In terms of our model, the value of the status quo—leaving the seat vacant—shifts late in the term, and so naturally does the range of possible agreement between the President and the Senate

Of course, the rational President recognizes this possibility and is likely to factor it into his calculations, making the nomination of a moderate nominee more likely. Conversely, a President at the beginning of his term may have incentives to gamble to nominate a candidate closer to his ideal point. The costs of failure are lower at that time because he has time to nominate a second or even third candidate.

Under a majority confirmation rule, in contrast, it is not clear that the President's ability to get his preferred nominees confirmed will usually wane toward the end of his term if his party has a majority. Indeed, the President may actually have more leeway to nominate a candidate close to his ideal point at the end of his term, because even his moderate party members will be loath to break ranks with their colleagues and cause the nomination to be given to the other party. To be sure, in a weak party system a President cannot be absolutely sure of his party's loyalty, and thus some Presidents may choose to moderate their preferences rather than play an end-of-term game of chicken.[113] But the fact remains that under majority rule, an end of the term nomination can in some ways strengthen the President's hand when his party has the Senate majority.[114]

---

[113] For a description of the "chicken" game and another legal application, see Douglas G. Baird et al, *Game Theory and the Law* 43–44 (1994).

[114] Other factors not discussed in our model may also weaken the President toward the

The increased importance of timing should also affect the timing of the Justices' retirement decisions. With no filibuster rule, Justices concerned to further their ideology consider the party of the President (and of the Senate majority) when deciding when to retire. With a filibuster rule, Justices would place additional weight on the length of time left in the President's term, the strength of the opposition party in the Senate, and even the prospect of further appointments.[115]

VII. Conclusion

The decisions of the Supreme Court are a consequence of its composition and its composition is shaped by the rules for confirming Justices. In this essay, we have discussed how the frequent resort to the filibuster—the most important change in judicial confirmation in generations if not since the beginning of the republic—may fundamentally alter the composition of the Court by making nominees more moderate and by encouraging the nomination of more stealth and uncertain candidates. In the course of our analysis, we have unpacked the countermajoritarian difficulty and showed that confirmation rules are at the heart of this salient issue of political theory. The supermajoritarian filibuster rule has the surprising effect of promoting majority-held principles and thereby ameliorating this central difficulty in constitutional law.

---

end of this term. As a lame duck he may not be able to offer patronage to get his nominees confirmed.

[115] As discussed above, the prospect of further appointments may make strategic filibusters more likely.

DENNIS J. HUTCHINSON

ASPEN AND THE TRANSFORMATION OF HARRY BLACKMUN

Anyone coming to grips with the judicial career of Harry A. Blackmun must reconcile two Blackmuns. First, is the "colorless, competent, conservative judge closely allied with his friend and sponsor,
Chief Justice Warren Burger,"[1] or, more harshly, as characterized
in the press at his nomination, as a "white Anglo-Saxon Protestant
Republican Rotarian Harvard man from the suburbs."[2] Finally, at
the end of his twenty-four-year tenure on the Supreme Court of
the United States, is the Justice lionized as champion of the social
outsider—prisoners, aliens, Native Americans, poor women, preg-
nant teenagers, gays and lesbians. Both Blackmuns are overdrawn,

Dennis J. Hutchinson is William Rainey Harper Professor in the College and Senior
Lecturer in Law, The University of Chicago.

AUTHOR'S NOTE: A preliminary version of this paper was delivered at a conference, Justice
Blackmun and Judicial Biography, sponsored by Brooklyn Law School, Sept 16, 2005. I
am very grateful to the participants at the conference for comments, to Kathryn Hutchinson for superlative research assistance, and for helpful suggestions to Al Alschuler, Douglas Baird, Jonathan Beere, Emily Buss, Gerhard Casper, David J. Garrow, Elliot Gerson,
Linda Greenhouse, Alice Henkin, Ralph Lerner, Tom Merrill, Richard Posner, David Roe,
David Sklansky, Michael Tonry, David Wigdor, and Diane P. Wood. I also thank Deans
John W. Boyer of the College and Saul Levmore of the Law School for underwriting my
archival research.

[1] John Jeffries, *Justice Lewis F. Powell, Jr.* 364–65 (Scribner's, 1994).

[2] John R. Waltz, *The Burger-Blackmun Court*, New York Times Magazine (Dec 6, 1970),
at 61. Blackmun later called the characterization "nasty," a "slur," Justice Harry A. Blackmun Oral History Project 115, 294 (1995) (Transcript, Manuscript Division, Library of
Congress) (cited below as OH). The Oral History must be used with caution. Blackmun
was famously uncomfortable before television cameras, and at age eighty-five suffered
from memory lapses from time to time. See, e.g., OH at 26, 295, 314, 351.

to be sure, but something happened to Harry Blackmun during his tenure, and the questions, obviously, are "when and why"?

It is too easy to identify, as some have, the election in 1980 of Ronald Reagan, who campaigned on an anti-abortion plank, and brought with his coattails eleven Senators elected with pro-life platforms, as the turning point for Blackmun. *Roe v Wade*,[3] the landmark abortion opinion in 1973 written by Blackmun, and which he quickly made his personal cause, was certainly in jeopardy, and the election seemed to portend major political changes in the country, but it was not determinative of the transformation of Mr. Justice Blackmun. Unlike the character in Moliere, who awakens one morning to discover that he has been speaking prose and not poetry for forty years, most of us, judges included, do not experience overnight conversions. Nor did Harry Blackmun. The transformation—there is no other word for it—from Warren Burger's "Hip-Pocket Harry" or "Minnesota Twin" was gradual and even more encompassing than his votes on the Court suggest.

As Hilary Spurling has recently emphasized in her lecture[4] occasioned by completion of her two-volume biography of Henri Matisse, defining moments for artists (perhaps no less for judges?) occur at points of great psychological vulnerability. If she is right, the place to begin to look for Harry Blackmun's transformation is the summer of 1979, more than a year before Reagan wrested the Republican nomination from a noisy field of competitors. Multiple factors exerted a powerful internal pressure on Blackmun at that time. As Linda Greenhouse has carefully documented,[5] Harry Blackmun and Warren Burger—lifelong friends and early Court allies—became estranged in 1974 over the internal blow-up in the Court over *United States v Nixon*.[6] By 1975, we are told, Brennan thought "Blackmun was continuing to drift away, not only from the Chief's influence but from his own conservatism, and he was determined to encourage it."[7] Blackmun's agonized and deeply reluctant support of the constitutionality of the death penalty had

---

[3] 410 US 113 (1973).

[4] Published as Hilary Spurling, *Matisse's Pajamas*, New York Review of Books 33 (Aug 11, 2004).

[5] Linda Greenhouse, *Becoming Justice Blackmun*, esp. ch 6 (Times, 2005) (cited below as Greenhouse.)

[6] 418 US 684 (1974). See OH at 228.

[7] Bob Woodward and Scott Armstrong, *The Brethren* 439 (Simon & Schuster, 1979, 2005).

been abandoned in 1977 when he agreed that capital punishment for rape was unconstitutional, a concession to recent precedent but the occasion for a bitter rebuke from Burger. By the time the October Term 1978 ended in June of 1979, Blackmun had voted with Brennan and against Burger in six bellwether cases involving civil rights and decided by a closely divided Court.[8] Blackmun was no longer in anyone's hip pocket, but his constitutional moorings seemed to critics to be ad hoc and perhaps even ad hominem.

Outside of the docket, his thin skin was being scraped both by criticisms of his surprising votes and by the prospect of being revealed, in an exposé due to be published at the end of the year, as a pathetic judicial mediocrity. Blackmun's agreement to be interviewed for *The Brethren*,[9] by Bob Woodward and Scott Armstrong, was perhaps a preemptive defense, but with little hope that the interview would allow him to escape severe criticisms of his abilities and his work. He felt that several Justices, especially Potter Stewart,[10] viewed him as inadequate,[11] and his suspicions that Stewart was a conduit to the press[12] (accurate, as it turned out[13]) only intensified his anxiety.

Deeper worries nagged Blackmun. He had arrived at the Supreme Court with little feel for constitutional law or theory, and he felt that his first several terms were on-the-job training in which he was both inadequate and behind. He needed to find his bearings, and he needed an environment less pressured and more supportive than what to him was the unremitting grind of the Court.

Almost by accident, he was thrown a life preserver, although it came from the mountains and not from the waters of the upper Midwest where he had begun to seek solace and a secluded place to "re-charge his batteries," as he often said, every summer. Joseph

---

[8] *Orr v Orr*, 440 US 268 (1979); *Davis v Passman*, 442 US 228 (1979); *United Steelworkers v Weber*, 443 US 193 (1979); *Gannett Co. v DePasquale*, 443 US 368 (1979); *Columbus Bd of Ed. v Penick, Dayton Bd of Ed. v Brinkman*, 443 US 449 (1979).

[9] Woodward and Armstrong (cited in note 7). Blackmun acknowledged being interviewed in his Oral History, OH at 292.

[10] OH at 166, 292.

[11] The Woodward-Armstrong book reports that William O. Douglas (p 209), William J. Brennan (p 211), and Stewart (pp 221, 229, 301) viewed Blackmun or his work as inadequate. Other passages emphasize Blackmun's weaknesses as a Justice: 143, 144, 206, 219, 220, 222.

[12] OH at 224.

[13] See generally David J. Garrow, *The Supreme Court and the Brethren*, 18 Const Comm 303 (2001).

Slater, president of the Aspen Institute, invited Blackmun to co-moderate a seminar on Justice and Society for two weeks in August of 1979.[14] The setting was perfect—spectacular outdoor vistas, which Blackmun adored, plus a music festival which he found both stimulating and soothing, and, most important, an informal and nonjudgmental atmosphere. The work was foreign, as he soon described in public and semi-public speeches, no less than a Great Books course in questions of the interrelationship between law and justice, and the relationship of justice and the action of the individual in society, based on texts from Plato to the present. Adventitiously, but crucially,[15] his co-moderator was Norval Morris, then Dean of the University of Chicago Law School and one of the leading scholars of criminal justice and penology in the country if not the world.

Morris, who had first met Blackmun four years earlier at Aspen,[16] quickly established an easy bond with Blackmun. Where Blackmun was hesitant and anxious, Morris was warm, charming, and acutely sensitive to his colleague. Morris was also a devoted opponent of capital punishment, a leading scholar in the field of penal reform, a professed liberal who declared in 1970, in one of his most quoted passages, "When the criminal law invades the spheres of private morality and social welfare, it exceeds its proper limits at the cost of neglecting its primary tasks."[17] He could be a mordant critic, but

---

[14] Blackmun had attended an Executive Seminar on Law and Society at Aspen in 1975 and again in 1977. Shortly thereafter he received an invitation to moderate a two-week seminar on Justice and Society in the summer of 1978. Blackmun to Krasney, Sept 30, 1977, box 1362, Harry Blackmun Papers, Library of Congress (cited below as HABLC). Worried over the amount of work, the proximity to the end of term, and his own limited knowledge, Blackmun resisted but was finally convinced that the workload could be shared and that the seminar could be scheduled late enough to avoid conflict with Court work. Recuperation from major surgery forced postponement of the first Justice and Society seminar until 1979. Blackmun to Slater, April 24, 1978, id. Robert McKay, then Director of the Program on Justice, Society and the Individual, and Slater wooed Blackmun throughout the process of establishing the new seminar, and Blackmun worked actively with the Aspen staff to review materials and scheduling for the seminar discussions.

[15] When Blackmun finally "succumbed" to Robert McKay's invitation to lead the seminar, he explained to Morris that the "clinching factor was your presence as moderator." Blackmun to Morris, May 11, 1979, box 1483, HABLC.

[16] Morris remembered that he had first met Blackmun in 1975 at a meeting in Aspen, Morris, 113 Harv L Rev at 22, but Blackmun did not recall meeting Morris until two years later in 1977 at an executive seminar under the auspices of the Aspen Institute. *Norval Morris Tribute*, May 5, 1994, box 1497, HABLC. Records of the Institute confirm Morris's recollection; I am grateful to Alice Henkin of the Aspen Institute for resolving the conflicting memories of the co-moderators.

[17] Morris and Gordon Hawkins, *The Honest Politician's Guide to Crime Control* 2 (Chicago, 1970). Morris and Hawkins advocated decriminalization of simple drug possession, gambling, abortion, pornography, and consensual, private sexual activities between consenting

he was also experimenting with fictions—what he called legal par-
ables—to explore, somewhat didactically, the roles of mental illness,
blame and guilt, and compassion in criminal law and punishment.
Morris was a shrewd teacher—insistent, witty, and deeply committed to what he viewed as a humane imperative for the legal
system. Compared to Blackmun's colleagues on the Court, Morris
was respectful, supportive, and curious about Blackmun's views. The
tone of the seminar, held for twenty-plus major figures in American
business, law, and government,[18] was informal, personal, and con-
genial, if sometimes raucous.[19] Each twelve-day session began with
what quickly came to be called the "Call me Harry" reception,[20]
hosted by the Justice and his wife, Dottie. The Morris-Blackmun
partnership was so successful, and valuable to the Aspen Institute,
that it was repeated sixteen more times, through 1995, a year after
Blackmun's retirement. Age and infirmity then made the annual
mountain trek too onerous.[21]

Aspen satisfied an acute need for Harry Blackmun. Insecurities
over his reputation inside and outside the Court, quickened by *The
Brethren*, impelled him to find ratification of his newly developing
views. He was at a psychological crossroads of no less than self-
definition if not self-worth. The most telling evidence is a letter
drafted but not sent to Burt Neuborne of New York University
School of Law and sometime legal director of the American Civil

---

adults including sodomy—homosexual and heterosexual. Id at 3. They declared: "We think
it improper, impolitic, and usually socially harmful for the law to intervene or attempt to
regulate the private moral conduct of the citizen. In this country we have a highly moralistic
criminal law and a long tradition of using it as an instrument for coercing men toward
virtue. It is a singularly inept instrument for that purpose." Id at 5. When Morris retired,
Blackmun said that one of the many things he learned from him at Aspen was that "we
seriously overuse the criminal law in this country." *Norval Morris Tribute*, May 5, 1994,
at 4–5, box 1497, HABLC.

[18] Participants in the 1979 session included four lawyers in private practice, two in
government, one corporate counsel, one judge, four academics, three from overseas, one
official from the American Bar Association, one college president, two community leaders,
and two members of the Aspen staff. The roster is filed in box 1483, HABLC. Blackmun
recalled, imperfectly, the roster in his retirement tribute to Morris. *Norval Morris Tribute*,
May 5, 1994, at 3, box 1497, HABLC. During the seventeen-year run, the Blackmun-
Morris seminar had 340 participants. Norval Morris, *H.A.B.: Integrity at Its Highest Level*,
113 Harv L Rev 21, 22 (1999).

[19] Id at 23.

[20] Id at 24. "'Yes, Justice Blackmun,' they reply," Morris later recalled. Morris, *H.A.B.*,
43 Am U L Rev 730 (1994). "[B]y the second week some of them did." Morris, 113 Harv
L Rev at 22.

[21] Without Blackmun, who had become a marquee attraction, the seminar was reduced
the following year from twelve days to one week, its current duration.

Liberties Union. In February of 1980, just weeks after the publication of the Woodward-Armstrong book, Neuborne published an admiring essay about Blackmun in the *National Law Journal* in which he traced Blackmun's "emergence as a significant centrist force on the court" who was "non-ideological, technically satisfactory, [and] intuitively fair,"[22] in the worthy tradition if not the technical mold of the late John Marshall Harlan. Despite Neuborne's reservations over Blackmun's "ability to express his results in a persuasive, doctrinally acceptable manner,"[23] the Justice was moved to write Neuborne a detailed thank-you note: "I write merely to express appreciation for your considerateness and understanding and 'tender' approach. I am not used to this kind of thing, especially from New England or the East. I shall do my best to fulfill the challenge which is implicit in your writing."[24] Blackmun proceeded to offer, "in partial self-defense,"[25] a numbered three-point explanation of his views, and concluded "that I appreciate the tone and content of your article. I presume to write this note to you to let you know specifically I am grateful."[26]

Blackmun left no evidence as to why he decided not to send the letter, but its contents reflect someone yearning for approval and grateful to receive even mixed praise, especially from what he viewed as the Eastern liberal legal establishment which had borne down so hard on him in his first few terms,[27] culminating in John Hart Ely's scathing critique of *Roe v Wade*.[28] Ely's essay inflicted a deep wound on Blackmun that never healed.[29] Neuborne's essay did not

---

[22] Neuborne, *Blackmun: Intellectual Openness Elicits Needed Respect for the Judicial Process*, Nat L J 18, 23, 24 (Feb 18, 1980).

[23] Id at 24.

[24] Blackmun to Neuborne, Feb 12, 1980, box 1437, HABLC (marked "not used").

[25] Id.

[26] Id at 2.

[27] Two early opinions for the Court made Blackmun a target of critical wrath from the left, *Wyman v James*, 400 US 309 (1971), which sanctioned a warrantless "visit" by officials to a welfare recipient's residence, and *United States v Kras*, 409 US 434 (1973), which upheld the constitutionality of bankruptcy filing fees for someone who claimed he could not afford them. See Greenhouse at 62–63, 108–10. *Wyman*, Blackmun's first opinion for the Court, was called "distressing . . . badly reasoned" and the "nadir of treatment for the poor in the years of the Burger Court." Robert Bennett, *Poverty Law*, in Vincent Blasi, ed, *The Burger Court* 46, 50 (Yale, pb ed, 1983). Blackmun remained defensive of *Kras* for the rest of his career, see OH at 190–91. "The academic world, I suppose, will always haunt me about United States v. Kras," Blackmun wrote in his unsent letter to Burt Neuborne in 1980. Blackmun to Neuborne (note 24 above) at 2.

[28] Ely, *The Wages of Crying Wolf: A Comment on Roe v. Wade*, 82 Yale L J 920 (1973).

[29] Cf. OH at 201, 493.

displace Blackmun's plodding reputation at a stroke, but journalists began to paint the Justice in a different light, and Blackmun even consented to a "rare interview"[30] with his hometown newspaper, the Rochester (MN) *Post-Bulletin*, in which he proclaimed, after a decade on the Court, that he hoped "I have a broader, more mature, more developed constitutional philosophy than I did in 1970."[31] Shortly after granting the interview, Blackmun returned to Aspen for the second Justice and Society seminar.

The impact of the first Aspen experience is almost immediately discernible, both on the bench and off, although the effect would only be fully realized over time. During his first decade on the Court, Blackmun was a frequent speaker to law schools, colleges, schools, bar groups, judicial conferences, and the like. His early speeches were highly lapidary, sometimes simply a collection of what he found to be meaningful quotations.[32] About the time he began his annual trek to Aspen, the themes became more pointed and more substantive, urging his audience to consider questions of justice, and, referring to Plato's injunction, as he did in his 1980 address at Hamline University's School of Law, to consider what constitutes a properly lived life.[33]

The Hamline address contains Blackmun's first public report of his work at Aspen:[34]

> We and the seminar participants studied Plato and John Locke, Thoreau and Martin Luther King, H. L. A. Hart and John Stuart Mill, John Rawls and Gerald Dworkin, Robert Nozick and Kai Nielsen, Alexander Bickel and McGeorge Bundy, among others. And "Billy Budd" and "Measure for Measure" were thrown in for sweeteners. We discussed and argued about civil disobedience, the relationship between law and morality, justice and the right to personal autonomy, distributive justice, racial discrimination, sex discrimination, retributive justice, the proper scope of the criminal law, and justice in an international context. And we

---

[30] Roger Runningen, *Blackmun Emerges as 'Independent' on Supreme Court*, Rochester Post-Bulletin (July 9, 1980), at 1.

[31] Id at 20.

[32] See, e.g., Blackmun, *Some Goals for Legal Education*, 1 Ohio N L Rev 403 (1974). Most of Blackmun's speeches during this period were not published.

[33] *Remarks of Harry A. Blackmun* (Dedication of New Law School Building, Hamline University School of Law, Oct 3, 1980), 1980 Hamline L Rev 177, 184 (cited below as Hamline Lecture).

[34] Id at 182.

concluded with Solzhenitsyn's address at Harvard and with some
thoughts about the just person.

Blackmun noted that the seminar consisted of two dozen professors
of law, federal judges, general counsels of national and international
corporations, government officials, and practicing lawyers. "The
interests," he said, "the devotion, and the dialogue were serious and
intense. After that experience, repeated for me twice now, no one
can convince me . . . that no one is concerned with what justice
is, or whether we really measure up, or how to achieve justice, or
how to make it available for the little person as well as the influential
one."[35] Blackmun closed his review with a characteristically modest
note that nonetheless highlighted his own sense of the seminar's
impact: "Perhaps we solved little or nothing, but each of us was
exposed to new approaches and new thoughts, and each was provoked to examining critically what usually is taken for granted, and
with a long view of the law, not just the exigency of the particular
case."[36]

Both the syllabus and the format were important to Blackmun,
which he tried to explain to Justice David Souter after announcing
his retirement. Blackmun was attempting to recruit Souter at Aspen.
"I have felt that it has been very good for me to get away from the
confinement of our cases here and to do so at a very beautiful place
in late summer," Blackmun wrote to Souter.[37] "[Aspen is] not more
of the same which we encounter here," Blackmun added in a follow-
up letter when Souter failed to respond. "It shook me up intellectually and, I think, was good for me."[38]

The sales pitch, which was unsuccessful, is revealing. Blackmun
defined himself to some extent, first as a court of appeals judge and
later in his first decade on the Supreme Court, as an assiduous
adherent to precedent and a master of the facts of each case he
encountered. At the same time, he admitted to knowing little con-

---

[35] Id.

[36] Id.

[37] Blackmun to Souter, Oct 17, 1994, box 1408, HABLC.

[38] Blackmun to Souter, Oct 26, 2004, box 1408, HABLC. Or as he told his Aspen
audience in 1992: "The seminar is another opportunity to look at the legal assumptions
we are prone to *accept* in day-to-day practice and in judging, and to examine those assumptions critically to see if they are really sound. . . . It is a shaking and somewhat
disturbing process. For me, it is well that we discover things are not so simple as to be
taken for granted." Blackmun, *Aspen* [Reading Text] 7, Aug 20, 1992, box 1483, HABLC.
Cf. Blackmun, Annual Proceedings 1992, American Law Institute, 411, 415.

stitutional theory when he arrived at the Court, and his first several terms constituted a monumental intellectual game of catch-up, a task with which he was uncomfortable if not overwhelmed, and which did not play to his self-defined strengths.

Aspen changed the focus and reframed the issues he faced, not only theoretically but also definitionally. He was fond of quoting Socrates' admonition to Callicles, with an implicitly self-deprecating reference: "The subject we are discussing is one which cannot fail to engage the earnest attention even of a man of small intelligence; it is nothing less than how a man should live."[39] He might have added: the subject is how a judge should live and what principles should guide him. Those principles, the seminar taught him, transcended precedent and legal theory. They included larger questions of justice and, as the interaction with the seminar participants annually illustrated, lawyer and layman alike expected the Supreme Court to serve those ends. If the initial break with Burger in 1974 over *Nixon* was liberating, as Linda Greenhouse's book illustrates, the liberation from the iron grip of precedent and cold case records must have been exhilarating. What the proper ends of justice were, as Blackmun acknowledged in his speech at Hamline, is highly contested and even indeterminate, but their pursuit, thanks to Aspen, had been authoritatively legitimized.

The Aspen syllabus (the version used in 1979 is reprinted here in facsimile as an Appendix) barely surfaced in Harry Blackmun's opinions, and Norval Morris is cited only twice: on the history of sentencing in 1989,[40] and—according to Blackmun—"one of the world's leading criminologists"[41]—on competency proceedings in criminal trials in 1992.[42] The syllabus is never far from the surface in Blackmun's work. The controversial comparison in *DeShaney v Winnebago County*[43] of the majority to the judges enforcing the fugitive slave laws derives from Robert Cover's influential book, *Justice Accused.*[44] Cover's work was taught at Aspen on the same day as

---

[39] Plato, *Gorgias* 500. Blackmun's translation appears to be Walter Hamilton (Penguin, 1960) at 106. Blackmun first quoted the passage in the Hamline Lecture at 184, and it became a staple in his public lectures. For a later published example, see *Movement and Countermovement (Remarks of Harry A. Blackmun)*, 38 Drake L Rev 747, 748 (1988).

[40] *Mistretta v US*, 488 US 361, 365.

[41] *Medina v California*, 505 US 437, 458.

[42] Id.

[43] 489 US 189, 212 (1989).

[44] Yale, 1984.

Regina v Dudley & Stephens,[45] a macabre example of the questions of necessity and criminal liability, which Blackmun assayed at length in *United States v Bailey*,[46] a case argued three months after the first Blackmun-Morris seminar. *Bailey* and *Farmer v Brennan*,[47] decided almost fifteen years later, both contain ringing condemnations of abusive prison conditions, a topic on which Morris was a foremost authority. The opinion that Blackmun viewed as his most important aside from *Roe* itself, the dissent in *Bowers v Hardwick*,[48] "borrowed much of its perspective," according to the clerk who wrote Blackmun's preliminary draft, "from H. L. A. Hart's position in the famous debate about the Wolfenden Commission's recommendation that Great Britain decriminalize sodomy; for nearly a decade, the Justice had discussed the Hart-Devlin debate"[49] at Aspen. In fact, the citation in Blackmun's *Bowers* dissent is telling: he refers to the version originally published by Hart in 1959,[50] which the Aspen syllabus highlighted (and still does), and not Hart's later and more sustained treatment of the issues in *Law, Liberty and Morality*, published four years later.[51] The Aspen materials were never far from Blackmun's mind, even if they did not often play conspicuous roles in his actual work product on the Court.

After Blackmun died, Morris speculated that Blackmun's thinking was deeply influenced in three areas by their annual partnership: the "law relating to mental illness," the "extent of racial discrimination in the criminal justice system," and the proper role for the Court in the administration of the death penalty. Race and the death penalty intersected, but, as Morris recalled, "after *McClesky [v Kemp* in 1987] there was not much talk about it." Morris believed that the "seminar ultimately influenced" Blackmun's position on the death penalty, and he explained how he tried, "inside and out of the seminar," to convince the Justice of the futility of constitution-

---

[45] 14 QBD 273 (1884). See A. W. B. Simpson, *Cannibalism and the Common Law* (Chicago, 1984). Blackmun first encountered the issue thanks to Edmond N. Cahn's *The Moral Decision* (Indiana, 1955). See Blackmun, *Thoughts About Ethics*, 24 Emory L J 3, 9–12 (1975) (discussing Cahn's treatment of *U.S. v Holmes*, 26 F Cas 360 (No 15,383) (CCED Pa 1842)).

[46] 444 US 394, 419 (1980) (Blackmun, J, dissenting).

[47] 511 US 825, 851 (1994) (Blackmun, J, concurring).

[48] 478 US 186, 212 (1986) (Blackmun, J, dissenting).

[49] Karlan, *A Tribute to Justice Harry A. Blackmun*, 108 Harv L Rev 13, 16 (1994).

[50] *Immorality and Treason*, 62 Listener 162–63 (July 30, 1959).

[51] Vintage, 1963 (1962 Harry Camp Lectures, Stanford).

ally distinguishing between murderers who deserved to die and those who did not:

> I pressed on him a vision of his brother Scalia directed by the legislature to dry up the Atlantic with a mop, sitting obediently by the water's edge in King Canute's chair directing operations. It seemed to me a perfect allegory for the charge given to the Court to distinguish the worse worse murderers from the merely worse murderers. A job, I thought, best left to Saint Peter and quite beyond human capacities, even the capacities of the Nine.

Harry Blackmun's modesty, candor, and accessibility readily made him the toast of the Aspen Seminar and prompted a local television station to request an on-camera interview in 1982. The request made Blackmun anxious. Although he had grown in confidence as a public speaker, in substantial measure thanks to the Seminar, television was another matter. Supreme Court Justices simply didn't do TV. He remembered that Warren Burger had been furious with Blackmun for granting a televised interview from Rochester when he was nominated in 1970.[52] Only two years before that, Justice Hugo Black had made front-page headlines in the *New York Times* when he criticized a leading Supreme Court decision during a lengthy television interview.[53] After Seminar officials endorsed the interviewer, Blackmun complied with the request.

One interview led to another. Daniel Schorr, the television and later radio journalist, had been a participant in the Blackmun-Morris sessions in 1982, and asked Blackmun to do an interview for the Cable News Network (CNN).[54] The step from local to national network television made Blackmun doubly nervous, but Schorr persisted, and a fifty-minute interview was taped on Thanksgiving Day 1982 in Blackmun's chambers at the Court. The Justice was discreet about decided cases but he sounded themes that would become staples for him on the stump in years to come: the Justices are

---

[52] *December 4, 1982, Cable News Network Broadcast 4* [Memo to File], box 1441, HABLC (cited below as CNN Memo).

[53] The *New York Times* used a four-column headline on page 1, Homer Bigart, *Black Believes Warren Phrase Slowed Integration*, New York Times (Dec 4, 1968), A1. Other coverage is rehearsed by Elizabeth Black in *Hugo Black: A Memorial Portrait*, Supreme Court Historical Society Yearbook 1982. *Justice Black and the Bill of Rights*, 9 Sw U L Rev 937 (1977) (transcript of CBS interview, Dec 3, 1968). The interview was especially controversial because Justice Black criticized the use of "all deliberate speed" in *Brown v Board of Education (II)*, 349 US 294, 301 (1955). See 9 Sw U L Rev at 941.

[54] CNN Memo at 1.

fallible human beings and even "prima donnas," Justice O'Connor—
beginning her second term—brought a conservative perspective to
the Court, and that he was initially hurt, before he developed a
"thick" skin, by anti-*Roe v Wade* mail condemning him as "Butcher
of Dachau, murderer, Pontius Pilate, King Herod, you name it."[55]
Schorr pressed Blackmun on what effect the Woodward-Armstrong
exposé, published three years earlier but still a hot topic wherever
Blackmun spoke, had on the Court. Blackmun conceded that "I
smell pretty bad" for the first thirty pages but felt the book "served
a purpose": after his daughter Susie read it, she said, "for the first
time in my life I think I have an idea of what your work amounts
to and what you're trying to do."[56]

When the CNN broadcast date was announced, Burger reacted
coldly toward Blackmun[57] but other Justices—William Brennan,
Byron White, and William Rehnquist—cheered Blackmun on. "I
suppose I've broken all the rules," Blackmun said to White.[58] "What
rules?" White grinned. "I think you enjoy doing it."[59]

Harry Blackmun was making his own rules: first, do no harm to
the Court as an institution, but, second, put an honest human face
on the institution—starting with his own—and explain how the
Court works and what moves him. While the Schorr interview was
in post-production, Blackmun agreed to be interviewed by John A.
Jenkins, a freelance writer for the *New York Times Sunday Magazine*.
Charmed by Jenkins, Blackmun sat for more than four hours of
audiotaped interviews over several days.

The resulting cover story in late February of 1983[60] was in many

---

[55] *A Justice Speaks Out: A Conversation with Harry A. Blackmun* (cited below as CNN
Transcript), Dec 4, 1982, at 18, on file in HABLC, box 1441. Quoting hate mail soon
became a frequent rhetorical trope for Blackmun, which he later explained in his Oral
History: "[I]t's kind of a good way to break the ice. My hearers enjoy my being insulted,
so it's a good way to start." OH at 305. In the interview with John Jenkins for the *New
York Times Magazine*, see text at note 60, Blackmun was quoted as saying: "Think of any
name, I've been called it . . . Butcher of Dachau, murderer, Pontius Pilate, Adolph Hitler."
John A. Jenkins, *A Candid Talk with Justice Blackmun*, New York Times Magazine (Feb
20, 1983), §6, 20, 26 (cited below as Jenkins). See also text at note 86. Over time, especially
to repeat hearers, the litany became garish. Images of martyrdom became a recurring
motif for Blackmun. In the first moments of his first Oral History interview, when asked
about his daily routine in chambers, he said that he liked to look out of his window, which
faced the front plaza of the Court, to "see who's picketing us." Id at 1.

[56] CNN transcript at 15.

[57] CNN Memo at 3.

[58] Id at 4.

[59] Id.

[60] Jenkins (cited in note 55).

respects Blackmun's Declaration of Independence. Where he had been guarded with Schorr and hesitant to characterize his colleagues or to delineate sharply the philosophical divisions within the Court, Blackmun was bluntly frank with Jenkins. One sentence is typical: "[H]e has emerged as the Court's most unlikely crusader, a jurist determined to make the Court responsive not only to individuals— 'One has to be aware that human beings are involved in all these cases,' he says—but also to 'prevent it from plunging rapidly to the right.'"[61] Jenkins observed that Blackmun's "unprecedented candor seems motivated not only by his political concern, but also by personal resentment. 'I have a little anger underneath it all,' he says"— anger from being characterized for a dozen years "'in a way that I think I never fit.'"[62]

The candor extended to colleagues. Jenkins included four lengthy anecdotes from Blackmun about Brennan, White, Thurgood Marshall, and Rehnquist.[63] Asked whether Burger felt betrayed by Blackmun's movement to the left, Blackmun replied, "I'm not going to be a No. 2 for anybody. I never have been, and I don't intend to be."[64] Jenkins pointed out to his readers that Blackmun voted 90 percent of the time with Burger during his first term but now voted 75 percent of the time with Brennan, the Court's most liberal member. And what of Justice O'Connor, who exchanged heated barbs with Blackmun in a case involving federal power and states' rights a few months before? Blackmun said she had "obviously settled down on the right side," and suggested that she might have a "political agenda."[65] Jenkins summarized Blackmun's understanding of his place on the Court: "He believes he is there to *do* justice, not merely to oblige its doctrinal demands, and his unprepossessing style serves to remind him of the constituency he has been sent there to serve."[66] Blackmun identified that constituency with a phrase that was becoming his battle cry, on and off the bench: "the world out there that we sometimes forget about."[67]

In a lengthy memorandum to his files, Blackmun recorded his

---

[61] Id at 20.

[62] Id at 23.

[63] Id at 24.

[64] Id at 29.

[65] Id at 57.

[66] Id at 23–24.

[67] Id at 24.

colleagues' reaction to the Jenkins article: "At noon that Sunday, Justice Marshall called me with his voice almost quivering. He said, 'Harry, thank you, thank you, thank you for saying what needed to be said.'" "Later that afternoon, Justice Brennan called with enthusiasm."[68] Justice White teased Blackmun about "being a good press agent for myself. SOC [Justice O'Connor] was cool for awhile and then sent me a note February 23 denying she had a 'political agenda.'"[69] For himself, Blackmun was extremely pleased with the article and sent complimentary letters to Jenkins and to his editor. Dozens of people wrote admiring letters to Blackmun,[70] including Ralph Neas, executive director of the Leadership Conference on Civil Rights, who declared he had "long admired your deep commitment to justice."[71] Blackmun warmly acknowledged the message: "Hearing from you at this time means very much to me."[72]

The break with Warren Burger was now not only complete but publicly acknowledged. Blackmun's new affinity with Brennan and Marshall was squarely on the public record and confirmed inside the Court. Coincidentally, almost at the same time that the Jenkins article was published, a student note in the *Harvard Law Review* documented "The Changing Social Vision of Justice Blackmun."[73] Outside the Court, the social and political forces that Blackmun felt were pushing the Court's "plunge to the right" accelerated. A month before the Jenkins article was published, President Ronald Reagan addressed the annual "Right to Life" rally and his remarks were printed in book form,[74] which his supporters noted was the only time a sitting president had published a book.

The threat to *Roe* was not the only issue that aroused Blackmun's passions during the 1982–83 Term. A majority of the Court was growing impatient with procedural delays in the imposition of death penalties, primarily from federal habeas corpus review of state court convictions. At the end of the Term, he published a scorching dissent

---

[68] *H.A.B.* [Memo to File], Feb 22, 1983, at 4, box 1440, HABLC.

[69] Id.

[70] Duly catalogued by Blackmun's staff. See Memo, Oct 26, 1983, box 1440, HABLC.

[71] Neas to Blackmun, Feb 21, 1983, id.

[72] Blackmun to Neas, Feb 24, 1983, id.

[73] Note, 96 Harv L Rev 717 (1983).

[74] Ronald Reagan, *Abortion and the Conscience of the Nation* (New Regency, 2000), originally published in *Human Life Review*, Spring 1983.

condemning "specious testimony of a psychiatrist"[75] at the penalty phase of a bifurcated capital trial that foreshadowed his eventual rejection of "tinkering with the machinery of death"[76] a decade later. Linda Greenhouse traces the path Blackmun followed,[77] properly noting that the turning point occurred in 1986 with *Darden v Wainwright*,[78] in which the Court denied relief to a death row inmate who Blackmun was convinced was either innocent or unfairly tried.[79] The opinion in *Darden* coincided with another dissent, which Blackmun later said was perhaps his best opinion: the carefully reasoned but impassioned argument for the constitutional invalidation of state anti-sodomy laws in *Bowers*.[80]

By 1986, Blackmun was deeply entrenched in the Brennan-Marshall camp on most issues involving the Bill of Rights, although he claimed that he was simply "trying to hold the center" as the Court was moving to the right.[81] Apparently Blackmun felt his views would enjoy more credence if he did not explicitly ally himself with the hard left on the Court, but the rhetorical strategy fooled no one.

And, each summer, Blackmun repaired to northern Wisconsin to "recharge his batteries," as he often put it, and returned to Aspen to join Morris. Yet by 1987 even Blackmun's work at Aspen had undergone a change at least in one respect. The highlight of the seminar had become Blackmun's annual lecture on *Roe v Wade* and the deliberations that led to the decision. "[F]or one session," Morris later explained, "the seminar abandoned its debating character and listened raptly to the Justice tell the story of his own involvement in the decision and what it meant to him. The presentation was a moving experience, and it became necessary to limit severely the number of auditors who each year had pressed for admission to our

---

[75] *Barefoot v Estelle*, 463 US 880, 916 (1983) (Blackmun, J, dissenting).

[76] *Callins v Collins*, 510 US 1141, 1145 (1994) (Blackmun, J, dissenting).

[77] Greenhouse, ch 7, esp at 165–74.

[78] 477 US 168, 188 (1986) (Blackmun, J, dissenting).

[79] Speaking off the record to the annual Eight Circuit Judicial Conference after the Term, Blackmun called *Darden* "result-oriented": "[I]f ever a man received an unfair trial, Willie Darden received an unfair trial." Transcript, box 1467, HABLC.

[80] At the same conference, Blackmun told the audience that the majority opinion in Bowers was "outrageous." Id.

[81] Neil Lewis, *Blackmun on Search for the Center*, New York Times (March 8, 1986), §1 at 7.

seminar room."[82] The lecture, which Blackmun also delivered at a summer school in 1986 at Aix-en-Provence, was full of detail, minor indiscretions, and agony. One witness in 1983 later remembered: "As he spoke, it became obvious that he was reliving the anguish and the torment, and when he finished talking, his voice was breaking and barely audible. He took no questions and left the room."[83] Four years later, a year after *Darden* and *Bowers* and a few weeks after *McCleskey v Kemp*,[84] the delivery remained essentially the same but Blackmun added the characterization of *Roe* as a "landmark[] on the road toward the full emancipation of women"[85] and changed his exit:[86]

> He spoke of the onslaught of mail that never let up, much of it addressed to Justice Blackmun by a nation that seemed to have missed the concept that a 7–2 ruling is a work of collaboration. "Pontius Pilate." "Murderous Madman." "I am praying for your slow, tortuous death. . . ." Then he said what he did about the emancipation of women and sat down quickly without ceremony. The room was silent for a moment. I think there was applause. But an interesting thing was happening, and no one knew what to do: every woman in the conference room started to cry. The women looked at Justice Blackmun and he looked at the women, and then, one by one, I can't tell you exactly why, maybe because he was there and the opinion he wrote had changed modern American history and he looked worn and sad, the women got up and made their way around the conference table and put their arms around him. He appeared slightly embarrassed but not displeased.

Three years later, "he got a standing ovation this time. The women had already begun to cry."[87]

Harry Blackmun did not keep a diary as such during his tenure on the Supreme Court, but each year he recorded—in pencil, on a sheet or more of lined foolscap—a "Chronology of Significant

---

[82] Norval Morris, *H.A.B.: Integrity at Its Highest Level*, 113 Harv L Rev 21, 24 (1999). The text of the version delivered by Blackmun in 1995 is appended to the Blackmun OH at 485–506. Earlier versions are contained in box 1363, HABLC.

[83] W. J. Frenza [*sic*: correct spelling is Fenza], *The Day Justice Blackmun Revealed His Anguish*, Morning Call (Allentown, Pa) (March 13, 1999), A35.

[84] 481 US 279 (1987).

[85] Cynthia Gorney, *Justice Blackmun, Off the Record*, New York Times (March 7, 1999), §4 at 15.

[86] Id. See also the final version of the annual Aspen lecture, OH at 492–93.

[87] Id.

Events."[88] "Aspen" dots the records, with a special notation for August 18, 1993: "National Treasure!" a response from the audience to his annual lecture on *Roe v Wade*.[89] Alice Henkin, who participated in the first Morris-Blackmun seminar and attended or participated in many more, most recently in her capacity as director of the Justice and Society Program, has recalled: "I think many who attended his seminar and heard his lecture came away feeling that he was a personification of justice and that if this was a person on the Supreme Court, the system could not be all bad. The event was an uplifting experience, although there was some romanticism involved, to be sure."[90] For Blackmun, the annual experience was both balm and validation.

How important was Aspen among the multiple forces that forged Harry Blackmun's transformation? The experience should not be underestimated. His participation, especially in the first few summers, came at a critical psychological fulcrum in his career: he had begun to diverge on the Court from his lifelong friend, Warren Burger, and the practiced judicial reflexes he brought to the Court had become moot. William Brennan patiently tried to coax Blackmun into the Brennan-Marshall fold, at least in non-criminal procedure areas. The "weary"ing drumbeat of cases picking at *Roe v Wade*, and his increasingly caustic defense of the decision, put Blackmun further on the left. The "root" of Blackmun's transformation, as John Jeffries has written, "lay in the natural concern of a parent for a child. The parent was Harry Blackmun and the child was Roe v. Wade. . . . It was Blackmun's defensiveness about Roe that led to his metamorphosis as a liberal."[91]

Aspen was a catalyst for the metamorphosis. Blackmun, the summa cum laude graduate in mathematics from Harvard College, was exposed to classical political theory and jurisprudence for the first time in more than four decades, and, perhaps really for the first time in his life. His interaction with Morris and the distinguished students in the yearly seminars allowed Blackmun to redefine his job, as a jurist committed to espousing the standards of a just society rather than as a judge simply navigating case law. He

---

[88] See box 1548, HABLC. A photograph of a portion of the record for October Term 1994 is reproduced in Greenhouse at 244.

[89] OT 1992 at 2, box 1548, HABLC.

[90] Interview with the author, Sept 6, 2005.

[91] Jeffries, *Justice Lewis F. Powell, Jr.* 366–68 (cited in note 1).

redefined his image as well, from the man out of his depth to the plainspoken tribune of the people, armed with both candor and media savvy. Aspen always awaited at the end of each term as an intellectual and emotional safe house where he could return as a local hero, as seminar leader, and even as narrator of "Peter and the Wolf" at the local music festival.[92] A final factor in the transformation, at least in tone if not direction, must be his choice of law clerks. Dating roughly from his earliest appearance at Aspen, Blackmun hired clerks who were eager to see law used as an instrument for social change, and their support, both intellectually and emotionally, helped keep his transformation on course.[93]

When Harry Blackmun retired in 1994, he was severely criticized as a creature of sentiment with no overarching theory of the Constitution; his dissent in *DeShaney* had recently been cited by Mark Tushnet as a prime example of "The Degradation of Constitutional Discourse."[94] Former Blackmun law clerks who had become academics came to his defense and argued that Blackmun grew on the Court through "empathy" with the "little people" in society,[95] which may or may not have been accurate but in any event begged the theoretical question. Harold Koh invited Blackmun to place his growth into a theoretical framework at several points during their forty hours of oral history, but the Justice wasn't interested. The critique of writing from compassion "doesn't bother me,"[96] he said,

---

[92] *Pleasing Opening for Aspen's Concert Hall,* Los Angeles Times (Aug 24, 1993), F8.

[93] Cf. David J. Garrow, *The Brains Behind Blackmun,* Legal Affairs (May/June 2005). Although Garrow's controversial essay lacks the evidence to sustain the claim that Blackmun was a creature of his clerks with respect to his vote, the essay contains substantial evidence—confirmed in case after case in the Blackmun Papers—that the clerks were the primary authors of Blackmun's opinions dating from the mid-1970s. Blackmun stated in his Oral History that "one of the keys to being a good justice is to get good clerks. The public will never know how much the law clerks contribute. Oftentimes they are the justice, I suppose some would say." OH at 455.

[94] Mark Tushnet, *Colloquy: The Degradation of Constitutional Discourse,* 81 Georgetown L J 251, 301 (1992).

[95] See, e.g., Harold Hongju Koh, *Tribute: Justice Blackmun and the "World Out There,"* 104 Yale L J 23 (1994); Pamela S. Karlan, *Bringing Compassion into the Province of Judging: Justice Blackmun and the Outsiders,* 97 Dickinson L Rev 527 (1993). What remains unexplained is how Blackmun chose the objects of his empathy. Dean Koh tried once during the Oral History interviews when he asked Blackmun if he had "any sympathy for, say, the parents whose children were being bused, or the white men usually who were affected by these affirmative actions programs?" OH at 290. "Well, I always had sympathy for the parents and the children who were in the middle of the controversy, but there it was," Blackmun replied. "We did the best we could do with it, and I wish there had been a happier solution to it." Id.

[96] OH at 15.

almost off-handedly, during the first interview. At other points, Blackmun seemed uninterested in "analyzing my thinking or attitudes,"[97] in drawing connections between thematically related opinions,[98] or in reconciling his change in emphasis between doctor-patient rights and the emancipation of women in the abortion cases.[99] The pose recalled what he told Jenkins more than a decade before explaining, as much as he ever did, what he thought his role and his lodestar were: "I think we're there to try to do justice to [the litigant] as well as to develop a great, overlying cloud of legal theory." Blackmun was happy, he told Koh, to be known as someone who fought for individual rights.

Harry Blackmun may have honestly believed that he could not locate his jurisprudence in theoretical terms that would satisfy academic critics. In any event, he never tried. Instead, in public he rhetorically defended what Morris called his "deeply held beliefs" with a degree of self-deprecation that approached self-martyrdom. A student of classical rhetoric would call the trope an appeal to ethos, trying to convince the audience by focusing on the character of the speaker. Unlike William Brennan, Harry Blackmun left no theoretical legacy, so his beliefs died with him. Like his listeners, whom he self-consciously softened up by recalling the cruel epithets that had been shouted or written to him, one is tempted to respond, "Poor Harry!" Yet if the Oral History demonstrates nothing else, for all the agony and melancholy, Harry Blackmun believed that he had satisfied Socrates' injunction about living a good life. When Blackmun died, he was interred at Arlington National Cemetery, but by his direction some of his ashes were spread privately at locations that he felt had shaped that life: the grounds of the Court, of his family home in Rochester, Minnesota, of the Mayo Clinic, of his vacation cottage on Spider Lake, Wisconsin, and of the Aspen Institute.[100]

---

[97] Id at 113.

[98] Id at 136, 209 ("never thought" about the connection between *Roe* and *Bowers*), 371 (same).

[99] Id at 205.

[100] Greenhouse at 248.

APPENDIX*

JUSTICE AND SOCIETY SEMINAR
Syllabus of Readings
July 15–28, 1979

BACKGROUND READINGS PRIOR TO SEMINAR

Justice is, or at least should be, the central concept of the legal system. The background readings introduce the two dominant themes of justice, utilitarianism and natural rights.

H. L. A. Hart, The Concept of Law, ch. VIII (excerpt)
John Stuart Mill, Utilitarianism, chs. 2, 5
John Rawls, A Theory of Justice, chs. I–III (excerpts)

PART ONE
PERSPECTIVES ON JUSTICE AND THE
RELATIONS OF LAW AND MORALITY

FIRST DAY

Civil disobedience as a statement of conscience raises the classic conflict between individual perceptions of justice and the regularity of the legal order. We consider initially the first occasion on which the issue was faced as a self-conscious philosophical issue, in Plato's Crito, and then in readings and cases that raise the problem in more modern form.

Plato, Crito
John Rawls, A Theory of Justice, ch. VI (excerpt)
Henry David Thoreau, On Civil Disobedience
Walker v. Birmingham, 388 U.S. 307 (1967)
Martin Luther King, "Letter from Birmingham City Jail"

SECOND DAY

The relationship between law and morality is raised in a highly pragmatic context when a judge must decide a hard case whose outcome depends on concepts of morality that are either not clearly defined in existing precedent or are defined in ways that are morally unacceptable to the judge. To what extent may the judge rely on his/her own concept or morality, and to what extent is the judge bound by the morality of the marketplace?

Regina v. Dudley and Stephens, Queens Bench Division, 1884, 14 Q.B.D. 273

---

* Syllabus, Justice and Society Seminar (1979), Aspen Institute, box 1483, HABLC (reproduced in approximate facsimile format). The syllabus is an expanded adaptation—by Morris, primarily, and Blackmun—of a preliminary reading list prepared by David A. J. Richards. Id. See also box 1367 id.

Lon L. Fuller, "The Case of the Speluncean Explorers," 62 Harv.
L. Rev. 616 (1949) (excerpt)
Repouille v. United States, 165 F.2d 152 (2d Cir. 1947)
Gregg v. Georgia, 428 U.S. 143 (1976) (excerpts)
Robert M. Cover, Justice Accused: Antislavery and the Judicial
Process, (1975) (excerpt)
Optional background reading:
Herman Melville, Billy Budd. (Cover, in Justice Accused, supra, argues
that the dilemma of Captain Vere in Billy Budd is modeled after the
dilemma faced by Melville's father-in-law, Justice Shaw, one of the an-
tislavery judges about whom Cover writes.)

PART TWO
JUSTICE AND INSTITUTIONAL COMPETENCE
(ADJUDICATION VERSUS LEGISLATION
AND/OR EXECUTIVE ACTION)

THIRD DAY
    If justice is the general moral aim of the legal system, how do
different institutions (courts, legislatures, executive branch officials) differ in their capacities to effectuate this aim? The Hart and Sacks readings
present the problem of the failure of New York State courts to develop
the tort right to privacy, the subsequent difficulties in developing the
right legislatively, and the related problem of the expansive judicial construction of a federal statute. Most lawyers agree with the Hart-Sacks'
criticism of the judicial failure to develop the right to privacy, but recent
commentary has questioned the general theory by which Hart and Sacks
supported their view: first, an attack on the theory's conservatism in view
of developments in public law litigation (Chayes); and second, an attack
on the theory's utilitarianism in view of the independent significance of
rights in the adjudication of hard cases (Dworkin).
    Hart and Sacks, The Legal Process (excerpt)
    Jones v. Alfred H. Mayer Co., 392 U.S. 409 (1968) (excerpt)
    Abram Chayes, "The Role of the Judge in Public Law Litigation,"
    89 Harv. L. Rev. 412 (1976) (excerpt)
    Ronald Dworkin, Taking Rights Seriously, ch. 4 (excerpt)

PART THREE
JUSTICE AND AMERICAN CONSTITUTIONALISM:
THE PRIORITY OF FREE SPEECH AND
LIBERAL TOLERANCE FOR ALTERNATIVE LIFE STYLES

FOURTH DAY
    American constitutionalism makes special claims about the pri-
ority of adjudication over legislative and executive power. The readings

for the fourth day examine recent moral arguments in support of this general claim, and the particular priority of free speech and religious tolerance among constitutional values. Two concrete free speech problems are examined: free speech versus the outrage of Holocaust victims, and free speech versus obscenity.

John Stuart Mill, On Liberty, chs. I–II (excerpt)

John Rawls, A Theory of Justice, ch. IV (excerpt)

Collin v. Smith, 578 F. 2d 1197 (7th Cir.), cert. denied, 99 Sup. Ct. 291 (1978)

Paris Adult Theatre I v. Slaton, 413 U.S. 49 (1973) (excerpt)

D. A. J. Richards, The Moral Criticism of Law (excerpt)

FIFTH DAY

Since John Stuart Mill's On Liberty, a central claim of liberalism, in addition to the primacy of free speech, has been that the scope of the criminal law must be restricted in order not to criminalize acts on the basis of conventional standards of disgust per se. In England the battle between liberalism and its critics took the form of the Hart-Devlin debate over the recommendation, now part of the law of England, to decriminalize consensual adult homosexuality and prostitution. In the United States, the issue has been posed by the recent failure of the Supreme Court to extend the constitutional right to privacy to consensual adult homosexuality. Would the same right to privacy apply to prostitution, use of soft drugs, cases of euthanasia, and the like, as some commentators claim?

John Stuart Mill, On Liberty, chs. III-IV (excerpt)

Patrick Devlin, The Enforcement of Morals, 4, 6–18, 20–23 (1959)

Edward H. Levi, "The Collective Morality of a Maturing Society, "30 Wash. & Lee L. Rev. 379 (1973) (excerpt)

H. L. A. Hart, "Immorality and Treason," 62 Listener 162–163 (July 30, 1959)

H. L. A. Hart, Law, Liberty and Morality (excerpt)

Gerald Dworkin, "Paternalism" (excerpt)

PART FOUR
DISTRIBUTIVE JUSTICE

SIXTH DAY

Since Aristotle, problems of justice have been divided into questions of distributive and retributive justice. Recent theories of justice focus on the justifiability of inequalities in distributive shares. These views range from the extreme egalitarianism of Marxism, to sharp constraints on inequalities in the form of Rawls' difference principle, to

Nozick's acceptance of extreme inequalities if they are the product of work-based merit.

John Rawls, A Theory of Justice, ch. V (excerpt)
Robert Nozick, Anarchy, State and Utopia (excerpt)
Kai Nielsen, "Class and Justice" (excerpt)
Arthur M. Okun, "Equality and Efficiency"

SEVENTH DAY

For Americans, a central case of injustice has been the deprivation of various benefits on the basis of racial prejudice. After Brown v. Board of Education, the courts and commentators struggled to articulate a neutral principle which might justify Brown while permitting the use of racial classifications for ameliorative purposes of compensatory justice. This problem is at the core of the recent Bakke decision and the Weber case.

Report of the National Advisory Commission on Civil Disorders (Kerner Commission Report) (1968) (excerpt)
Vann Woodward, The Strange Career of Jim Crow (excerpt)
Herbert Wechsler, "Toward Neutral Principles of Constitutional Law," 73 Harv. L. Rev. 1 (1959) (excerpt)
Alexander Bickel, The Least Dangerous Branch (excerpt)
Alexander Bickel & Philip Kurland, Brief of the Anti-Defamation League of B'Nai B'Rith Amicus Curiae, De Funis v. Odegaard (excerpt)
University of California Regents v. Bakke (excerpt)
McGeorge Bundy, "Beyond Bakke," Atlantic Monthly (Nov. 1978)
Brief for the United States and the Equal Employment Opportunity Commission, United Steelworkers of America v. Weber (excerpt)

EIGHTH DAY

Is the injustice of sexism on a par with the injustice of racism? Should the constitutional tests, designed to combat racism, be comparably used against sexism? What are the relevant differences, and how should policies combating sexism take account of them? The readings for the eighth day begin with John Stuart Mill's and Virginia Woolf's remarkable attacks on sexism and then address the contemporary constitutional issues.

John Stuart Mill, The Subjection of Women (excerpts)
Virginia Woolf, A Room of One's Own (excerpts)
Frontiero v. Richardson, 411 U.S. 677 (1973)
Richard A. Wasserstrom, "Racism, Sexism, and Preferential Treatment: An Approach to the Topics," 24 U.C.L.A. L. Rev. 581 (1977) (excerpt)

PART FIVE
RETRIBUTIVE JUSTICE

NINTH DAY

A central issue of retributive justice is the degree to which the criminal law may justly be used in the regulation of wrongdoing, in particular, the appropriateness of criminal punishment for a strict-liability offense imputed to a corporate officer. The classical view in criminal law is that it is unjust to apply criminal sanctions to strict-liability offenses (Packer), yet the Supreme Court has permitted such sanctions. Should criminal penalties be more aggressively used against corporate wrongdoing in order to increase the level of personal responsibility in corporate bureaucracies?

Herbert Packer, The Limits of the Criminal Sanction (excerpt)
United States v. Park, 421 U.S. 658 (1975) (excerpt)
Christopher Stone, "Why the Law Can't Do It," in Where the Law Ends
Arthur S. Miller, "Courts and Corporate Accountability" (excerpt)
Gilbert Geis, "Deterring Corporate Crime"

TENTH DAY
INTERNATIONAL JUSTICE AND HUMAN RIGHTS

To what extent can or should concepts of justice be applied to the relations between and among states? Presumably, the idea of just wars implies that some range of principles of justice are internationally applicable (Walzer). If so, should these ideas apply to international economic distribution? (Tucker).

The Universal Declaration of Human Rights and related covenants indicate an international consensus on the weight and, to some extent, on the scope of the idea of human rights (Henkin). Nonetheless, political sovereignty may in various ways blunt the critical edge of the idea of human rights as applied to states (Emerson). In addition, some commentators from the West believe that the coinage of international human rights is debased by the inclusion of social and economic rights and question the Carter human rights policy to the extent it does not discriminate among kinds of violations of human rights and possibly endangers larger political goods like détente with the Soviet Union (Frankel).

Michael Walzer, Just and Unjust Wars (excerpt)
Robert W. Tucker, The Inequality of Nations (excerpt)
Universal Declaration of Human Rights
Louis Henkin, The Rights of Man Today (excerpt)
Rupert Emerson, "The Fate of Human Rights in the Third World," World Politics, July 1975
Charles Frankel, Human Rights and Foreign Policy (excerpt)

ELEVENTH DAY
JUSTICE AND THE LAWYER'S ROLE
If justice is the central aim of the law, what is the proper role of the lawyer in effectuating justice? Are lawyers professionally required to do things which would be unethical if they were private persons? (Monroe Freedman). Or, does our system of justice wrongly insist that lawyers be too adversarial and judges too passive? (Judge Frankel). Certainly, in some contexts, the adversarial conception of the lawyer's role is clearly misplaced (Hazard). In general, can the role of lawyers as professionals be defended? (Wasserstrom). If the lawyer is the necessary instrument of justice, should legal services be regarded as a public good that should be equitably distributed, as Judge Frankel has recently urged?

> Monroe H. Freedman, "Professional Responsibility of the Criminal Defense Lawyer: The Three Hardest Questions," 64 Mich. L. Rev. 1469 (1966).
> Marvin E. Frankel, "The Search for Truth: An Umpireal View," 123 U. Pa. L. Rev. 1031 (1975) (excerpt)
> Geoffrey C. Hazard, Jr., Ethics in the Practice of Law (excerpt)
> Richard Wasserstrom, "Lawyers as Professionals: Some Moral Issues," 5 Human Rights 1 (1975) (excerpt)
> Marvin E. Frankel, "Justice: Commodity or Public Service" (1978)

TWELFTH DAY
Review and critique.

RONALD K. L. COLLINS
AND DAVID M. SKOVER

CURIOUS CONCURRENCE: JUSTICE
BRANDEIS'S VOTE IN WHITNEY v
CALIFORNIA

> From the tenor of the opinion . . . one would anticipate that
> Justice Brandeis must end up in dissent. In fact, however, he
> concurs in affirming the conviction of Miss Whitney. This
> outcome leaves us with a train of puzzles as to what he has been
> saying. (Harry Kalven, Jr.)[1]

On May 16, 1927, a unanimous Supreme Court affirmed California's conviction of Charlotte Anita Whitney for criminal syndical-

Ronald K. L. Collins is Scholar, First Amendment Center, Arlington, Virginia. David M.
Skover is Dean's Distinguished Research Scholar and Professor of Law, Seattle University
Law School.

AUTHORS' NOTE: We sincerely thank Geoffrey Stone, who encouraged this article and
then shepherded it through the editorial process, and Martin Redish and Hans Linde,
who gave valuable suggestions to improve the piece. Our appreciation goes, as well, to
Dean Elena Kagan of the Harvard Law School, and David Warrington and Edwin Moloy
of Special Collections at the Harvard Law School Library, for permission to reprint various
items from the Louis Brandeis Papers. We are grateful to William Eigelsbach of Special
Collections at the University of Tennessee Library, who assisted our research in the Edward
T. Sanford Materials Collection, and to Vanessa Yarnell, who enabled our research at the
U.S. Supreme Court library. This article is dedicated to our friend and colleague Steven
Shiffrin—a wonderful soul who, like Harry Kalven before him, honors the "worthy tra-
dition" by keeping alive the fighting spirit of dissent. Steve: this one is for you.

[1] Harry Kalven, Jr., *A Worthy Tradition: Freedom of Speech in America* 164 (Harper &
Row, 1988).

ism.[2] The patrician social activist was known both for her family's privileged status and for her allegiance to Leftist principles. She was a member of California's Communist Labor Party, which led to her arrest for organizing and participating in a group that advocated criminal syndicalism. After the Court's ruling, the fifty-nine-year-old dissident faced up to fourteen years in prison. Only a gubernatorial pardon would change her fate.

Justice Louis Brandeis—the great dissenter, advocate of civil liberties, and champion of free speech—joined in that judgment. Nonetheless, he penned a remarkable concurring opinion, now hailed as "a brilliant exposition of the new philosophical defense of political dissent."[3] The opinion has been celebrated as one of the most conceptually influential and rhetorically powerful justifications for First Amendment liberties. That seminal concurrence has been described as "arguably the most important essay ever written, on or off the bench, on the meaning of the first amendment,"[4] and as "rank[ing] among the most frequently cited [opinions] ever written by a Supreme Court Justice."[5]

Brandeis's memorable concurrence has been the focus of much scholarly analysis. In 1988, Vincent Blasi authored a Talmud-like line-by-line exegesis of most of Brandeis's words.[6] Other commentators, such as Bradley Bobertz,[7] Ashutosh Bhagwat,[8] David Rabban,[9] and Cass Sunstein,[10] wrote of the significance of the *Whitney* concurrence in the evolution of First Amendment theory and doctrine. Still others, like Thomas Emerson[11] and Rodney Smolla,[12]

---

[2] *Whitney v California*, 274 US 357 (1927).

[3] Mark A. Graber, *Transforming Free Speech: The Ambiguous Legacy of Civil Libertarianism* 100 (California, 1991).

[4] Vincent Blasi, *The First Amendment and the Ideal of Civic Courage: The Brandeis Opinion in Whitney v. California*, 29 Wm & Mary L Rev 653, 668 (1988).

[5] Bradley C. Bobertz, *The Brandeis Gambit: The Making of America's "First Freedom," 1909–1931*, 40 Wm & Mary L Rev 557, 645 (1999) (footnote omitted).

[6] See Blasi at 668–97 (cited in note 4).

[7] See Bobertz at 641–47 (cited in note 5).

[8] See Ashutosh A. Bhagwat, *The Story of Whitney v. California: The Power of Ideas*, in Michael C. Dorf, ed, *Constitutional Law Stories* 418–520 (Foundation, 2004).

[9] See David M. Rabban, *Free Speech in Its Forgotten Years* 365–71 (Cambridge, 1997).

[10] See Cass R. Sunstein, *Democracy and the Problem of Free Speech* 26–28 (Free Press, 1993).

[11] See Thomas I. Emerson, *The System of Freedom of Expression* 106 (Vintage, 1970).

[12] See Rodney A. Smolla, *Free Speech in an Open Society* 105–06 (Knopf, 1992).

depicted Brandeis's handiwork as a brilliant foreshadowing of a more promising future for freedom of speech.

Neither these nor the many other commentaries on the *Whitney* case, however, have devoted extensive attention to the following question: Given Brandeis's faith in speech freedoms, why did he *concur* in the judgment of the Court in *Whitney v California*? When commentators have addressed that question at all, they have given variations on the same simple answer: Brandeis (joined by Holmes) concurred with the majority, "but *only* because the question of freedom of expression had not been raised sufficiently at trial to qualify as an issue on appeal."[13] Virtually everyone has accepted, with little or no question, Justice Brandeis's assertion[14] that jurisdictional impediments necessitated his vote in the case.[15]

But what if those commentators (and many others) were too credulous? What if such jurisdictional impediments were more deliberately chosen than doctrinally compelled? Or what if there were jurisdictional problems, but of a rather different order than Justice Brandeis had suggested? What if Brandeis were wrong in the reasons he tendered for voting to uphold Ms. Whitney's conviction? Such queries raise yet larger questions: Is it possible that the *Whitney* case was far more complex than Brandeis's concurrence suggested?

Much as we admire Louis Brandeis's eloquent and compelling First Amendment jurisprudence in *Whitney*, we find his jurisdictional and substantive arguments suspect. For that matter, we find it difficult to believe that the learned Brandeis was entirely unmindful of the shortcomings of those arguments. Given such shortcomings, we consider Brandeis's opinion to be a most curious concurrence. It is curious in its depiction of the facts and the law of the case, and it is equally curious when considered alongside other

---

[13] Juliet Dee, *Whitney v. California*, in Richard A. Parker, ed, *Free Speech on Trial* 38–39 (Alabama, 2004) (emphasis added).

[14] 274 US at 379–80 (Brandeis concurring).

[15] See, e.g., Daniel A. Farber, *The First Amendment* 61 (Foundation, 1998); Martin Shapiro, *Whitney v. California*, in Leonard W. Levy, Kenneth L. Karst, and Dennis J. Mahoney, eds, *The First Amendment: Selections from the Encyclopedia of the American Constitution* 135 (Macmillan, 1990); Philippa Strum, ed, *Brandeis on Democracy* 238 (Kansas, 1995) ("Brandeis wrote a concurrence rather than a dissent because Whitney's lawyers had not argued that the statute was an unconstitutional limitation on speech that presented no clear and present danger to the state, which were the grounds on which he would have overturned the conviction. Brandeis felt constrained to follow the Court's rule that it would not decide a case on the basis of an argument not made by the attorneys."); Kermit L. Hall, William M. Wiecek, and Paul Finkelman, *American Legal History: Cases and Materials* 419 (Oxford, 1991).

opinions penned by Justice Brandeis. For those reasons, we aim to provide a more searching examination of Brandeis's vote in *Whitney*.

It is a largely overlooked fact: what Brandeis did in *Whitney* must be viewed against the backdrop of what he did in *Ruthenberg v Michigan*, a 1927 unpublished First Amendment case. In his *Ruthenberg* dissent, Brandeis first introduced the lofty free-speech principles that later found their way into his *Whitney* concurrence. More important for our purposes, however, is the irony that the far more radical creed, conduct, and associations of Charles Ruthenberg won Brandeis's First Amendment toleration, whereas the relatively benign behavior and associations of Anita Whitney did not; and that similar criminal syndicalism prosecutions resulted in different votes by Brandeis. Why is this so?

The answer to that question is tied to the fact that the First Amendment story of Anita Whitney is inextricably linked to that of Charles Ruthenberg. And a fascinating story it is, both in law and history. It involves, in various ways, an array of characters ranging from a U.S. Supreme Court Justice (James McReynolds) to a lawyer for the Hearst newspapers (John Francis Neylan) to two civil liberties appellate lawyers (Walter Pollak and Walter Nelles) to a Brandeis law clerk (Walter Landis) to an Alameda County prosecutor (Earl Warren) and finally to a California governor (Clement Calhoun Young). More significantly, this story establishes that generations of lawyers and scholars remained oblivious to the obvious, and let Brandeis's rhetoric divert them from what they might otherwise have noted about his reasoning. Finally, this story shows how, even as Brandeis sought to justify his concurrence on procedural grounds, he ended by concluding that Ms. Whitney's conviction had to be sustained *on the merits*.

I. The Free-Speech Story of Charles Ruthenberg and Anita Whitney

Charles Emil Ruthenberg and Charlotte Anita Whitney both castigated the abuses of American capitalism and imperialism, and demanded that the constitutional guarantees of free speech and association protect their right to do so. Both suffered the indignities and penalties of social intolerance, police harassment, criminal prosecution, and judicial sanction for advocating dissident beliefs and associating with communist groups. And both asked the United

States Supreme Court to safeguard their expressions of defiance, and were rebuffed.

Their similarities notwithstanding, the differences between them were stark and significant. Ruthenberg was a commoner from an immigrant family; Whitney was upper-middle class and from a distinguished bloodline. Ruthenberg found his radical roots early on in life—preaching on street corners, supporting labor strikes, organizing antiwar demonstrations, recruiting and training party workers, and campaigning for office as a socialist candidate; Whitney came to her dissident beliefs much later, after devoting years of service as a social worker, probation officer, political lobbyist, suffragette, civil rights activist, and civic league president. As national executive secretary of the Communist Party, Ruthenberg gained a reputation as the "most arrested red in America,"[16] reportedly with more than sixty indictments pending against him at one time; Whitney was arrested only once, on charges of aiding and abetting criminal syndicalism as a member of the Communist Labor Party of California, and that after having delivered an address to the Women's Civic Center of Oakland about the economic and political disenfranchisement of African-Americans and the nation's abhorrent practices of lynching. And, more central to our purposes, Justice Brandeis raised a First Amendment lance in Ruthenberg's defense against criminal syndicalism charges, but raised a shield for the state when Whitney was similarly charged. The free-speech story of Charles Ruthenberg and Anita Whitney is a study in contrasts, and an ironic tale of how a notorious dissident was lost to legal history whereas a minor figure was catapulted into it.

A. THE YOUNGER YEARS

On July 7, 1867, Charlotte Anita Whitney was born in San Francisco into an influential and refined family. She could count five Mayflower pilgrims on her father's side; on her mother's side, the Dutch Van Swearingen family, who settled in 1640 in Maryland, could claim two American Revolutionary officers, one a colonel in the Virginia militia who produced a line of genteel slave

---

[16] This title was coined by the *Chicago Daily Tribune* in a report on Ruthenberg's arrest in Chicago after a telegram informed the Illinois authorities that he had been indicted in New York for violation of the state's criminal syndicalism act. See *Most Arrested Red "in America" Is Seized Again*, Chicago Daily Tribune (Dec 2, 1919), p 5 ("It is said at present he has more than sixty indictments pending against him.").

owners. Anita's father, who suffered health conditions, escaped the climate of New England by migrating to California in the 1860s to begin a successful legal practice; there, he met his wife, and raised his children in an environment of comfort and culture. In the fall of 1885, George Whitney packed his daughter off to the East Coast to be educated at Wellesley. She spent her holidays with her aunt and uncle-in-marriage, the conservative Supreme Court Justice Stephen J. Field.[17]

Three years before Whitney entered college, Charles Ruthenberg was born in Cleveland, Ohio, in a small wooden-framed house. His birth on July 9, 1882, added a ninth child to the immigrant family that had left Germany only four months earlier. "Worker August Ruthenberg," as his father's name was recorded on his marriage license, was a longshoreman who raised his family in one of Cleveland's poorer districts. A socialist who believed in organized labor, August never seriously engaged in radical politics but exposed his son to Sunday afternoon discussions with his blue-collar friends on the philosophy of Schopenhauer, Hegel, and Schelling. Though Charles had wanted to go to high school and college, his father's premature death of typhoid on August 23, 1898, forced him to earn money for the family. He became a carpenter's assistant, working ten hours a day for $9.00 per week.[18]

In 1892–1893, while Ruthenberg learned his fourth- and fifth-grade lessons, Whitney engaged in social work at the College Settlement on New York's lower east side, where she was first exposed to real poverty. Anita had found "at last . . . something vital to be done."[19] Returning to California in 1901, she began a lengthy stint in charitable work. She served as secretary for the Associated Charities of Alameda County from 1903 to 1910, and spearheaded a successful campaign to oust racetrack betting. As

[17] The essential facts in this paragraph are substantiated in the two most important biographical works on Charlotte Anita Whitney. See Al Richmond, *Native Daughter: The Story of Anita Whitney* 17–21 (Anita Whitney 75th Anniversary Committee, 1942); Lisa Rubens, *The Patrician Radical: Charlotte Anita Whitney*, 65 Cal History 158, 160 (1986). See also Clare Shipman, *The Conviction of Anita Whitney*, 110 The Nation 365 (1920).

[18] The essential facts in this paragraph derive from the major biographical work on Charles Ruthenberg. See Oakley C. Johnson, *The Day Is Coming: Life and Work of Charles E. Ruthenberg* 7–15 (International Publishers, 1957). Lesser works on Ruthenberg include Elizabeth G. Flynn, *Debs, Haywood, Ruthenberg* (Workers Library, 1939), and Jay Lovestone, *Ruthenberg: Communist Fighter and Leader* (Workers Library, 1927). See also Theodore Draper, *American Communism and Soviet Russia: The Formative Period* 13–28, 40–57, 243–47 (Vintage, 1986).

[19] Quoted in Shipman at 160 (cited in note 17).

the first probation officer of Alameda County, she established efficient methods that set the standards for her successors. She helped orchestrate the 1911 victory for women's suffrage in California. As president of the California Civic League, she strove for laws securing minimum wages for women and children, the pasteurization of milk, the abatement of red-light prostitution districts, and the right of women to serve on juries.[20]

Not social work, but socialist work was the toil of Charles Ruthenberg in his early adulthood. At twenty-six years of age, he took the pledge at a Socialist Party meeting in January of 1909. That summer, he gave street-corner soapbox speeches on socialist principles, including the need to secure rights for laborers, women, and racial minorities. Somewhat self-conscious and halting as a speaker, he nevertheless demonstrated the knowledge, earnestness, and commitment that qualified him to head the Socialist ticket as a mayoral candidate in 1911 and a gubernatorial candidate in 1912. Ruthenberg used the power of his campaign to publicize the corruption of capitalist politics and to endorse the struggles of striking workers. Although he lost both elections, Ohioans cast more socialist votes in 1912 than any other state, and Ruthenberg's tally for the governorship was only a little less than the 89,930 for Eugene Debs's presidential candidacy. As organizer and secretary of Local Cleveland, Ruthenberg focused in 1913 on the induction of new party members and mass circulation of leaflets informing the public of socialist platforms. Late in that year, he was arrested for the first time at one of his street-corner speeches; though he was released without charge, this event marked the beginning of his ascent in the public consciousness—and police vigilance.[21]

Perhaps nothing propelled that ascent more than Ruthenberg's mobilization of public opinion in favor of worker strikes and in opposition to "imperialist wars." In 1914 (the same year that Anita Whitney joined the Socialist Party, after having witnessed the vicious treatment of organizers for the International Workers of the World), Ruthenberg initiated a statewide crusade on behalf of Ohio coal miners. In the week that World War I broke out in

---

[20] The facts on Anita Whitney's social and civic work are substantiated in Bhagwat at 409 (cited in note 8); Rubens at 160–61 (cited in note 17); Shipman at 365 (cited in note 17). See also Franklin Hichborn, *The Case of Charlotte Anita Whitney* 3 (unidentified publisher, 1920) (pamphlet on file with authors).

[21] The essential facts in this paragraph were derived from Johnson at 21–25, 28, 39–41, 44–45, 70–71, 80–81, 86 (cited in note 18).

Europe, he mounted a demonstration in Cleveland attended by 3,000 people who applauded his rebuke of war launched by capitalist profiteers. "Capitalism," he charged, "is fighting to replace democracy in this country with a military machine."[22] And Ruthenberg was prepared to fight back for the minds and bodies of Americans who might listen to his provocative rhetoric.[23]

B. THE WAR YEARS

"You Will Pay in Blood and Suffering" read the leaflet distributed by the Socialists of Cleveland on April 1, 1917. It was one of many warnings delivered at a series of antiwar rallies organized by Charles Ruthenberg to protest America's impending entry into World War I. When Congress declared war on Germany five days later, he composed a "Manifesto Against War," which the *Socialist News* published. "In all history," Ruthenberg wrote, "there has been no more unjustified war than that which this nation is about to engage in. . . . No greater dishonor has been forced upon a people than that which the capitalist class is forcing upon this nation against its will."[24] The Manifesto urged workers to engage in a general strike that would trammel the war economy and force the government to remain neutral.[25]

Ruthenberg had long foreseen public counteroffensives to suppress socialist demonstrations against American war policy. "We are being tested by fire," he notified the readers of the *Socialist News*.[26] Still, the heat had not yet been directed against him personally. That was to change in June of 1917. Under the pressure of local businesses and newspapers, the Printz-Biederman Company forced Ruthenberg to choose between his political activities or his purchasing-agent job; he chose socialism, and was fired. Even worse, a Cleveland federal grand jury indicted him, along with two of his colleagues, for obstructing the Conscription Act. The prosecution's star witness was a young man unknown to him, Alphons J. Schue, who had pled guilty for refusing to register after

---

[22] Quoted in Johnson at 103–04 (cited in note 18).

[23] The facts in this paragraph are found in Bhagwat at 409–11 (cited in note 8); Rubens at 161–63 (cited in note 17); Johnson at 87–91 (cited in note 18).

[24] Quoted in Johnson at 113 (cited in note 18).

[25] The essential facts in this paragraph were derived from id at 109–16.

[26] Quoted in id at 110.

having been induced by Ruthenberg's speeches not to comply with the law. With an unsympathetic jury, a guilty verdict was no surprise. Before his sentencing, Ruthenberg addressed the court: "I am not conscious of having committed any crime. The thing I am conscious of is having endeavored to inspire higher ideals and nobler lives. If to do that is a crime in the eyes of the Government, I am proud to have committed that crime."[27] He was sentenced to one year in the workhouse at Canton, Ohio.[28]

Out of jail on bail pending the appeal of his conviction, Ruthenberg mounted a vigorous mayoral campaign under the slogan: "For Socialism, Peace and Democracy." His address to an audience of 10,000 sympathetic listeners at the Cleveland Federation of Labor's picnic on Labor Day was meant to be one of the campaign's highlights. As Ruthenberg spoke, however, a cluster of rowdy soldiers pushed their way to the front of the crowd and demanded that he step down; they climbed onto the stage, shoving and punching anyone who tried to stop them. They succeeded in breaking up the assembly as thousands fled into the streets. Ultimately, Ruthenberg was not elected mayor, although he ran in third place with 27,865 votes, more than double his tally for the prior mayoral election. Two months later, in January of 1918, he entered prison after his antirecruitment conviction was upheld by the U.S. Supreme Court, with Justice Brandeis joining a unanimous judgment that rejected a host of alleged criminal procedural errors.[29] He was released in December of that year, after serving ten months on good behavior as a clerk-typist in the prison office.[30]

1919 proved a life-transforming year for both Charles Ruthenberg and Anita Whitney. That year, both left socialism to become communists, participated actively in the formation of communist party branches, and were arrested under state criminal syndicalism or anarchism statutes. In June, Ruthenberg joined ninety-four delegates from twenty states at the Left Wing Conference in New York to debate the means of overtaking the Socialist Party and transforming it into a Marxist working-class party governed by communist principles. At the September national

---

[27] Quoted in id at 121.

[28] The essential facts in the paragraph were derived from id at 117–21.

[29] See *Ruthenberg v United States*, 245 US 480 (1918).

[30] The essential facts in this paragraph were derived from Johnson at 122–37 (cited in note 18).

convention of the Socialist Party in Chicago, the left-wingers abandoned the convention to begin the American Communist movement, but the movement divided at birth into the Communist Party of America (the more radical branch, led by Ruthenberg as National Secretary) and the Communist Labor Party of America (with Alfred Wagenknecht as Executive Secretary). The CLP's National Program called for a "unified revolutionary working class movement in America," recommended the general strike as a political weapon, and endorsed the Industrial Workers of the World by declaring: "In any mention of revolutionary industrial unionism in this country, there must be recognized the immense effect upon the American labor movement of the propaganda and example of the Industrial Workers of the World, whose long and valiant struggle and heroic sacrifices in the class war have earned the affection and respect of all workers everywhere." It was this tribute to the IWW that would later prove to be Whitney's tribulation.[31]

Returning to California, the left-wing delegates were eager to win over the Socialists for the newly formed Communist Labor Party. Anita Whitney was among those who voted to change their affiliation. The first convention of the Communist Labor Party of California assembled at Loring Hall in Oakland on November 9; Whitney was selected as a member of the credentials and resolutions committees. After morale-boosting preliminaries—three cheers for the Bolsheviki and some spirited singing—the convention got down to business. Most of the convention's energy was consumed in a dispute over a resolution recognizing "the value of political action." Whitney strongly backed the "political action" resolution, but the majority feared that it represented no more than a reversion to the parliamentarianism of the Socialist Party and rejected it in favor of the more belligerent language of the CLP National Program. That vote did not deeply alienate Anita: she remained at the convention until it adjourned and subsequently attended at least one state executive committee meeting of the newly created party.[32]

---

[31] The facts in this paragraph are substantiated in Draper at 17–20 (cited in note 18); Johnson at 145–46 (cited in note 18); Richmond at 76–77, 110 (cited in note 17); Rubens at 163–64 (cited in note 17); Blasi at 3 (cited in note 4).

[32] The facts in this paragraph are substantiated in Richmond at 77–78 (cited in note 17); Blasi at 3–4 (cited in note 4); Shipman at 365 (cited in note 17); Friend William Richardson, *Case of Anita Whitney* 2–3 (California gubernatorial papers, Nov 28, 1925) (on file with authors). The official Communist Labor Party songbook included such wildly

The *Oakland Enquirer*'s next-day description of the convention set off chain reactions for months to come. "The American flag hung in one corner of the room," the story read. "But, during the noon hour, a huge red cloth was hung so that the American flag was no longer visible while the radicals prepared to adopt their un-American constitution." On November 11, 400 American Legion members and sympathizers raided Loring Hall; the rioters hurled furniture, pictures, charters, and insignia from the Communist Labor Party office windows, and set the place ablaze. (On the same day, a Legionnaire raid of the IWW hall in Centralia, Washington, ended in a lynching of one IWW member.) In all of this, the flames were fanned by national hysteria: having ordered his infamous "red raids," Attorney General Mitchell Palmer declared on November 14 that he had a list of 60,000 individuals, both citizens and aliens, under Justice Department investigation.[33]

Two weeks after the Loring convention, eleven key figures in the Communist Labor Party of California were arrested and charged with criminal syndicalism. Effective on April 30 of 1919, California's criminal syndicalism statute had been presented to the legislature as an emergency measure for the "immediate preservation of the public peace and safety," and had passed by unanimous vote of the senate and with only nine dissenting votes in the assembly. The act defined "criminal syndicalism" as "any doctrine or precept advocating . . . the commission of crime, sabotage . . . or unlawful acts of force and violence . . . as a means of accomplishing a change in industrial ownership or control, or effecting any political change"; and it provided that any person who "organizes or assists in organizing, or is or knowingly becomes a member of, any organization, society, group or assemblage of persons organized or assembled to advocate, teach or aid and abet criminal syndicalism" is guilty of a felony punishable up to fourteen years in prison.[34] The act's chief target was the International Workers of the World. The IWW had not only been

---

outlandish musical propaganda as the following: "Onward, Chrisian Soldiers! Rip and tear and smite! / Let the gentle Jesus bless your dynamite . . . . Onward, Christian Soldiers! Eat and drink your fill. / Rob with bloody fingers, Christ O.K.'s the bill."

[33] The facts in this paragraph were drawn from Richmond at 83–89 (cited in note 17); Hichborn at 11 (cited in note 20); *Oakland Veterans Raid Communists*, New York Times (Nov 13, 1919), p 1.

[34] For an annotated text of the California criminal syndicalism act, see 23 *California Jurisprudence* 1101–33.

instrumental in orchestrating labor strikes and slowdowns to improve conditions for industrial laborers and migratory farm workers, but it was suspected of more nefarious and surreptitious deeds in California: destroying hop kilns, burning wheat and hop fields, placing phosphor bombs in haystacks and barns, among other activities. With the criminal syndicalism law, California state authorities now had a forceful weapon against the IWW, and strike back it did: almost immediately, James McHugo, the IWW secretary in Oakland, and dozens of IWW adherents were indicted under the act. But the IWW was not to be the only target of prosecution for criminal syndicalism, as Charles Ruthenberg and Anita Whitney came to understand only too well.[35]

Ruthenberg was arrested on two separate occasions and under two separate state laws before the turn of the year. Shortly after Ohio's state legislature enacted its syndicalism statute, he was arrested in July of 1919 at the Cleveland Socialist headquarters and charged "with circulating copies of the *Messenger* . . . which advocates the Soviet form of government." With that indictment still pending, Ruthenberg was arrested again on December 1— this time in Chicago, following a telegram from New York authorities that he had been indicted under New York's 1902 Criminal Anarchy Law for publishing the Left Wing Manifesto, adopted at the June conference, that advocated the forceful eradication of established government. Whereas the Ohio charges were quietly dismissed, the New York prosecution was set for trial in October of 1920.[36]

In contrast, Anita Whitney could not have anticipated her criminal syndicalism arrest. The Oakland Civic Center, an organization of conservative middle- and upper-class "club women" who were the wives of distinguished doctors, lawyers, professors, and public officers, had asked the patrician communist to address them on November 28. She delivered a dynamic speech on "The Negro Problem in America," recounting the shameful history of slavery, deconstructing the theory of black inferiority, and comparing cur-

---

[35] The essential facts in this paragraph were drawn from Richmond at 82–83, 88 (cited in note 17); Richardson at 1 (cited in note 32); Woodrow C. Whitten, *Trial of Charlotte Anita Whitney*, 15 Pacific Historical Rev 286, 292 n 36 (1946).

[36] The essential facts in this paragraph derived from Johnson at 147–48 (cited in note 18); *Most Arrested Red "in America"* at 5 (cited in note 16); *Two Convicted of Anarchy: Ferguson and Ruthenberg Given State's Prison Sentences*, Washington Post (Oct 30, 1920), p 4; *Radicals' Release Ordered by Court*, New York Times (April 20, 1922).

rent disparities in the economic and political power of the races. What most grabbed Whitney's audience, however, was her shocking statistics on and descriptions of the abhorrent practice of lynching. Coming to a rousing conclusion, Whitney figuratively wrapped herself in red, white, and blue: "It is not alone for the Negro man and woman that I plead, but for the fair name of America that this terrible blot on our national escutcheon may be wiped away. . . . Let us then both work and fight to make and keep her right so that the flag that we love may truly wave 'O'er the land of the free / And the home of the brave.'"[37]

The club ladies applauded her; but upon her exit, she was arrested. Detective Fenton Thompson informed the stunned fifty-two-year-old communist stalwart that she was charged with criminal syndicalism. Although Whitney was at that time the treasurer of the Labor Defense League, an association formed to defend and employ counsel for penniless defendants, she had sacrificed so much of her own funds that she had insufficient resources to make bail for herself. While her friends scrounged for bond money, she was led to a cell, searched, and divested of her jewelry. To her indignant allies, she had a characteristically humble answer: "Why worry about it? They do it to others—hundreds of others. Why not to me?" On December 30, Whitney's information was filed: five counts, all drawn in the language of the relevant statute. The first count charged: "the said Charlotte A. Whitney . . . unlawfully, wilfully, wrongfully, deliberately and feloniously organize[d] and assist[ed] in organizing, and was, is, and knowingly became a member of an organization, society, group and assemblage of persons organized and assembled to advocate, teach, aid and abet criminal syndicalism." A demurrer to the information was overruled, her request for a bill of particulars was denied, and trial was set for January 27 of 1920. Thus began the case that would later be known as *Whitney v California*.[38]

---

[37] The essential facts in this paragraph were drawn from Richmond at 90–96 (cited in note 17); Reubens at 163–64 (cited in note 17); Shipman at 365–66 (cited in note 17); Anna Porter, *The Case of Anita Whitney*, New Republic (July 6, 1921), pp 165–66.

[38] The essential facts in this paragraph derived from Richmond at 96–98 (cited in note 17); Porter at 165–66 (cited in note 37); Shipman at 365–66 (cited in note 17); Brief for Plaintiff-in-Error, *Whitney v California*, U.S. Supreme Court October Term, 1925—No 10 (Sept 4, 1925), pp 7–9 (available at http://curiae.law.yale.edu).

C. WHITNEY'S WOES

Thomas H. O'Connor—a stocky man of intense energy, sharp intellect, and charm—was one of San Francisco's legal "stars," a criminal defense lawyer with a reputation for strategic brilliance and rhetorical eloquence. His friend, Fremont Older (the social activist editor of *The Call*), had so interested O'Connor in Anita Whitney's case that he offered to represent her pro bono as lead counsel. In contrast, his associate counsel, J. E. Pemberton (an aging Socialist and country judge), was much less confident of his competence as a trial lawyer. The O'Connor-Pemberton duo would be up against John U. Calkins and Myron Harris as the prosecuting attorneys, the latter a flag-waving orator. When O'Connor first entered the courtroom of Superior Judge James G. Quinn on Tuesday, January 27, 1920, the attorney did not appear his typically vigorous and assured self. Explaining that the distress and distraction caused by his young daughter's illness with influenza had prevented him from preparing sufficiently for trial, O'Connor asked Quinn for a continuance. The jurist would have none of it, and demanded that the trial commence. On the second day of voir dire, O'Connor himself was stricken with influenza, but the judge showed no mercy: the jury of six women, six men, and a female alternate had been chosen and were being held day and night in custody at the state's cost,[39] so the court was ready to hear opening statements.[40]

Myron Harris promised to prove the syndicalist nature of the national Communist Labor Party with which Anita Whitney was associated:

> We will show that although she, herself, in expressions of opinion, may have said that she was for changes by political action, . . . that her every attitude and everything that she has done

---

[39] Indeed, the jury's seclusion did cost Alameda County a pretty penny, although Judge Quinn might never have imagined the extent of the damages. One account puts it colorfully: "[The jury] left Alameda County aghast with a bill of $3,000 [recall: in 1920 dollars] to cover its expenses. . . . [T]hose who did the condemning ate hearty breakfasts, dinners and suppers, smoked fine cigars, kept themselves well groomed [with expensive haircuts, shaves, and toilet articles], dipped into popular magazines at random. . . . One paper commented: '[N]ext time it is anticipated that a trip to Palm Beach or the Canadian Rockies may be thrown in as a sort of diversion.'" Richmond at 113–14 (cited in note 17).

[40] The facts in this paragraph are substantiated in id at 98–101; Shipman at 366 (cited in note 17); Whitten at 288 (cited in note 35).

showed her to be a radical, not of the conservative Socialist
Party, but a member of the Communist Labor Party, which is
in violation of this law.[41]

When Harris mentioned the Third International at Moscow and
the International Workers of the World, it became clear that the
prosecution aimed to associate Whitney with the Communist
Party of California, through it with the national party, and through
the latter with the Russian party and the radical IWW. The theory
of the state's case, in short, was "stacked up like the House that
Jack Built. Miss Whitney was a member of the Communist Labor
party, this party had endorsed another party, and members of that
other party had been convicted of 'criminal syndicalism.'"[42]

O'Connor immediately objected: Without charging Whitney
with membership and participation in a group that itself engaged
in criminal syndicalism, the prosecution's case rested solely on
guilt by a nebulous chain of associations. He moved for a directed
verdict after the prosecution's opening statement, but Judge Quinn
denied the motion. Now, it was O'Connor's turn to show the
defense's hand. Whitney's innocence would be demonstrated by
her own political beliefs and personal interactions with the Communist Labor Party of California, all of which exhibited no purpose or objective that might be characterized, beyond a reasonable
doubt, as criminal syndicalism.[43]

On Saturday, February 7, O'Connor died of influenza. Without
O'Connor to resist them, the state's attorneys transformed Anita
Whitney's trial into a prosecution of the IWW. A mountain of
evidence—approximately 60 percent of that introduced by the
prosecutors—substantiated the IWW's syndicalist character.
There was everything from IWW songs to excerpts of IWW-
circulated literature to testimony by professional witnesses of the
IWW's suspected destruction of industrial and agricultural prop-
erty. The twenty-some witnesses for the prosecution had built a
formidable case against the IWW. But the IWW's connection to
Anita Whitney hung by a slender thread: the Communist Labor
Party of California, of which she was an organizing member, had

---

[41] Quoted in id.

[42] Shipman at 366 (cited in note 17). See also Brief for Plaintiff-in-Error at 10 (cited
in note 38).

[43] The essential facts in this paragraph were derived from id at 10–11; Whitten at 288–89
(cited in note 35).

adopted the Communist Labor Party of America's platform, which in its section on industrial unionism endorsed the IWW as an example of "the revolutionary industrial proletariat of America." In short, Anita Whitney was criminally responsible because of this tenuous nexus to the alleged syndicalist activities of certain members of the IWW.[44]

The defense relied on only two witnesses. First, there was Max Bedacht, a National Executive Committee member for the Communist Labor Party of America, who testified to a resolution passed at the national convention[45] that might cast doubt on the state's characterization of the CLP as a violent or terrorist organization. Second, there was Anita Whitney. Taking the witness chair on February 19, she asserted, in essence, that although she was a member of the Communist Labor Party of California, she neither understood nor intended it to be a vehicle of criminal syndicalism, and it was neither her purpose nor that of the state party to engage in violence, terrorism, or violation of any law.[46]

At the end of the trial, Judge Quinn instructed the jury as to the California law of criminal syndicalism, but refused several of the defense's requests for instructions. He did not instruct the jury that Whitney could be convicted only if she specifically intended to act in a way forbidden by the law.[47] Whitney's lawyer did not request that the court give an explicit "clear and present danger" instruction—that is, whether at the time of Whitney's active association with the Communist Labor Party of California, its activities (including the endorsement of the IWW) created a clear and present danger of the sort of sabotage, terror, or violence

---

[44] The essential facts in this paragraph were derived from Richmond at 109–12 (cited in note 17); Whitten at 291–92 (cited in note 35); Shipman at 366 (cited in note 17); Richardson at 11 (cited in note 32); Brief for Plaintiff-in-Error at 10–17 (cited in note 38). It should be noted that the U.S. Supreme Court record in *Whitney v California* (on file in the Supreme Court library) contains no complete transcript of the entire trial, although it does contain transcripts of excerpted testimony by a substantial number of the prosecution's witnesses.

[45] The resolution read in relevant part: "[T]he Communist Labor Party proclaims that the term 'direct action' is not associated with terrorism, violence or any other perverted meaning which capitalist lawmakers have given this phrase, but by it is meant such united action by the workers on the job which they may use in forcing concessions from the employing class directly without the use of the capitalist state." Cited in Whitten at 293 n 39 (cited in note 35).

[46] The essential facts in this paragraph derived from id at 292–93; Shipman at 366 (cited in note 17).

[47] See Brief for Plaintiff-in-Error at 15–17 (cited in note 38).

prohibited as "criminal syndicalism" by California law. The importance of that missing instruction would later become pivotal.

It took six hours on Friday, February 20, for the twelve jurors to reach consensus: guilty on count 1 (knowing membership or organization of an association "assembled to advocate, teach, aid and abet criminal syndicalism"). After the court refused to extend Whitney's bail of $2,000 pending an appeal, she was immediately taken to the county jail. When she returned to Judge Quinn's courtroom four days later to receive her sentence, the chamber was packed. "As (Anita) entered," reporter Alma Reed described in a special story for the *New York Times*, "I was present to witness the silent tribute of 300 men and women prominently identified with the leading social service and public welfare agencies of the state. They arose as she passed down the aisle to her seat, and they remained standing until sentence had been pronounced." Whitney's allies were pained to hear the penalty: imprisonment of one to fourteen years in San Quentin.[48]

Whitney's conviction and sentence inspired sharply worded critique by the press on both sides of the divide. The *Sacramento Bee* censured her for betraying her social and cultural status to consort with outlaws. In contrast, the *San Francisco Call* commended her: "The colonists were wrong when they burned witches; the people were wrong when they spat upon the abolitionists. And the people of California may be equally wrong when they send Anita Whitney to prison."[49] Moreover, a host of distinguished voices rose up to condemn the injustices done to Whitney. Religious leaders, politicians, and civic and civil rights organizations pointed to the Whitney case as a telling example of the perils of indiscriminate red-baiting.[50]

Anita Whitney was fifty-two years old when she was convicted, and she would be sixty years of age before she finally emerged from the shadow of prison. Her trek in the appellate process would prove arduous, unpredictable, and long, lasting more than seven years. The team of three who led that journey in its earliest stages were John Coghlan and J. E. Pemberton, her trial lawyers, headed

---

[48] The citations from Alma Reeds's narrative in this paragraph and the next were taken from Richmond at 114–16 (cited in note 17).

[49] The two newspaper quotations were reprinted in Reubens at 164 (cited in note 17).

[50] The facts in this paragraph derived from Richmond at 119–23 (cited in note 17).

by John Francis Neylan. A "respectable, conservative California legal talent," Neylan was a "Hearst lawyer and a prominent counsel for a large number of local corporations."[51] Whitney's appellate team filed an opening brief (July 21, 1920) and a closing brief (April 8, 1921) before the District Court of Appeal of California in San Francisco, one of the state's six intermediate courts of review.[52] Those briefs laid out a plan of attack against the criminal syndicalism statute itself, and against its application to the "refined, cultured, intellectual woman who has spent her life and private fortune in charitable and philanthropic work for the relief and betterment of her fellowmen."[53]

The appeal moved along three strategic fronts:

1. *The criminal information did not state the acts constituting a public offense with enough particularity or in ordinary and concise language:* Thus, Whitney was denied "the right to be sufficiently informed of the nature of the accusation against her, to enable her to prepare her defense."[54]

2. *The evidence presented by the prosecution at trial was insufficient to justify the verdict:* Anita Whitney may have held unconventional beliefs, but "mere opinion cannot be punished as a crime."[55] Moreover, "[t]here is not one scrap of evidence even remotely suggesting that she ever endorsed any act of violence either by [the Industrial Workers of the World or the Bolsheviks of Russia] or by individuals belonging to these organizations."[56]

---

[51] Paul L. Murphy, *The Constitution in Crisis Times: 1918–1969*, 85–86 (Harper & Row, 1972). But see Roger W. Lotchin, *John Francis Neylan: San Francisco Irish Progressive*, in *The San Frisco Irish: 1850–1976*, 86–110 (Smith McKay, 1978). Even so, this "progressive" was highly critical of FDR: "[T]he nation and its people have been brought to the verge of disaster by President Roosevelt." *Addresses by John Francis Neylan: The Politician, The Enemy of Mankind* (privately printed pamphlet, 1938).

[52] Appellant's Opening Brief in the California District Court of Appeal, First Appellate District—Division One, *The People of the State of California v Charlotte A. Whitney*, Criminal No 907 (July 21, 1920), reprinted as Exhibit A in Brief for Plaintiff-in-Error (cited in note 38); Appellant's Closing Brief in the California District Court of Appeal, First Appellate District—Division One, *The People of the State of California v Charlotte A. Whitney*, Criminal No 907 (April 8, 1921), reprinted as Exhibit B in Brief for Plaintiff-in-Error (cited in note 38).

[53] Appellant's Opening Brief at i (cited in note 52).

[54] Id at iii–xviii.

[55] Id at xix. See generally id at xix–xx.

[56] Appellant's Closing Brief at xxiv (cited in note 52). See generally id at xxiv–xxviii.

3. *The California criminal syndicalism act is void for vagueness:* If
it were "permissible to introduce in evidence manifestoes of
the Bolshevist Party of Russia to show the character of the
Communist Labor Party of Oakland," then the statute's
terms are too vague and indefinite to be susceptible to reasonable definition.[57]

All three arguments identified classic due process violations. No
specific First Amendment violations were alleged. Before the appellate court rendered its ruling, however, Whitney's counsel filed
a supplemental brief[58] to emphasize the federal unconstitutionality
of the California criminal syndicalism act and Whitney's conviction. "We desire at this time to raise herein a federal question,"
the brief asserted. "[M]ere membership in an organization, without
the doing or commission of any overt act is not a crime; it is a
constitutional right and privilege; and the legislature cannot otherwise provide. . . . By attempting to punish her for the exercise
of her legal and constitutional right, the state is abridging the
privileges and immunities of a citizen of the United States."[59]

None of the appellant's claims struck a chord with the California
District Court of Appeal. A three-judge bench unanimously upheld Whitney's conviction on April 25, 1922.[60] Running merely
five paragraphs, the opinion largely relied on California Supreme
Court precedent[61] to reject the appellant's due process claims. The
only memorable section of the opinion was the court's depiction
of Whitney's purposes, if only because of its overheated rhetoric:

> That this defendant did not realize that she was giving herself
> over to forms and expressions of disloyalty and was, to say the
> least, lending her presence and the influence of her character
> and position to an organization whose purposes and sympathies
> savored of treason, is not only past belief but is a matter with

---

[57] Id at xlvii.

[58] Supplemental Brief for Appellant in the California District Court of Appeal, First
Appellate District—Division One, *The People of the State of California v Charlotte A. Whitney*,
Criminal No 907 (July 21, 1920), reprinted as Exhibit C in Brief for Plaintiff-in-Error
(cited in note 38).

[59] Id at lvii–lviii.

[60] *People v Whitney*, 57 Cal App 449, 207 P 698 (1922).

[61] See *People v Taylor*, 187 Cal 378, 203 P 85 (1921) (upholding a criminal syndicalism
conviction on the basis that sufficient evidence existed for the jury to find that the Communist Labor Party of California, of which the defendant was an organizer and member,
constituted a syndicalist group within the meaning of the California law).

which this court can have no concern, since it is one of the conclusive presumptions of our law that a guilty intent is presumed from the deliberate commission of an unlawful act.[62]

The worst fears of her appellate counsel had come true: Unless this appellate ruling were overturned, Whitney had been tried and convicted, and her conviction might stand, "not for any act of her own," but because others with whom she was not proven "to have had the slightest dealings started fires and carried poisons in other parts of the State."[63] The California Supreme Court denied Whitney's petition for review[64] without issuing an opinion.[65]

Despite the slim chances for any case to be considered by the U.S. Supreme Court, there were good reasons why the Court might be interested in *Whitney v California*. The case had the potential to make new law. The Court had yet to decide whether the First Amendment rights of political speech and association applied against the states through the Fourteenth Amendment; it had yet to hold state regulation of expressive liberties to a higher standard than reasonableness; and it had yet to determine the circumstances in which a member of an organization should be held responsible for the group's unlawful conduct.

To raise the odds of winning, John Francis Neylan needed some heavyweights in the appellate bar to assist him. There was Walter Heilprin Pollak of New York, who would soon argue before the U.S. Supreme Court in *Gitlow v New York*[66] and later in *Powell v*

---

[62] 57 Cal App at 452, 203 P at 699.

[63] Appellant's Opening Brief at xxi (cited in note 52).

[64] Appellant's Petition for a Hearing by the Supreme Court, *The People of the State of California v Charlotte A. Whitney* (June 3, 1922) (available at http://curiae.law.yale.edu).

[65] Brief for Plaintiff-in-Error at 2 (cited in note 38).

[66] 268 US 652 (1925). The *Gitlow* decision upheld the conviction of a radical Socialist, who assisted the publication of the Left Wing Manifesto and the organization of the Communist Labor Party of America, under New York's criminal anarchy statute. In dicta, Justice Sanford's opinion of the Court *assumed* that liberties of speech and press were protected by the Fourteenth Amendment's Due Process Clause against impairment by a State. The majority determined, nevertheless, that a State, in the exercise of its police power, could punish utterances tending to incite crime or disturb the public peace. Enunciating what is known as the "bad tendency test," Sanford's opinion reasoned that a State might "suppress the threatened danger in its incipiency." He declared: "[The State] cannot reasonably be required to defer the adoption of measures for its own . . . safety until the revolutionary utterances lead to actual disturbances of the public peace of imminent and immediate danger of its own destruction."
New York's criminal anarchy statute was understood to import the legislature's determination that such utterances were so inimical to the general welfare and involved such danger of substantive evil that they could be penalized under the police power, and every

Alabama[67] (one of the famous Scottsboro cases).[68] Walter Nelles of New York also came on board. As counsel for the National Civil Liberties Bureau, he had edited a book on the federal Espionage Act cases[69] before his involvement in *Whitney*; he would argue *Gitlow* with Pollak; and subsequently he taught jurisprudence at the Yale Law School.[70]

The Supreme Court granted a writ of error. After the case record had been transferred to the Court, an unusual procedural twist occurred. Whitney's attorneys filed a stipulation of the parties before the California District Court of Appeal, and the court issued an order on December 9, 1924, that amended the record by including the following statement:

> The question whether the California Criminal Syndicalism Act (Statutes 1919, page 281) and its application in this case is repugnant to the provisions of the Fourteenth Amendment to the Constitution of the United States, providing that no state shall deprive any person of life, liberty, or property, without due process of law, and that all persons shall be accorded the equal protection of the laws, was considered and passed upon by this Court.[71]

---

presumption had to be indulged in favor of the validity of the statute. Because the statute did not penalize the utterance of abstract doctrine or academic discussion but rather denounced the advocacy of action for accomplishing the overthrow of organized government by unlawful means, it was constitutional as applied to the Left Wing Manifesto's advocacy of mass action progressively leading to industrial disturbances, mass strikes, and revolutionary mass action aimed at destroying organized parliamentary government.

[67] 287 US 45 (1932). See generally Dan T. Carter, *Scottsboro: A Tragedy of the American South* (Louisiana State University Press, 2nd ed, 1984).

[68] See *W. H. Pollak Dies; Leader at Bar, 53*, New York Times (Oct 3, 1940), p 25. First Amendment scholar Zechariah Chafee remarked of Pollak after his death: "It is hard to realize that a person so much alive as Walter Pollak can be dead. . . . He radiated generous enthusiasm for justice, delight in mental activity, unexpected flashes of wit. We have lost him when we need him most." Zechariah Chafee, Jr., *Walter Heilprin Pollak*, The Nation (Oct 12, 1940), pp 318–19. For an account by his son (later Dean of the Yale and University of Pennsylvania Law Schools and a federal judge), see Louis H. Pollak, *Advocating Civil Liberties: A Young Lawyer Before the Old Court*, 17 Harv CR-CL L Rev 1 (1982).

[69] Walter Nelles, *Espionage Act Cases: With Certain Others on Related Points* (National Civil Liberties Bureau, 1918). Nelles also edited *Law and Freedom Bulletins* (National Civil Liberties Bureau, 1920), including discussion of the 1917–20 prosecution and appeal of IWW members in Chicago under the federal Selective Service and Espionage Acts. See *Haywood v United States*, 268 F 795 (1920).

[70] See *Prof. Walter Nelles of Yale Law School: An Expert on Labor Injunction and Former Lawyer Here Is Dead at Age of 53*, New York Times (April 1, 1937), p 23.

[71] Petition for Rehearing, *Whitney v California*, U.S. Supreme Court October Term, 1925, No 10 p. 2 (available at http://curiae.law.yale.edu).

Securing such a state court "certificate" and amending the case record for federal high court review was a lawyerly move that Walter Pollak and Walter Nelles knew well. Indeed, they had done exactly that in *Gitlow*.[72] Now, once again, the savvy appellate advocates were looking down the road to avoid any possible procedural hurdles. The adequacy of the California District Court of Appeal "certificate" was an issue that would cause legal delay and confusion, but ultimately would make the Supreme Court's review possible.

D. RUTHENBERG'S RUIN

While Anita Whitney's criminal syndicalism case was still under consideration in the California District Court of Appeal, Charles Ruthenberg's criminal anarchy case was just beginning in the New York State trial court system, where he faced charges for his activities as national secretary of the Communist Party of America. The prosecution relied heavily upon Ruthenberg's publication of the Left Wing Manifesto that appeared in *The Revolutionary Age* on July 5, 1919. Ruthenberg's defense "was to present frankly and fully his reasons for thinking and acting as he did,"[73] ensuring that the state did not mischaracterize his views as incitement for violence. The jury convicted him, and he was sentenced to five to ten years of hard labor at the Sing Sing state penitentiary. Eighteen months later, the New York Court of Appeals reversed Ruthenberg's conviction on a technical statutory ground.[74]

Forty days later, Ruthenberg found himself once again on the wrong side of the bars—this time in St. Joseph, Berrien County, Michigan. The central executive committee of the Communist

---

[72] See note 66; see also Philip B. Kurland and Gerhard Casper, eds, 23 *Landmark Briefs and Arguments of the Supreme Court of the United States: Constitutional Law* 530 (University Publications of America, 1990).

[73] Johnson at 149 (cited in note 18).

[74] The essential facts in this paragraph derived from id at 149, 152–53; *Gitlow, Anarchist, Gets Limit Sentence*, New York Times (Feb 12, 1920), p 15; *Grand Jury to Pass upon Radicals Here*, New York Times (July 14, 1919), p 15; *New York Judge Orders Two Chicago Reds to Prison Cells*, Chicago Daily Tribune (Oct 30, 1920), p 12; *Two Convicted of Anarchy*, Washington Post (Oct 30, 1920), p 4; *Lawyer, a Convict, Argues for Release*, New York Times (April 15, 1922), p 6; *Radicals' Release Ordered by Court*, New York Times (April 20, 1922), p 15; *New York v Ferguson*, 234 NY 159, 136 NE 327 (1922) (reversing Ruthenberg's conviction because the jury was wrongly allowed to infer that he was a manager or proprietor of *The Revolutionary Age*, and thus subject to prosecution under the New York criminal anarchy statute).

Party of America had called a national delegate convention for late August of 1922. In advance of the convention, the seventy-five delegates began gathering on Tuesday, August 15, at an isolated summer resort in Bridgman, near St. Joseph; Ruthenberg aimed to reconcile differences among various factions to ensure united support at the convention for the newly formed Workers' Party. A veil of secrecy covered the event: the delegates met in a sand-dune amphitheater surrounded by woods; every individual was given an alias and a numbered portfolio for documents; all portfolios were collected and stored at night in two barrels that were sunken in the ground and covered with sand and natural debris; and all outside contact was forbidden.[75]

Delegates from the Comintern of Moscow, the Red Trade International of Moscow, and the Hungarian federation were there; but so was a mole, a delegate clandestinely working for the Bureau of Investigation in the U.S. Department of Justice. From August 15 to 22, the delegates debated and voted—until federal agents, tipped off to the event, were spotted near the meeting place. Suspecting an incipient police raid, the foreign delegates quickly exited and many others hurried off. Deputy U.S. marshals appeared on the morning of August 22 to arrest the assembly.[76]

The information filed against Ruthenberg charged that he "did voluntarily assemble with a certain society, group and assemblage of persons, to wit, the Communist Party of America, formed to teach and advocate the doctrines of criminal syndicalism."[77] The prosecution's main witness at trial was Francis Morrow, or "K-97," the government agent who was a delegate to the Communist Party's national convention. K-97 testified that Ruthenberg had attended the Bridgman convention as a member of the Central Executive Committee of the Communist Party of America, contravening the defense's claim that Ruthenberg had attended the meeting as an advocate for the adoption of an open and legal Workers' Party.[78]

---

[75] The essential facts in this paragraph were drawn from *People v Ruthenberg*, 229 Mich 315, 321–22; 201 NW 358, 359–60 (1924); Johnson at 154 (cited in note 18); *C. E. Ruthenberg, Head of Communists, Dead*, Washington Post (March 3, 1927), p 8.

[76] The essential facts in this paragraph derived from Johnson at 154–56 (cited in note 18); *People v Ruthenberg*, 229 Mich at 323–23; 201 NW at 360 (cited in note 75).

[77] *People v Ruthenberg*, 229 Mich at 320; 201 NW at 359 (cited in note 75).

[78] The essential facts in this paragraph derived from Johnson at 163 (cited in note 18); *Accused Burns in Red Trial*, New York Times (April 21, 1923), p 15; *Links Ruthenberg to*

Ruthenberg testified about and entered into evidence the proposed program of the Workers' Party that he had introduced to the delegates at Bridgman. On the one hand, as the defendant pointed out, the program insisted that the party's function was to be overtly political, rather than covertly subversive: "The class struggle must take the form of a political struggle, a struggle for the control of the government." On the other hand, there was text that, at least in its tone, might be read as more threatening: "The Workers' party declares one of its chief immediate tasks to be to inspire in the labor unions a revolutionary purpose and to unite them in a mass movement of uncompromising struggle against capitalism." Similarly, the resolutions of a committee that Ruthenberg had steered, which were adopted unanimously at the Bridgman convention, had the same ambivalent quality; some appeared to distance the Workers' Party from the illegal Communist Party ("A legal C.P. is now impossible. Should conditions change only a convention can change the party's policy.") and others seemed to maintain that integral link ("The illegal Communist party must continue to exist and must continue to direct the whole Communist work.").[79]

Striving to dispel any negative implications that might be drawn from the Workers' Party program and resolutions, Ruthenberg insisted that, although the program endorsed the ultimate control of the American government by the working class, it did not advocate or teach crime, sabotage, violence, or other illegal forms of terrorism as the means to bring about that end. At most, the program did "nothing more than to predict that force, violence, civil war and bloodshed will be the inevitable consequence of the class struggle"[80] between the working class and the capitalist state. But Ruthenberg's characterization of his personal and his party's purposes was challenged, not only by K-97, but also by the damning inferences that could be derived from the illegal Communist Party's effective control of the legal Workers' Party agenda. To

---

Reds: "K-97" Asserts He Was a Delegate at Raided Convention, New York Times (April 24, 1923).

[79] All of the quotations in this paragraph referring to the Workers' Party program and the adjustment committee's resolutions derived from *People v Ruthenberg*, 229 Mich at 332–33, 336–37; 201 NW at 363–65.

[80] Transcript of Record in the Supreme Court of the United States, October Term, 1926, *Charles E. Ruthenberg, Plaintiff in Error v The People of the State of Michigan*, No 44, p 189 (filed Feb 19, 1925) (brief on file at the Library of the U.S. Supreme Court, Washington, DC).

that extent, the testimony of Jay Lovestone, the national secretary of the Communist Party of America, who had participated actively at the Bridgman convention, undercut the defense's theory of the case. Addressing the purposes of the Workers' Party, Lovestone stated unequivocally that "the members of the open party were to carry out the policies of the Communist party" and the "Workers' party . . . was in all respects a Communist organization."[81]

Throughout the trial, the defense had argued that Michigan's criminal syndicalism act, both on its face and as applied to Ruthenberg's participation at the Bridgman convention, violated state constitutional and federal Fourteenth Amendment guarantees of political speech and association. The defense would find yet other grounds for objection when Judge White denied its specific requests to charge the jury in conformity with its claims of constitutional liberties.

In view of the existing state of federal free-speech law, the trial court judge's instructions to the jury might well have been deemed relatively unassailable. The judge began by enumerating the task for the jurors:

> It is not disputed that the convention held near Bridgman was a meeting of the Communist Party of America, nor is it disputed that the respondent was present at that meeting; which leaves for your consideration these three questions: 1st. Was the Communist Party of America, at the time the respondent assembled with that organization . . . a society formed to teach and advocate criminal syndicalism? 2d. Was the Communist Party at the time and place in question an assemblage to further the alleged unlawful purposes of the organization? 3d. Did Charles E. Ruthenberg assemble with the Communist Party voluntarily, that is to say, with the conscious purpose and design to further and aid the teaching and advocacy by the Communist Party of the doctrines of criminal syndicalism?[82]

In regard to the first question, the judge elaborated on the difference between advocacy of communist sociopolitical theory and advocacy of criminal syndicalism:

> In order to establish that the Communist Party was at the time and place in question an organization which taught and ad-

---

[81] *People v Ruthenberg*, 229 Mich at 337–38; 201 NW at 365.

[82] Transcript of Record at 190 (cited in note 80).

vocated criminal syndicalism, the prosecution must satisfy you
from the evidence beyond a reasonable doubt, not alone that
this party taught the theory that the social forces now in operation would of their own momentum bring about an encounter of force between opposed social classes, but also that
this party taught and advocated crime, sabotage, violence and
terrorism as the method or one of the methods of accomplishing
the changes in the organization of society desired by the communists.[83]

Significantly, however, the judge refused two instructions requested by the defense that aimed to infuse the "clear and present
danger" test into the interpretation of the statute.[84] Considering
the evidence and the instructions, few were surprised when the
jury reached a verdict of guilty on May 2, 1923.[85]

Ruthenberg's brief to the Michigan Supreme Court was filed
on September 19, 1924.[86] It challenged the criminal syndicalism
act as unconstitutional on its face and as applied, under both the
Michigan Constitution and the federal Fourteenth Amendment,
on several grounds:[87]

---

[83] Id at 191.

[84] Rejected request no. 12 read:

> You are instructed, in further definition of the doctrines of criminal syndicalism,
> that the statute is directed against the teaching and advocacy of crime, sabotage,
> violence and other unlawful methods of terrorism as an immediate program of
> action. If you find from the evidence that the Communist Party, at the time and
> place alleged, was an organization which taught the desirability of revolutionary
> changes in our social institutions, but did not teach or advocate that anyone
> should proceed presently to commit acts of crime, sabotage, violence, or ter-
> rorism, then it is not established that the assemblage in question constituted a
> violation of the statute and you should declare the respondent not guilty.

And rejected request no. 13 read:

> [For there to be teaching and advocacy within the contemplation of the statute,]
> the time and circumstances must be such that the teaching or advocacy of the
> prohibited doctrines presents a clear and imminent danger that acts of crime,
> sabotage, violence or terrorism may result from the advocacy. If you find . . .
> that no circumstances have been presented in evidence making manifest a clear
> and imminent danger of such acts of criminal injury on account of the teachings
> and advocacies of the Communist Party, then your verdict should be not guilty.

Id at 199.

[85] Id at 237.

[86] *Ruthenberg Files Appeal*, New York Times (Sept 20, 1924), p 18.

[87] In addition to the claims enumerated in the text, Ruthenberg alleged that the trial
court erred by (1) overruling the defendant's challenge to a juror, (2) denying the defendant's motion for a bill of particulars, and (3) denying the defendant's motion to suppress
evidence found in his suitcase at the Bridgman convention on the basis that the state

1. *On its face, the Michigan criminal syndicalism act is void for vagueness:* the provisions of the Michigan statute "are too vague, uncertain and indefinite to form the basis of a prosecution for crime."[88]

2. *On its face, the Michigan criminal syndicalism act violates freedoms of speech and association guaranteed by the state constitution and the Fourteenth Amendment:* the Michigan statute punishes "as a felony the enunciation of a doctrine without the intent, the occasion, . . . or the imminent result of such enunciation," in violation of state and federal guarantees of free speech and association.[89]

3. *As applied, the Michigan criminal syndicalism act violates Ruthenberg's freedoms of speech and association guaranteed by the state constitution and the Fourteenth Amendment:* by the information or evidence adduced by the state at trial, it does not appear (*a*) "that the assemblage in question by any teaching or advocacy gave rise to imminent danger of criminal injury to any persons or property, or to any governmental establishment or operation, or to the public peace or welfare in any respect," and (*b*) "that there was any attempt or intent, either by the alleged unlawful assemblage or by [Ruthenberg] as a participant therein, to solicit, induce, incite or promote any acts of criminal injury under circumstances involving a clear and present danger of the consummation of such injury."[90]

These arguments were brushed aside by the Michigan Supreme Court. On December 10, 1924, the court unanimously upheld Ruthenberg's conviction. To the claim of vagueness, the court declared: "The naivete of this should make a Communist smile. One need read but little to discover what the terms sabotage and violence mean . . . . Sabotage has had a well understood meaning ever since French industrial workers threw their sabots, or wooden shoes, into machinery."[91] Ruthenberg's second claim of facial un-

---

violated his constitutional right against a wrongful search and seizure. The Michigan Supreme Court rejected these claims with dispatch. See *People v Ruthenberg*, 229 Mich at 326–31, 201 NW at 361–63.

[88] Transcript of Record at 236 (cited in note 80).

[89] Id.

[90] Id.

[91] *People v Ruthenberg*, 229 Mich at 325; 201 NW at 361.

constitutionality fared no better: "This statute reaches an abuse of the right to freely speak, write and publish sentiments, and is squarely within the accountability allowed to be exacted . . . . The reasons advanced here against the constitutionality of the act have been urged against similar acts in other jurisdictions and found to have no merit."[92]

Most of the court's vehemence was reserved for Ruthenberg's as-applied argument. Excerpting lengthy passages from the Workers' Party program and resolutions adopted at the Bridgman convention, borrowing pieces from Jay Lovestone's testimony, and much more, the court painted as colorful a portrait as possible of Ruthenberg's syndicalist status:

> Defendant was acting under orders from Moscow. He was pledged to obey such orders and, under this record, it taxes credulity too far to believe he was endeavoring to bring Communist doctrines and tactics within the law. . . . [His purpose] was to further the ends of the underground or illegal party, and that purpose and such ends center upon the destruction of republican or parliamentary form of government by direct action and criminal force.[93]

And what of "clear and present danger"? This, too, was dismissed with fervor:

> The Communists say they are but prophets of disorder, violence and destruction eventually to come. In the sweet bye and bye, they say, resistance to their schedule will lead to the shedding of blood but the guilt will rest upon those who fight to maintain government under the Constitution of the United States. But they are militant prophets, to say the least, with present activities toward fulfillment of what they prophesy. Prophecy of violence to come does not mantle present militant organization and criminal activities to hurry its advent.

> Quaint Old Thomas Fuller, 275 years ago, hit off defendant's plea of present innocent advocacy of eventual force and violence when he said: "It is dangerous to gather flowers that grow on the banks of the pit of hell, for fear of falling in; yea, they which play with the devil's rattles will be brought by degrees to wield

---

[92] *People v Ruthenberg*, 229 Mich at 323–24; 210 NW at 360.

[93] *People v Ruthenberg*, 229 Mich at 331–32, 339–40; 210 NW at 363, 365–66.

his sword; and from making of sport, they come to doing of mischief."[94]

On January 5, 1925, Ruthenberg was sentenced to serve between three and ten years in the Jackson state prison. He served only twenty days of his term before he was released. His attorneys had petitioned Justice Louis Brandeis for a writ of error enabling them to seek review in the U.S. Supreme Court of the Michigan court's judgment in *People v Ruthenberg*. Brandeis granted the writ of error on January 19, ordering that the writ would operate as a supersedeas upon providing a bond for $7,500. (Earlier, Justice James C. McReynolds had refused to grant Ruthenberg such a writ.) The bail bond was delivered and approved on January 26, and Ruthenberg was once again at liberty—just in time to deliver an address at the first annual Lenin memorial meeting in Madison Square Garden.[95]

II. THE SUPREME COURT STORY: THE TWO MINDS OF LOUIS BRANDEIS

The story of the Whitney and Ruthenberg appeals is the story of the two minds of Louis Brandeis. One case he didn't want to decide, but was forced to; the other he did want to decide, but was unable to. One case impelled him to apologetic concurrence; the other provoked him to uninhibited dissent. One case was to be resolved by procedural rules; the other on the merits with a new vision of the First Amendment. All of this changed unexpectedly—and the two minds of Louis Brandeis melded into one.

A. IF AT FIRST YOU DON'T SUCCEED . . .

With Anita Whitney's case still pending before the Supreme Court (and held over to be considered along with *Ruthenberg v Michigan* in the October term of 1925), her legal team mulled over the arguments that might finally win the day. Their brief focused

---

[94] *People v Ruthenberg*, 229 Mich at 353–54; 210 NW at 370.

[95] The essential facts in this paragraph were drawn from Johnson at 164–65 (cited in note 18); *Ruthenberg Is Sentenced*, Los Angeles Times (Jan 6, 1925), p 1; *U.S. High Court to Hear Plea of Ruthenberg*, Chicago Tribune (Jan 23, 1925), p 10; *Ruthenberg May Win Review by High Court*, New York Times (Jan 23, 1925), p 2; Order Allowing Writ of Error, in Transcript of Record at 241 (cited in note 80); *Ruthenberg Out on Bail: Released Pending Appeal, He Will Speak at Lenin Meeting Here*, New York Times (Jan 27, 1925), p 10.

on the state's infringement of Whitney's liberties of assembly, speech, and association protected under the Due Process Clause of the Fourteenth Amendment. Specifically, the brief contended that a "statute which is applied to attach penal consequences to joining an organization still in its formative stage, because that organization subsequently acquires over defendant's protests a questionable character, imposes a 'previous restraint' upon the right of assembly." Moreover, the brief argued that the Communist Labor Party of California's convention of November 9, 1919, had no quality of incitement, and that Whitney's conviction would have violated due process even if she had participated in all the purposes and activities of the convention. This was so because nothing short of "incitement to violent action" can be punished without infringing the rights of free speech and assembly. Distinguishing Whitney's case from *Gitlow*, in which the Left Wing Manifesto was held to be a call to illegal mass action, the brief stressed that the program of Whitney's party (recognizing the "long and valiant struggles and heroic sacrifices" of the IWW "in the class-war") was no more than a "generalized statement of collective sympathy," and could not be construed as any type of incitement, much less the "direct incitement" found in *Gitlow*.[96]

Whitney's counsel anticipated that the trial record could be viewed as providing scant basis for the Supreme Court's assertion of federal question jurisdiction. The brief, accordingly, emphasized the "certificate"—the stipulation of the parties and order of the California intermediate court of appeal—in establishing that jurisdictional basis:

> In the District Court of Appeal and also upon her application for leave to appeal to the Supreme Court of California, Miss Whitney contended that the statute "and its application in this case is repugnant to the provisions of the Fourteenth Amendment of the Constitution of the United States . . . ." (*Stipulation and addition to the record*, filed Dec. 16, 1924). That contention "was considered and passed upon" by the District Court of Appeal—the highest California Court to which appeal was permitted—and was overruled by that court (*Order amending record*).[97]

---

[96] See note 66. The essential facts of this paragraph derive from Brief for the Plaintiff-in-Error at 66–84 (cited in note 38).

[97] Id at 4 (omitting page numbers for the transcript of record).

Two years after the Court had agreed to review *Whitney v California*, oral arguments were finally heard on October 6, 1925. From the tenor of the Justices' questions, they appeared most concerned over the precise character of Anita Whitney's involvement with the Communist Labor Party of California. They closely questioned counsel as to whether Whitney had attended party meetings after the Loring Hall organizing convention, and whether she had put her weight behind any syndicalist proposal or action. Given the Court's parsing of the merits, it must have been a surprise when its decision was rendered thirteen days later. The Court's one-line per curiam opinion dismissed the case for want of jurisdiction.[98]

However bleak things looked at that time, Anita Whitney still had a chance in the court of public opinion. Talk of pardon was everywhere in the California air, and an "Anita Whitney Committee" was soon formed to rally public support. But Whitney would have none of it. "I'm not going to ask for a pardon," she told an Associated Press reporter. "If the Governor is disposed to pardon anyone, let him liberate the poor men who are now imprisoned for violation of this same law and whose guilt may be less than mine." In any event, Governor Friend W. Richardson released a thirteen-page statement denying the pardon. For the governor, the simple truth was that Anita Whitney had assisted the Communist Labor Party, an organization that had engaged in "sedition and disloyalty amounting to almost treason."[99]

Whitney's lawyers were confident that the Supreme Court had not fully appreciated the jurisdictional base for appeal that they laid when they had sought a certificate from the California District Court of Appeal. Accordingly, they filed a petition for rehearing.[100] "This court acted under a misapprehension of the facts," the petition explained. The state intermediate appellate court's "order and the stipulation upon which it was entered did not constitute an attempt to confer jurisdiction upon this court by consent."

---

[98] The essential facts in this paragraph derived from *State Act Up in Highest Court*, Los Angeles Times (Oct 7, 1925), p 3; *Whitney v California*, 269 US 530 (1925).

[99] The essential facts of this paragraph were drawn from *Woman Syndicalist Will Not Seek Pardon*, New York Times (Oct 22, 1925), p 7 (AP story); *War Group in Whitney Case*, Los Angeles Times (Nov 4, 1925), p 7; *Whitney Case Details Given*, Los Angeles Times (Nov 27, 1925), p 6; Richmond at 131–36 (cited in note 17); Richardson at 13 (cited in note 32).

[100] Petition for Rehearing (cited in note 71).

Rather, "the stipulation and order stated the actual facts concerning the raising of . . . Federal questions in the California District Court of Appeal, and the stipulation was entered into and the order was made for the purpose of enabling these actual facts to appear in the record."[101]

It is unusual for the Supreme Court to grant review in a case, hear oral arguments, and then withdraw its jurisdiction. It is still more unusual for the Justices to rehear such a case when their jurisdiction remains highly doubtful. But on December 14, 1924, the Court agreed to take a second look at *Whitney v California*. The Justices, or a majority of them, wanted to decide this case, and they were unwilling to let possible jurisdictional barriers stand in their way. Rehearing was rescheduled for March 15, 1926.[102]

B. BRIEFLY PUT

In late February of 1926, Ruthenberg's lawyers filed their brief for plaintiff in error in the U.S. Supreme Court.[103] Mindful of procedural snags, they devoted several pages to establishing federal jurisdiction based on what had been expressly claimed at various stages of the case. Before proceeding to the specific "errors intended to be charged," the brief stressed the issue of imminence:

> Under the interpretation of the statute given to the jury, it made no difference that the assembly at Bridgman did not *then* and *there* advocate the doctrines of criminal syndicalism. . . . It is enough that *somewhere and [sometime]* there had been formed a party to teach and advocate the doctrines of criminal syndicalism, and that this meeting at Bridgman "was called and for the purpose of promoting, carrying out and furthering the fundamental general designs and objects of the party." (emphasis in original)

---

[101] Id at 2.

[102] Briefs were filed by Whitney's counsel and the state's attorney reiterating the same arguments, substantive and procedural, that they had made in earlier briefs, although to some degree with stronger analysis and precedential authority. See Supplementary Brief for Plaintiff-in-Error, *Whitney v California*, U.S. Supreme Court October Term, 1925— No 10 (available at http://curiae.law.yale.edu); Brief of Defendant-in-Error on Rehearing, *Whitney v California*, U.S. Supreme Court October Term, 1925—No 10 (March 10, 1928) (available at http://curiae.law.yale.edu).

[103] The following summary of Ruthenberg's arguments derives from Brief for Plaintiff-in-Error, *Ruthenberg v Michigan*, U.S. Supreme Court October Term, 1925—No 44 (Feb 27, 1926), pp 2–8, 13–14, 16–19, 21–24, 33–36, 42–46, 53 (brief on file at the Library of the U.S. Supreme Court, Washington, DC).

Addressing that point more fully, the brief emphasized that the "record presents, in a general way, three versions of the doctrines of the Communist Party." One of those doctrines ("Marxian theories") was largely philosophical, while another (derived from isolated passages selected from isolated documents collected by the prosecution) was inflammatory, while yet another version of Communist Party doctrine (proffered by the defense) was innocently organizational. If, indeed, there were *three* versions of Communist doctrine, could the State select one, ignore the others, and proceed to convict Ruthenberg without violating his right to due process?

Among the arguments offered by Ruthenberg's lawyers were the following:

1. *First and Fourteenth Amendment Rights of Assembly Violated:* This argument distinguished *Gitlow* and made several specific points, such as

   - *Crime of Assembling*: "The crime of 'assembling' is an absolute novelty in American law. *This is the only case of record in all our law books . . . in which the judgment depends solely on a charge of assembling with a society devoted to the propagation of a certain form of doctrine.*" (emphasis in original). That is, the "act of 'assembling' takes its criminal quality from the antecedent character of the society with which the accused assembles, not from any actual advocacy of criminal syndicalism that is aided or instigated by his act of assembling."

   - *Opinion vs. Incitement*: "One may be an anarchist and give frequent expression to his anarchistic belief without running afoul of the [criminal syndicalism] statute. An utterance without *incitement-quality* and *incitement-intent* is not criminally punishable." Indeed, "*[u]ntil opinion by its form and intent passes over this realm of incitement it is beyond the reach of the police power.*"

   - *Conspiracy*: The crime with which Ruthenberg was charged smacked of the more traditional crime of conspiracy, which the brief was quick to distinguish: "the charge laid out in this case and the evidence by which it is supported do not fall within the classification of conspiracy. It was not alleged or proved that the plaintiff in error, at the time and place of the supposed felony, entered into a certain plan and agreement with other persons to undertake the future dissemination in some form of the doctrine of criminal syndicalism." If the idea of conspiracy can be detached from the logic of the state syndicalism law, what then is the purpose of such a law other than to penalize beliefs?

2. *State Syndicalism Law is Beyond the "Police Power"*: The brief explained that the Michigan law contravened the State's lawful police powers because the "statute does not require that the said act of assembling shall present or manifest a clear and present danger of overt criminal injury or public disturbance."

3. *The State Law is Impermissibly Vague:* The "provisions of the said statute," the brief concluded, "are too vague, uncertain, and indefinite to provide an ascertainable standard of guilt, in contravention of the due process provision of the Fourteenth Amendment."

The State's brief made the standard arguments of the day in a standard way. It tendered two basic arguments:[104]

1. *Limited Scope of Right to Assembly:* The Fourteenth Amendment right of assembly urged by Ruthenberg is limited to "peaceable assemblies to perform the duties or exercise the privileges of citizens to petition the legislature for a redress of grievances." It does not extend, by contrast, to "advocacy of the doctrines of armed mass action, insurrection and civil war for the violent and forcible overthrow and destruction of organized government, . . . which are the fundamental tenets of the Communist Party of America."

2. *Valid Exercise of "Police Power"*: "The right 'peacefully to assemble,'" the brief maintained, "does not deprive the state of Michigan of the primary and essential right of self-preservation, nor does the Fourteenth Amendment limit the power of the State of Michigan to deal with crimes, and this is true even though the statute makes intent unnecessary as an element of the offense."

---

[104] The summary of the State's arguments derives from Brief for Defendant-in-Error, *Ruthenberg v Michigan*, U.S. Supreme Court October Term, 1925—No 44 (April 26, 1926), pp 6–11 (brief on file at the Library of the U.S. Supreme Court, Washington, DC).

Notably, the State's brief lacked any detailed discussion of exactly how Ruthenberg's association with the Communist Party of America amounted to the kind of criminal syndicalism likely to produce a clear and present danger.

As the draft opinions in *Ruthenberg v Michigan* were circulated for consideration, one thing was becoming increasingly obvious: It would be *Gitlow v New York* all over again—Sanford writing for the majority with Brandeis and Holmes in dissent. Justice Sanford was moving along the same tracks that he had in *Gitlow*, wherein he wrote:

> Every presumption is to be indulged in favor of the validity of the statute. . . . And the case is to be considered "in the light of the principle that the State is primarily the judge of regulations required in the interest of public safety and welfare"; and that its police "statutes may only be declared unconstitutional where they are arbitrary or unreasonable attempts to exercise authority vested in the State in the public interest."[105]

The *Ruthenberg* majority had not moved a doctrinal inch from its position in *Gitlow*, in which Justice Sanford approvingly echoed the view of others:

> "Manifestly, the legislature has authority to forbid the advocacy of a doctrine designed and intended to overthrow the government without waiting until there is a present and imminent danger of the success of the plan advocated. If the State were compelled to wait until the apprehended danger became certain, then its right to protect itself would come into being simultaneously with the overthrow of the government, when there would be neither prosecuting officers nor courts for the enforcement of the law."[106]

And *Gitlow* was nothing if not a reaffirmation of the bad tendency test: "In such case it has been held that the general provisions of the statute may be constitutionally applied to the specific utterance of the defendant if its natural tendency and probable effect was to bring about the substantive evil which the legislative body might prevent."[107]

---

[105] 268 US at 669.

[106] Id at 669–70 (quoting *People v Lloyd*, 304 Ill 23, 35, 136 NE 505, 512 (1922)).

[107] Id at 671.

What was different in *Ruthenberg* was that Brandeis, rather than Holmes,[108] was now penning the dissent (App. A).[109] Brandeis, like Holmes before him, refused to yield to Sanford's reaffirmation of the bad tendency test. But Brandeis was doing something more than reaffirming the clear and present danger test; he was moving beyond it—and with Holmes's approval.

Brandeis spoke of Holmes's "clear and present danger" formulation as if it were the starting point of his constitutional analysis, and stressed the importance of analytical clarity: "We must bear in mind . . . the wide difference legally between assembling and conspiracy, between advocacy and incitement, between preparation and attempt." Before proceeding to either his own reworking of Holmes's test or any application of the law to the facts of the case, Brandeis's *Ruthenberg* dissent informed his readers of the values to be safeguarded by his notion of the First Amendment. He wrote with the grace and democratic fervor of Walt Whitman: "In a democracy public discussion is a political duty. This principle lies at the foundation of the American system of government. Freedom to think as you will and to speak as you think are means indispensable to the discovery and spread of political truth. Without free speech and assembly discussion would be futile."[110] Combining that poetic elegance with Enlightenment reasoning, he went on to add what would become memorable lines:

> Those who won our independence by revolution valued liberty both as an end and as a means. They believed liberty to be the secret of happiness and courage to be the secret of liberty. They recognized that the greatest menace to freedom is an inert people; that the greatest menace to stable government is repression; and that the fitting remedy for evil counsels good ideas. Believing in

---

[108] Id at 672–73 (Holmes dissenting).

[109] The quotations in Brandeis's *Ruthenberg* dissent that follow derived from Unpublished Draft of Brandeis Dissenting Opinion in *Ruthenberg v Michigan*, dated Oct 1, 1926, in *The Louis Brandeis Papers: Part I, 1916–1931* (Harvard Legal Manuscripts, Harvard Law School Library), microfilm reel 34, frames 00351–00360.

[110] What David Cole said of Brandeis's concurrence in *Whitney* holds equally true for his draft dissent in *Ruthenberg*: "As Holmes had done in *Abrams*, Brandeis retained the outline of the *Schenck* clear and present danger test, but filled it with new meaning, substituting an essentially political justification for Holmes's quasi-economic reliance on the discovery of truth through free trade in ideas. Brandeis, who never used Holmes' market metaphor, shifted the focus of the First Amendment from the pursuit of transcendent truth to subjective individual freedom and intersubjective political deliberation." David Cole, *Agon at Agora: Creative Misreadings in the First Amendment Tradition*, 95 Yale L J 857, 888 (1986) (footnote omitted).

the power of reason as applied through public discussion, they eschewed silence coerced by law—the argument of force in its worst form. Recognizing the occasional tyrannies of governing majorities, they amended the Constitution so as to guarantee free speech and assembly.

Returning to doctrine, Brandeis categorically rejected *Gitlow* and the majority in *Ruthenberg*: "Only an emergency can justify repression. Mere bad tendency of the utterance cannot." Tweaking Holmes's test while giving it greater staying power, Brandeis then declared: "[N]o danger flowing from speech can be deemed clear and present, unless the incidence of evil apprehended is so imminent that it may befall before there is opportunity for full discussion." Moreover, "even imminent danger cannot justify resort to prohibition of functions essential to effective democracy, unless the evil apprehended is relatively serious."

Brandeis's draft dissent was equally striking in the lengths to which it went to apply the Justice's vision of the First Amendment to the facts in the case. The discussion of Communist doctrine was so extensive in *Ruthenberg* that it might have made the petitioner happy to have such information readily available in a nationally distributed government document. "The [Party] teaching is that American Democracy is a fraud," wrote Brandeis, "that not merely the practice, but the form of our government makes it the effective instrument of capitalist control." Such descriptions might have struck some as out of place, because their very presentation might be understood as an expression of sympathy. But the progressive Brandeis spared no adjectives in expressing his disdain for the Party's "foul" or "noxious doctrine" made possible by the "dictatorship of the proletariat." Even so, he felt the need to remind Americans: "Those who won our independence by revolution valued liberty both as an end and as a means." In other words, the ideal of revolution need not be judged as un-American.

The draft of the *Ruthenberg* dissent was relentless in its demonstration that the Communist Party of America, as constituted in 1922, posed no "imminent danger that some evil might result from Ruthenberg's assembling with [it]." More accurately, no such danger reasonably could have been inferred from the record as presented in the case. Drawing on that record and on matters of "judicial notice," Brandeis declared:

- "There is no suggestion of sabotage. In fact, the Party rejects as absurd the theory that the revolution can be accomplished by the direct seizure of industry without first overthrowing the capitalist state."

- "The predicted use of force in the final struggle by which the communist state is to be substituted in America for the capitalistic was in 1922 a remote contingency."

- "The Party had then less than six thousand members, scattered throughout the United States. Of these, all but five thousand were foreign born—persons apparently of small means and unfamiliar with the English language."

- "Even if all the resources, intellectual and financial, of the Russian Soviet Republic were to be devoted to propaganda here, the process of converting any substantial portion of the thirty million American workers to revolutionary views would necessarily be a slow one."

- "If the only evil apprehended was illegal violence in the final struggle, there could be no basis for a claim that mere assemblage with this society, although formed to advocate the noxious doctrine, would create imminent danger of the evil."

- "[W]hile the criminal state of mind was to be developed, the time was apparently not then deemed ripe for putting foul doctrines into practice, either as a means of preparation and education or otherwise."

- "There is not even a suggestion that Ruthenberg had, in any connection, committed, or attempted or conspired to commit, or had incited any other person to commit, any act of violence or terrorism."

- "[There was not] a particle of evidence [introduced] that these delegates, or any of the Party's officers, had advocated resort in the near future to crime, sabotage, violence or other unlawful methods of terrorism as a means of preparation for accomplishing industrial or political reform, or for any other purpose, either in Michigan or elsewhere in the United States, or had attempted or conspired or threatened to resort, or had incited any other person to resort to such means of preparation."

Little remained to be done, save perhaps some last minute proofing by the clerks. Sanford and his colleagues had prevailed again, but at least this time Brandeis had raised a formidable lance in dissent. This dissent would be remembered much the same way that Holmes's dissent in *Abrams*[111] would be remembered. Brandeis dissenting in *Ruthenberg*—it would in time become a familiar phrase in American law.

It had been 10 months since the Justices heard oral arguments in *Ruthenberg v Michigan*. The time had arrived for the Court printer to release the opinions. But something unexpected happened. On March 3, 1927, there was a story in the *Washington Post* bearing the headline: "C. E. Ruthenberg, Head of Communists, Dead."[112]

His death came as a complete surprise, except to a few in his inner circle. A week or so earlier, while Ruthenberg was in New York, he had doubled up in pain in his hotel room, this in the presence of friends who expressed concern and urged him to see a doctor. "No," he replied, "I've got to get to that meeting in Chicago." When the pain subsided, he was off on a train to the windy city to attend another Party meeting. His friend and ideological ally, William Z. Foster, was concerned at how pale he looked when they met in Chicago. "You look sick, Charley," he said. To which came the reply: "Yes, Bill, I'm kind of under the weather." A few hours later Ruthenberg collapsed and was taken immediately to the American Hospital. The doctors performed an emergency appendectomy, but to no avail. Three days later, on March 2, 1927, Charles Emil Ruthenberg was dead at forty-four—acute peritonitis.[113]

An honor guard flanked the body as it lay in state at the Ashland Boulevard Auditorium in Chicago. A long line of mourners passed by. There was a funeral march to Graceland Cemetery Chapel. Later Ruthenberg's body was cremated and his ashes were taken in a bronze urn to New York's Manhattan Lyceum. Later still, the urn (inscribed,

---

[111] 250 US 616, 624–31 (1919) (Holmes dissenting).

[112] Washington Post (March 3, 1927), p 8.

[113] The facts in this paragraph derived largely from Johnson at 177–78 (cited in note 18); Draper at 243–47 (cited in note 18).

"Our Leader, Comrade Ruthenberg") was taken by a special guard wearing red shirts and black armbands to memorial meetings at Carnegie Hall, Central Opera House, and the New Star Casino. Some 10,000 comrades flocked to the memorial events to stand, one last time, with Ruthenberg. In Russia, too, they saluted him. At the official request of the Communist Party of the Soviet Union, his ashes were sent to Moscow to rest beneath the Kremlin wall. He was the last American to receive that "honor."[114]

The case that had been so important to Brandeis—both in terms of articulating his vision of First Amendment law and in applying it—was now lost. Within a week, the writ of error in *Ruthenberg v Michigan* (No. 44) was dismissed.[115]

C. CHANGING HORSES IN MID-STREAM

Even before Charles Ruthenberg died and his writ of error was dismissed, the Court divided along the same lines in its treatment of *Whitney*. Seven Justices intended to dispose of *Whitney* on the merits, presumably along the same lines of reasoning as in *Ruthenberg*,[116] and Justices Brandeis and Holmes planned to concur in the judgment alone. Brandeis prepared a lackluster two-paragraph opinion (App. B)[117] largely contesting the majority's assumption of jurisdiction. After noting the petitioner's failure to raise the issue of clear and present danger in the state courts, Brandeis obliquely declared: "[T]here was evidence on which the court or jury might have found that such [a clear and present] danger existed." Accordingly, he conceded that "the judgment of the state court cannot be disturbed."

Had Brandeis left his draft concurrence in *Whitney* untouched, the history of First Amendment law would have been deprived of

---

[114] The facts in this paragraph derived largely from Johnson at 177–78 (cited in note 18); Draper at 243–47 (cited in note 18); Arthur Schlesinger, Jr., *Hitched to a Red Star*, New York Times (July 24, 1960), Book Review, p 3.

[115] *Ruthenberg v Michigan*, 273 US 782 (1927).

[116] We can only speculate here, since we have been unable to locate the original majority opinion in *Ruthenberg* and the earliest drafts of the majority opinion in *Whitney*. Nevertheless, given the arguments made by Justice Brandeis in his unpublished *Ruthenberg* dissent, it is clear that the majority had planned to reach the merits. Likewise, the unpublished early draft of Brandeis's *Whitney* concurrence establishes that the majority had never planned to dismiss the case for procedural reasons.

[117] A draft of Brandeis's original concurrence in *Whitney* is contained in his papers, and is virtually identical to what was set out in the final two paragraphs of the published opinion. It is reprinted as Appendix B.

"one of the great majestic, stirring tributes to freedom of expression."[118] But he did not. He seized much of his rhetoric and reasoning in *Ruthenberg*, and reworked it. Sometimes lifting whole passages with minor modifications, sometimes rearranging phrases and sentences, and sometimes inserting new observations, Brandeis infused brilliance, vitality, and eloquence into his *Whitney* opinion.

On May 16, 1927—more than five years after the start of Whitney's trial—the Court issued its decision in *Whitney v California*.[119] Whitney's conviction was upheld by a unanimous Court. Justice Sanford, the author of *Gitlow*, wrote for the majority of seven Justices who viewed *Whitney* as tantamount to a *Gitlow* "bad tendency" case.[120] Little need be said here about the majority's opinion, other than that in its unusually generous grant of review, Sanford felt obliged to declare: "[T]he usual course here taken to show that Federal questions were raised and decided below is not to be commended . . . ."[121] In contrast, the opinion was ungenerous in its grant of free-speech protection. The Fourteenth Amendment notwithstanding, the opinion was highly deferential to state statutory determinations of dangerous expression. Such determinations "must be given great weight. Every presumption is to be indulged in favor of the validity of the statute . . . ."[122] Only patently unreasonable laws or laws unreasonably applied[123] could be set aside as violations of due process.

Brandeis's concurrence, joined by Justice Holmes, rejected the "bad tendency" test in favor of the "clear and present danger" standard. Brandeis perceived Sanford's constitutional analysis as devoid of any meaningful First Amendment restraints: "I am unable to assent to the suggestion in the opinion of the court that assembling with a political party, formed to advocate the desira-

---

[118] Smolla at 106 (cited in note 12).

[119] 274 US 357 (1927)

[120] See note 66.

[121] 274 US at 361.

[122] Id at 371.

[123] In the same term as the *Whitney* decision was rendered, a unanimous opinion (per Justice Sanford) set aside a criminal syndicalism conviction on the grounds that the law as applied violated due process. *Fiske v Kansas*, 274 US 380 (1927). The conviction of Harold B. Fiske, an IWW organizer, was reversed because it was obtained "without any charge or evidence that the organization in which he secured members advocated any crime, violence or other unlawful acts or methods as a means of effecting industrial or political changes or revolution." Id at 387.

bility of a proletariat revolution by mass action at some date necessarily far in the future, is not a right within the protection of
the Fourteenth Amendment."[124] On the procedural side of the
ledger, Brandeis rejected the majority's assumption of jurisdiction.
"Our power of review in this case is limited . . . to the particular
claims duly made below, and denied."[125] Finding no clear and
present danger issue raised by Whitney's counsel in the state court
proceedings, Brandeis added: "We lack here the power occasionally exercised on review of judgments of lower federal courts to
correct in criminal cases vital errors, although the objection was
not taken in the trial court. . . . Because we may not inquire into
the errors now alleged, I concur in affirming the judgment of the
state court."[126]

Substantively, the similarities and differences between Brandeis's opinions in *Ruthenberg* and *Whitney* are notable. Taken together, they provide a fuller view of Brandeis's ideas—both as
conceptualized and applied—than has heretofore been known.
Brandeis's *Ruthenberg* opinion lacks some of the polish that made
his *Whitney* concurrence so remarkable. Understandably, *Ruthenberg* does not contain at least one memorable passage found in
Whitney: "Men feared witches and burnt women."[127] And *Ruthenberg* is not as comprehensive in its formulation of the clear and
present danger test. What *Whitney* lacks, in contrast, is precisely
what *Ruthenberg* proffers: an extended and forceful application of
Brandeis's approach to the facts of the case.

Given Brandeis's jurisdictional concerns in *Whitney*, he did not
examine the *application* of his test to the facts. As Brandeis explained in *Whitney*:

> Whether in 1919, when Miss Whitney did the things com-
> plained of, there was in California such clear and present danger
> of serious evil, might have been made the important issue in
> the case. She might have required that the issue be determined
> either by the court or the jury. She claimed below that the
> statute as applied to her violated the federal Constitution; but
> she did not claim that it was void because there was no clear
> and present danger of serious evil, nor did she request that the

---

[124] 274 US at 379 (Brandeis concurring).

[125] Id at 380 (Brandeis concurring).

[126] Id.

[127] Id at 375.

existence of these conditions of a valid measure thus restricting the rights of free speech and assembly be passed upon by the court or a jury. On the other hand, there was evidence on which the court or jury might have found that such danger existed.[128]

Among possible reasons for such failures of proof, two stand out as most likely. First, Whitney's trial lawyers focused on her personal innocence rather than on the criminal culpability of the group. In contrast, Ruthenberg's lawyers built a strong record concerning the legal character of the Communist Party of America. Second, since the First Amendment had not at the time of the trial been applied to the states, Whitney's counsel may not have believed it necessary to request a clear and present danger jury instruction. Ruthenberg's attorneys, however, requested (though were denied) a clear and present danger jury instruction. Hence, the jurisdictional problems that plagued *Whitney* were absent in Ruthenberg's case.[129]

One other difference between what Brandeis wrote in *Ruthenberg* and *Whitney* is worth some reflection; it concerns the question of the burden of proof in criminal syndicalism cases argued after *Schenck v United States*.[130] Specifically, which side (the prosecution or the defense) bears the burden of making such a showing of "clear and present danger" to the trier of fact? In *Ruthenberg*, Brandeis seemed to be saying that such a burden rested with the state: "The jury [was] not instructed that there must be clear and present danger of immediate violence to justify conviction." In *Whitney*, Brandeis appears to point in the other direction: "The legislative declaration" of the California syndicalism statute creates "a rebuttable presumption" that the clear and present danger "conditions have been satisfied." By that measure, the state need not

---

[128] Id at 379.

[129] An interesting (and professionally important) question is whether a court (and specifically a Justice such as Brandeis) should hold counsel to an obligation to make legal arguments that prior opinions have not encouraged or have rejected—for instance, that the First Amendment (via the Fourteenth Amendment) should bind the States exactly as it does Congress—or rather should understand an invocation of the Fourteenth Amendment generously to encompass whatever the court is prepared to make of it. This point is discussed more fully in Part III.

[130] 249 US 47 (1919). Rejecting a First Amendment challenge to a conviction under the Espionage Act of 1917, Justice Holmes's opinion of the Court in *Schenck* reasoned: "The question in every case is whether the words used are used in such circumstances and are of such a nature as to create a clear and present danger that they will bring about the substantive evils that Congress has a right to prevent. It is a question of proximity and degree." Id at 52.

offer such proof as part of its case in chief. Rather, it would be incumbent on the defense to rebut the presumption of danger. Since Whitney's lawyers had neither offered rebutting evidence nor sought a jury instruction challenging the legislative presumption, the Supreme Court (Brandeis insisted) was unable to take the matter up de novo in a state case.

Had Ruthenberg lived, the *Whitney* concurrence would have been far more modest. It would have been a short and technical opinion, and devoid of the luster that made it famous. In other words, it would have been lost to history.

D. THE PHOENIX RISES

Eugene Debs predicted in 1925 that "Anita Whitney will not go to prison."[131] By 1927, after the Supreme Court's affirmance of her conviction, that prediction seemed fanciful. But a few days before the Court granted a rehearing in *Whitney v California*, something unusual happened. It was something that caught the attention of Anita Whitney's lead appellate counsel, Walter Pollak. One of Pollak's former clients, Benjamin Gitlow, who six months earlier had lost his First Amendment case in the Supreme Court, was pardoned by the governor of New York.[132]

Shortly thereafter, in June 1927, California Governor Clement Calhoun Young pardoned Whitney,[133] an act of clemency that surprised many. Few governors, let alone a Republican governor like Young, ever pardoned a "Red" at a time when Communists were so demonized. So, why was Anita Whitney pardoned? The answer is every bit as curious as almost everything else in her case.

The pardon application and much of the campaign were spearheaded by Whitney's former California appellate lawyer, John Francis Neylan. The Hearst lawyer who looked out for the interests of management,[134] Neylan was a man of power. From his plush suite at the Palace Hotel, he developed legal arguments to

---

[131] Quoted in Richmond at 137 (cited in note 17).

[132] The facts in this paragraph are substantiated in *Gitlow v New York*, 268 US 652 (1925); *Gitlow Is Pardoned by Governor Smith as Punished Enough*, New York Times (Dec 12, 1925), p 1; *Gitlow, Set Free, Rejoins Radicals*, New York Times (Dec 13, 1925), p 18.

[133] *Miss Whitney Granted Pardon in California*, Washington Post (June 21, 1927), p 1 (AP story).

[134] See *John Francis Neylan, 74, Dies in San Francisco*, Washington Post (Aug 22, 1960).

save the liberty of a client whose political creed was antithetical to his professional existence.

He also recruited others to his cause. The list of those who endorsed a pardon for Whitney was a Who's Who of captains of commerce. Politicians also stepped forward to advance the pardon campaign. "Were I Governor, I would pardon her at once," declared U.S. Senator Hiram Johnson (R-CA). University professors, social workers, economists, and civic and religious leaders followed suit. Even Walter J. Peterson, who had been in charge of the detail that arrested Whitney, said that her arrest was a mistake:

> I investigated Anita Whitney's record in 1919 . . . . I found that she had always done an enormous amount of good in the community. . . . She was one of those idealists who want to make the world better for everyone. I ordered Fenton Thompson not to arrest her. But he was so zealous he went over my head to Commissioner J. F. Morse and the arrest was made. No constructive good can be done by making a martyr of Anita Whitney. She should never have been held to answer in the first place.[135]

The beneficiary of the pardon, however, resisted these efforts. "I have done nothing to be pardoned for," she told a reporter for the *Oakland Tribune* in May of 1927. "I have no intention of asking for a pardon." And then, in allegiance to her ideological comrades, she declared: "I have nothing to complain of in comparison with Sacco and Vanzetti."[136] The editors of the *Los Angeles Times* were so taken aback by her response that they remarked: "If Anita Whitney will not sign her own petition for leniency, there isn't much reason why anyone else should."[137]

While this campaign was building momentum, Ms. Whitney was still out on bail on her $10,000 bond. She probably would have been rearrested and ordered to start her prison time at San Quentin had it not been for the hesitancy of the Alameda District Attorney, Earl Warren.[138]

---

[135] Richmond at 139 (cited in note 17).

[136] All of the newspaper references come from or are quoted in *Miss Whitney Won't Ask Pardon*, New York Times (May 17, 1927), p 31.

[137] *Has an Interest*, Los Angeles Times (June 21, 1927), sec A, p 4.

[138] See *Miss Whitney Won't Ask Pardon*, New York Times (May 17, 1927), p 31.

On June 20, 1927, Governor Young pardoned Anita Whitney. His reasons for issuing the pardon:

- "Because I do not believe under ordinary circumstances this case would have ever been brought to trial."

- "Because the abnormal conditions attending the trial go a long way toward explaining the verdict of the jury."

- "Because I feel that the criminal syndicalism act was primarily intended to apply to organizations actually known as advocates of violence, terrorism, or sabotage, rather than to such organizations as the Communist Labor Party," and

- "Because the judges who have been connected with the case as well as the authors and some of the strongest advocates of the law under which Miss Whitney was convicted unite in urging that a pardon be granted."[139]

The pardon apparently won the approval of Louis Brandeis. Shortly after it was issued, the Justice wrote to his friend, Harvard Law Professor Felix Frankfurter: "The pardon of Anita Whitney was a fine job."[140] A few weeks later, Whitney celebrated her sixtieth birthday. She was now a free woman, thanks largely to conservative capitalists.[141]

In her last years, Anita Whitney remained true to her stripes. She still passed out leaflets at factory gates, picketed at the German Consulate, and took to a "soapbox in Dolores Park to talk about the Japanese internment."[142] Even at eighty-three, when she was frail, she allowed longshoremen to carry her to a political rally where she spoke in defense of her fellow activists in the labor movement. In February of 1955, she died at her home in San Francisco,[143] having lived just long enough to hear the news about

---

[139] Quoted in *Miss Whitney Granted Pardon in California* at 1 (cited in note 133).

[140] Melvin I. Urofsky and David W. Levy, *"Half Brother, Half Son": The Letters of Louis D. Brandeis to Felix Frankfurter* 293 (Oklahoma, 1991) (letter dated June 26, 1927).

[141] Richmond at 140 (cited in note 17).

[142] Rubens at 169 (cited in note 17).

[143] See *S.F. Woman Supporter of Reds Dies*, Los Angeles Times (Feb 5, 1955), p 2; *Anita Whitney, Old-Time Communist Dies at 87*, Washington Post (Feb 6, 1955), sec A, p 14. Her private papers appear to have been destroyed by an unsympathetic relative. See Rubens at 167 (cited in note 17).

the Court's landmark ruling in *Brown v Board of Education*.[144] Whereas Charles Ruthenberg's death had robbed him of a lasting name in the law, it made Whitney's name memorable. And whereas the Court had not given Whitney her liberty, it gave her a legacy.

III. Brandeis's Vote Against Whitney: Procedural and Substantive Faults

Justice Brandeis voted for Charles Ruthenberg on both procedural and substantive grounds, and voted against Anita Whitney on both procedural and substantive grounds. We find it difficult to accept such different outcomes.

The final two paragraphs of Brandeis's concurrence in *Whitney* usually have been ignored. They stated, in full:

> Whether in 1919, when Miss Whitney did the things complained of, there was in California such clear and present danger of serious evil, might have been made the important issue in the case. *She might have required that the issue be determined either by the court or the jury.* She claimed below that the statute as applied to her violated the Federal Constitution; but *she did not claim that it was void because there was no clear and present danger of serious evil, nor did she request that the existence of these conditions of a valid measure thus restricting the rights of free speech and assembly be passed upon by the court or a jury.* On the other hand, *there was evidence on which the court or jury might have found that such danger existed.* I am unable to assent to the suggestion in the opinion of the Court that assembling with a political party, formed to advocate the desirability of a proletarian revolution by mass action at some date necessarily far in the future, is not a right within the protection of the Fourteenth Amendment. *In the present case, however, there was other testimony which tended to establish the existence of a conspiracy, on the part of members of the International Workers of the World, to commit present serious crimes; and likewise to show that such a conspiracy would be furthered by the activity of the society of which Miss Whitney was a member. Under these circumstances the judgment of the state court cannot be disturbed.*
>
> Our power of review in this case is limited not only to the question whether a right guaranteed by the Federal Constitution was denied, *Murdock v. City of Memphis*, 20 Wall. 590; *Haire v. Rice*, 204 U.S. 291, 301; but to the particular claims duly made below, and denied. *Seaboard Air Line Ry. v. Duvall*, 225

---

[144] 347 US 483 (1954).

U.S. 477, 485–488. We lack here the power occasionally exercised on review of judgments of lower federal courts to correct in criminal cases vital errors, although the objection was not taken in the trial court. *Wiborg v. United States*, 163 U.S. 632, 658–660; *Clyatt v. United States*, 197 U.S. 207, 221–222. This is a writ of error to a state court. *Because we may not enquire into the errors now alleged, I concur in affirming the judgment of the state court.*[145]

At the outset, note that Brandeis offers two kinds of arguments as to why he votes to affirm Whitney's conviction—jurisdictional and substantive. Generally speaking, this two-track line of argument suggests that even if one were to grant arguendo that there were no jurisdictional impediments, Brandeis was nonetheless prepared to vote against Whitney on the substantive merits. On both tracks, we think Brandeis had it wrong, and we surmise that he may well have known it.

A. JURISDICTION

Louis Brandeis's noted biographer, Alpheus Thomas Mason, echoed the *Whitney* concurrence when he wrote: "Miss Whitney had not, as she might have done, raised the question whether there was in fact a 'clear and present danger' manifest in her acts."[146] That echo has reverberated down the halls of academe for almost eight decades; it is the conventional wisdom. That "wisdom," however, both assumes too much and understands too little. For the matter is much more complicated. Brandeis was right to flag jurisdictional problems, but wrong in the way he resolved them.

From the beginning, *Whitney* was not a case that Brandeis wanted to hear. Recall that the Court first had denied jurisdiction over the appeal, and granted a rehearing only after Whitney's counsel maintained that the California court's certificate established jurisdiction. Even then, Brandeis might have been disinclined to hear the case, as revealed in his astute clerk's thirteen-page typed memorandum. Had Brandeis's brethren paid allegiance to the law tendered in James Landis's memo, *Whitney* could not have remained on the Court's docket.

According to that memo, there was no basis for finding a federal

---

[145] 274 US at 379–80 (Brandeis concurring) (emphasis added).

[146] Alpheus Thomas Mason, *Brandeis: A Free Man's Life* 565 (Viking, 1946).

question in the *Whitney* trial and appellate court record. Among
the reasons presented, the following were most significant:[147]

No federal claim raised at trial: Examining the trial record,
only a demurrer to the information remotely suggested a constitutional claim. The demurrer asserted generally "that the facts
stated do not constitute a public offense, for the reason that the
purported statute therein referred to is void, invalid, and unconstitutional." Citing six Supreme Court rulings, Landis emphasized "the doctrine that a mere assertion of unconstitutionality and invalidity will be taken to have had reference to the
state and not the federal constitution."

No federal claim raised by the certificate: Landis found the certificate suspect: "[T]he certificate in this case is really a stipulation by counsel approved by the court (not signed by any
member of the court). Its effect is thus considerably weaker than
the usual type of certificate signed by the presiding justice of
the state court." Moreover, the certificate alone was "incom-
petent to originate [a federal] question." The only value of a
certificate was to make more specific the federal claim that was
already in the record.[148]

No federal question necessarily decided by the state court: Landis
acknowledged that Supreme Court jurisdiction would lie if a
state court actually decided a federal question but attempted to
conceal its decision by failing to mention the federal claim in
its opinion. Regarding the existing state of First Amendment
law, however, Landis concluded: "[T]here must be something
in the record (including the opinion) that the state court was
led to suppose that the plaintiff in error claimed protection

---

[147] The references to James Landis's memorandum, the synthesis of the arguments
therein, and the supporting quotations are drawn from James M. Landis, *In re #10—
Existence of a Federal Question in the Record* (undated memorandum to Justice Brandeis
regarding jurisdictional hurdles in *Whitney v California*), in *The Louis Brandeis Papers: Part
I, 1916–1931* (Harvard Legal Manuscripts, Harvard Law School Library), microfilm reel
34, frames 00325–00337.

[148] Notably, Landis took pains to distance *Whitney* from another case argued by Walter
Nelles and Walter Pollack, *Gitlow v New York*, 268 US 652 (1925), in which a certificate
from the New York Court of Appeals had been used to establish the existence of a federal
question for Supreme Court jurisdiction. The *Gitlow* case was readily distinguished on
the grounds that the federal First and Fourteenth Amendment claim had been specifically
raised in and ruled upon by the New York trial and appellate courts. See Kurland and
Casper at 521–531 (cited in note 72).

under some specific clause of the constitution. In view of the fact that the claim for protection in this case . . . is by no means fully and specifically developed by the decisions of the Supreme Court of the United States, it would seem to be highly erroneous to assume that the state court . . . necessarily decided that the statute was not in conflict with the federal constitution."

Thus, Landis (who would later serve as dean of the Harvard Law School) submitted that Whitney's writ of error should be dismissed. Surprisingly, Brandeis dismissed the sound advice of his law clerk, and signed onto the majority's dubious grant of jurisdiction to reach the federal First Amendment claim.

Instead, Brandeis faults Whitney's counsel for failing to raise a clear and present danger claim at her state court trial. But could that fault be fairly charged? At the time of Whitney's trial, neither the First Amendment nor the Supreme Court's "clear and present danger" test had been applied to the states. Whitney's trial took place in early 1920. But as late as 1922, the Court insisted that "neither the Fourteenth Amendment nor any other provision of the Constitution of the United States imposes upon the states any restrictions about 'freedom of speech.'"[149] Dicta to the contrary did not come until June of 1925 in *Gitlow v New York*.[150] The *holding* of *Stromberg v California*[151] explicitly applying the First Amendment to the states through the Fourteenth Amendment did not come until May of 1931, and the First Amendment right of assembly that was at the core of the *Whitney* case was not imposed on the states until 1937.[152]

---

[149] *Prudential Insurance Company of America v Cheek*, 259 US 530, 543 (1922).

[150] 268 US 652, 666 (1925).

[151] 283 US 359, 368–69 (1931) (striking down on First and Fourteenth Amendment grounds a California statute criminalizing the display of a red flag as a statement of "opposition to organized government"). In *Fiske v Kansas*, 274 US 380 (1927) (a unanimous decision filed on the same day as *Whitney*), the Court set aside a Kansas syndicalism conviction of an IWW organizer because the State's indictment and prosecution failed to introduce any real evidence of the group's unlawful purposes. As applied, the law was "an arbitrary and unreasonable exercise of the police power of the state, unwarrantably infringing the liberty of the defendant." Id at 387. *Fiske* has been understood by some distinguished First Amendment scholars to be the first case to uphold a defendant's claim to protection of the First Amendment. See, e.g., Emerson at 103 (cited in note 11). See also Zechariah Chafee, Jr., *Free Speech in the United States* 352 (Harvard, 1941). Professor Chafee does observe, however, that "[i]t might be assumed that the court did nothing more than declare that a man cannot be convicted for a crime which is neither charged nor proved." Indeed, this narrower construction of *Fiske* strikes us as the more accurate one.

[152] *DeJonge v Oregon*, 299 US 353 (1937).

Given the state of the law, the "clear and present danger" test was not likely to be invoked by Whitney's defense counsel, and the California courts would not likely have granted a request for such an instruction.[153] Thus, Brandeis's declaration that Anita Whitney "might have required that [the First Amendment's "clear and present danger"] issue be determined either by the court or the jury" asked too much of trial counsel.[154]

So, why did he do it? Charles Ruthenberg's death on March 2, 1927, must have frustrated Brandeis. The formidable dissent that he had drafted for *Ruthenberg* stood to be lost to history. The solution might have seemed obvious: adapt the *Ruthenberg* dissent to the facts in *Whitney*. But Landis's memorandum powerfully argued that the Court lacked jurisdiction in *Whitney*. Recall that Brandeis originally had prepared a two-paragraph opinion dispensing with Whitney's appeal for procedural reasons. If he continued down that course after Ruthenberg's death, there would then have been no reason for him to reach the First Amendment. When the *Whitney* majority leaped over the federal jurisdictional hurdles to reach the merits of the case[155] (and reinvigorate the

---

[153] The fact that Ruthenberg's trial and appellate attorneys explicitly raised federal constitutional speech and assembly claims and requested trial court instructions on those issues, which were predictably refused, in no way undercuts our point. After all, Ruthenberg and his counsel had faced scores of criminal indictments, and were extremely familiar with all the procedural and substantive gambits that might conceivably be used in his defense. In that respect, their particularized expertise far exceeded that of Whitney's state trial and appellate counsel.

[154] Strictly speaking, Brandeis appears misleading when he suggested that Anita Whitney should have raised a First Amendment clear and present danger defense, for that constitutional reference masked an analogous *statutory* burden that Whitney's counsel did not satisfy. Brandeis's concurrence presented the California legislature's explanation of the contemporary conditions threatening public order and justifying the enactment of an emergency measure. He read the California statute as creating a presumption of public harm arising from syndicalist activities—a presumption that could be rebutted by the defendant with sufficient evidence that no such imminent danger existed. Essentially, the statutory burden and the constitutional one mirrored each other; in all likelihood, a defendant who rebutted the statutory presumption would have made an argument quite similar to a First Amendment clear and present danger defense. But the two are different in this important respect: if Anita Whitney had prevailed on statutory grounds, a court would not thereafter entertain any constitutional challenge to the same effect. See, e.g., *Siler v Louisville & Nashville R. Co.*, 213 US 175 (1909). By the same logic, if Whitney failed to raise a state statutory defense, she could not thereafter assert a federal First Amendment claim. This is but another reason why Brandeis ought to have restrained himself from waxing long on the First Amendment.

[155] "Sanford did not explain why the justices bent their rules in this case; most likely, the conservative majority wanted to warn political radicals that not only could publishing calls for revolution be punished—as *Gitlow* had ruled—but that simply joining a 'revolutionary' group could lead to prison." Peter Irons, *A People's History of the Supreme Court* 290 (Penguin, 1999).

"bad tendency" test[156]), Brandeis felt obligated to counter both
their jurisdictional and substantive arguments. The result was his
curious concurrence in *Whitney*.

B. SUBSTANCE

The links between Miss Whitney, the mild-mannered political
reformist, and the hot-headed IWW radicals were so tenuous as
to be farcical. But Brandeis chose to lend his name to that farce.
Consider the following passage from his concurrence: "there was
other testimony which *tended* to establish the existence of a conspiracy, on the part of members of the International Workers of
the World, to commit present serious crimes, and likewise to show
that such a conspiracy would be furthered by the activity of the
society of which Miss Whitney was a member." In other words,
there was evidence in the record that *might* establish: (1) that some
extremists in the IWW conspired to commit immediate and dangerous illegal acts; (2) that the Communist Labor Party of America
"furthered" that conspiracy by recognizing in its National Program the "long and valiant struggle and heroic sacrifices" of the
IWW; (3) that the Communist Labor Party of California additionally "furthered" that conspiracy by adopting the National Program of the Communist Labor Party of America; and (4) that
Anita Whitney could be prosecuted for her otherwise lawful membership and innocent participation in the Communist Labor Party
of California.[157]

Under that application of the California statute, the "evils" of
the IWW are imputed to Anita Whitney in such a way that its
criminal acts stain her. She is sullied by her mere assembly with
the CLPC, regardless of her own intent in assembling and regardless of whether or not that assembly meaningfully furthers
the conspiratorial schemes of the IWW. This theory of culpability
posits, with Brandeis's approval, that if the IWW's activities produce an imminent danger of serious violence, then responsibility

---

[156] See Rabban at 17–18, 118–19, 132–34, 193–200, 256–58, 282–85, 291–92, 320–26
(cited in note 9).

[157] Remember that, under the California statute, her criminal culpability was completed
by her membership in the CLPC, her presence at its organizing convention and involvement in its committees, her grudging acceptance of the CLPC's rejection of her reformist
"political action" resolution, her continued active attendance at the organizing convention,
and of course her willingness to entertain silly radical songs.

for that danger "flows" to Whitney. Such logic removes any semblance of actual causation from the constitutional equation. That Brandeis understood this problem is evidenced by his *Ruthenberg* dissent, where he wrote that there must be a "proximate relation of cause to consequence of which alone the law commonly takes account." That language did not find its way, however, into his *Whitney* concurrence. To the extent that Brandeis abandoned that concept in *Whitney*, his heroic First Amendment formulation collapses into a variation of the majority's "bad tendency" test.

Indeed, the Justice's own law clerk, James Landis, cautioned Brandeis about this problem. In his October 27, 1926 memorandum on the *Whitney* case, Landis incisively observed:

> [I]t may be argued that we have a situation where [the IWW's] industrial crimes were likely to occur whether the Communist Labor Party of California existed or not; [but] that the danger of such crimes was substantially increased by (a) the existence of a group like the CLP which, while it did not advocate sabotage, yet justified violation of law as a remedy for the ills of the proletariat, the same ills, to a certain extent, which disturbed the IWW, or by (b) expression of approval given by the CLP, or (c) by both together. The argument of course assumes that the evil tendency of the speech or assembly is enough to remove it from the protection of the fourteenth amendment . . . . But in any case where there is no direct incitement, it is very dangerous to allow a limitation on the right of free speech or assembly to be based on an evil tendency, whether to create a danger or to increase an existing danger. Many innocent activities, certainly protected by free speech, might be condemned under such a rule. . . . Hence we ought to require at least a clear demonstration of the effect or tendency of the acts punished in increasing the danger.

Landis went on to apply his understanding of the "imminent incitement" test to the *Whitney* facts:

> Such a demonstration doesn't exist here. . . . (i) The reference in the National Program of the CLP of America to the IWW is nothing more than a statement of approval; a pledge of "whole-hearted support" in a political platform may be disregarded. The statement is in very general terms, it may or may not be understood to refer to the criminal activities of the IWW, [and it] was not communicated directly to the people whom it is here argued it will influence. . . . Hence it is very doubtful whether the Cal. Party's statement of approval . . . would carry

a dynamic quality such as would lead to action on the strength of it. (ii) I find more plausible the idea that the very existence of the CLP of Cal., a group with similar ultimate aims and an ethic which excuses law-violation, would lend encouragement to these active syndicalists. The suggestion may indicate the danger of the whole theory which would uphold the statute.[158]

What, then, was Justice Brandeis thinking? One is left to wonder why he proceeded beyond the jurisdictional analysis to the substantive discussion that could prove so problematic.

IV. History in the Making

> Having much, of course, makes one want more, and this appears
> true for Brandeis scholarship as well. (Melvin I. Urofsky)[159]

However Brandeis voted in *Whitney*, the final result in the case would have been the same. And while a vote in her favor might have made the pardon campaign on her behalf easier, it proved unnecessary. So why is it important which way Brandeis voted as long as he wrote what he did?

It is a truism, but one worth repeating nonetheless: context gives words their fullest meaning. Context puts flesh on skeletal words. The idea was not foreign to Brandeis; it is a leaf out of his book: "No law, written or unwritten, can be understood without a full knowledge of the facts out of which it arises and to which it is to be applied."[160] The same, of course, holds true for Brandeis[161] and

---

[158] Memorandum on *Whitney v California*, October 27, 1926, pp 5–6, in *The Louis Brandeis Papers: Part I, 1916–1931* (Harvard Legal Manuscripts, Harvard Law School Library), microfilm reel 34, frames 00307–00312. This memorandum was unsigned. Based on our understanding of the record of correspondence between Brandeis and his clerks at the time, we assume that James Landis authored it; if it were not Landis, then it would have been Robert Page.

[159] Melvin I. Urofsky, *The Brandeis Agenda*, in Nelson L. Dawson, ed, *Brandeis and America* 132, 147 (Kentucky, 1989).

[160] Louis D. Brandeis, *The Living Law*, 10 Ill L Rev 461, 467 (1916).

[161] Professor Urofsky makes a telling point:

> . . . I keep coming back to the man, to his life and work. On several occasions
> I thought I had finished, and each time I would run across something new, a
> letter or an opinion or a source I had not seen before, and suddenly there would
> be a new idea, a new appreciation of what he stood for. I am not done exploring
> Brandeis, but it is a vast territory, and those of us working it there welcome
> company.

Urofsky at 148–49 (cited in note 159).

what he wrote in *Whitney*.

While others have written thoughtfully on the meaning of the words of Brandeis's great concurrence,[162] they have done so with too little historical backdrop. We have attempted to provide a measure of context heretofore missing, or missing in the sense that much of the available historical information had not been collected in a single place.

We came to this juncture by asking: "Why did Brandeis concur in *Whitney*?" That question led us back not only to the life and times of Charlotte Anita Whitney, but also to those of Charles Ruthenberg. At the end of this inquiry, some may sense that we have done little more than return to the place from whence we began, namely, that Brandeis concurred in *Whitney* for jurisdictional reasons. Even if that were true, it does not discount the importance of a fuller and more informed understanding of *why* Brandeis did what he did.

As rhetorically rich and intellectually astute as Brandeis's concurrence was, we submit that it might have been better still had he *applied* those insights to the facts of *Whitney*, much as he had done in his *Ruthenberg* dissent. In light of his jurisdictional concerns, he might have voted to remand the case for further proceedings.

Be that as it may, it is enough, for our purposes anyway, that the story of Brandeis's concurrence has been told more fully than ever before. And what an amazing story it is in the history of free speech in America.

---

[162] See, e.g., Blasi (cite in note 4); Robert M. Cover, *The Left, the Right, and the First Amendment*, 40 Md L Rev 349 (1981).

Appendix A[†]

SUPREME COURT OF THE UNITED STATES

No. 44 — October Term, 1926

| Charles E. Ruthenberg, | In Error to the Supreme Court |
| Plaintiff in Error | of the State of Michigan. |

vs.

The People of the State of
Michigan.

Mr. Justice Brandeis, dissenting.

Ruthenberg was tried, convicted and sentenced for the crime of voluntary assembling with the Communist Party of America, a society "formed to teach or advocate the doctrines of criminal syndicalism" — and for that crime only. This new felony of voluntarily assembling is very unlike the ancient misdemeanor of unlawful assembly. Its criminal quality does not arise from immediate danger of breach of the peace incident to a gathering at a particular time and place under particular circumstances. It inheres, as the statute is construed by the Supreme Court of Michigan, in every gathering of a society, formed to advocate the obnoxious doctrine of criminal syndicalism. 229 Mich. 315. The mere act of assembling is given the dynamic quality of crime. The accused is to be punished, not for violence or threat of violence, not for attempt, incitement or conspiracy, but for a step in preparation which, if it threatens the public order at all, does so only remotely. There is guilt, although there was no present act of promulgation of syndicalism. What the society had done before the accused attended the meeting and what the assemblage did later, are of no significance except as evidence to establish the purpose of the meeting and his election to join it. The felony is complete at the moment the accused becomes part of the particular assemblage, whatever the time, place or circumstance, however remote the danger appre-

---

[†] © Harvard University Law School Library. This unpublished draft opinion is located in *The Louis Brandeis Papers: Part I, 1916–1931* (Harvard Legal Manuscripts, Harvard Law School Library), microfilm reel 34, frames 00351–00360, and is reproduced with permission of the Harvard Law School Library. It was not contained in Alexander M. Bickel, *The Unpublished Opinions of Mr. Justice Brandeis* (Harvard University Press, 1957) or elsewhere. This draft was dated October 1, 1926, and appears to be the last complete version that was sent to the printer. Apparently, at some subsequent but unspecified date, Justice Brandeis penned modifications in the margins of the October 1ˢᵗ draft, but the changed draft was never printed, possibly because of the dismissal of Ruthenberg's case. See *The Louis Brandeis Papers: Part I, 1916–1931* (Harvard Legal Manuscripts, Harvard Law School Library), microfilm reel 34, frames 00361–00362, 00365–00369. In any event, based on the information available to us, it is impossible for us to know whether or not Justice Brandeis would finally have adopted those modifications or any others. The bold and bracketed numbers in the text refer to the original printed page numbers in the dissent.

hended, and however improbable that serious evil will eventually befall. Is the statute so construed and as here applied consistent with the due process clause?

[2] The right to liberty obviously does not prevent a State from taking action reasonably required to protect itself from destruction or serious political, economic or moral injury. To this end, it may, in the exercise of its police power, ordinarily adopt any measure which the governing majority deems necessary and appropriate. But, despite arguments to the contrary which had seemed to me persuasive, it has been settled that the State's power, so far as its exercise involves fundamental rights of the citizen, is restricted by the due process clause in matters of substantive law as well as in procedural law. Whether a particular measure is reasonable and appropriate, may therefore present a justiciable federal question. In this case, the matters requiring consideration are whether the right to peaceful assembly is one of the fundamental rights; if so, what its limits are; and whether these have been invaded by the statute as construed and applied. As to the first of these enquiries, there seems little room for doubt. The right of assembly partakes of the nature of the rights to free speech, to a free press, and to teach — the fundamental rights with which it is closely associated. See *Meyer v. Nebraska*, 262 U.S. 390; *Bartels v. Iowa*, 262 U.S. 404; *Pierce v. Society of Sisters*, 268 U.S. 510. The protection extended by the Constitution to the right of assembly must, therefore, be as broad as that enjoyed by these other fundamental rights. Like them, it may be restricted only if, and to the extent that its exercise involves clear and present danger.

The novelty in the prohibition introduced is that the statute aims not directly at the practice of criminal syndicalism, but at the preaching of it. The practice of "sabotage, violence or other unlawful methods of terrorism as a means of accomplishing industrial or political reform" had already been made a crime. So had conspiracy, and incitement to others, to use such means. But no attempt was made to prove any such overt act in Michigan, or elsewhere in the United States, nor to show danger of breach of the peace at the assemblage. The convention was held in a remote and secluded spot supposed to be known only to a few trusted delegates who attended it. There was not even danger that the obnoxious doctrine would be taught at the convention. All the delegates were familiar with it.

[3] Since the attack made upon the statute as construed and applied, our decision of this question must depend upon the specific facts. *Dahnke-Walker Milling Co. v. Bondurant*, 257 U.S. 282. But, before these can be examined profitably, it is necessary to determine generally, when a danger shall be deemed clear; how remote the danger may be and still be deemed present; and what degree of evil shall be deemed sufficiently substantial to justify resort to abridgement of free speech and assembly as the means

of protection. To reach sound conclusions on these matters, we must bear in mind why a State is, ordinarily, denied the power to prohibit dissemination of social, economic and political doctrines which a vast majority of its citizens believes to be false and fraught with evil consequences; in other words, why free speech and assembly were made constitutional rights. We must bear in mind, also, the wide difference legally between assembling and conspiracy, between advocacy and incitement, between preparation and attempt.

In a democracy public discussion is a political duty. This principle lies at the foundation of the American system of government. Freedom to think as you will and to speak as you think are means indispensable to the discovery and spread of political truth. Without free speech and assembly discussion would be futile. With them, discussion affords ordinarily adequate protection against the dissemination of the noxious doctrine. Those who won our independence by revolution valued liberty both as an end and as a means. They believed liberty to be the secret of happiness and courage to be the secret of liberty. They recognized that the greatest menace to freedom is an inert people; that the greatest menace to stable government is repression; and that the fitting remedy for evil counsels good ideas. Believing in the power of reason as applied through public discussion, they eschewed silence coerced by law — the argument of force in its worst form. Recognizing the occasional tyrannies of governing majorities, they amended the Constitution as to guarantee free speech and assembly.

To self-reliant men, with confidence in the power of reason applied through the process of popular government, no danger flowing from speech can be deemed clear and present, unless the incidence of evil apprehended is so imminent that it may befall **[4]** before there is opportunity for full discussion. Only an emergency can justify repression. Mere bad tendency of the utterance cannot. If authority is to be reconciled with freedom this rule must prevail.[1] Moreover, even imminent danger cannot justify resort to prohibition of functions essential to effective democracy, unless the evil apprehended is relatively serious. Pro-

---

[1] Compare Z. Chafee, Jr., 'Freedom of Speech,' pp. 24–39, 207–221, 228, 262–265; H. J. Laski, 'Grammar of Politics,' pp. 120, 121. See Thomas Jefferson: "If there be any among us who wish to dissolve the union or change its republican form, let them stand undisturbed as monuments of the safety with which error of opinion may be tolerated where reason is left free to combat it." First Inaugural Address. Also: "We have nothing to fear from the demoralizing reasonings of some, if others are left free to demonstrate their errors and especially when the law stands ready to punish the first criminal act produced by the false reasonings; these are safer corrections than the conscience of the judge." Quoted by Charles A. Beard, The Nation, July 7, 1926, Vol. 123, P. 8. And Lord Justice Scrutton in Rex v. Secretary for Home Affairs, Ex parte O'Brien, (1923) 2 K. B. 361, 382: "You really believe in freedom of speech, if you are willing to allow it to men whose opinions seem to you wrong and even dangerous; . . . " Compare Warren, "The New Liberty Under the Fourteenth Amendment," 39 Harvard Law Review, 431, 461.

hibition of free speech and assembly is a measure so stringent that it would be inappropriate as the means for averting a relatively trivial harm to society. A police measure may be unconstitutional merely because it is an inappropriate means of protection. Thus, a State might, in the exercise of its police power, make any trespass upon the land of another a crime, regardless of the results or of the intent or purpose of the trespasser. It might, also, punish an attempt, a conspiracy, or an incitement to commit the trespass. But it is hardly conceivable that this Court would hold constitutional a statute which punished as a felony the mere voluntary assembly with a society formed to teach that pedestrians had the moral right to cross unenclosed, unposted, waste lands and to advocate their doing so, even if there was imminent danger that advocacy would lead to a trespass.

In the case at bar, the evil feared was obviously not a trivial one. But the question for decision is whether there was reasonable ground for fear. No such ground existed, unless there was in 1922 imminent danger that some evil might result from Ruthenberg's assembling with the Communist Party of America, and unless the [5] evil which might reasonably be apprehended was one sufficiently serious to make denial of free speech and assembly an appropriate remedy. These matters require consideration not only of the doctrine to be advanced, but also of the circumstances under which it was to be preached.

The Program and other documents introduced at the trial establish that the doctrine to be taught and advocated by the Communist Party of America was "criminal syndicalism." The Party teaches that workers are now exploited and oppressed; that the interests of capital and labor are irreconcilable; that the low condition of labor results from the fact that existing government, municipal, state and national, constitutes government by and for the capitalist class; that the class struggle is inevitable; and that to secure adequate relief, the class struggle must take the form of political struggle — a struggle for the control of government. The Party declares that the ultimate goal is destruction of existing government and substitution of a proletarian dictatorship; that, as the workers are dependent for life, liberty and happiness upon the ownership and control of the raw materials and machinery of production, this dictatorship will take these from capitalists; that it will establishment ownership; that with such ownership it will develop management of the industries by the workers; and that it will, in time, include as workers the whole adult population.

There is no suggestion of sabotage. In fact, the Party rejects as absurd the theory that the revolution can be accomplished by the direct seizure of industry without first overthrowing the capitalist state. The teaching is that American Democracy is a fraud, that not merely the practice, but the form of our government makes it the effective instrument of capitalist control; that effective control by the workers can be secured only through destroying the existing government and substituting therefore the dictatorship of the proletariat, in the form of workers' councils or Soviets; that this indispensable revolutionary change can be achieved through the mass power of the exploited class, provided its members are united in unshakable loyalty to the principles and leaders of the Party; but that the capture of political power cannot be effected by the ballot alone; that to overthrow capitalist government, resort must eventually be had to the same kind of armed force which **[6]** is now used by the ruling class to keep the working class in subjection; and that in the transition period from Capitalism to Communism force must and will be used to establish and to maintain the dictatorship of the proletariat.

The predicted use of force in the final struggle by which the communist state is to be substituted in America for the capitalistic was in 1922 a remote contingency. The Party had then less than six thousand members, scattered throughout the United States. Of these, all but five thousand were foreign born — persons apparently of small means and unfamiliar with the English language. The aggregate of a year's expenditures for all its activities was $185,715. Even if all the resources, intellectual and financial, of the Russian Soviet Republic were to be devoted to propaganda here, the process of converting any substantial portion of the thirty million American workers to revolutionary views would necessarily be a slow one. Before the predicted cataclysm could supervene, there would be ample time and opportunity to meet false assertions by evidence and fallacious reasoning by sound argument. If the only evil apprehended was illegal violence in the final struggle, there could be no basis for a claim that mere assemblage with this society, although formed to advocate the noxious doctrine, would create imminent danger of the evil. There was absent that proximate relation of cause to consequence of which alone the law commonly takes account.

The claim seriously urged is a different one. It is that the Communist Party of America advocates, as a means of preparation for the final struggle, the immediate commission of criminal acts of violence or other unlawful methods of terrorism; and that the possibility of such immediate preparatory acts constitutes clear and present danger which justifies denial of the right of assembly. The Program supplies ample evidence that the Party plans to propagate immediately the criminal state of mind. It proclaims boldly the foul doctrine that the end justifies the means. It declares that the party does not feel itself bound by existing laws, because these were forced upon the workers by the "bourgeois class state." It states that it will prepare the workers for the ultimate armed insurrection incident to overthrowing the capitalist state, by teaching **[7]** its members and other workers, that during the intermediate period of preparation, the fighting proletariat must come into open conflict "with bourgeois justice and the organs of bourgeois state apparatus." But, while the criminal state of mind was to be developed, the time was apparently not then deemed ripe for putting foul doctrines into practice, either as a means of preparation and education or otherwise.

The Party announces its purpose to unite industrial workers, farm laborers, working farmers and negroes, and to build a United Front of the whole exploited class, so that its direct mass power may become a factor in the class struggle, which is eventually to culminate in armed insurrection and civil war. It declares, that in order to educate members of the Party to assume leadership of the mass, its tentacles should reach out into every form of workers' organizations; that it will strive to control these organizations and the workers; and that its members should participate in elections and endeavor to revolutionize both organized and unorganized labor. But neither in the record, nor in matter of which we take judicial notice, is there any basis for a contention that in 1922 the time and conditions were deemed by the Party opportune for any form of immediate violence, or that there was any reason for belief on the part of the state authorities that the Party deemed it to be so. So far as it appears, neither the Party, nor any member of it had therefore resorted to any act of violence, or had attempted, threatened, or conspired to do so; or deemed that immediate acts of violence were then advisable.

The Party propagation of the criminal state of mind by its teaching, and its program of violence as a means of preparation, bring the danger incident to formation of the society nearer than it would be, if the only violence to be apprehended were that involved in the predicted final struggle. Every denunciation of existing law tends in some measure to increase the probability that there will be some violation of it.[2] Condonation of a breach enhances the probability. Expressions of approval add to the probability. Advocacy heightens it still further. But even advocacy of violation, however reprehensible morally, is not a justification for [8] denying free speech, where, as here, the advocacy falls short of incitement. Here, there is nothing to indicate that the advocacy would be immediately acted on. To support a finding of such danger it would have to be shown either that immediate violence was, in fact, advocated, or that the past conduct of Ruthenberg, or other delegate furnished reason to believe that such advocacy was then contemplated. The documents introduced showed little more than what sort of people were gathered at the convention, their beliefs and their hopes.

Ruthenberg was not an obscure or mysterious person. He and his history were well known. He was nearly forty years old. Continuously

---

[2] Compare Judge Learned Hand in Masses Publishing Co. v. Patten, 244 Fed. 535, 540; Judge Amidon in United States v. Fortuna, Bull. Dept. Justice No. 148, pp. 4–5; Chafee, "Freedom of Speech," pp. 46–56, 174.

since his birth he had been a citizen of Cleveland, Ohio. From 1909 to 1919, he had been an active member of the Socialist Party. He had several times been its candidate for mayor. He had been its candidate, also, for state treasurer, for governor, for representative in Congress and for United States senator. It is true that he had been arrested repeatedly in Cleveland and elsewhere. But no prosecution had ripened into final sentence, except one. That was for violation of the Selective Draft Act by inducing another to fail to register. See *Ruthenberg v. United States*, 245 U.S. 480. All other prosecutions were likewise for political speeches or for the circulation of political literature. There is not even a suggestion that Ruthenberg had, in any connection, committed, or attempted or conspired to commit, or had incited any other person to commit, any act of violence or terrorism.

The past conduct of the others in attendance at the Bridgman convention afforded likewise no basis for apprehending immediate violence. Every person present was a duly accredited delegate. All that these men had done, and all that they planned, had presumably been learned by the State. For ever since the organization of the party in September, 1919, Francis A. Morrow had been employed by the Department of Justice as a spy upon its operations. In that capacity, he joined the Party and had become active in its counsels. Being active and trusted, he had been elected as a delegate to this convention. It was he who became their chief witness. But neither through his testimony, nor otherwise, was there introduced a particle of evidence that these delegates, or any of the Party's officers, had advocated resort in the near future to crime, sabotage, violence or other unlawful methods of terrorism as a means of preparation for accomplishing industrial or political reform, or for any other purpose, either in Michi[9]gan or elsewhere in the United States, or had attempted or conspired or threatened to resort, or had incited any other person to resort to such means of preparation.

The secrecy of the meeting was not, under the circumstances, evidence of any such illegal purpose. Secrecy was resorted to, not because the formation of the Party was believed to be illegal, or because some act in violation of some law of Michigan or of the United States was contemplated, but for a very different reason. Those who formed the Communist Party of America at Chicago in 1919 had done so openly. The organization meeting and its later proceedings had been as public as those of other political parties. Without change of platform or general plans, the Party was converted later into a secret organization, because the Secretary of Labor had ruled meanwhile that mere membership in it by an alien authorized his deportation under the Act of Congress, October 16, 1918, c. 186, § 2, 40 Stat. 1012, amended June 5, 1920, c. 251, 41 Stat. 1008; and because several thousand persons resident in the United States had been arrested through operations of the Department of Justice, on the charge that they were aliens liable to deportation because of membership in the Communist Party of America. See *Colyer v. Skeffington*, 265 Fed. 17.[3] As most of the members of the Party were aliens, the Secretary's ruling, and the occurrences of January, 1920, led the Party to believe that secrecy was essential to its existence.[4]

The jury were not instructed that there must be clear and present danger of immediate violence to justify conviction. It is contended that neither the jury nor this Court has any concern with the question whether the existence of this weak political party did in fact furnish a reasonable basis for the belief that assembling with it constituted a clear and present danger of serious evil; that it was the function of the legislature of the State to determine **[10]** whether, under then existing conditions, voluntary assembly with a society formed to advocate the overthrow of organized government by force and violence constituted a clear and present danger of substantive evil; and that, by enacting the measure, the legislature had impliedly decided that question in the affirmative. Compare *Gitlow v. New York*, 268 U.S. 652, 668–671. The legislature must, obviously, determine, in the first instance, whether a danger exists which calls for the particular protective measure which it enacts. But where the statute enacted is valid only in case certain conditions exist, the enactment cannot alone establish the facts which are essential conditions of the statute's validity. This is not a case like *Hawes v. Georgia*, 258 U.S. 1, where the prosecution relies upon the statute as creating a rebuttable presumption.

Statutes enacted under the police power, which imposed merely absolute prohibition, as distinguished from regulation, have been repeatedly held invalid in cases involving the liberty to engage in business.[5] The power and duty of this Court are no less where the liberty involved is that of free speech and assembly.

---

[3] Among the members so arrested were many citizens, but all these were immediately released as soon as the fact of citizenship was ascertained. This action by the Government showed that there was no reason to believe that the persons arrested had violated either any federal or state law, since in making the arrests agents of the Department of Justice cooperated with the state authorities. "The Deportations Delirium of Nineteen Twenty," by Louis F. Post, pp. 51–55.

[4] "The Deportations Delirium of Nineteen Twenty," by Louis F. Post, pp. 80–153.

[5] Compare Frost v. R.R. Comm. of California, 271 U.S. __; Weaver v. Palmer Bros. Co., 270 U.S. 402; Jay Burns Baking Co. v. Bryan, 264 U.S. 504; Pennsylvania Coal Co. v. Mahon, 260 U.S. 393; Adams v. Tanner, 244 U.S. 590.

Appendix B[†]

SUPREME COURT OF THE UNITED STATES

No. 3 — October Term, 1926

Charlotte Anita Whitney, Plaintiff in Error *vs.* The People of the State of California.	In Error to the District Court of Appeal, Appellate District, Division One of the State of California

Mr. Justice Brandeis, concurring.

This writ of error was allowed under §237 of the Judicial Code solely on the ground that a right guaranteed by the Federal Constitution was denied. Our power of review in this case is necessarily limited to the question, *Murdock v. City of Memphis*, 20 Wall. 590; *Haire v. Rice*, 204 U. S. 291, 301; and as to it, there can be no review unless, and except so far as, the claim of right was duly made below, and the denial was followed by appropriate exceptions. *Seaboard Air Line Ry. v. Duval*, 225 U. S. 447, 485–488. For the writ of error is to a state court; and we, therefore, lack the power occasionally exercised on review of judgments of lower federal courts to correct in criminal cases vital errors, even although the objection was not taken in the trial court. *Wiborg v. United States*, 163 U. S. 632, 659–660; *Clyatt v. United States*, 197 U. S. 207, 221–222.

The claim mainly urged is that the Criminal Syndicalism Act as here applied violates the right of free speech and assembly. It was not disputed that the defendant became a member of the Communist Labor Party; was on its committee of resolutions; and attended its meetings in California from time to time. The evidence was directly largely to the issue whether the organization was of such a character as to bring it within the class of organizations prohibited by the statute. For reasons stated

---

† © Harvard University Law School Library. This unpublished draft opinion is located in *The Louis Brandeis Papers: Part I, 1916–1931* (Harvard Legal Manuscripts, Harvard Law School Library), microfilm reel 34, frames 00370–00371, and is reproduced with permission of the Harvard Law School Library. It was not contained in Alexander M. Bickel, *The Unpublished Opinions of Mr. Justice Brandeis* (Harvard University Press, 1957) or elsewhere. This draft was the printed version of revisions that Justice Brandeis made on January 3, 1927. It appears to be the last draft of the *Whitney* concurrence that Justice Brandeis composed before Charles Ruthenberg's death on March 2, 1927, the dismissal of Ruthenberg's writ of error on March 14, and the subsequent incorporation of text from Brandeis' *Ruthenberg* dissent into his expanded *Whitney* concurrence. In any case, based on the information available to us, it is impossible for us to know whether or not Justice Brandeis would have made further modifications to the January 3rd draft opinion in *Whitney* if the events concerning the *Ruthenberg* case had not occurred. The bold and bracketed number in the text refers to the original printed page number in the concurrence.

by me in *Ruthenberg v. Michigan*, decided this day, the statute is, in my opinion, invalid, if applied at a time when there did not exist clear **[2]** and present danger as there defined. Whether in 1919, when Miss Whitney did the things complained of, there was such danger in California, might have been made the important issue in the case. The defendant might have required that either the court or the jury determine that issue. But she made no specific request to that end. She did not even make a general request for a directed verdict. On the other hand, there was evidence on which the court or jury might have found that such danger existed. Under these circumstances the judgment of the state court cannot be disturbed.